THE QUEST FOR NATIONALITY

Benjamin T. Spencer

THE *Q*UEST FOR

NATIONALITY

AN AMERICAN LITERARY CAMPAIGN

Syracuse University Press 1957

The publishers gratefully acknowledge
financial assistance from its FORD FOUNDATION grant
in publishing this book.

Library of Congress Catalog Card Number: 57-12017

© 1957 Syracuse University Press

to VMS
_____
and MLS

Foreword

> This land was ours before we were the land's.
> She was our land more than a hundred years
> Before we were her people. She was ours
> In Massachusetts, in Virginia,
> But we were England's, still colonials,
> Possessing what we still were unpossessed by,
> Possessed by what we now no more possessed.
>
> ROBERT FROST

This book is a history of the attempt of American authors, critics, and patriots to design and foster a national literature during the three centuries after the first settlements. Based as it is on explicit critical comment, it is concerned rather with literary intention than result; it is a record of the course of the national literary will rather than a reckoning of the full achievement of the American imagination. The extent of this achievement has already been admirably measured by such works as F. O. Matthiessen's *American Renaissance,* Alfred Kazin's *On Native Grounds,* and (since the completion of the present manuscript) R. W. B. Lewis' *The American Adam,* which traces the fulfillment during the nineteenth century of an earlier prescription which I have described as "the romance of the future." Moreover, with varying criteria of nationality, the indigenous stamp has been the focal theme of numerous volumes on individual American authors, the most notable of which is perhaps James's *Hawthorne;* and the intricate involvement of nationality with the literary fortunes and ambitions of New York writers in the 1840's and 1850's has recently been recounted by Perry Miller in *The Raven and the Whale.* These assessments show how the land, in Frost's terminology, gradually "possessed" the mind of the native writer—how it entered, often without his awareness, into his symbols and imagery, into the very pace and stresses of his style. The American writer's attempt, on the other hand, to "possess" the land, to design a literary strategy which would comprehend his new culture, is another though not an unrelated story; and it is this story which the present study seeks to tell.

The basic pattern of the present volume has been determined primarily by the changing emphases of literary nationalism as each literary generation has felt them. In other words, it is descriptive rather than normative in approach; it has rather sought to define the nature of nationality in American literature by presenting the full play of conflicting doctrines and, indeed, of counternationalistic currents, than by weighting the material in support of a personal predilection or thesis. "Nationalism," writes Mr. Boyd C. Shafer in his recent *Nationalism: Myth and Reality,* "is what the nationalists have made it; it is not a neat fixed concept but a varying combination of beliefs and conditions." Though the term "nationality" is somewhat more stable, generally signifying as it does a common language and historical tradition and culture, it, too, is scarcely a "fixed concept"; and the convergence of nationality and literature in what is usually called "literary nationalism" confronts one, as it were, with a double variable whose processes are complex indeed. Nationality in American literature thus becomes a changing counter, a perennial compromise between the autochthonous national character on the one hand and prevailing literary doctrines on the other. The term has been and must be redefined from generation to generation as the concepts of the two entities, America and literature, shift under realignments in political power and under fresh emphases in literary criticism.

Although explicit critical pronouncements naturally provide the majority of the data for tracing these doctrines, I have also utilized poems, fiction, and drama whenever these belletristic sources bear directly on the issue of nationality. I have not, however, in general proceeded to infer and elaborate an author's theories from works which have no reference to the issue. It would be possible, of course, to infer and develop from "Young Goodman Brown" or "Benito Cereno" or *Bracebridge Hall* a nationalistic or antinationalistic principle, respectively, for Hawthorne, Melville, and Irving. Yet in each case the deduction would likely be at variance with the many explicit utterances of these authors on the subject; and in this study of a conscious literary quest authorial statement has seemed to be deserving of more weight than such inferences. As a consequence, some authors who loom large in the national literature are all but absent from these pages simply because they left scant record of their participation in the quest for nationality: Emily Dickinson and Mark Twain do not appear so often as Bayard Taylor and John Neal.

In order to convey the texture as well as the pattern of the quest, I have at times made liberal use of the phrasing and idiom of the authors themselves. For the pursuit of nationality was no mere dispassionate critical search; it was in large part a campaign involving national pride and hence a persistent use of affective language. Moreover, the terminology itself often provides the surest clue to the distinctive critical atmosphere which nurtured a particular brand of nationality. The contrasting assumptions of Mather, Neal, Whitman, and Leland, for instance, emerge in the very style and diction through which these authors conveyed their views; and, by the same token, the essence of the diverse nationality of successive literary generations is at last comprehensible only through the shifting overtones of their own language.

At its best the quest for nationality was a concern for literary integrity—for delivering American writers from the sterile obligation to express what their own experience had not nurtured and what their own society did not require. Even when its prescriptions were most extravagant, they undoubtedly served to create an atmosphere increasingly reassuring to the hesitant talents of the young nation. Abundant testimony from many American writers shows that the numerous declarations of literary independence like Emerson's "The American Scholar" played no small part in invigorating the literary imagination and elevating the national literary morale. The importance of the conscious pursuit of nationality is in a measure suggested by the fact that scarcely a native author of any importance before 1900 failed to engage in the inquiry and to declare himself publicly on its issues.

As a terminal date for the major phase of the quest, the year 1892 emerges as an all but inevitable choice. During that year and the preceding one, the deaths of Whittier, Lowell, Curtis, Melville, and Whitman had marked the end of a literary generation which had done much to establish an indigenous literary tradition. Concurrently

Howells' *Criticism and Fiction* appeared to expound the principles of a democratic, realistic literature whereby the diverse textures of American life were being comprehended by a host of native writers of the postwar generation. Of even more import for literary independence, perhaps, was the first international copyright law of 1891. It was no accident, therefore, that in the 1890's American novelists began to see their works selling by the hundred thousand. In this confident literary atmosphere Stedman could with justice proclaim that "our novitiate has ended."

The succeeding decades were to see, of course, consolidations and revaluations. Literary colonialism lingered here and there, even to the middle of the twentieth century. Moreover, two international wars and the great economic depression during the intervening years impelled correlates in regionalism, proletarianism, or a nostalgic nationalism. But these revaluations of the twentieth century are an aftermath of the major and intensive quest for nationality which had been successively concluded before 1900, and their history belongs to another volume.

The part which others have played in bringing to completion this study has been large and indispensable. The greatest debt I owe to my wife, whose contributions have been so sustained and varied that they cannot be properly described within the space at hand. Roy Harvey Pearce and Alfred Ferguson, who read the completed manuscript in its first draft, offered detailed and judicious criticism which effected substantial improvements in the final version. For continuous encouragement and interest over many years I am grateful to Robert Bolwell, Edwin Cady, Harry Hayden Clark, and F. DeWolfe Miller.

Much of the research for the study was made possible by a Grant-in-Aid from the Library of Congress (from a special subvention from the Rockefeller Foundation) for Studies in the History of American Civilization. Both for the grant and also for the courtesies extended by the Library during an entire year I wish to record my appreciation.

For permission to quote copyrighted material at some length I should like to make the following acknowledgements: From *Complete Poems of Robert Frost,* copyright 1930, 1949, by Henry Holt and Company, Inc., copyright 1936, 1948, by Robert Frost, by permission of the publishers. From the *Journals* of Emerson, edited by E. W. Emerson and

W. E. Forbes, and the *Journal* of Thoreau, edited by Bradford Torrey, The Houghton Mifflin Company. From *The Notebooks of Henry James,* edited by F. O. Matthiessen and K. B. Murdock, the Oxford University Press.

Benjamin T. Spencer

Delaware, Ohio
July 4, 1957

Contents

CHAPTER ONE

Anticipations, Colonial and Revolutionary (1607-1782)

> I have therefore here but briefly touch't every thing with an American Pen. . . .
>
> COTTON MATHER, 1689

The Sense of Nationality

Almost from the beginning there was a sense of distinctive nationality. Decade by decade the diversity among the colonists in manners and religion, in race and tongue, gradually was subordinated through a century and a half to the stronger bond wrought by common risks and hopes in a new society in a new land. To this developing sentiment of New World nationality New England gave the most persistent expression. Barely half a century after the *Mayflower* had landed, ministers like William Stoughton were convinced that the "Lord's promises . . . have singled out New England . . . above any nation or people in the world"; and chroniclers like John Higginson and Thomas Thacher were proclaiming the need of "a *compleat history of the united colonies of New-England*" so that God might have fitting praise for the care of his people and that present and future generations might understand their divine heritage.

The *Magnalia* of Cotton Mather a generation later (1702) may not have been the *"compleat history"* which Higginson and Thacher envisioned, but through its epic design it consciously tendered the richest of tributes to the unique character of what its author called "our little

New-English nation." "Let it be known that America can *enbalm* great persons, as well as produce them," wrote Mather as spokesman for the New World, "and New-England can bestow an *elegy* as well as an *education* upon its heroes." In this desire to commemorate a common culture and heroic past, one may perceive the first aspirations toward a national literature.

This sense of New World nationality, focused largely in New England chronicles and sermons during the first century of the colonial period, appeared with increasing insistence in other sections in the decades preceding the Revolution. That this cisatlantic diversity from Europe might nourish the seeds of political disunion, however, few of the apologists for American character and manners seriously considered. Acknowledging George III as the "best of Kings," they could also speak of their concern for their "country" and for "national sins," as did President Samuel Davies of the College of New Jersey at the outbreak of the French and Indian War; or, espousing the "idea of British religion and British government," like the prominent Philadelphian William Smith, editor of the *American Magazine,* they could at the same time repudiate any literary work which would "weaken us as a nation" or which would be incompatible with what a *"free people* have the right to expect." Such loyal subjects fondled a regenerate New World society with the left hand, as it were, and took the oath of allegiance with the right. In the arts and sciences Heaven has "glorious purposes to serve thro' America," Smith said in 1766; yet Heaven's purposes, he was sure, were to be accomplished through a "perpetual union" between Britain and her American colonies.

The Revolution, of course, effecting the emergence of America into the first of the modern nations, abruptly cancelled the traditional assumptions of such men as Mather and Davies and Smith that the New World society might have a distinctive flowering in the cisatlantic air while firmly rooted in British institutions and sheltered by British power. Undoubtedly before 1776 the sense of nationality, of cultural divergence from the mother country, was far more pervasive and insistent than the desire for "nationhood," for political divergence. The French immigrant Hector St. John de Crèvecoeur was not alone in at once envisioning a "new race called Americans" and shrinking from a revolutionary struggle committed to establishing an independent state. Crèvecoeur's French romantic background may have weighed more heavily than cisatlantic experience in his portrayal of the eighteenth-century American as a "new man who acts upon new principles"; and his wish may have in part been father to his thought that from a "promiscuous breed" the inhabitants of the colonies were evolving into a "pleasing uniformity" from the new air they breathed, the generous government they obeyed, the religious tolerance they found about them, and the free labor in which they might engage. But as the Revolution approached, the immigrant Crèvecoeur's view that the colonists, for all their diversity, were becoming "Americans in general" was shared by native writers as well. In New England young Timothy Dwight, making his "Valedictory Address" at Yale in 1776, was equally certain that the colonists had acquired a homogeneous national character. Unlike Crèvecoeur, however, he felt impelled to help erect a new political structure more sensitive to the distinctive aspirations of this "people, who have the same religion, the same manners, the same interests, the same language, and the same essential forms and principles of civil government. . . . A people, in all respects one, . . . indeed a novelty on earth."

The Songs of the New Zion

Inasmuch as the question of nationalism was of little moment in the literary principles of seventeenth- and early eighteenth-century Europe, it would not be surprising to find the small band of Colonial writers ignoring the issue entirely. Nevertheless, with the increasing pride in themselves as a "people," the colonists were insistently concerned that such literature as they did produce should be consecrated to their New World destiny—a destiny which seemed to them to involve the pure and absolute realization of dreams and designs from the Old Testament, or from Milton, or from Locke. As in Milton's envisioned commonwealth the hymns of the saints blended with high strains instructing the nation in Truth, so an America sanctified by God's blessing and untouched by tyrannical institutions could be expressed only through the loftiest of songs. The corruptions of sense and unreason would have their utterance only in the Old World; in the New World poetry and history alike would be the exultation of a millennial society.

That America was to be the new Zion, that "God himselfe is the founder, and favourer of this Plantation," was the conviction of such Virginians as Alexander Whitaker, the minister at Henrico in 1613, as well as of the theocrats who were to appear later in New England. Yet it was the Puritans, of course, who through the rest of the century most zealously fostered a rejection of European modes, social and literary, by shaping "a new plantation whose design is religion," a New England which should be "an Habitation of Justice and Mountain of Holiness." In such a society of saints all might sing, John Cotton conceded in 1647, but the "grounds of Singing" were to be only God's "soveraignty" and the "greatness of God's works of Creation and Providence"; for "the end of singing is to praise the Lord for his goodnesse, and to stirre up our selves and others to serve the Lord. . . ." Soon after the turn of the century Benjamin Colman, the minister of Brattle Street Church, somewhat less soberly urged "every chearful heart, and skilful Ear or Hand, to let God have the Voice he gave and which he claims, to tune our *Harps* to the Songs of Zion." And foreseeing the time "when the *Messiah* shall have gathered his Sheep belonging to this *American* Fold," Judge Samuel Sewall heard the whole universe ringing "with seraphick Acclamations":

> So Asia, and Africa
> Europa with America;
> All four, in consort join'd shall Sing
> New Songs of Praise to Christ our King.

Thus the first prescriptions for American writing were attentive to its "national" import: it was to be dedicated and distinct, to be free from the impurities of that of the Old World. It was to be the medium of the divine; and thus to sing the new nation was to sing the heavenly plan. Foreshadowing the conviction of many a nineteenth-century republican author that all history must be rewritten from an American point of view, such chronicles as Hubbard's *A Narrative of the Troubles with the Indians* (1677) were avowedly undertaken to show the Providential hand at work in the New World and thus to remind posterity of God's kindness to "our *little Sion*." Like the poet Edward Taylor, each "sweet singer of Israel" was to become a "crumb of Dust . . . designed/ To make my pen unto thy praise alone"; he was to indite "heavenly verses" which should "be passed like to the handker-chief carryed from Paul to help and uphold disconsolate ones." Indeed, so pervasive was this sense of a divine dispensation, as Joshua Scottow reported from abroad, that Grace itself seemed to have "dropt down into the Pens of private Christians . . . ; [and] a letter then from New-England . . . was Venerated as a Sacred Script, or as the Writing of some Holy Prophet." Thus the song and chronicle were utterances not so much of individuals as of a people tracing in communal thanksgiving the "windings of Divine Providence"; for, as Benjamin Colman said, no people can *"sing of his Mercies and Judgments in the Inspired* Phrase *with more direct and pertinent self Application than we can do."*

The "Virtuous and Religious Use" to which Colman supposed the Muse in America should be uniquely consecrated was of course some-what modified by the currents of the Enlightenment as they reached cisatlantic shores. But usually the millennial spirit remained, with an admixture of secular components. Even as the Revolution was at hand, Joel Barlow envisioned the heroic poet of the New World as one who would repudiate the "vengeful chiefs and furious gods" of Homeric tradition to sing of "milder themes." Only in the sublime air of Amer-ican society could the modern poet

> From Angel-harps . . . catch the inspiring God.
>
> .   .   .   .
>
> Seraphs and system'd worlds around him shine,
> And lift his mortal strains to harmony divine.

In Barlow the New Jerusalem became the reign of Reason, for he supposed that the Scriptural millennium might be "introduced with-out a miracle." But like the Puritans he regarded America and hence the American writer as uniquely ordained to redeem mankind; and in this process of redemption the old arts of the imagination as prac-ticed in Greece seemed to him, as to Cotton Mather, corrupt and hazardous influences. Thus the colonists consciously fixed the pattern which two centuries later Lord Bryce still found characteristic of the American mind: Christianity is an "important ingredient" both in the national character and "in the literature which those Americans who are least colored by European influences produce."

The American Muse

That American Muse whose "strong and diverse heart" seemed in a later century to Stephen Vincent Benét to have so long defied understanding had her birth among the colonists. That her future was to be a unique one the colonial writers were certain, for in the Puritan cast of her infant features they could discern lines which presaged a purer character than that of the courtly Muses of Europe. Indeed, in renouncing the pagan literary divinities of antiquity, many a pious seventeenth-century poet joined the popular author of "The Day of Doom," Michael Wigglesworth, who vowed to "invocate" only the "Dearest Dread, most glorious King":

> For I do much abominate
> To call the Muses to mine aid:
> Which is th' Unchristian use, and trade
> Of some that Christians would be thought. . . .

In writing an "Elegie" for the eminent minister Thomas Shepard, Urian Oakes refused to ask "Apollo's leave," for he supposed that David's lament for Jonathan contained a "Diviner Warrant"; and when, in turn, Cotton Mather composed a memorial poem to Oakes, he sustained the Puritan intransigence toward the classical Muses, applauding the "Sweet *New-England-Poet*," Wigglesworth. Even in the next century Thomas Walter continued to disclaim the need of cisatlantic authors for "a Draught from the muddy Source of *Helicon*" or for "the impure and carnal Conceits of the profane *Greeks* and *Romans*" or for the aid of the "fancied *Muses* of the Heathen."

With the increasing affluence and leisure of the colonists in the eighteenth century, however, the American Muse frequently abandoned Zion for secular and humbler habitations. In New England in the 1730's she was assured by a local poet at Watertown (Francis Knapp?) that she might find waters at a neighboring fresh-pond superior to those of "famed Castalian or Pierian well." Farther south the satirical poet Ebenezer Cook would claim no such superiority for the cisatlantic scene in *The Maryland Muse* (1731). This Muse, he knew, "Did never drink of the Castalian *Springs,/ Or bath'd her Limbs in* Heliconian *Streams*." To command the utterance of themes suitable to "this meridian," Cook conceded, the Muse were best attired in "Home-spun Vestments" plain as those worn by the girls of rural Maryland.

With these homely native Muses, however, whether Puritan or rural in cast, some pre-Revolutionary American writers preferred to have nothing to do. They inclined rather toward the literary goddesses with a traditional guise and appearance, as did Benjamin Franklin when he expressed the hope that through further translations of the classics Philadelphia might become the "seat of the *American* Muses." Another Philadelphian, Jacob Duché, Chaplain of the Continental Congress, proffering three pieces of American poetry to an English lord as "the finest efforts of an infant muse," also felt obliged to add a neoclassic apology rather than a cisatlantic defense for the "frequent incorrectness both in sentiment and language" in the poems. Rather than trust America's literary future to an indigenous Muse, both Franklin and Duché seem to have preferred to import the mature goddesses of the Old World. Such, indeed, had been the friendly charge nearly two centuries earlier in England from Michael Drayton to the early Virginian poet George Sandys:

> Entice the Muses thither to repair;
>
> Entreat them gently; train them to that air;
>
> For they from hence may thither hap to fly.

An American Style

If the Muses were to be trained to the American air, as Drayton had urged, they would of necessity acquire an American accent. Unconcerned with belles-lettres though the founders of the New Zion may have been, nevertheless they acknowledged their reliance on the word and, drawing on such authorities as Ramus and Talon, they devoted many a preface and passage to rhetorical considerations. The norms of expression which they evolved, however, were framed on no rhetorical absolutes; they were dictated by the distinctive character of the New World society for which and to which they spoke. With one accord they renounced the ornate as incompatible with the truth on which the New Zion was founded. *"New-England,* happie in her new true stile," needed but a "plaine" Muse, William Morrell had decided by 1625; and soon thereafter Francis Higginson agreed that the truth in *New-Englands Plantation* might be found "without any frothy bumbasted words, or any quaint new-devised additions." As to the authors of the Bay Psalm Book God's truth was an altar whose brightness needed not their polishings of verbal elegance, so to Richard Steere "*Naked* truth in plain simplicitee" seemed less obscured when "wrapt in raggs" than when "Cloath'd with *Academick* Skill,/ Or lofty raptures of a *Poet's* Quill."

Thus the seventeenth-century writers, correlating their expression with the stark purity of their New Zion, in effect proclaimed plainness as the national style and manifested a taste and tradition that did not easily die. For here probably were the roots of Emerson's later distrust of ornament; and here certainly was a formative influence on Thoreau, who paid unabashed tribute to the "strong, coarse, homely speech [of the early Puritans Josselyn and Wood] . . . which brings you very near to the thing itself" and is most admirable when it most "outrage[s] common taste and the rules of composition." Thoreau's words were, indeed, but an indigenous echo of such early historians as Major John Mason, who in writing of the Pequot War avowed *"Truth and Plainness"* and censured those who *"have wrote in a high Stile"* their *"vain narration,"* or Daniel Gookin, who "endeavoured all plainness" rather than "elegancy of words." These and many more might well have subscribed to Roger Williams' conclusion: "Truth is a Native, naked Beauty."

This American preference for a plain style was of course shared by some contemporary English writers of similar religious persuasion, and it was later reinforced by the example and prescriptions of Sprat, Tillotson, and others who in England were fostering lucidity and simplicity. Yet the same insistent commitment to the plain style was not to be found among contemporary English authors. It was from the astringent cultural climate of the New Zion rather than from the neo-classic, rationalistic, or scientific atmosphere of English culture that the "new true stile" took its cisatlantic course.

If the American Zion prescribed a plain style, the American wilderness seemed to the colonists to compel also a rude one. Many an American author, even later than colonial days, was to feel with George Sandys, translator of Ovid in the forests about early Jamestown, that his work would be a "Stranger" in polite society because it had been "bred in the New-World, of the rudenesse whereof it cannot but participate." Yet to the New World mind this rudeness, like Puritan plainness, could be reckoned an asset if popular communication were the end of style. Unlike the "daintinesse of speech" in England, American writings *"are* not to *dazle, but direct the apprehension of the meanest,"* wrote Thomas Hooker; and hence he did not conceal a certain democratic pride in the *"homely dresse and course* [*sic*] *habit"* of his own discourse: *"It comes* out of the wildernesse, *where curiosity is not studied. Planters if they can provide cloth to go warm, they leave the cutts and lace to those that study to go fine."* American writers in colonial days knew that their milieu would scarcely allow them to "go fine," whether in New England or elsewhere.

To the south in Virginia the historian Robert Beverly, aware even in the early 1700's of the distinctive styles effected through diverse national cultures, recognized the futility of aspiring in the New World to write *"Poetical Stories"* and *"Romance"* such as those to which the French were by temper and tradition addicted. *"I am an* Indian, *and don't pretend to be exact in my Language,"* Beverly explained: *"But I hope the Plainness of my Dress, will give him* [the reader] *the kinder Impressions of my Honesty, which is what I pretend to. Truth . . . depends upon its own intrinsic Value, and, like Beauty, is rather conceal'd, than set off by Ornament."*

Among this array of colonial authors who accepted the necessity of adapting style to milieu, none did so more persistently and proudly than Cotton Mather. As a young writer, committing himself to the principle that a proper New World style is one comprehensible by the great body of readers, he resolved to touch "every thing with an American Pen"—that is, as he explained, to abjure "Ostentation" and learned discourse on "Platonic Notions" as not "Profitable for those Plain Folkes, whose Edification I have all along aimed at."

Mather's *Magnalia*, prefaced by commendatory "nationalistic" poems by his fellow ministers, undoubtedly stands as the most impressive proof that his was indeed an "American Pen"; but his awareness of the distinctive quality of American writing emerged more explicitly in his address to English subscribers to the *Biblia Americana*. Such an *"American Work,"* he felt, was like "a Tree, that grew on the Western side of the *Atlantic"* from English seedlings, but in passing "unto the *American Strand,"* the English seed and stock were nourished into richer flowering than they could have attained in the Old World: "Nor will it be New or Strange, if some things happen to be *Meliorated,* and made more *Sweet* and *Fine,* by passing over this mighty Ocean. Or, to address you under *another Figure;* The Writers whom you made much of [while at home] . . . certainly, will not lose your Favour, for having *Travelled Abroad,* and now *Returned Home* in *Company;* tho' with their *Habit* and *Language* having something of an *American* change upon it." Mather was of course willing to concede *"That the Style and Manner of the New-England Writers does not equal that of the Europeans"* and that his countrymen might well cultivate some of "those *ingenuous* and *Mollifying Arts"* through a study of the classics. Nevertheless, he also proclaimed the inevitability and the propriety of American Pens expressing *"American Sentiments"* in a *"Habit* and *Language"* with an *"American* change" upon them. In such convictions in the early 1700's one reaches the peak of literary independence in the colonies, of pride in a "national style." For over half a century thereafter American writers increasingly yearned to lose the plainness and rudeness of the New World in the denationalized style of "polite letters."

With the coming of the Revolutionary decade, however, pride in a native texture and style reasserted itself. Meanwhile, from the Scottish philosophers and rhetoricians had come doctrines of nature and the arts to encourage an utterance of the New World as the vision of the New Zion had done a century earlier—doctrines which affirmed that for the highest species of poetry and the grandest reaches of the imagination the vigorous temper of a youthful people was a more likely soil than that of "polished" nations.

It was out of the convergence of this cultural concept and the sense of colonial unity preceding and during the Revolution that the Scotsman John Witherspoon, President of the College of New Jersey and signer of the Declaration of Independence, formed a slender bridge of cultural nationalism linking Cotton Mather and Noah Webster. "The state of society then, is what gives a particular color to the style," he wrote by way of a general premise; and then he proceeded to the corollary that whereas "a pompous swelling and compliment" are occasioned by the obsequiousness inherent in absolute monarchies, "boldness and sometimes ferocity" are characteristic of republican states. But Witherspoon was not content with this generalized apology for the tone of American writing as distinguished from that in the tyrannical atmosphere of the Old World; for he perceived that a new range and order of language might be needed to express the life of men in a new continent and society. Distinctive American usage, such as "clever" and "fellow countrymen," he dared to defend as the consequence of neither ignorance nor inelegance, but rather of "American . . . growth." With a cultural independence consonant with the political atmosphere about him, Witherspoon proclaimed that Americans need not "be subject to the inhabitants of that island [Britain], either in receiving new ways of speaking, or rejecting the old." To crown, as it were, his case for linguistic freedom, he coined the term "Americanism."

If through Witherspoon some of the implications of the Scottish common sense philosophy for an American style were made clear, through Crèvecoeur some of the expectations of French romanticists also became manifest. Through the character of the minister in his *Letters from an American Farmer* Crèvecoeur identified the "particular color" of a republican style with a quality consonant with the romantic belief in America as a land where the salutary forces of nature might at last be freely expressed. If your letters to England "smell of the woods and be a little wild," the minister assured the simple farmer, so much the greater is their merit: "But perhaps you will be a more entertaining one [correspondent] dressed in your simple American garb, than if you were clad in all the gowns of Cambridge. You will appear to him something like one of our wild American plants, irregularly luxuriant in its various branches, which an European scholar may probably think ill placed and useless." Yet this "exuberance" is but a "proof of fertility" of the American literary soil, said the minister, and the American farmer should by no means be dissuaded by an awe of learning and taste from conveying in his writing the flavor and beauty of "a few American wild cherry trees." Like other men, he too may express the "genuine dictates" of his mind, following the "spontaneous impressions which each subject may inspire" and the "line which nature has herself traced" for him. Thus, with disarming obliqueness, Crèvecoeur by espousing the "local and unadorned" anticipated Emerson's famous plea that American writers be not intimidated by the courtly Muses of Europe but dare to treat the "meal in the firkin, the milk in the pan."

The Birth of Literary Pride

During the latter half of the eighteenth century the foundations of a national literature which the Puritans had so firmly but narrowly laid in their songs of the New Zion were extended and enlarged to accommodate a prophetic variety of American themes; and with this variety was nurtured the sense of literary self-sufficiency and independence. By the 1750's an *American Magazine* had been inaugurated with editorial policies which its title would seem to imply. Readers "who would discourage genius in their own country, and prefer any thing from abroad, how mean soever," wrote the editor William Smith, betray themselves to be "equally bad men and bad citizens." By the 1770's this pride in American authorship was sufficiently diffused through the colonies for the printer James Rivington to project an anthology of American poems on the model of Dodsley's English collection.

As the Revolution took its triumphant course, distrust and exclusion of European works emerged as corollaries of an encouragement of native productions. Accordingly, Hugh Henry Brackenridge designed his *United States Magazine* (1779) to show the world that Americans were not *"so many Ouran-Outans of the wood"* but were *"able to cultivate the belles lettres, even disconnected with Great Britain"*; and Tom Paine, confident that Americans were able enough to fill the pages of their own journals, both deplored European wit as "one of the worst articles we can import" and also pleaded for the establishing of magazines to develop American genius. To protect and nurture the literary efforts of the infant nation, Paine and Webster even before the end of the Revolution had begun a campaign for strong copyright laws which was to persist for over a century.

Though this nationalistic eagerness *"to cultivate the belles lettres"* pathetically outdistanced literary realization for many decades, by the end of the Revolution the colonists had at least made critical sorties to discover the likeliest passage to a distinctive New World literature. They were obliged, of course, to proceed from premises and modes already established in Europe, or to find some Old World ideal or ultimate peculiarly congenial to the New. An early and indeed an abiding hope they placed in the American landscape, for in what they took to be its intrinsic beauty and its ranging majesty seemed to lie unprecedented reserves of that eighteenth-century aesthetic desideratum, the sublime. Happily unsullied by "piles of rubbish," by "mystic obelisk, or storied wall," by "ruin'd statues" and "crumbling arch," as David Humphreys observed, American nature seemed in primitive and naked grandeur to sound the tone for the loftiest song. Early in the eighteenth century the Connecticut poet Roger Wolcott pitied the ancients whose inspiration could but lie in "high *Olimpus*" rather than in those New England peaks whose "looks alone are able to Inspire/ An Active Brain with a Mercurial Fire." From their majesty Wolcott was certain that the Muses would an "ample Dew Distill" far purer than that from the ivy-topped hills of the Old World. Here perhaps was the first American enunciation of what may be called the neoclassic "topographical fallacy" which Lowell and other critics were to try to expose repeatedly in the nineteenth century: the assumption that grandeur in scenery would issue in sublimity of poetic vision and loftiness of style—that into the very tone and texture of American writing, as even Thoreau and Whitman and Simms and the Romantics continued to say at times, would be inevitably infused the sweep of the prairies, the majesty of the Rockies, and the thunder of Niagara.

For those whose imaginations were not aroused by sheer sublimity, however, "moral associations" were not difficult to discover. Colonists who were cool to the prospect of a New Zion frequently were responsive to the new Eden that seemed to lie in the innocence and richness of a virgin continent. Early settlers and explorers like John Smith and Jacob Steendam reported the land to be a very Eden; and after a century this first impression, enriched through literary associations classic and neoclassic, flowered into the expectation of an idyllic society with its appropriate pastoral utterance. Though this "new *Arcadia*" might arise on the "woody Banks" of almost any American stream, its most confident prophets placed it in the Middle Atlantic States. The most considerable young poet of the middle years of the century,

Nathaniel Evans, thought some son of Pennsylvania might well "sing of swains, whose snowy lambkins feed/ On Schuylkill's banks," with an inspiration as divine as that of Denham or Pope; and young Freneau likewise supposed that the "lambs and lambkins which sport on every plain" of "our western world" were enough to raise both the fancy and the fire of its poets.

Sublimity and Arcadia, based as they were on the undeniable grandeur and purity of American nature, no doubt appeared to most eighteenth-century poets to offer a sufficient and exemplary range of operation for the native imagination. At any rate, in other literary resources the New World was clearly at a disadvantage. A "usable past" capable of evoking a common response across the diverse colonies had scarcely been achieved in the brief span of the pre-Revolutionary epoch. Yet in a narrower range the "New England nation" before the end of the seventeenth century found in the Pequot War something of a heroic past deserving a commemorative literature; and a native-born poet and a "Well-wisher to his Countrey," Benjamin Tompson, complained that *"Harvardine* quils" remained silent "While *Mars* triumphant thunders on our hills" and "whole towns" perish without "an *Elegy*." Like MacLeish two centuries later, Tompson in behalf of a New World cultural tradition, censured the academic "irresponsibles" of his day whose art had become so private that their "Eloquence [was] confined/ To no man's use but the mysterious mind." Within a generation, however, Tompson's desire for a commemoration of New England heroism had its fulfillment in Mather's *Magnalia* (1702), which, as Nicholas Noyes observed, through its eulogy of "national" worthies, drew on the past to establish a heroic code for the New Zion. Such tributes to Puritan heroism were not undertaken without conscious emulation of the classical epic tradition. An American who celebrated the Pequot War, the Reverend John Bulkley reminded his compatriots, was comparable to those olden poets who properly sought "to raise up Monuments to, and eternize the Names and Actions of their Admired Heroes."

With the Revolution this sense of a heroic past impelling literary commemoration widened and deepened across the colonies. Indeed, even earlier the French and Indian War had effected a sense of unity and of Providential care in "this new World of America" sufficiently strong for the Reverend Nathaniel Appleton to exclaim after the victory at Montreal: "We are called to sing a *New* Song; a Song that neither We nor our Fathers were ever able to sing before. . . ." In the severer test of colonial unity during the Revolution the *"New Song,"* however, became imperative. The "classic stream" and "sportive song" of the academy were of necessity abjured for "war inspiring theme." The "blood-bought fame" and "thirst of glorious death" became "the rich theme that wakes th'enraptur'd song." By hymning the acts of Revolutionary heroes, future bards would set the pattern of national virtue, Brackenridge prophesied, and wandering over the scenes of Revolutionary battles they would fix heroic associations in the minds of coming generations.

"Thy native land is big with mighty scenes," wrote Mercy Warren in 1782 to a young American in France; some poet, she added, must "retrace, and recollect the days,/ When, by the margin of the Western tide,/ Young empire sprung from proud oppression's side." Looking to the future, Revolutionary writers could find in their own present the seeds of a "usable past." All but immersed in this "past" though they were, they yet occasionally ventured to exemplify its use. It was in such an atmosphere that the Abbé Robin found Harvard students in 1781 enacting tragedies derived from "their national events"—tragedies which he found more moving than those of the French theater because "those manners and customs are delineated, which are peculiar to themselves."

There was a remoter past with tragic implications, of course, in the legends of the aborigines. Yet the colonists, bent on expulsion if not extermination of the Indian, could effect in their own imaginations little conjunction with his myths and his art. Few could accept, as did the poet at Watertown (Francis Knapp?), the intrusion of a dark aboriginal past into the confident air of the early eighteenth century:

> During the dark, if poets' eyes we trust
> These lawns are haunted by some swarthy ghost.
> Some Indian prince who, fond of former joys,
> With bow and quiver thro' the shadow plies.

Yet if they could not assimilate the Indian to their own imaginative uses, they could at times recognize from afar the authenticity of his art. Through the Indian treaties, transcribed by official clerks and interpreters and published by Cadwallader Colden and William Smith, they caught, however tenuously, some hint of the "poetical language," of the "divine Enthusiasm," of the "untaught Eloquence" which marked Indian speech and song.

Such pristine beauty, however, could not countervail the blessings of Progress. If the rough gem throw out some sparks, Smith argued in the 1750's, how will it shine when polished! And though he was conscious of a translator's inability to do "justice to the laconic spirit and manly force of the alleged original," he nevertheless did not hesitate to adapt it "to modern ears." Even the young Freneau, sufficiently moved by aboriginal tales to attempt to portray a domestic tragedy which befell the Hudson Bay Indians, could scarcely compound an Amerindian poetry. Indeed, the Indian past with its poetic utterance was long to remain fundamentally alien to the American author.

Finding his own colonial past thin in imaginative associations and the aboriginal past culturally alien, the colonial writer nevertheless at length discovered a temporal alternative which became a fixed article in American literary faith. Associations, he concluded, might cluster about the future as well as the past; and since the New World was clearly the best hope of man, the indigenous path of American writing lay toward the roseate prospect of ages to come. "I tread the hallowed soil with far higher pleasures from *anticipation* than your classic enthusiasts feel from *reflection* . . . ," declared the fictional correspondent of Jacob Duché's *Caspipina's Letters* (1774) in this first pronouncement of the revised associational strategy for American writers. While European empires faded, Duché's correspondent predicted, cisatlantic authors would evoke emotions more intense and pure from images of future perfection than those stirred by pictures of some shadowy Golden Age of the Old World past. But this Old World past had "painful and useless" memories as well, Crèvecoeur's romantic spokesman in the *Letters* reminded American writers in the 1770's, and to these "melancholy reflections" the American imagination happily need not be bound. A richer fund of associations, the spokesman concluded, lay in the "anticipated fields" of future improvement than in Roman ruins.

Although this new strategy of association from prospect rather than from retrospect was impressively used in such later works as Whitman's "Passage to India," it scarcely became a cardinal element in American fiction and poetry. Nearly a century later Hawthorne was forced to confess, in *The Marble Faun,* that these improved American fields, with their happy firesides, were not so readily amenable to the designs of the romantic imagination as Crèvecoeur had supposed, and that Italy with all her bloody past must still command his fealty as artist if not as citizen.

Thus even before the Revolution American literature was in a measure committed to the idea of Progress. The prospect of a more humane world in turn yielded the expectation of a sublimer art. As early as the 1730's the almanac-maker Nathaniel Ames wondered that his own poetic accents were so feeble when his muse was so indubitably "inspir'd with Nobler Themes" than the "Old, forsaken, Threadbare, Grecian Lies" and the "silly gods" from which Homer had wrought heroic verse. Later, in the Revolutionary years, Joel Barlow elaborated Ames's premise. The "soaring bard" in the new society governed by Reason, Barlow was confident, could discard "vengeful chiefs and bickering gods" and bid the world attend his song of "Virtues and loves and heavenly themes." The arts of the imagination which flourished in Greece tended, alas, little to the improvement of mankind and hence have had their day, he concluded. In contrast, the songs of America, he said with the prophets of the New Zion, would be the messianic hymns of universal peace. The distinctive mission of the New World bard was thus to celebrate those "moral beauties" first realized here. In such an art "patriot views and moral views [became] the same."

Inevitably during the Revolutionary years Liberty emerged not only as the prime "moral view" to be hymned and expounded by the patriot writer but also as his all-sufficient muse. "That spirit of freedom . . . hath given birth to Orators and Poets . . . ," Duché assured his compatriots in the early 1770's, even as John Witherspoon applauded the "boldness" of style which among republicans supplanted the "pompous swelling" of monarchical writers.

As the course of the conflict brought increasing assurance of independence, it brought as a corollary the prospect of an imminent golden age of literature; for *"liberty is of so noble and energetic a quality,"* as Brackenridge explained, *"as even from the bosom of war to call forth the powers of human genius, in every course of literary fame and improvement."* A similar faith in the power of liberty led the eminent physician and historian of Charleston, David Ramsey, to prophesy that with the establishment of republican institutions men would at last appear as they really are, that the arts in America would no longer languish "under the low prospects of subjection," but that there would emerge an "elevation of soul" which would be expressed in a classic excellence long stifled by the artifice of monarchies. Even in London the American Charles Wharton, publishing a poem to Washington, defiantly explained that his poetic bark was propelled by *"Liberty's* inspiring gale." Like Wharton, many another author before the end of the Revolution had vowed that as an American he would throw off the yoke of the "servile Muse" that lived in the Old World institutions.

Colonial Misgivings

If it is clear that American literature before the 1780's was not in either practice or theory one vast plain of colonial imitation, it is equally clear that the foothills of literary independence were scattered. The small cluster about Cotton Mather at the turn of the first American century soon leveled off into the colonial abasement of the majority of mid-eighteenth-century authors. The earlier New World pride in a dedicated purity or in honest rudeness faded for a time into an obsequious lament for transatlantic elegance.

As the eighteenth century brought wealth to the colonists, it also brought through varied media an intercourse with European culture which could not fail to awaken a sensitiveness to cisatlantic crudity and a longing for polite society and literature. Colonial libraries in Virginia frequently displayed the classics on more than a third of their shelves; the *New England Weekly Journal* boasted that its contributors and editors were "considerably improv'd by their Travels into distant Countries" and aimed at the "Encouragement of Wit and Politeness"; Old Father Janus of the rival *New England Courant* "wou'd refin'd Poetry impose," uncolleged though he was; in the *Virginia Gazette* Arabella Slys and Helena Fidgets measured American manners, and the Meddlers' Club of the *South Carolina Gazette* appeared with hopes that such "Attempts of Carolinians, tho' weak," would please as much as "foreign Pieces of a more refined Sense, since our Intentions are good, tho' our Capacities small." With Augustan yearnings the American Muse of a poet like Francis Knapp, no longer independently plain, confessed herself "presumptuous" and "feeble" in daring to sing of British worthies; and young Benjamin Franklin was scarcely willing seriously to controvert "the Complaint of many Ingenious Foreigners . . . *That good Poetry is not to be expected in New England*."

This literary abasement in mid-eighteenth-century America was not the humility which is born of an intent reading of the classics of Western Europe; it proceeded rather from an excessive yet narrow and modish adulation of current English literary fashions which could have little relevance to the temper of American life. Thus Mather Byles could inform Pope that the "Polite and learned Part of my Country-men" looked upon "such exalted Genius's [*sic*] as Mr. Pope . . . in the same light, in which you behold the admired Classicks" and thought of him as belonging to a "Race of Superior Beings." However much in this adulation may be disregarded as formal compliment, at mid-century writing with an *"American* change upon it" no longer found Mathers to champion it. "And if I shine 'tis his reflected Light," said Byles, in further deference to "mighty Pope," though at times he aspired to the "glitt'ring Language" of Milton. By essay and poem, therefore, he sought to "encourage a Spirit of Politeness and Delicacy in this Country" to supplant the "rude Rust" which he so intensely deplored:

> Rough horrid Verse, harsh, grated thro' the Ear,
> And jarring Discords tore the tortur'd Air;
> Solid, and grave, and plain the Country stood,
> Inelegant, and rigorously good.

That "Extravagance of Imagination," that "boisterous, wild, and irregular" style of earlier American authors he could scarcely accept as a proper correlate of a vigorous and experimental society; this "Genius run wild" he would subject to the "rules of art" so that American writing might shine "with . . . Purity and Elegance."

In this yearning for Augustan elegance Byles bespoke the pervasive distaste of his time for the indigenous tradition which had been assuming substance and shape in the seventeenth century. Americans no longer were to sing a new song; they were to be measured and moulded by an alien one. They were to cultivate polite literature, which was especially desirable in America, young John Trumbull said in his valedictory oration at Yale, because it gave delicacy and refinement and polished away "that rugged ferocity of manners, which is natural to the uncultivated nations of the world." If they wished to be original authors, they were no longer to prefer honesty in rags but, as the jurist Jeremiah Gridley reminded them, to acquire "easiness of mind and a competent fortune. . . . Travel and the most refined conversation. . . ." Amid such cosmopolitan aspirations it is not surprising that Franklin should have throttled the homely poetic inclinations of his Poor Richard: " 'Tis methinks a poor Excuse for the bad Entertainment of Guests, that the Food we set before them, tho' coarse and ordinary, is *of one's own Raising, off one's own Plantation,* &c. when there is Plenty of what is ten times better, to be had in the Market."

Thus, while England fed on classic and continental literature, America at mid-century fed chiefly on the Augustans. Occasionally some literary prophet descried new Homers and Virgils arising in the New World; and Shakespeare, Milton, and other pre-Augustan authors of course had their American disciples. Yet transcending all was "heav'nly Pope," as young Freneau called him; and the mid-century American Muse, as William Smith suggested, could fancy no choicer habitation for herself than "other Twit'nams in each bowery wood." Indeed there was much truth in the claim of a South Carolinian in 1731 that America had become merely a "Province" in his "Empire." Perhaps few English authors could have so completely diverted American literature from the native channel which it had begun to cut during its first century.

In the shadow of the neoclassic ideal America became a dull land whose inelegance rendered it unfit to inspire or receive literary treatment. Henry James's famous indictment of American aesthetic barrenness was only an amplified echo of Richard Lewis' complaint, a century and a half earlier, that *"Here,* rough Woods embrown the Hills and Plains,/ Mean are the *Buildings,* artless are the Swains." How could Maryland, where a *"bare subsistence* claims our Utmost Care," asked Lewis, evoke the *"soft enchanting Strains"* or "Thoughts sublime" which the "kind Climate" and "pompous Piles" of Italy inspire! In Pennsylvania James Sterling, longing for Alexis' (Pope's) pipe, likewise pronounced "Our *Indian* woods, as yet unus'd to sing" and "Nothing . . . wanting but *Poetic* ground." In New York William Smith prefaced his history of that Province (1757) with a warning that "the little Transactions" of his Colony could afford no *"illustrious Characters,* [or] . . . grand Events" to delight "Gentlemen of this Taste." On the frontier at Fort Henry, Thomas Godfrey despaired in his courtship of a Muse who viewed "with contempt the rude unpolish'd shade" and preferred woods and lawns in "beauteous order" to dark and dreadful forests and "trembling peasants." And at Harvard a coterie of college poets, singing in 1761 the praises of the newly crowned George III, lamented that the mocking bird was "America's sole boast" among the birds of song.

To such mid-century devotees of polite literature, moreover, the public no less than the landscape seemed callow. Before the Revolution Nathaniel Evans summarily flung at a mercenary populace an indictment which was to be echoed by American writers for nearly two centuries:

> And we are in a climate cast
>
> Where few the muse can relish;
>
> Where all the doctrine now that's told,
>
> Is that a shining heap of gold
>
> Alone can man embellish.

In such a land, Evans observed, one may "loiter in poetic bliss,/ And go without a dinner." And from "this disastrous shore" Freneau, like many later expatriates, dreamed of departing for a Europe where "Poets may flourish." Indeed the common people, as John Adams observed, could scarcely be expected to provide men of letters with the necessities, conveniences, and ornaments of life. Yet if the indifference of the philistine masses was disheartening for the early American poet, the distrust of the imagination among men of affairs was equally obstructive. Hence it is not surprising that solicitous friends of Joel Barlow should have warned him in his early poetic career that Americans are not sufficiently "refined, enriched, and improved" to support even a Pope or a Milton, and that the "most that can be expected from our countrymen in this age is 'Be ye warmed and be ye filled.' "

The sanguine Barlow, conceding the temporary dominance of "blustering characters," prophesied an era of refinement after the new nation became settled in the ways of peace. So long as such hopes rested on the transplanting of the neoclassic in America, however, the "inclement clime" would continue to forbid "the plants to bear."

The Rising Glory of America

To dismiss as mere naïveté the confidence of authors like Barlow in an imminent flowering of belles-lettres in America is to ignore the cultural determinism accepted by the educated men of the era. How axiomatic a principle the westward course of empire, of which Berkeley had sung in the 1720's, came to be to the eighteenth-century American mind is attested by John Adams: "There is nothing, in my little reading, more ancient in my memory than the observation that arts, sciences, and empire had traveled westward; and in conversation it was always added since I was a child, that their next leap would be over the Atlantic into America."

The suspicion of the Renaissance that man and his world were old to the point of death seemed invalidated by the fresh vigor of a New World which was increasingly confident of its destiny to complete the cycle of culture long ago begun in the Orient. Looking back across the Atlantic in the 1760's John Trumbull could report the decline of polite letters in Britain owing to a "luxurious effeminacy, which hath caused the decay of genius." When he looked about him, however, he saw neither the "sordid ignorance of peasants" nor the "unthinking dissipation of the great" debasing the genius inherent in the dominantly "middle station" of American society. And it was from this homogeneous people that another Connecticut Wit, Timothy Dwight, envisioned a rising sun of glory to which the older cultures were as the twinkling of a day-star: "Here the progress of temporal things toward perfection will undoubtedly be finished. Here human greatness will find a period."

Certain though they were that the Muses would find "soft retreats" in American plains and forests because a "Western course has pleas'd . . . [them] all along," the eighteenth-century prophets could scarcely design for them in any detail a New World guise. And eagerly though they sought to discern the character of the immigrant Muses, even the more eminent men of letters, like Francis Hopkinson and William Smith, could achieve no more exact description than the humble and anonymous contributors to Isaiah Thomas' *Royal American Magazine* who from time to time envisioned a cisatlantic Muse on "daring wings" inspiring "new ideas." One and all, they inclined to reiterate a faith that in the westward cycle of culture other Newtons and Shakespeares and Popes would arise, that the Ohio would become another Avon, and that each "sylvan flood" would emerge as another Tiber. Yet at times the New Zion fused with the westward course of empire in the image of millennial perfection. To this New Jerusalem Freneau supposed that only American bards might compose the "blissful prelude," and to hymn its eventual appearance in the New World Barlow heard "unborn Joshuas" rise in future song.

These colonial prophets of America's destined pre-eminence in letters did not evade the final implication of their belief in the westward course of the arts. Even before the Revolution the almanac-maker Nathaniel Ames was convinced that the vast trans-Allegheny territory might become "the Garden of the World" and that in its progressive cycle "Humane Literature" would pass beyond the Eastern seaboard "to the Western Ocean." "O! Ye Unborn Inhabitants of America!" Ames cried in rapture over the eminence which in succeeding centuries the Arts and Sciences were to attain in the vast new continent, ". . . you will know that in Anno Domini 1758, we dream'd of your Times." Long after Britain should be laid in the grave, a contemporary of Ames agreed, the Arts would be perfected in "th' utmost Bourne/ Of California" and America, closing the cycle of culture begun long ago in the East, would stretch her domination as far as "proud Japan."

As surely as the political direction of the American republic was cumulatively set in colonial days, so the literary imagination glimpsed the general categories in which it was to work for two centuries. A new land and a new society, the colonial writers affirmed again and again, would require an American Muse. She was to be a child of the future rather than of the past, they suspected; and if she lacked the dignity of the Old World Muses, she was free of their dubious associations. Through the ensuing centuries, they predicted, she would achieve a distinctive idiom in which to utter the fresh grandeur of

American nature and the humane impulses of American society. Like Shakespeare's Miranda, she would in her isolated milieu incarnate the perfect fusion and flowering of the Hellenistic and Hebraic traditions and inspire her poets to sing of the brave new world which the older cultures had envisioned. By the end of the Revolution something of her emergent cisatlantic character had become evident.

CHAPTER TWO

The Search for National Modes and Principles (1783-1814)

> Were I at liberty my plans to choose,
> My politics, my fashions, and my muse
> Should be American. . .
>
> JUDITH SARGENT MURRAY, *The Gleaner,* 1798

The Impulse Toward Literary Independence

When in *Over the Teacups* Holmes paid his final tribute to "The American Scholar" (1837) as the new nation's "Declaration of Literary Independence," he seems to have regarded Emerson's pronouncement as an unheralded revelation suddenly come from America's literary Over-soul. Actually, of course, there had been scores of similar declarations during the half century between the Revolution and Emerson's address. In fact, the movement toward cultural autonomy which had been already reflected before 1783 in such projects as Webster's *Grammatical Institute* was sharply accelerated by the successful termination of the war; and throughout the late 1780's and 1790's the determination of the young country to have a self-sufficient culture was signified not only by numerous demands for an independent literature but also by nationalistic research in the fields of American history and American diseases.

Within a few years after the Treaty of Paris the phrase "American literature," rare before the 1780's, had become a familiar one. Generally it signified not merely belles-lettres but rather more inclusively philosophic, historical, scientific, and political writings as well. In numerous orations like that of one Mr. Sanborn at Dartmouth in 1786 "the encouragement of American literature" in the inclusive sense was "strongly and elegantly recommended." Moreover, many editors and publishers, sharing this nationalistic literary sentiment, opened their pages to aspiring native authors: the first issue of the *Boston Magazine* in 1783 boasted that one third of its pieces were "original"; and Mathew Carey announced that though he would not exclude foreign selections from his *American Museum,* "American publications . . . shall always meet a preference." The *Massachusetts Magazine* found space in 1789 for *Amelia: . . . An American Novel,* and two years later, despite an admitted decline in originality, maintained proudly that "a decided majority of our present Magazine is at least *American."*

Originality thus quickly became almost a byword among those editors who felt that America might achieve a literary independence as readily as she had won her political freedom. Her learned men needed only to cease trying to shine "in borrowed beams," they believed in the 1780's, and her great and "original literary characters" would become manifest. In this all but absolute confidence in native genius the historian Ebenezer Hazard could announce his intention of making "the most, if not the whole" of the *American Magazine and Register* *"original,"* and the editors of the *Massachusetts Magazine,* professing *"Originality"* to be their aim, could risk a large investment of copperplates on "domestick subjects" rather than copy sketches from Old World masters. Though this editorial pursuit of originality abated somewhat at the turn of the century, it revived as the second war with Britain again whetted national pride.

In 1812 even the sometime Anglophile *Port Folio,* eager to become a national magazine, besought from its contributors "original composition" based on the study of Nature as they found it in their immediate environment. In these war years *Polyanthus* became equally "ardent in the defense of *original genius,"* convinced that American writers must sever all extraneous ties and stand on their *"own basis."* Meanwhile, however, American writers had been consistently attempting to display "original genius." Like Mrs. Sarah Wood, author of *Dorval,* they wrote novels which made claims of being *"Founded on Recent Fact"* and of being "wholly American" in sentiment, character, and manners. Indeed, this impulse toward a national culture was substantial enough to lead a committee of the Pennsylvania Assembly to declare in the late 1780's that an American theater with native productions was "a natural and necessary concomitant" of political independence.

A literature which ventured "to portray American manners, to celebrate American achievements, or to record American events," as the dramatist James Nelson Barker noted, inevitably became the object of contempt among Anglophile critics who, nevertheless, could be charmed by Yorkshire rusticity. Indeed, such critical sneers were to be met "on every side" by any "son of Columbia [who] attempts to cultivate a natively poetical soul," sighed the poet Eaglesfield Smith of New York soon after the turn of the century. Yet the sneers did not prevent Smith from issuing in Emersonian accents his own declaration of literary independence nearly a generation before "The American Scholar":

> The same sun which shines on the Old World illumines the New.
> . . . The Americans eat, drink, walk, sleep, study, and think, in the
> same manner as English men. The well-educated young men of this
> country are as susceptible of fine emotions, and as capable of accurate
> description, as any . . . of their polite travelers.

And in the nationalistic atmosphere of the War of 1812 even Irving sufficiently relaxed his devotion to traditional literary modes and standards to give precedence to native efforts, however crude:

> We would rather hear our victories celebrated in the merest doggerel
> that sprang from native invention, than beg, borrow, or steal from
> others, the thoughts and words in which to express our exaltation. By
> tasking our own powers, and relying entirely on ourselves, we shall
> gradually improve and rise to poetical independence. . . .

It was Noah Webster, however, who between the wars with Britain most unremittingly insisted that "America must be as independent in *literature* as she is in *politics*," though belletristic authors could find among his exhortations disappointingly few hints as to how such independence might be achieved. "For America in her infancy to adopt the present maxims of the old world," he wrote in Part I of *A Grammatical Institute* in 1783, "would be to stamp the wrinkles of decrepid age upon the bloom of youth and to plant the seeds of decay in a vigourous constitution." To found American literature on the literary taste and manners of Europe seemed to him as ill advised as an attempt to erect "a durable and stately edifice . . . upon the mouldering pillars of antiquity."

Though Webster was careful to state that Americans must utilize the experience and wisdom of all nations and ages, he supposed that they had little to learn from modern Europe, which had "grown old in folly, corruption and tyranny" and had allowed literature to decline. Accordingly, convinced that national opinions are contingent on a national language, he toiled at lexicography in order to free America from a reliance on English opinions and English books. "In truth," he wrote Barlow, "we shall always be in leading strings till we resort to original writers and original principles instead of taking upon trust what English writers please to give us." Like many of his contemporaries, Webster thus encouraged an "original" American literature; yet he made clear that his conception of "originality" did not involve mere novelty but rather an alignment with what he considered to be a fundamental set of moral and aesthetic values evolved in human experience and expressed in the older classics. America and her culture were to be, as Whitman was to say later, consonant with Nature. American literature, reasserting Nature through a return to "original principles," would thus afford a standard of redemption from the decadence of modern Europe. It was with this inclusive cultural concept that Webster sustained his attack against a colonial mentality: "Americans, unshackle your minds and act like independent beings."

Among the many anxious attempts to evoke an independent literature, some chauvinistic inflation of American authors was inevitable. But to counterbalance every injudicious literary boast, one might easily adduce an injudicious colonial detraction, such as the Anglophile William Cliffton's characterization of America as "these cold shades . . ./ Where Fancy sickens, and where Genius dies." Between these occasional extremes of naïve puffery and intemperate reaction flowed the main critical current of firm confidence in America's literary future. There was praise for those who were attempting to "naturalize" the Muses by adapting their steps to a New World terrain; there was assurance that genius need "No more . . . roam,/ For scenes of fiction, scenes remote from home"; there was satisfaction "To think at last, that out owre these Pennsylvania's woods,/ Amang the summer trees and buds,/ A bardie should spring up, a musie,/ A genuine Parnassus pousie. . . ." In short, most of the nation's small band of editors and critics inclined with the poet John Blair Linn to admit contemporary shortcomings but to compare American poetry to an infant Hercules that would grow strong through the nourishment of our plains, our waters, and our mountains: "These regions were not formed, only to echo the voice of Europe; but from them shall yet sound a lyre that shall be the admiration of the world."

The Rejection of the Old World

The pervasive demand for "originality" in American literature had its inception in diverse influences varying in nature and complexity. Some of the editors who espoused it seem to have had little beyond cisatlantic novelty in mind, and their concern for it was grounded in national pride and journalistic rivalry rather than in any well-considered literary principles. Others, like Noah Webster, more reflectively attached the concept to the germinal origins and classical mainstream of Western thought. With the advent of the Romantic movement and the publication of such works as Edward Young's *Conjectures on Original Composition* (1759), however, a new emphasis on spontaneity, natural genius, and uniqueness appeared in English criticism and found echoes in America in the post-Revolutionary era. But perhaps the greatest encouragement to cisatlantic originality, as will be seen, came from the highly esteemed Hugh Blair of the Scottish school, with his faith in the promptings of the heart.

Before the post-Revolutionary writers explored the imaginative liberty implicit in any doctrine of originality, however, they inclined to draw up a literary bill of particulars against European literary practices. Like their political compatriots, they could more readily list their grievances against the mother country than formulate a new bill of rights and principles.

Throughout the colonial period, of course, those who viewed America as a New Zion had condemned the importation of the impurities which they supposed to be inherent in most of the books of the Old World; and they had proposed that New World writing should have as its single object divine approval. With national independence, however, this simple principle was broadened to the comprehensive postulate that distinctive fashions, manners, language, and political and social attitudes must be shaped to accord with the new republicanism. The responsibilities of a national literature in this shaping process emerged with a ready logic: imported novels and dramas and poems reflected and therefore instilled alien modes; consequently, for the integrity of American culture, the reading of recent European belles-lettres must be discouraged and an indigenous literature aligned with both the resources and the ideology of the new republic must be created. As the influential Judith Murray wrote in *The Gleaner:* in sentiment, fashion, and politics Americans must "radically throw off every foreign yoke." To her and to most of her literary contemporaries belles-lettres seemed a prime agent in this inclusive cultural emancipation.

How subtly the Old World biases of European fiction might infect American youth Charles Brockden Brown illustrated in *Clara Howard* through his Philip Stanley, "a mere country lad" who by his reading was led into an unfortunate reverence for royalty and a contempt for American "peasantry." Yet generally adjudged more susceptible than such young gentlemen as Stanley to the taint of "foreign usages" were the young ladies. English books might contain some valuable observations, as William Hill Brown's Mrs. Holmes remarked in *The Power of Sympathy,* but their "local descriptions" were "not always applicable to the situation of an *American* lady," and their denigration of learning in women was an outmoded "trans-Atlantick idea." But especially pernicious for American girls, the *Massachusetts Magazine* judged, were the "splendid palaces, dignified epithets, magnificent retinues, and all the dazzling scenes painted by novelists" of Europe. Distrust of such influences led even so judicious an author as Royall Tyler to question whether the more sophisticated literary taste that was being cultivated throughout the new nation was altogether a matter for pride; for he feared that while the American fancy was being enchanted, the heart was being corrupted. Especially the English novel, said Tyler, "impresses on the young female mind an erroneous idea of the world in which she is to live. It paints the manners, customs, and habits of a strange country; excites a fondness for false splendor; and renders the homespun habits of her own country disgusting." In view of such cultural dislocations, the duty of American writers seemed clear; and the deliberate attempts of Enos Hitchcock, William Hill Brown, Charles Brockden Brown, Mrs. Hannah Foster, Mrs. Sarah Wood, and others to portray for American girls manners and sentiments and codes consonant with the national milieu were grounded in much the same cultural realism as Howells' more comprehensive attack on romantic fiction a century later.

Although most of the apprehension over foreign modes was focused on England, it occasionally embraced the Continent and ancient Greece as well. Europe appeared to Freneau scarcely a source from which his countrymen might derive "learning or grace"; it was a "damnable place" where "reason and wit" were stifled by "popes and pretenders." Federalists like the poet T. G. Fessenden of course were disposed to fix the center of cultural infection more specifically in France—a country which had fed America on "whipped syllabub" and "vile fricasees of foreign trash," on "trumpery novels, . . ./ A windy wild and wordy waste/ To suit the ruling vitious taste." Some authors who could countenance no literature which did not subserve New World humanitarianism even looked at Homer askance. For all his "variety, animation, and sublimity," Joel Barlow concluded, "in a view of philanthropy," Homer's work has been "a serious misfortune to the human race." To counteract the *Iliad* Barlow demanded an American epic which would disseminate the love of liberty and would discourage the passion for violence and war. The moment had come in America, he felt, to direct poetry and all the arts to the end "that true and useful ideas of glory may be implanted in the minds of men here, to take place [*sic*] of the false and destructive ones that have degraded the species in other countries."

There were reasons other than the humanitarian scruples of Barlow for an especial American devaluation of the classics. In an excessive veneration for the ancients Benjamin Rush saw the chief inhibition to originality and the creative impulse. Only by ceasing the study of the sublime authors of antiquity, he maintained, could American writers equal them. What course literary "originality" in America might take Rush did not venture to say. But his words presage "The American Scholar" as surely as Barlow's prefigure both Whitman's uneasiness over the feudalism of Shakespeare and Twain's disgust at the reactionary influence of Scott.

Literature in America

Though the phrase "American literature" achieved a quick prominence in the post-Revolutionary generation, it rarely bore for the writers of that time the dominantly belletristic implications which it held later for Longfellow or Whitman or Howells or MacLeish. The literature of a nation, Simms wrote in 1841, is of two kinds: "It is that which distinguishes and illustrates, especially, the fortunes, tempers and peculiar characteristics of the people with whom it originates; or, it is that which is produced by native writers, from the common stock of human knowledge, in a fair competition with the reflective minds of other nations." Though Simms and his contemporaries were generally concerned with a "national literature" of the first type, it was with the latter signification that many of the pleas for an American literature before 1815 were made.

This second kind of American literature might be belletristic writing produced in America but adhering to universal ideas and forms; or it might be a mature composition in any field of intellectual endeavor in the young country. When the historian John Bristed in the early years of the century predicted that the United States would become the "bulwark and ornament of literature," when Noah Webster wrote Barlow that he would be happy to receive his opinion on any subject "favorable to American literature," and when John Quincy Adams discovered that in Europe Americans had a "sad reputation on the article of literature"—all were thinking of learned publications in the widest sense. The context of scores of similar statements shows that often in its early stages the campaign for "American literature" involved scarcely more than an attempt to stimulate the pursuit of the arts and sciences in America. It involved the assumption that Apollo had crossed the Atlantic not to express a unique national mind, but rather to "light up the West" with universal principles—that in their new cisatlantic home the Muses would not renounce their traditional character. Those who held such assumptions—and many did—were not disposed to look for any indigenous outlines on the American

Parnassus; and even those who dared to hope that they might discern such outlines were generally obliged to view them through the critical lenses of the neoclassicists and the Scottish rhetoricians. Of these critical authorities the most influential in the post-Revolutionary generation were Lord Kames (Henry Home) and Hugh Blair.

With his belief in a taste allied to the moral sense and "governed by principles common to all men," Kames undoubtedly deflected the current of American writing from the uniquely national or the concretely local. Certain grand and elevated objects, and certain qualities like regularity and proportion, Kames adjudged universally and naturally agreeable; and the fact that these objects and qualities were to be abundantly found in America may well have encouraged cisatlantic literary aspiration. Yet the treatment of these objects and qualities he proposed to evaluate by "general rules" derived from universal principles. By Kamesian doctrines American modes and materials were suitable only so long as they conformed to that "standard of taste" common to all nations; American idiom was admissible only to the extent that it moved within "certain inflexible laws." Under the dominance of Kames, therefore, even staunch foes of many Old World attitudes like Timothy Dwight often felt obliged to transcend the American scene in order to represent "such manners, as are removed from the peculiarities of any age, or country, and might belong to the amiable and virtuous, of every age." How pervasive was the authority of Kames's doctrines may be seen in the frequency with which the *Port Folio* relied upon his rules of criticism to establish poetic merit. Intimidated by these canons, many a native writer turned away from his own experience and milieu toward the abstract plane of universals.

Even more frequently, however, belletristic issues in the post-Revolutionary generation were settled by recourse to the dictates of Hugh Blair. Like Kames, Blair supposed taste to have the same foundation in all nations. But Blair was less austere; and in grounding his universality in that which "touches the heart," in insisting that a good heart is a "requisite to taste," he seemed to afford America and her authors a fairer literary prospect than did the Kamesian rules. Moreover, by his encomiums on genius, the sublime, and figurative language in the writings of ruder stages of society, he encouraged American authors to believe that the utterances of the young nation, unpolished though they were, might surpass in imaginative power the more sophisticated productions of Europe. And in his dictum that a good poet will eschew foreign scenes and exhibit the landscape peculiar to his own country, he encouraged a kind of indigenous reference which Kames scarcely seemed to sanction.

Blair, to be sure, did not altogether abandon a neoclassic devotion to elegance and propriety; but he did place new stress on the imagination and assign its cultivation to nature rather than to tradition; he did deplore the "servile imitation of any author"; he did foster experimentation by asserting that no one could be a good writer unless he had "some degree of confidence to follow his own genius." Further, in his view that the liberty afforded by republican institutions offers the most propitious of all literary climates, he lent additional support to nationalistic literary prophecies. Indeed, American writers who wished to utter their own sentiments and exhibit their own scenes may well have perceived in Blair their most valuable transatlantic apologist.

As early as 1783, when the *Boston Magazine* began publishing excerpts from his criticism, American writers were utilizing Blair to loosen the hold of a neoclassicism which was clearly incompatible with the national temper. Soon thereafter, he was hailed as a "national acquisition" and his views were incorporated into the critical pronouncements of both poets and prose writers. For the young poet Joseph Ladd he served as a formidable ally in an attack on the Latinisms and swelling periods of Johnsonian style. For John Blair Linn, who frequently cited him, he must have stood as the prime authority for the belief that the style of a writer should be one which "nature dictates." And in Charles Brockden Brown's praise for the American author "who paints, not from books, but from nature, who introduces those lines and hues in which we differ, rather than those in which we resemble our kindred nations beyond the ocean," one may detect recurrent echoes of Blair.

Other European critics played a part, of course, in the attempts of America's first literary generation to achieve a native though not specifically a national literature. Few American critics of the time seem to have escaped the dominance of Kames and Blair, but occasionally literary reckonings of the future were taken from the sturdy postulates of neoclassicism. By such postulates "originality" was to be neither desired nor expected in American letters, as the patriotic classicist Colonel John Parke concluded after reading Boileau and Addison. Since the best writing had always consisted not so much in " 'advancing things that are *new* as in giving things that are *known* an agreeable turn,' " it seemed to Parke that the American author had better bend all his efforts to representing the "common sense" of history rather than the peculiar experience and principles of the new republic.

Sharing the same Boileau-Addison distrust of originality, Dr. Benjamin Waterhouse, of the *Monthly Anthology,* soon after the turn of the century confessed his own preference for "transatlantick silk and fine-twined linen" over "tow-cloth," and advised his countrymen to abandon their concern over plagiarism and "to express old things in a new way." Indeed, in the early 1800's when disillusion over America's slow literary development had begun to fix itself in the minds of erstwhile nationalists like Charles Brockden Brown, there was no little comfort to be derived from Boileau and Pope, whose neoclassic voices seemed to say that, after all, originality was a mere "chimaera" which was to be found in no "judicious work," that good sense is the same in all ages, and that a "new thought" is merely a fresh and lively statement of this good sense.

The impact of other European critical systems on the nation's first literary generation was less pronounced. The associationist psychology of Locke and Hartley left its mark on Thomas Odiorne, but he did not trace its implications for cisatlantic writers so explicitly as did Bryant and later authors who read the associationist Alison. In fact, Alison's influence, like that of A. W. Schlegel, Herder, and Madame de Staël, with their espousal of the organically national as opposed to the neoclassical universal in art, was scarcely to be felt until after 1815. By that time the views of Madame de Staël especially had begun to be disseminated. In 1813 the *Analectic* carried excerpts from her work, in which diversity in national tastes was defended and literature was viewed as the product of changing social and political forces rather than as the exponent of absolute reason. Those Americans who perceived the implications of her *Influence of Literature Upon Society,* issued in Boston in 1813, may well have indulged in a new confidence in the nation's literary future. Yet the first literary generation were obliged for the most part to construct their critical theories without the benefit of her historical and nationalistic point of view. Encouraged toward originality though they were by some of the social and aesthetic theories of the Scottish philosophers, they were as often impelled by neoclassic postulates to aspire toward literature in America rather than an American literature.

The Ties of Tradition

Committed to a neoclassical reverence for Nature or for universal Reason, the conservative man of letters before 1815 ventured only with the greatest caution beyond the "rules" of the pre-Romantic "English school." Fenimore Cooper was surely right in observing, in his later years, that until 1812 England was the "idol" of America's "literary adoration." Even the cultural nationalist, for all his desire to emancipate American letters from current British modes, usually considered himself no more obliged to declare his independence of Addison and Steele than the founding fathers had felt obliged to renounce William and Mary. It is not surprising, therefore, that in creating the Bloomsgrove family to exemplify American propriety in education and manners in the 1790's, the Revolutionary chaplain Enos Hitchcock should have specified that young Bloomsgrove should adorn his mind with "elegant literature" and "elegance of taste." This was the same elegance which Noah Webster, for all his exhortations to cultural independence, found so thoroughly characteristic of the *Spectator* that he advised American girls to give Addison the first place in their libraries. In the South the republican William Wirt echoed Webster in pronouncing the *Spectator* a means to virtue and enlightenment, and in lamenting the "contempt for everything that is old" which has thrown the ancient authors into oblivion.

Implicit in such a view as Webster's or Wirt's was the assumption that political nationalism did not involve cultural isolation—that the new republicanism of America, indeed, was ultimately to be valued in proportion as it permitted a freer access to Virtue and Reason and Taste. It was on this premise that Irving could proclaim his allegiance both to his country and to the "good old orthodox writers" who, as "adopted citizens," formed a sort of literary Nile whence America might derive "riches, beauty, fertility." Even the War of 1812 could scarcely persuade him to poison "with political virulence, the pure fountains of elegant literature," for the high mission of such literature, he thought, is to unify rather than to divide the human family. As the projectors of the *American Review* phrased the issue in 1811, the "relish for elegant literature" is not to be vitiated by the infusion of political bias, for only upon the scaffolding of English literature may the superstructure of a reputable American literature be erected. No doubt that early anthologist of American literature, Dr. Elihu Smith, spoke for most of young Irving's generation when he spoke of the belles-lettres of all nations as agents of universal taste uniting mankind in "one vast brotherhood/ In equal bonds of knowledge and of right." In such a view American literature would best become American by embracing those universals which the national life seemed destined to exemplify more positively than that of any civilization of the past.

To accept American literature as the perfected organ of universal taste was also, even for many a literary nationalist, to accept the corollary of a universal English style, whose values and harmonies and usages had been fixed by the Augustans in permanent standards of "elegance and correctness." From these standards cisatlantic works were not to deviate; they were to be measured "by rules precisely such as Tooke, Harris, Kaimes [*sic*], Blair, or Lowth would have applied to British efforts of genius"; their style was to be adjudged "perspicuous or obscure, nervous or feeble, harmonious or discordant, &c."

More specifically, American poems were to be judged by the "laws of English Prosody" which, as the poet-critic Charles Prentiss declared, had been "settled by Dryden and Pope." Such "laws," of course, could scarcely admit to legitimacy any of the changes in linguistic and prosodic values which might be suggested by Indian place names, or by the speech of racially diverse immigrants, or by the dialects of the Negroes. Any such linguistic pressures from a new society were to be resisted as "gross corruptions"—as the Babel of a disunited species. The "notion of an American tongue, or of gaining our idiom from the mouths of the illiterate," the *Monthly Anthology* could regard only

with horror; the "irregular" was not to escape the knife because it was
of domestic growth, Noah Webster's etymological arguments for innovations notwithstanding.

Even the most patriotic men of letters often drew the line at projecting American independence into the linguistic frontier of Americanisms. Like the eminent Princeton theologian, Samuel Miller, in
A Brief Retrospect of the Eighteenth Century (1803), they would at
once affirm their "partiality" for America and yet resent recent London
observations on Franklin's "American style of writing," hastening to
assert that Franklin was free from provincial taints, that he had used
Addison as his model, that he was not guilty of "unauthorized terms
and phrases, which characterize too many American writers in later
times."

A few native writers and critics, of course, relied upon the ancient
rather than the English classics for their standards of universal taste.
Not content to become American Augustans, they ventured to associate themselves with the loftier company of the older masters. Even
on the wild New York frontier during the Revolution, the poet-nov-
elist Eliza Bleecker supposed it appropriate to invoke Apollo and to
contrast her lot with Virgil's. Not far away, at the "College at She-
nectady" [*sic*] John Blair Linn prayed that "Homer's awful fire . . .
bless our infant land." And in Boston Robert Treat Paine became
Menander that he might fittingly correspond in verse with his Philenia (Mrs. Morton), whom he flattered as "the American Sappho"
who wove "Pierian webs" and turned Beacon Hill into a new Parnassus. Indeed, amid innumerable prophecies that new Homers and
Terences would be inspired by "FREEDOM'S patrons," occasional attempts were made to adapt the American materials to classic models.
Yet two thousand years proved too large a gulf for the old forms and
idioms to span, and hence such experiments as Colonel John Parke's
paraphrases of Horace (1786) with the use of American scenes soon
yielded to the more suggestive pattern of Scott.

The vogue of Scott's narrative poetry after 1805 served as a prelude
to the appearance of *Waverley* (1814), which, in the words of Samuel
Goodrich, was to make a "greater sensation in the United States than
. . . some of the battles of Napoleon." By the end of the War of 1812
there were renewed hopes for the "Genius of this unfam'd land;/ In

lofty strain, like wizard Scott, to soar,/ And court the muses to this foreign strand." Soon the very clouds in the Western sky began to assume the shapes of castled cliffs and mouldering towers. The romantic mode of Scott promised a more congenial path than neoclassicism to an American literature which would be both indigenous and respectable.

American Differentiae: Themes and Materials

Since the concept of an organic nationalism, with its allowance for diversity in idiom and cultural values, was not widely entertained on cisatlantic shores before 1815, the first literary generation were ineluctably obliged to chart a course for American literature within the bounds of what was adjudged to be universal taste. An "original" literature therefore was likely to imply for even the most zealous literary patriot not a startling mutation but rather a reordering of European ideas, a purification of Old World genres, or a realization of the literary dreams of ancient cultures in the ideal atmosphere of the New World. Within approximately such a range of assumptions, the post-Revolutionary writers proceeded busily to sketch the outlines of a literature which they supposed would not only have proper national attributes but would also be the glory of the world.

To an age which regarded the incisive generalization as inherently poetic, the clue to a legitimate Americanism in literature might well seem to lie in the explicit ideological content of a work. Certainly such early poets as Humphreys and Barlow proceeded on the assumption that to serve the best literary interests of their country their own work should involve a direct expression of American ideas and sentiments —yet ideas and sentiments not at odds with universal Reason. Therefore, the two of them undertook, respectively, such projects as "A Poem on Industry" and *The Columbiad* with the avowed purpose of writing "patriotic" poetry in which both poetical and moral objects, as the current phrasing had it, were to be kept in view. Humphreys' "moral object" was to affirm the especial benefactions of national industry; Barlow's was to "nerve" his country with the "patriot lay" through the inculcation of republican principles and "true and useful ideas of glory"—a moral object which he thought might well lift his epic above the *Iliad,* since that ancient poem espoused inhumane social and ethical attitudes. Since America "must now be considered as the depository and guardian of the best interests of mankind," Barlow reasoned, an American poem can be properly national only if it bespeaks "genuine philanthropy," and the patriot mind and the moral mind become one and the same.

To the early essayists and novelists no less than to the poets, the American writer seemed obligated to express his country's mission and glory. To young Charles Brockden Brown, as to Barlow, the "most precious morsels" of literature seemed to be those "strains which have a peculiar relation to the political or religious transactions" of an author's country. There were difficulties for the "story-telling moralist" in America, Brown acknowledged, because the country's political system and social maxims were part of a "new and untrodden field"; and, in Virginia, William Wirt conceded that America's fluid society confronted the native essayist with a similar problem. Yet by virtue of this very fluidity, Wirt confidently asserted, such an essayist might "aspire without vanity or presumption, to occupy an higher rank in the scale of public estimation and moral utility, than any of his European models and precursors" could hope to attain. The American essayist in his view was to be, like Barlow's American poet, a republican moralist. He was to help restore the simplicity and dignity of manners characteristic of the ancient republics and to help eradicate that predilection for those luxuries "which constitute the baubles of our colonial childhood, the badges of aristocratical distinctions we have abjured, and the idols of the abominable passions, which we have sworn on the altars of the revolution to expunge from our souls."

On the most elementary level this conscious effort to express national ideas resulted in the patriotic song such as "Hail, Columbia," which, as Hopkinson said, was written "to get up an American spirit. . . . It was truly *American* and nothing else. . . ." But poetry had a more complex mission, as Timothy Dwight remarked, than that performed by such songs: it was to augment the welfare of the nation by improving its manners and its political, economical, and moral sentiments. In an America "by heaven design'd [to be]/ Th' example bright, to renovate mankind," Dwight supposed that "rising bards" were all but traitors to the national destiny if they should fail to inculcate a cisatlantic piety—if they should "soil the page refin'd" with "sickly spot" or "taint the artless mind" or cause the "meek virgin" to blush.

Novelists and dramatists as well as "rising bards" construed the moral bearing of their works in nationalistic terms. The Anglo-American Mrs. Rowson, dedicating her *Slaves in Algiers* (1794) to the citizens of the United States, assured her audience-readers that in drawing forth the tear of sensibility her play utilized *"no one sentiment, in the least prejudicial, to the moral and political principles of the government under which I live."* Her earlier *Charlotte Temple* (1791), written in England and designed to save American girls from misery rather than to earn the applause which might be given a more sophisticated work, set the pattern, of course, for a whole school of fiction sentimentally and consciously committed to a national standard of virtue for "Columbian Young Ladies." Perhaps because the theater was under especial attack for its alleged licentiousness, native dramatists eagerly affirmed their obligation to fix "the impressive moral in the heart" and thereby to safeguard cisatlantic mores. Even the American "comic muse," as William Dunlap said, was required to be "sportive . . . in moral mode;/ Proud of her dwelling in our new made nation/ She's set about, a serious reformation/ For faith she'd almost lost her reputation." This homespun, modest Muse seemed to Dunlap all the sturdier for having abstained from the "high season'd food" of Europe; she could better be nurtured on the "Fruits of your country's growth, food for the mind,/ Where moral truth and sentiment are join'd."

This current of literary concern for a national standard of morality in such writers as Dwight, Dunlap, and Mrs. Rowson undoubtedly had its fountainhead in the New Zion; but during the eighteenth century it was fed by the streams of neoclassicism, by the Enlightenment, and by romantic sensibility. Hence to early literary prophets like Dwight, Freneau, and Barlow, as to the later Whitman, American literature seemed destined to become the autochthonous voice of a nation which for the first time in history had manifestly embraced a belief in both God and Reason.

As Whitman's "divine literatus" was to be "kosmic," so Barlow's native bard was to "ken the total God" and to prepare for the coming of the Prince of Peace to a world united by love—but a love which had been matured through the agency of Moral Science and Reason. As to the nature of this Reason which America was to exemplify for all mankind, undoubtedly such diverse minds as Freneau and Dwight would scarcely have agreed; but the two authors did concur in declaring the American writer to be her most authentic voice. Since America is a land where "Reason shall enforce her sway," said Freneau, her representative writers must resist all collusion with the superstition and tyranny of Europe. And Dwight in *Greenfield Hill* (1794) had a similar vision of an America where "rising bards" would celebrate Reason's first great national triumph. These poets would be the voice of a Reason, however, unknown to Hume and Voltaire; their Reason would involve a scheme of science and morals based on "God's own word." But whatever divergent conceptions of Reason may have existed among Barlow and Freneau and Dwight, they were all agreed that the American poet could have no traffic with the irrationalism of classical mythology. All could have accepted Mrs. Sarah Morton's affirmation that *"Columbia's native minstrel"* would scorn the use of "Pagan deities," since Reason and Truth disdain them. Rather it was the "mystic mandate" of the "patriot muse," said Mrs. Morton, to spread the "mental light" of "equal freedom."

To the numerous nationalistic authors who inclined to abjure the classic wars and deities in behalf of "equal freedom," the Revolution seemed to supply a heroic action consonant with both universal Reason and American destiny. It not only contained novel scenes and episodes to which transatlantic authors could lay no claim; it also involved inclusive principles which might well re-enforce epic or tragic sublimity. From the Revolution, indeed, one might glimpse Divinity itself; for in the American victory such patriots as Hazard, Belknap, Barlow, and Dwight perceived the same Providential hand that Edward Johnson and Cotton Mather in the previous century had seen in cisatlantic affairs. Indeed, for any author whose pen might hesitate to trace a pattern in the manifold details of such recent history, there were historians and divines at hand to supply the underlying argument for a large national work based on the Revolution. Even with the coming of peace President Ezra Stiles of Yale proclaimed that "none but Americans can write the American war"; and he had no doubt that the "future *Homers, Livys,* and *Tassos* of our country" would "drop a tear upon those mighty ones, those *beauties* of *Israel,* who have fallen in battle," for they fell in the "wars of the Lord."

The poets, too, perceiving the Divine hand at work in the Revolutionary victory, were equally sure, as Samuel Low prophesied, that some "Heav'n-taught" American bard would "chant the memorable tale,/ How Freedom fought, and did at last prevail." Such a war for Freedom, Freneau added, had a higher claim on genius than any previous conflict and should issue in the grandest poetry in history; for the old heroic poems were written on a "comparatively narrow basis." If barbarous and petty ancient wars could be "aggrandized" by Homer and Virgil, so the reiterated argument went, how much greater would be a Revolutionary epic supported by "all the solidity of philosophy." The fallacy of such positivist literary arguments is, of course, attested by the dearth of good poetry based on the Revolution. Nevertheless, they bred a national literary confidence which led Mrs. Rowson to affirm that, having "matchless Washington" as the subject for a "Eulogy," she need have no envy of Homer, who, after all, had only "barbarous chieftains."

The Revolution was claimed almost as soon for the dramatist as for the epic poet and the elegist. Yet here the problem of historic distance continued to be a troublesome one. William Dunlap, struggling nine years over his *André* (1798), finally yielded to the prevailing opinion that "recent events are unfit subjects for tragedy" and reluctantly decided to give a didactic rather than a tragic treatment to his Revolutionary materials—or, as he said, to instruct the men that are by singing of men as they were, and to expose the true nature of British oppression. Even after the passing of a generation the "prevailing opinion" which had thwarted Dunlap continued to discourage both dramatists and romancers who desired to treat the larger figures and events of the Revolution. As Daniel Jackson incisively stated the issue in *The Asylum* (1811):

> Romance, founded on great events, and embracing eminent characters and important achievements, cannot be written, with any considerable degree of interest and effect, where the scenery is laid, and the drama cast, in America; because, should it be attempted, the theatre must be erected on the field of the revolution, an era not sufficiently remote, and comprising occurrences too recent, to be arrayed in the vesture of

fiction. It will, however, furnish materials, and the most brilliant apparatus, to a writer of some succeeding century.

Despite the cogency of Jackson's argument, literary patriots closer to the Augustan tradition persisted in their faith that the inherent sublimity of the Revolutionary struggle was a theme which needed no hallowing through the mists of time. A decade after the conclusion of the war Richard Snowden found it all but incredible that the Revolution had not appeared in "a poetical address"; and accordingly he resolved to write *The Columbiad* (1795), in order to break ground for some abler poet, who might thereby more readily sing of Bunker Hill and make "Columbia o'er Europa shine." With a more realistic appraisal of public taste, however, the women writers of the day claimed the recent war for less pretentious treatment. Conceding that the sublime and heroic strains were outside their scope, they nevertheless supposed, as Mrs. Judith Murray remarked, that "the interesting events of the revolution, may become the exercise of humbler talents; and garbed in simple language, may, for a certain class of readers, possess peculiar charms." As if to prove the validity of Mrs. Murray's dictum, that "humble minstrel" Mrs. Sarah Morton, contrasting herself with the proud bards of ancient times, announced at the end of the century that she had written with few of the "ornaments of Poetry" a tale founded on the actual events of the Revolution, *The Virtues of Society*.

While Mrs. Morton was eschewing poetic ornaments in her Revolutionary narrative and while Richard Snowden was envisioning "some future *Humphreys*" sublimely singing Bunker Hill, the living David Humphreys was attending to the more specific purposes and formal problems which the composition of a heroic treatment of the war might involve. The ancient languages, he could but admit, were superior in figures and sounds for "glowing descriptions of battles"; yet he was confident that selected phases of Revolutionary warfare were available to the American poet for keeping alive the "fire of heroism" necessary for the defense of free states. Such an explicitly patriotic use of poetry, Humphreys believed, was thoroughly in accord with the ancient and exalted tradition of the art; and not a few of his contemporaries shared his devout hope that some inspired bard "with rapture rolling eyes" would do justice to the Revolutionary warriors. Such bards, said no less a figure than Washington himself, are the keepers of "the gate by which Patriots, Sages and Heroes are admitted to immortality. Such are your Antient Bards who are both the priests and door-keepers to the temple of fame. And these . . . are no vulgar functions."

It was inevitable that the majority of early American writers should have placed their hopes for a national literature in the expression of a distinctive sociopolitical ideal, whether the ideal was linked to the Revolutionary past or the vision of future glory, rather than in a delineation of native manners; for while the prevailing Augustan tradition sanctioned both literary modes, American society clearly possessed the earnestness to sustain the former rather than the brilliance and the contrasts requisite for the latter. Nevertheless, a few post-Revolutionary authors were convinced that in a mirroring of republican manners the freshness of the image would compensate for any crudeness and would afford the most distinctive type of national literature. It was undoubtedly the "boldness of a youthful muse," as the dramatist Barnabas Bidwell expressed it, that led these writers to eschew flights toward the sublime for a more modest concern with the "true"—the domestic circumstances of the "common life" that they knew. And certainly in the dominantly Augustan literary atmosphere of 1800 no little courage was required to assert, as did Charles Brockden Brown, that the American novelist might well discount his obligations to the universal in order to introduce into his fiction "those lines and hues in which we differ, rather than those in which we resemble our kindred nations beyond the ocean" and thereby trace "all that is genuine and peculiar in the scene before him."

The motive for such realism, of course, often transcended the desire merely to exploit cisatlantic novelty. To "portray American manners, . . . record American events" and "delineate American . . . customs, opinions, characters" was, as the dramatist J. N. Barker perceived, to provide a potent counteragent to alien modes of thinking. Yet the norm of American manners was not easy to determine. In the early 1790's Timothy Dwight, remarking the need of a national style of clothing, saw three distinct sets of manners crystallizing along the coast: those of Virginia, of South Carolina, and of New England. Since those of the Southern states were dependent on slavery, he was confident that the "patriotic mind" would rejoice that New England manners were spreading across the country and thus were in process of becoming the national standard. However far the "plain manners" of New England may have spread geographically before 1812, they certainly dominated, by virtue of the section's literary pre-eminence, the early literature in this genre.

The Maine writer, Mrs. Sarah Wood, who for all her Gothicism avowedly sought in *Dorval* (1801) "to catch the manners of her native land" in order to counteract the fashions of Europe, surely assumed with Dwight that the mores of New England might best represent the nation as a whole. The more comprehensive devotion to the variety of American behavior which led St. John Honeywood to portray the "Shaking Quakers" and to sigh for Shakespeare's pen to do them justice was not common. But whatever their differences in estimating the authentically native, Mrs. Wood and Honeywood must have shared with Royall Tyler a conviction that, in view of the corruption of American hearts by foreign novels, "There are two things wanted . . . : that we write our own books of amusement, and that they exhibit our own manners."

No group of native writers at the turn of the century stood to gain more by Tyler's view than the dramatists, who saw an occasion to elevate the status of the American stage by claiming that an especial moral and patriotic force resided in their depiction of republican manners. In *The Gleaner* (1798) the influential Mrs. Murray observed that "every patriotic moralist" ought to be concerned with the *"utility"* of the stage, and she urged that the American theater be supplied with native scenes so that "Columbian Shakespeares" might yet arise. Mrs. Murray's well-intentioned generalities were given a sharper focus by the dramatist George Watterston, who perceived the advantages of a native comedy of manners for both the stage and the national culture:

> Most of the *few* dramatists of this country seem to have mistaken the principal object of comedy, and have, accordingly, laid their scenes in foreign nations. To satirize the prevailing vices and follies of mankind, is evidently the design of this species of dramatic composition. It becomes the peculiar duty of those who devote their attention to the comic muse, to confine themselves particularly to their own nation,

and to satirize such vices and follies as are there most frequent and common.

Whether Watterston considered the plane of republican manners a sufficiently lofty one from which to launch "the shaft of ridicule" at human follies is not clear; but he leaves no doubt that he judged American behavior had been unduly neglected on the stage.

Among the post-Revolutionary proponents of a national literature, however, far less attention was accorded to American manners than to that resource and stimulus which has appeared more consistently than any other through nearly three centuries of cisatlantic literary aspiration—the American landscape. Especially to the mind formed by neoclassic or Augustan doctrines, American nature seemed to offer the firmest assurances of unrivaled literary achievements. Supported by the current postulate that "sentiments of the mind bear some proportion to the objects that surround it," that grand mountains "fill the mind with a dignity and sublimity of sentiment peculiar to the western continent," post-Revolutionary critics lost no time in amplifying the earlier colonial literary faith in the regenerative power of American nature. Even without the rugged grandeur of the Far West, young writers like John Blair Linn and Samuel Knapp found innumerable scenes which seemed to them pregnant with the "spirit of inventive enthusiasm" or calculated to "hurry" the imagination into "poetical enthusiasm."

Yet despite this "poetical enthusiasm" no fund of poetry was forthcoming, and early nineteenth-century critics could but wonder why the Muse slumbered amid such scenes. "We have skies, which give us the varied and kind returns of seasons," went a typical lament at the turn of the century; "we have winds, which one would think would blow the spark of genius into flame; we have waters, which should allure to their banks the vagrant foot of enthusiasm; and we have mountains, which furnish us with all that is grand and elevating in prospect." So long as nationalistic critics relied on America's winds to blow native genius into flame, they were of course doomed to reiterate such disconsolate reports on the nation's literary achievements. More judiciously young Irving, reflecting on the success of Campbell's "Gertrude of Wyoming," realized that while "sweet nature" might furnish inspi-

ration and imagery, she could not afford full sustenance for the poetic
or philosophic mind. American poets needed no dryads, satyrs, nightingales, and other "hackneyed materials," he observed; but, in addition to the "simple beauty or wild magnificence" of nature, they required an awareness of the "human mind . . . in new and striking
situations." For this reason Irving did not suppose, as did the Southern poet Daniel Bryan, that any noble soul would break into "rhapso-
dies of divinest enthusiasm" while walking through Columbia's forests or hearing the roar of her rivers or gazing on the grandeur of her
mountains. Indeed, said Bryan, only the excessive "lucrative exertion"
of his countrymen kept them from beholding, as he had done a thousand times in fancy, "the Genius of Columbian Poesy" on "the wildest
cliffs of Allegany [*sic*], . . . warbling . . . the sweetest raptures of
Inspiration."

This faith of Bryan's that an elevated landscape would produce an
elevated poetry persisted through both the neoclassic and the romantic
phases of American literary development. Later it was expressed in
Whitman's assertion that America itself is a great poem and hence
the poet's first care must be to allow the physical magnificence of the
land to "embouchure" into his sensibilities. It was essentially to the
validity of this process that David Humphreys testified when, in ac-
counting for the success of his post-Revolutionary poems about America, he declared that the very novelty and grandeur of his country's
topography had not only provided him with "magnificent images"
but also given "energy to the language" which expressed his "sensa-
tions." Nature itself, as it were, had guaranteed both the substance and
the spirit of the poems. In this climate of critical opinion it was inevitable that a century of effort to transmute Niagara into the grand American poem should have begun. Even as the Revolution ended, critics
turned the attention of literary aspirants toward this "immense spectacle," arguing that it could not "fail of raising lofty and sublime ideas"
and hence of inspiring "a very fine original poem." Other "immense
spectacles" across the nation, of course, were in turn acclaimed by
regional devotees with equal confidence. The mountains of New
Hampshire seemed to the historian Jeremy Belknap to contain the
unparalleled and intrinsic stuff of sublimity:

A poetic fancy may find full gratification amidst these wild and rugged scenes. . . . Aged mountains, stupendous elevations, rolling clouds, impending rocks, verdant woods, chrystal streams, the gentle rill, and the roaring torrent, all conspire to amaze, to soothe and to enrapture. To the ornithologist Alexander Wilson, who had traveled through many of the states, the whole continent sang so rapturously that the failure of any native poet to catch its lofty mood seemed all but incredible:

> Our western world, with all its matchless floods,
> Our vast transparent lakes and boundless woods,
> Stamped with the traits of majesty sublime,
> Unhonoured weep the silent lapse of Time,
>
> . . . .
>
> While scarce one Muse returns the songs they gave,
> Or seeks to snatch their glories from the grave.

Perhaps because the rivers of the Old World had flowed so steadily through the poems of the past, America's "matchless floods," as Wilson called them, were more frequently proposed than either Niagara or the Alleghenies as the most propitious of themes. If such "insipid brooks" as the Arno and Thames can inspire, if "brooks of half a mile/ Can rouse the thousand bards of Britain's Isle," so the reiterated argument ran, should not the mightier Hudson or Schuylkill command a grander commemoration? Decade by decade successive literary centers proclaimed the quantitative and hence aesthetic superiority of their regional streams to those of Europe. Before the Revolution the Muse was generally declared to have abandoned Europe in order to inhabit the banks of the Schuylkill; but by 1815 she apparently had been charmed by the palisades of the Hudson and, indeed, had been occasionally lured into the tributary Mohawk. To sing the charms of such a river as the Hudson, Eliza Bleecker's daughter, Margaretta Faugères knew that her own "trembling lyre" was no fit instrument, but she foresaw "some loftier poet" in the light of whose tributes the Nile and Tiber and Danube's tides would be forgotten. Neither St. John Honeywood nor John M'Kinnon was so lofty a poet as Mrs. Faugères envisioned, but each bespoke the unprecedented charms of the Mohawk and Hudson, the one denying that "*Roman Tiber, or Brittania's Thames,/* Survey more beauties than our silver streams," the other invoking the Muse to "scent/ The wild perfume of transatlantic pines,/ The lilies of the misty Mohawk's vales." Such Eastern streams could claim both a wild and cultivated beauty along their shores to tempt the poet; but in the West "sublime Ohio" throughout the post-Revolutionary generation rolled "his deepening tide" like an almost mythical stream, sweeping through dark forests in primitive splendor.

Though it was the grandeur of American mountains and rivers that usually encouraged native bards to poetic "enthusiasm," the less spectacular agrarian landscape with its air of simple well-being did not go entirely unrecognized as a distinctive mutation of a traditional genre. An authentic portrayal of rural American life, a few authors were convinced, would crown the long tradition of pastoral poetry. "Arcadia itself is not more beautiful nor yet more sonorous than Pennsylvania," proclaimed the *Port Folio;* and, even as he composed *The Columbiad,* Richard Snowden invoked the Arcadian Muse of Sidney in order that he might properly sing of the revolving year and of forest and Indian lore and pastoral scenes. Such was the scene that John M'Kinnon, too, wished to celebrate: "a landscape gravid with the wealth/ Of future years, the blended charms of land,/ And sea, and skies autumnal."

It was David Humphreys, however, with his usual concern for the critical premises of his works, who provided the most "seasonable arguments and reflections" on the proper nature of an American pastoral. This distinctively New World poem, he said, would comprise the "process and result" of the American conquest of the wilderness, the description of how "forests fell, houses rose, and beautiful scenery succeeded"—changes "like those in a garden of enchantment." The inhabitants of this "garden," he insisted, must belong to the "middle station" in culture; as the golden mean between the excessively rude and the polished, they would be the "new actors for a golden age." In essence Humphreys was sketching a republican, middle-class pastoral. As a patron of the "Genius of Culture" rather than of primitivism, he sought to fuse agrarian achievements with an agrarian ideal in order to guide his countrymen toward that equable society which he thought the Revolution had opened to them.

Occasionally, amid the customary preoccupations with sublime or pastoral landscapes, the post-Revolutionary imagination turned toward the familiar world of American flora and fauna. "I have often regretted," wrote Alexander Wilson in the early 1800's with regard to the mild and pleasing manners of the bluebird, "that no pastoral Muse has yet risen, in this western woody world, to do justice to his name, and endear him to us still more by the tenderness of verse, as has been done to his representative in Britain, the Robin Redbreast." In his day Wilson was almost alone in sensing fresh cisatlantic subjects in "our charming warblers" and in proposing that American poets "faithfully pourtray/ The various pipes that hymn our rising day!" Yet even as Wilson was making his claims for American warblers, there was initiated (apparently by the Anglophile Joseph Dennie) the long literary war against the nightingale. The truly American poet, declared Dennie's *Port Folio* in 1805, leaves "to European poets their *Nightingales* and *Skylarks,* and their *dingles* and *dells.* He makes no mention of yews and myrtles, nor echoes a single note of either Bullfinch or Chaffinch, but faithfully describes American objects. . . ."

To the alien company of the nightingale James Kirke Paulding soon consigned the glow-worm. The whippoorwill and firefly, he insisted, could well replace them. Through the use of such simple and distinctive creatures from the native scene, Paulding predicted, not only would the individual character of America be reflected, but poetry itself would also become genuine and imaginative. In the whippoorwill, he reminded his literary compatriots, they had "a rare poetical bird," for about him had gathered many stirring tales of national superstition; and in the firefly they indeed had a "treasure" which provided them "new imagery," whereas poets in "the other three quarters of the globe . . . are drained to the very dregs."

Like the whippoorwill, the Indian with difficulty achieved status as a component of an American literature. Despite occasional appearances in pre-Revolutionary poetry, drama, and songs, he was not readily assimilated into the apostrophes to American nature or into a poetry of republican ideas or into delineations of native manners. In almost any version of a national culture before 1815 he was an alien. In the American epic he assumed an unheroic and antinational guise; and when the Indian wars were acclaimed as a theme fit for an American Homer, as Timothy Dwight believed them to be, it was the "gallant deeds" of the Puritan invaders and not the traits of the aborigines which were to guarantee the New World flavor. Long before Henry

James, Dwight reckoned with European skepticism with regard to belletristic materials in a country devoid of magnificent villas and palaces, of variety in character and manners, of hierarchical order in society and church. His retort was that the American writer had as a scene "a novelty in the history of man": the colonization of a wilderness by men with mild manners, Christianity, the arts, and learning. Such a "combination of enterprise, patience, and perseverance" seemed to him to "compensate the want of ancient castles, ruined abbeys, and fine pictures." Yet in all this "combination" the Indian was to appear only as grist for the conqueror's mill, not as a sensitive being fit for tragic, epic, or lyric treatment in his own right. Indeed, post-Revolutionary authors with a Puritan heritage were scarcely sympathetic with suggestions such as Colonel John Parke's that "Indians . . . Deep couching in the midnight wood" might serve as an appropriate theme for an American poem. Like Jeremy Belknap, they might note the existence of Indian legends about the White Mountains, only to exclude such "fictions" from an inventory of local themes appealing to the "poetic fancy."

In view of this prevailing disregard of the aborigines, it is not surprising that Mrs. Sarah Morton should have remarked in 1790 that Indian themes and subjects are so simple and limited that they have scarcely been touched. Convinced that such themes might enable her to compose a work both "original" and "wholly American," Mrs. Morton composed *Ouâbi,* a tale that illustrated the "Virtues of Nature" better than the actual conditions of aboriginal life. Yet, whatever the sentimental defects of the tale, she perceived something of the Indian's place in the national literature; and Charles Brockden Brown was no less eager for "the partial eye of the patriot" when he introduced the red man into a longer prose work. The Indians of his *Edgar Huntly* (1799) were in part, he asserted, the creatures of national literary pride, the proof that America could provide "numerous and inexhaustible . . . sources of amusement to the fancy and instruction to the heart, that are peculiar to ourselves." In the Indian wars and frontier perils Brown perceived indigenous materials which would provide the American author with incidents involving a passion and terror far more powerful than that which they could derive from "Puerile superstition and exploded manners, Gothic castles and chimeras." Yet even here the Indian remained a creature of "hostility" outside the positive current of national sentiment. In general, until the 1820's he continued to be an incidental though indigenous example of the diabolic or primitive or pathetic—a national antihero "whose passions civilization had not yet put under any restraint."

Differentiae: Style and Forms

Confident of his ability to create a literature characteristic of America through theme or idea or setting, the post-Revolutionary author was disposed to accept his English heritage of diction and style as inevitable and incidental rather than as primary limitations upon a national literature. The insistence that an autochthonous tone and texture and idiom pervade the very nuances of expression marked a later stage of the aspiration for an American literature. Yet even before 1815 two contrasting styles professing indigenous claims struggled for dominance. One style moved toward simplicity—an ideal which, though at variance with much in national literary practice, could trace a literary ancestry in the strong and explicit devotion to a plain style among colonial writers as well as in the neoclassic stress on perspicuity. This tradition led Ezra Stiles to suppose that the English mother tongue might slough off its "rough sonorous diction" in America and "grow up, with the present American population, into great purity and elegance, unmutilated by the foreign dialects of foreign countries." In behalf of this same purity Dr. Benjamin Rush attacked Johnson's "turgid stile" and Gibbon's "purple glare" and Junius' "thick set metaphors" as unfit to "be admitted into our country." With Rush's dictum that "The present is the age of simplicity of writing in America" Noah Webster agreed, extolling Franklin and Witherspoon as the worthiest models for the native writer inasmuch as they bestowed their labor on ideas, not words. To Webster "ornament" seemed un-American, as it did also to the Virginian George Tucker, who warned his countrymen against European affectation and proposed that they should strive for a "manly species of writing" which should emphasize substance and precision and force.

Yet this very effort to nationalize simplicity as the true genius of American style was indicative of a contrary bent in popular expression. Between the wars with Britain, as George Tucker observed, novels, romances, Fourth of July orations, and newspapers had increasingly indulged in such vulgar and florid strains that anyone who cherished simplicity could only conclude that both the English language and common sense had been put "to the rack" by high-sounding inanity. Of this luxuriant rudeness in American writing Joseph Dennie was perhaps the most persistent and indignant critic. A generation before the vogue of Jack Downing and Sam Slick announced the ascendancy of a native humor, he showed his contempt for the genre by satirically concocting an illiterate letter from one Ichabod Flash in "the militia style, so justly in vogue in this happy country." To Dennie this "militia style" seemed little else, as he said in one of his numerous attacks upon it, than a "vile alloy of provincial idioms, and colloquial barbarism."

Yet other cisatlantic alloys were apparently more disconcertingly prevalent than the "militia style." At times even the staunch literary nationalist could but shudder at Fifth of March orations in what Timothy Dwight called the *"Boston Style . . .* a phrase, proverbially used throughout a considerable part of this country to denote a florid, pompous manner of writing." It was no doubt a bit of similarly barbarous native prose that evoked from the obscure Carolinian poet George the derisive sneer: "It is not *English* that he writes, Sir; it is *American.* His periods are accompanied by a yell, that is scarcely less dismal than the war-hoop [*sic*] of a Mohawk." Though Washington Irving was equally aware of this taste for "rant" and "fustian" and violent metaphor prevailing in the early 1800's, he had enough historical perspective to see that much of it was the inevitable correlate of a young country. Hence, whereas Dennie and George fastidiously ostracized the unchaste American Muse from all respectable literary circles, Irving humorously recognized her as "a pawnbroker's widow, with rings on every finger, and loaded with borrowed and heterogeneous finery." With an even more explicit allowance for stages of infancy, youth, and manhood in a nation's sensibility, William Wirt was disposed to tolerance toward the American palate for a "gorgeous load of ornaments" and for "variegated pinks and blushing roses."

The articulation of this national sensibility, or more properly the imaginative demands of American experience, could scarcely be fulfilled by allegiance to the decorum of neoclassic style. Minor issues, like the use of Indian names, and major issues, like the use of American images, exerted constant and indigenous pressure against transatlantic strictures of correctness. As early as the 1670's Benjamin Tompson had foreseen the difficulty that American poets would face in adapting Indian cacophonies into euphonious English verse; and nearly a century and a half later young Edward Everett still found efforts toward indigenous verse thwarted by what seemed to his neoclassic ear the barbarous names of Indian places. By the time of the Civil War, however, the example of Cooper, Irving, Whitman, Longfellow, and many another had turned the neoclassic liability into a romantic asset by making the old savage names resound with varied tones of suggestion.

Of more import than euphony, however, was the indigenous image. Soon after the Revolution Benjamin Rush, perceiving that the American imagination could never operate flexibly or boldly from the base of inherited metaphors, proposed that native authors "borrow imagery from the many useful and well-known arts which have been the inventions of modern ages, and thereby surpass the ancients in the variety and effect of our compositions." To Rush's pre-Emersonian warning against an excessive worship of the ancients, to his confidence in a perennial fund of inspiration from the changing arts as well as unchanging nature, even Dennie's conservative *Port Folio* (1801) subscribed. Only dullness has resulted, the *Port Folio* essayist (Dennie?) realized, from the "fashion among our American versifiers, to copy servilely, images and expressions, which however pertinent in Italy or England, are most ridiculous, when associated with description of our own *home-bred* nature"; hence American *"versemen"* might better "enter into a sort of non-importation agreement" and rely on the "fertile storehouse" of images perennially before their eyes. The very tones of the *Port Folio*'s affirmation that names of native birds are as soft to the ear as *Philomel* and that "Oak and elm are as good wood to supply poetical fire, as cypress and yew" were to be echoed by Emerson's "The American Scholar" a generation later.

To more avowedly nationalistic minds like those of Noah Webster and J. K. Paulding, however, the use of indigenous imagery did not constitute a sufficient literary emancipation. "As an independent nation," wrote Webster, "our honor requires us to have a system of our own, in language as well as government. Great Britain . . . should no longer be our standard; for the taste of her writers is already corrupted, and her language on the decline." A new country, new institutions, new associations, new combinations of the arts and sciences, and intercourse with peoples unknown abroad—all seemed to him to enforce a separate "American tongue"; and for the consolidation of a truly national language no other country in history, he argued, had had so excellent an opportunity as post-Revolutionary America. To discard the rich English vocabulary he knew, of course, would be folly; but this heritage he proposed to nationalize by simplifying orthography, by allowing cisatlantic additions, and by standardizing usage from an American center. By such processes he hoped both to effect a bond of national union among his countrymen and also to diminish their "astonishing respect" for current British literature and art.

But Webster also realized that language is "not framed by philosophers," and hence for all his sweeping defiance of British standards, he always deferred to the pure style of Temple, Addison, and Swift. In fact, his aim was evidently to follow both the "best English writers" and the "general practice," that is, to find a common denominator of national usage in the English Augustans and the American yeomanry, whom he credited with speaking the purest English in the world. In this aim he was joined by the authors of a dozen and a half American grammars before 1800. Even a literary conservative like the poet-critic Charles Prentiss, who in his later years found "unauthorized words" and such an "arrant Americanism" as the word "applicant" sufficiently "painful" to damn the poetry in which they were employed, in his early criticism defended Webster's proposed dictionary and conceded respectability to a growing number of indigenous words and to the peculiar American signification of many others common to both England and America. Whether he would have considered such Americanisms as "freshet," "lengthy," and "intervale" reputable enough for belletristic use is not clear; but for a time, at least, he reflected the post-Revolutionary impulse toward linguistic independence by refusing to pursue what Royall Tyler called that *"ignis fatuus* of the learned of Europe," a standard fixed by an academy.

Since the bolstering of the union against diversity was always a salient motive in the advocacy of a standard "American tongue" by such Federalists as Webster, the favor which Republicans accorded a cisatlantic variety of English generally involved more flexible cultural and political principles. Sufficiently conversant with the history and growth of the English language to write an Anglo-Saxon grammar, Jefferson could scarcely avoid concluding that an "American dialect" would inevitably emerge from the diversity and novelty of life in the rapidly expanding nation. "The new circumstances under which we are placed," he declared, "call for new words, new phrases, and for the transfer of old words to new objects." Moreover, such dialectal mutation, he argued from Burns and classic Greek literature, constitutes "the riches of . . . language" rather than adulterates it. In the more zealous Republican view of James Kirke Paulding, however, the American tongue was not to be permitted to lag in a slow organic growth. Chagrined that the language of his country was currently without a "national physiognomy," he proposed in humorous desperation to "make a French revolution among the alphabet," to invent a dozen more letters, to demote "aristocratic A" and "put honest Z in its place." For America could never be "truly independent," he insisted, "till we make our own books, and coin our own words—two things as necessary to national sovereignty, as making laws and coining money."

Yet in any dictionaries of the *"American vulgar tongue,"* whether Federalist or Republican in principle, the Anglophile Dennie could see only an ominous indulgence toward "colloquial meanness" and a vulgar degradation of literary diction. Words like "lengthy" he sneeringly relegated to that "Indian vocabulary" of "wigwam words" frequently employed by provincial writers who model their style on Fourth of July orations and the Declaration of Independence. And while at the turn of the century Dennie's *Port Folio* denounced Alexander's *Columbian Dictionary* as a "record of our imbecility," the *Palladium* complacently concluded that, since the English language was at its zenith, it required no new words, especially no coined Americanisms like "belittle" and "sot" and other similar barbarisms of a *"Columbian"* language." Although Timothy Dwight and John Quincy Adams were favorable to a slow alteration of the English language by the infusion of new terms necessitated by unique American conditions, they regarded Webster as an extremist and shared Dennie's assumption that there was a special literary diction established in England to which an American writer was obliged to conform, as Dwight said, "in good degree." That the subsequent literary practice of American authors followed this principle rather than some of the extreme proposals of Webster and Paulding or the Anglophile purism of Dennie is now a matter of history.

Though most American authors thus ventured toward linguistic innovations as a device for cultural autonomy, few called into question the hierarchy of genres established by the Old World tradition. This tradition dictated the grandiose attempts to compose a Columbian epic. "I should hope to live to see our young America in Possession of an Heroick Poem, equal to those the most esteemed in any Country," wrote John Adams to Trumbull in 1785, urging him to think of a subject which would employ him for many years and "afford full scope for the pathetic and sublime." In such a spirit of emulation Barlow and Snowden undertook their *Columbiads*. But America's heroic tradition was so ill defined that it might embrace Washington (as in Snowden), Columbus (as in Barlow), or the saints of Israel (as in Dwight). None of these mortal figures satisfied the doctrinaire Freneau, who asserted that the emancipation of the Western world had a greater claim than any other subject on the epic poet. The Revolution itself should be the setting, he specified; but he could accept no Revolutionary leader as being of epic stature. As a heroic example for the imminent glory of America no mortal figure of the past would suffice; only the pure concepts of "rational government, equal liberty, and . . . temporal felicity" would serve to attune the national mind to republican virtues.

For the accommodation of American principles and experience to other traditional genres there were of course occasional proposals and specifications. The essay, for instance, seemed both to Wirt in Virginia and to the author of *The Friend* in New England to have a fairer field in America than in any previous society. Yet on the politically conscious American mind of the post-Revolutionary decades the oration acquired a firmer hold than the essay; for oratory was regarded as "a sort of governing Genius, moulding the mind of man," as Dennie phrased it, and many an American youth apparently felt that "the elegant figure of Eloquence" was to be preferred "before sceptres and thrones." The literary esteem accorded eloquence in Roman antiquity, its traditional association with republicanism, and its functional presence on innumerable patriotic occasions in the new republic all combined to focus attention on the oration as a national mode of expression. Perhaps the most complete analysis of the desiderata for American eloquence came in John Quincy Adams' *Lectures on Rhetoric and Oratory* (1810) given at Harvard. Believing as he did that speech was ultimately the adjunct of Reason, Adams deplored both the excessive "fertility" of native oratorical genius and an uncritical reliance on foreign models. In view of the American jury system he inclined to allow a certain indigenous lack of refinement in judicial eloquence; and for the American pulpit he sanctioned an even more distinctive cisatlantic development, since for the Protestant sermon the churchless ancients could afford no guidance whatsoever and French models presupposed an infallible church. Having allowed American circumstances and institutions these general modifying influences, however, Adams deferred to Blair and Locke and Kames on the minutiae of rhetoric and style, apparently indifferent or hostile to the indigenous idiom and metaphor which, even more than the larger structure, were increasingly to lend the oratory of the New World a distinctive tone and texture.

Yet however limited their view of the national imagination, the persistent yearning of the post-Revolutionary writers for an independent literature is attested by the recurrent use of the epithet "American" in titles and subtitles. Immediately after the Revolution Mathew Carey, acclaimed in his own day for his "repeated exertions for the encouragement of American literature," planned to publish an edition of all well-known American poets. This projected anthology had to await other hands, although in a section of his *American Museum* entitled the "Columbian Parnassiad" Carey did succeed in preserving many early native poems. With Elihu Smith's *American Poems* (1793) and a rival collection *The Columbian Muse* (1794), compiled though they both were with the loosest sort of nationalistic criteria, the new republic's divers poetic achievements were at last displayed. Caleb Bingham's selection of native pieces in *The Columbian Orator* (1797) reflected more substantially and explicitly a distinctive national turn of mind. Yet the honorific epithets "American" and "Columbian" were not reserved for anthologies alone. When the editors of the *Massachusetts Magazine* in 1789 began the publication of *Amelia . . . An American Novel* and subsequently published other selections described as "An American Ballad" or "An American Tale," they inaugurated the practice of employing the nationalistic subtitle—a practice which was to persist for a century and a half as an integral part of the long campaign for an American literature.

New Bases in Criticism

Although Lowell's famous dictum ". . . before we have an American literature, we must have an American criticism" evidenced the maturer insight of a later literary generation, the post-Revolutionary writers were not unaware of the cogency of such a view as Lowell bespoke. If America was to have a distinctive literature, many of them realized, her authors must feel the assurance that only a sound critical validation of national diversity could provide. Already the first steps toward this validation were being taken when an essayist in the authoritarian *Monthly Anthology* (1810) dared to state that "If there be principles of taste which should be common to all nations, it is almost impossible to ascertain them." Once this skepticism regarding the sanctity of neoclassic universals was widely diffused, a new set of literary principles consonant with cisatlantic culture might be devised. Meanwhile, as T. G. Fessenden complained, American critics were likely to have "a taste too pure/ To relish native literature."

A substantial and contagious declaration of the literary implications of American nationality was, in the main, to await the Transcendentalists and Whitman; but even before the Constitution was adopted, that New England essayist who called himself "The Friend" (either Timothy Dwight or Josiah Meigs) had already begun to suspect that the "colonial depression" and "meanness of soul" among his literary compatriots was ultimately attributable to their easy assumption that the transatlantic "rules" of literary excellence were absolute. In attacking this assumption through a series of articles, the "Friend" argued in an appropriately American vein that the concept of progress may be applied to the arts as well as to the sciences—that as new views of poetical objects expand the perspective of criticism, criticism accordingly must advance toward perfection by a new catholicity. Since the stock of poetical images is as "infinite" as "the natural and moral creation" itself and since the modes of exhibiting these images are as various as the modes of perception, he added, why should a single specimen be erected into an authoritarian species to inhibit the roving imagination? Convinced that American genius would be liberated if "nature" were "consulted in preference to Aristotle," the "Friend" joined that numerous company who a generation before "The American Scholar" proffered their declarations of literary independence by an appeal to cisatlantic experience:

> In our own happy state of society, disjointed from the customs and systems of Europe, commencing a new system of science and politics, it is to be ardently hoped, that so much independence of mind will be assumed by us, as to induce us to shake off these rusty shackles, examine things on the plan of nature and evidence, and laugh at the grey-bearded decisions of doting authority.

In this pre-Emersonian attempt to establish American literature on experience rather than on Aristotelian or neoclassic formulas, the New England "Friend" was joined by the prominent Pennsylvanians Benjamin Rush and Charles J. Ingersoll, who could not see why "an American poet, breathing the air of liberty . . . [should] fall down before this calf of criticism." No doubt such concerted questioning of English neoclassicism was rooted in national pride; but it was certainly projected beyond a mere chauvinistic outburst into a sustained and rational search for literary principles consonant with a new republican culture. It seemed clear that without a proper concession to the influence of American "climate, plants, animals, arts, manufactures, manners and policy" on the inherited language and literature, as Webster remarked, the indigenous literary efforts of the coming decades would continue to be held in "unmerited contempt." Hence Webster's avowed effort "to dissolve the charm of veneration for foreign authorities which facinates [*sic*] the mind of men in this country." Hence the pleas of the dramatist James Nelson Barker that his "plain-palated, homebred" drama not be expected to "lisp the language of Shakespeare," that it not be "chid with undeserved severity" and "indiscriminating censure," that American critics not timidly remain silent awaiting the decision of the *Edinburgh Review*. Undoubtedly many such supplications involved an exploitation of patriotic bias rather than a disinterested concern for critical justice. Yet there was also some validity in the satirist Fessenden's charge that "Columbian genius lies prostrated,/ Because its fairest fruits are rated/ By hearts of flint and heads of block."

Although many post-Revolutionary writers thus were convinced that they must abandon a blind deference toward transatlantic dicta, they were less certain of the critical principles which should define a cisatlantic mode. Such admonitions as Dwight's that critics should consider "the *subject, scope, or end*" of a work were little more than echoes of Pope. Perhaps in espousing a plain style Noah Webster was expressing something closer to a national aesthetic, for in so doing he was not merely reiterating the traditional Puritan distrust of ornament but also anticipating the functional principles of Thoreau, Emerson, and Horatio Greenough. "Remember that sublimity and elegance do not consist principally in words," wrote Webster to some "Yung Gentlemen" in 1790, "az the modern stile of writing would make us beleev. Sublimity consists in grand and elevated ideas; and elegance iz most generally found in a plain, neet, chaste phraseology." Indeed, Webster was willing to discard "variety" as an aesthetic criterion if it were incompatible with the more inclusive standard of utility; and hence the regularity of Philadelphia seemed to him more beautiful than Boston's irregularity, because the latter could not readily accommodate men in business as a city should do. This emphasis on function Constance Rourke would later make the touchstone of American culture; yet how much of his belief Webster derived from indigenous example and how much from Kames's distinction between intrinsic and relative beauty, it is all but impossible to say.

Rather than rely on any fixed judicial principle, however, many nationalistic critics inclined to trust the flexible response of public taste as the only criterion ultimately consistent with republicanism. As Cotton Mather had with cisatlantic pride consciously adapted his style to the understanding of his hearers and readers, so the post-Revolutionary author often acknowledged the American public as the proper arbiter of his literary fate. That the absence of aristocratic patrons would hamper certain elegant arts perceptive critics like Charles In-

gersoll well knew, but they were also convinced that a widely disseminated common learning would provide a more solid groundwork
for good literature. Hence the literary jurist William Austin after a
sojourn in England could rejoice that America was not an aristocracy
but a republic of letters, where knowledge was broadly linked to common sense; and John Pope after traveling through much of the new
nation could profess his faith in the voluntary "assentation" of independent Americans as opposed to the flattery which accompanies patronage. Such pronouncements did not proceed from a sense of resig-
nation but from an active confidence in the moral and aesthetic sensibilities of the American people. Indeed, said a contributor to Freneau's
Time-Piece (1797), more than the inhabitants of any other nation the
Americans are disposed "towards everything belonging to taste."

Yet however well disposed toward "taste" the post-Revolutionary
public may have been, clearly this disposition could be made even
more responsive to native works through judicious critical guidance.
Such guidance was attempted early in the century when Brown's
Monthly Magazine and American Review apportioned a section for
the consideration of American books; and soon thereafter the *Monthly
Anthology,* declaring that the native literary landscape was being mis-
takenly adjudged barren because no map showed its actual character,
inaugurated a new department to treat forgotten and neglected American works. With the death of these periodicals and the depression of
American letters in the early part of the century, the need for some
critical center which would be at once informed without being alien
and American without being provincial became even more evident.
Accordingly in the winter of 1814-15 Willard Phillips, William Tudor,
E. T. Channing, J. T. Kirkland, R. H. Dana, and others projected the
North American Review in order "to foster American genius, and, by
independent criticism, instruct and guide the public taste." In this
journal American criticism had at last found a stable though not wholly
indigenous base.

Retarding Forces

Though the considerations of native literary themes and modes were
numerous before 1815, as many attempts seem to have been made to

analzye America's literary backwardness as to construct cogent proposals for the development of a national literature. Logically enough, perhaps, post-Revolutionary critics supposed that they must be certain that the creation of literature was possible in America before they ventured to discuss its nature. Nor was this order of precedence a mere critical gesture; for literate Americans in that day heard much from transatlantic "scientists" about the disintegrating influence of climate on American intelligence and about the degeneration of the species in the Western Hemisphere; or they heard from foreign visitors about a vulgarity in American social life which would stifle all aesthetic impulses. The very phrasing of such aspersions stamped itself on the minds of sensitive American authors and became a stock element in discussions of America's literary prospects. The Carolina poet George was thus merely echoing the clichés of current controversy when he asked John Davis whether he "did not think that it was some physical cause in the air, which denied existence to a poet on *American* ground. No snake . . . exists in Ireland, and no poet can be found in *America."* By the end of the century, however, most American authors were convinced that it was not "some physical cause in the air" but chiefly the social milieu that retarded the national literature. As a consequence, indictments of this milieu appeared by the score, and many of them contained motifs on which variations of discontent were to be played by restive American authors and critics for a century and a half.

By the turn of the century the mercenary spirit of the new land, even then incarnate in the bold entrepreneur, had been singled out by the American writer as a major threat to his art. Considering the size of the population at the time, the outcry against American Philistinism was as loud in the early 1800's as in the 1920's among the Lost Generation; nor did the passage of a century and a quarter essentially alter the bill of particulars made by that perennial kind of literary plaintiff whose art, however much he professes to be uninterested in popular favor, actually is motivated by the hope of social plaudits and rewards. Yet on more legitimate grounds, as Whitman observed, the writer in a democracy must be able to expect a degree of sympathetic receptiveness in his national audience, and hence many a literary patriot has with justice lamented public indifference or hostility to his work. In the post-Revolutionary generation authors of both parties attributed the national apathy toward literature to an obsessive "love of gain." As a Republican, Peter Markoe charged that his country-men, tainted by Hamiltonian principles, were "to curs'd luxury un-wisely prone" and "Rewarded ev'ry artist" but their own. As a Fed-eralist, Dennie anticipated Ezra Pound's attack on usury by reporting "Americans . . . [so] engrossed with Jewish bargains . . . and such great speculators, that they neither know inventers [*sic*] and authors, nor commend nor remunerate their services." And if the Federalist Daniel Webster in his Phi Beta Kappa oration in 1809 could trace literary apathy in America to the "grovelling, dust-loving propensity" to gold, the Republican Joel Barlow could give cynical support to the indictment by threatening to conform to a public attitude which rel-ished bank notes more than his *Columbiad*: "I'll be rich too; I'll despise my literary labors, which tend to build up our system of free government, and I'll boast of my bank shares, which tend to pull it down. . . ."

The threat which the national penchant for "luxury" and "bargain-ing" held for the belletristic authors, however, lay not merely in the failure of their countrymen to "remunerate their services"; more se-riously, in an obsessively mercenary society indifference toward men of letters often passed into ridicule and contempt. Even so prominent a figure as John Quincy Adams, having promised to contribute to Dennie's *Port Folio* in order to help remove the "foul-stain [*sic*] of literary barbarism" from his country, felt obliged to request that his "poetical trifles" remain anonymous because "no small number of very worthy citizens among us [are] irrevocably convinced that it is impos-sible at once to be a man of business and a man of rhyme." In Virginia the mercenary atmosphere seems to have been scarcely less oppressive, for there William Wirt never dared have his drama *The Path of Pleas-ure* either published or acted, because he questioned whether "the circumstances of its being a play is likely to do me any injury with the world, either as a man of business or as a man pretending to any dignity of character." His friend Judge St. George Tucker was certain that it would surely not advance him in the public estimation *"but may have the contrary effect."* But that hardy literary pioneer Freneau, boldly defying what Adams called the "Cherokee contempt of litera-

ture" by becoming a professional man of letters, chose for a time
openly to indict the national Philistinism with which the more respectable Adams and Wirt were willing to compromise. When such
rich, conceited merchants as Robert Morris disparage native poets, he
wrote, then "Low in the dust is genius laid—/ The *Muses* with the
man in trade." With the passing of the years, however, Freneau felt
his attacks to be futile in "this bard-baiting clime." In Charleston he
sadly watched the "prudent Muse" competing with "a dancing bear"
and paying obedience to "sleepy squires, that damn all plays." Convinced at last that poetry could not flourish in his own time in America, he placed his final hope in a kind of cultural determinism which
postulated that a people must be near "their meridian of opulence and
refinement, before they consider the possessors of the fine arts in any
other light than a nuisance to the community." As for the immediate
future: it would merely "be an age of prose:/ When sordid cares will
break the muses' dream."

A few post-Revolutionary authors, of course, were able to accept the
utilitarian bias and the distant cultural meridian of their country with
more composure than did Freneau. In the settlement of a vast new
land it seemed only natural to the popular author William Austin that
a talented young man "scarcely hesitates whether to prefer a habitation
on the fertile banks of the Mississippi to a more elevated seat on Parnassus." Yet rarely were they inclined to extol in a positive accent
what the poet John M'Kinnon euphemistically called the "interesting
labours that promote her [America's] high/ And amiable prosperity."
In fact, no generation in America's literary history has applied more
scathing epithets to the national character. To Dennie the new republic seemed to be a "region covered with Jewish and canting descendants of [Puritans]" where "men of liberality and letters [can] expect
but such polar icy treatment as I have experienced"; to one poetic
admirer of Scott her vast stretches were but "these . . . wild domin-
ions,/ Where Avarice holds her tyrant sway"; and to the young Anglophile poet William Cliffton they were but "these cold shades . . ./
Where Fancy sickens, and where Genius dies."

Though the spirit of gain was to persist as a permanent threat to
the literary imagination in America, the post-Revolutionary author was
additionally and peculiarly beset by party strife and rancor. Soon after

the war Anna Eliza Bleecker, upon discovering that the inspiration of "spiral pines" and "airy mountains" on the New York frontier could not countervail the distractions of a society in conflict, lamented that "Faction has chac'd away the warbling Muse"; and as internecine party bitterness succeeded the hostility to Briton and Indian (of whom Mrs. Bleecker presumably spoke), many an aspiring writer was wont to excuse his own literary ineptitude by echoing her words. Certainly DeWitt Clinton bespoke the consensus of his generation when he declared in 1814 that the distraction of party spirit "has spread a morbid gloom over our literature, has infected the national taste." In this inflamed atmosphere authors discovered that the public of the early 1800's had little interest in works not filled with political invective. As a result, as those New England literary arbiters Joseph Buckminster and William Tudor respectively reported in Phi Beta Kappa orations, native literary talents were diverted to the "service of a vulgar and usurping faction," and in the recurring heat of elections literary energies were frittered away on "temporary perverseness."

For all their animadversions against political activity and the spirit of gain, the authors of the post-Revolutionary generation neither ignored the economic bases of the national literature nor declined to engage in the political efforts necessary to convert these bases to their own interest. With justice they observed that the infant literature of America, like her infant industries, required federal protection if it were to prosper. Even as the Revolution ended, Noah Webster, Jeremy Belknap, Tom Paine, and Joel Barlow were arguing the necessity of a copyright law if the rewards of authorship were to be substantial enough to sustain a professional man of letters. During the Revolution, Tom Paine observed, literature had been "a disinterested volunteer . . . and no man thought of profits"; but for the normal eras of peace, he insisted, laws must be enacted "to prevent depredations on literary property." Only by such legislation giving "laudable direction to that enterprizing ardor of genius which is natural to our stage of society," Barlow added, could America hope for that distinctive literature which would crown her national character. By the end of the century Brockden Brown and other advocates of copyright were able to point to the large importations of British books and to cheap American reprints thereof as the most obvious explanation of the fact that there was not one full-time professional man of letters among four million Americans. Among American publishers national pride clearly had its limits, and the hundreds of pleas for a national literature were not cogent enough to induce them to pay obscure native writers substantial sums for works which would have a negligible sale, when popular British books could be reprinted without remuneration to their authors. The campaign to correct this injustice to both British and American writers was to continue for a century before it achieved its objectives.

The innumerable essays and orations which dealt with these retarding forces—the mercenary spirit, the absence of a polite society, party factionalism, and the lack of copyright protection—were at last but diverse attempts to account for one salient fact in post-Revolutionary America: the man of letters was neither honored nor respected by the majority of his compatriots. Hence belletristic writing faltered because it lacked the motivating power of social approval. This literary climate was recognized and deplored by Daniel Webster when he remarked that genius "will be wooed," and by Fisher Ames when he more explicitly declared that, since the chief inducement to literature is the applause of others, "at present the excitement to genius is next to nothing." As American authors looked about them, they singled out the various social agents of their frustration: Dennie blamed the "Userer, Speculator, or Jew" and also the Southern planter, whose literary interests seemed to be confined to advertisements for fugitive slaves; Alexander Wilson included "most of the pretended literati in America," whose taste and imagination he thought inferior to those of "an ignorant ploughman in Scotland"; James Nelson Barker felt himself the victim of those "hypercritics" who could be pleased only by the "mellow tints which distance gives to every foreign object." Like most later generations of American authors, this first generation often considered itself "lost" and traced its plight to a society whose values were too confused and crude to sustain a mature literary art.

As Romantic perspectives displaced Augustan postulates in the American mind, certain eighteenth-century native deficiencies appeared less crucial, but others loomed in their stead. For the cisatlantic writer perhaps the most disheartening of these Romantic prerequisites was the possession of a legendary past, about which associations of heroism or terror or fantasy had clustered to form a common fund of allusion. Aware that America was a land virtually without a history, early national poets like David Humphreys could only concede that "Erato's seat, alas! can't here be found,/ Columbia's barren, 'tis unhallow'd ground." In some "era . . . sufficiently remote," as the novelist Daniel Jackson perceived, events like the Revolution might well furnish "the most brilliant apparatus" for romantic works. But such prospects of future literary glory afforded little consolation to other novelists like Brackenridge who, reading "The Lady of the Lake" on the banks of the Ohio, lamented that he was "cut off from romantick base," that in his dale no memorable deeds had been done, and that among his hills were none conducive to song:

> Here neighboring to the savage tread
> Inglorious I must bend my head,
>
> . . . .
>
> Though in my bosom burns the flame
> That in a happier age and clime
> Might have attempted lofty rhyme.

An America of barbarous Indian names, "vulgar history," and brick-kilns, young Edward Everett agreed, could scarcely awaken those "high strains of feeling" induced by the Old World where "every sod" has felt some "valiant foot" and where the castle's "broken wall" makes "man feel feeble as he views its fall."

Thus new problems for the American author were adumbrated by the aesthetic of the associationists whose critical ideas, stemming from Locke and Hartley, held increasing authority in American literary thought during the first four decades of the nineteenth century. To stir the deepest poetic feelings, the associationists contended, the author requires objects and scenes which may reliably serve as symbolic reminders of the range of human destiny and the instability of human hopes. For the lack of such associations the "great scale" of nature in America could not compensate, as Humphreys observed; the imagination required not merely grandeur but rather scenes hallowed by deeds of "magnanimity, wisdom, and patriotic virtue." Although in the early 1800's the jurist Joseph Story, the poet Thomas Odiorne, and the novelist-historian George Tucker all pondered this doctrine of association with its "airy train" of "successive thought," they did not assess its implications for the American writer. It was left to Irving to chart the most constructive course for early nineteenth-century authors who felt inclined to bemoan the deficiency of romantic association in their native land: their very function, he asserted, was to establish such association, as Campbell in exemplary fashion had done in "Gertrude of Wyoming." Insignificant hills and turbid streams in Europe, he reminded his literary compatriots, were sources of national pride only because "history and moral fiction" had made them so; "our majestic rivers roll their waters unheeded, because unsung." For the American author to demand a hereditary fund of tradition as the *sine qua non* of his own writing was to forget that he was to develop the fund as well as use it, that chiefly through him and the historian were local associations to evolve. How well Irving invested his own region with "poetical feelings" was attested a century later by Henry James, who discovered on his return to the Hudson that America, not Europe, had become for him the romantic world.

Prospects

Although the authors of the post-Revolutionary generation realized few of their aspirations for a national literature, an undercurrent of confidence in the eventual pre-eminence of American letters persisted steadily below the successive waves of controversy and eddies of despair. To a generation who accepted the Berkeleyan principle of the westward cycle of culture and who were familiar with the Scottish philosophers' correlation of poetry and civilization, America's ultimate literary glory seemed manifest destiny. "Nations, like individuals, have their progress from infancy to maturity, from maturity to age . . . ," wrote Paulding; and perceiving in his own America the "endearing modes of early youth," he supposed that to the new nation, an obeisance from the countries of the Old World was due like that accorded Joseph from his older brothers. To the more conservative mind of Webster this youthfulness seemed rather the happy prelude to that cultural meridian from which England was now declining into corruption—that meridian which "in every civilized nation" is a "particular period of time" when "language and taste arrive to purity." Yet whatever their differences of emphasis in interpreting the optimum point of the cultural cycle, both Paulding and Webster would no doubt have agreed with the historian John Bristed that the United States would conjoin the heritage of Europe with its own fresh genius and, avoiding the extremes of aboriginal barbarism and Old World decadence, would become "the bulwark and ornament of literature."

Not only from this theory of the cultural cycle but also from those doctrines which linked literature to Nature did the post-Revolutionary author derive reassurance. Although frequently construed in the Augustan sense of Order or Reason, Nature came to signify increasingly for the American author that "pure impulse" of the heart of which the unsophisticated author in a simple society might have the most authentic experience. In Edward Young's *Conjectures on Original Composition* the American writer was assured of the worth of the spontaneous outpourings of untutored genius, and from Blair's *Rhetoric* he received sanction for the "native effusions of his heart." With such doctrines in mind American writers confidently began to reassess their literary resources—resources which had generally been reckoned liabilities under Augustan systems of computation. In this reassessment Nature became the critical touchstone. Relying on the "uncultur'd taste" which resides in Nature, eclectic poets like Paul Allen and John Blair Linn prophesied that Genius would "awaken in this new-born land." If poetry is the "natural language of man, and has its origin in the mild virtues of the human heart," as Freneau's *Time-Piece* (1797) asserted, and if it is enriched through a relation to the "new appearances" of "pure and simple Nature" across the continent, as the Boston critic S. C. Thacher contended in the *Monthly Anthology* (1805), then surely American authors might well conclude that they were peculiarly endowed with "a fair and stable basis" on which to "erect the grandest moral and literary structures."

Finally, in his republican institutions the post-Revolutionary author frequently saw a distinctive factor which could help him to eclipse the authors of Old World monarchies and to rival the ancients. Nor was such a view merely the uncritical fabrication of American pride. Blair had correlated political freedom and literary excellence and had quoted Longinus: "Liberty . . . is the nurse of true genius; it animates the spirit, and invigorates the hopes of men; excites honourable emulation, and a desire of excelling in every art." For the American author, therefore, republican freedom was to be both theme and inspiration.

Yet with all these advantages of epoch, nature, and institutions, few post-Revolutionary authors were so chauvinistic or so naïve as to expect in their own time a native literature rivaling the classics. Like Emerson and Whitman later, most of those who eagerly espoused an indigenous literature were aware that it was contingent on the development of a well-defined national character. The "political and literary independence . . . [of America are] two very different things," wrote Freneau in the 1780's—"the first was accomplished in about seven years, the latter will not be completely effected, perhaps, in as many centuries." In this concession to the slow processes of cultural maturation Brockden Brown concurred: "It is only the gradual influence of time, that by increasing our numbers, and furnishing a ready market for the works of domestic hands and heads, that [*sic*] will, at length, generate and continue a race of artists and authors purely indigenous, and who may vie with those of Europe." Yet regardless of these judicious and realistic estimates, during the next generation the attempt to accelerate the birth of an indigenous literature was to reach its greatest intensity.

CHAPTER THREE

The Sweep of Confidence:
Transatlantic Realignments (1815-1860)

> Give us, then, *nationality* . . . ; give us excess of it. Let us love the yet barren hills of our own literature, and we shall learn to make them wave and smile with harvests. Let our authors . . . strike their roots into their native soil and spread themselves to their native sun, and . . . they will flourish.
>
> CHARLES INGERSOLL, 1837

> The truth is, that in one point of view this matter of a national literature has come to such a pass with us, that in some sense we must turn bullies, else the day is lost, or superiority so far beyond us, that we can hardly say it will ever be ours.
>
> HERMAN MELVILLE, 1850

Nationality: The Pervasive Theme

Like most literary generations, that which comprised the writers of America between the War of 1812 and the Civil War inclined to disparage its immediate predecessors. In the expansive air of national security which swept across the land after the second war with Britain, such men of letters as Charles Ingersoll, William Tudor, and Peter Du Ponceau discounted previous accomplishments in the development of a national literature and propounded the view which has all too generally persisted ever since: that the post-Revolutionary decades were a sterile period when Americans, to use Ingersoll's words, "had . . . not yet even thought of shaking off the mental yoke." Underestimating as they did both the literary problems and progress of the antecedent period, they also for a time overestimated the impact of the recent military success and its politico-economic consequences on the texture and habits of the national mind. By the 1840's, however, they were less disposed to echo the assured pronouncement of the editor of the *North American,* William Tudor, soon after the war: "A subservience to foreign opinions is destroyed." As mid-century approached, it was clear that England still exerted on the American mind an influence so strong that Simms was willing to term it "pernicious."

For the intensified campaign for a national literature conducted by numerous American periodicals in the decade after the second peace with Britain, the new political unity induced by the era of good feeling provided an explicit and inclusive motivation. But to enter fully into the American imagination, this political nationalism had to be reenforced and clarified by other circumstances which happily coincided with the expansive postwar temper: the founding of new magazines more extensively devoted to criticism; the impressive example of Scott's treatment of scenes and events which appeared analogous to those in America; the "literary war" of the 1820's and 1830's bred by the aspersions of English travelers and by Sydney Smith's sneer, "Who reads an American book?"; and the influx from the Continent of a nationalistic and relativistic critical theory which encouraged writers to express their own time or indigenous tradition rather than universal Reason. It was the convergence of such streams of influence as these that increasingly swelled the current of national literary ambition and diverted it from Britain in the ante-bellum decades. Accelerated in the 1820's and 1830's by an increasingly powerful and articulate popular press on the one hand and by impulses from the transcendental Over-soul on the other, the tide reached its crest in the mid-1840's. Diffused by academic skepticism and sectional dissension, it receded in the 1850's. After the Civil War and again during the First World War new cultural and political forces converged to effect a resurgent nationality in American letters of a somewhat different character. But between 1815 and 1860 the tide of literary nationalism was at the full and, for all the diversity that played on its surface, its deeper currents flowed in a single massive stream.

In the midst of this nationalistic tide American authors of the antebellum generation were inevitably impelled toward a high degree of self-consciousness about the indigenous flavor of their work. From Phi Beta Kappa and Fourth of July orations, from the Lyceum, from the schoolmaster's rostrum, from discourses before historical societies, from preface and editorial and essay, and even from the mouths of fictional characters, they were ceaselessly apprised both of their obligations to the national literature and of the sustenance which they could derive from indigenous experience and sentiments. Furthermore, however remote from topical interests the curricula of the day may seem to have been, the universities and colleges felt a far greater responsibility for a serious literature of public relevance than they felt a century later. Emerson's "The American Scholar" was only the most brilliant link in a long chain of academic discourses in which Phi Beta Kappa orators bespoke the interdependence of literature and national welfare. Nor was this national perspective absent from the classroom. From Professor T. C. Upham at Bowdoin both Hawthorne and Longfellow learned of the values inherent in native themes; and as a student Longfellow devoted an oration to the benefits to be derived from a national literature. Whether Emily Dickinson in her brief academic life heard similar discourses is not a matter of record; but that she reflected upon nationality in literature is probable, for she read Longfellow's *Kavanagh,* into which a long dialogue on the subject had been injected; and she must have listened at least once to her brother Austin's commencement oration at Amherst on the perennial topic: "The Elements of our National Literature."

Yet if isolated young writers like Emily Dickinson were not confronted with the issue through novel or academy, they could scarcely have escaped it in some American periodical. Like the policy of many post-Revolutionary journals, that of the major magazines in the decades after 1812 was avowedly nationalistic. Immediately after the war, journals with Democratic inclinations, such as the *Analectic, Niles' Weekly Register,* and especially the *Portico,* zealously if often naïvely argued that America could as readily demonstrate her power in the literary as in the military sphere. Erstwhile Federalists joined with almost equal zeal in the campaign; and the *North American Review,* founded at the end of the war on an explicit policy of encouraging nationality in American letters, sustained this policy so earnestly that Joseph Story was moved to declare a decade later that the journal had "done as much to give a solid cast to our literature, and a national feeling to our authors as any single event since the peace of 1783." In the ensuing years even such a slight *"new bud* in the *garden of literature"* as Morris and Woodworth's *New York Mirror and Ladies' Literary Gazette* (1823) was willing to stake its future on being *"literally* and *emphatically,* AMERICAN"—a policy which its editors construed as meaning that "all the *images* reflected from our *Mirror* . . . [would] be in accordance with our national habits, patriotism, and modes of thinking." Among the scores of such editorial avowals, there were of course variations in nationalistic tone. But no editor was more uncompromising than John Neal, who, in editing *Brother Jonathan* (1843), cried for "Authors . . . American to the back bone —American in speech—American in feeling—American through life, and all the changes of life—and American, if it must be so . . . in death." A few periodicals, such as the sporting journal *Spirit of the Times* (1847), went so far as to discontinue all British articles in favor of "articles truly American, . . . presenting the peculiar characteristics of, and illustrating scenes and incidents throughout 'the Universal Yankee Nation,' from the St. Lawrence to the Rio Grande." Yet most of the magazines did not push their nationalistic policies to this exclusive point, rather contenting themselves, like the early *Knickerbocker,* with the more flexible aim of reflecting the "indigenous feelings of our country" and "the blended radiance of a whole people's mind."

When viewed against the background of this insistent campaign among the periodicals for a national literature, single discourses like Emerson's "The American Scholar" assume a somewhat less salient position in the American critical landscape. Indeed, in the very year in which Emerson made his memorable assault on the colonial mentality of his compatriots, Charles Fenno Hoffman and the popular novelist Robert Montgomery Bird were exchanging views on how to convert the *American Monthly* into a truly national magazine which would counteract the flood of foreign periodicals and would strengthen the public interest in indigenous subjects and attitudes. Undoubtedly

Hoffman and other editors lacked the cogency and eloquence of Emerson in stating the case for literary emancipation; but those in Emerson's audience who read, say, the first issue of the *Democratic Review* three months later must have found no great disparity between the Harvard discourse and the argument advanced by the magazine that the democratic "genius" must rally the literary mind of America "from the state of torpor and even of demoralization in which so large a proportion of it is sunk."

Although later in the 1850's major journals like *Putnam's* and the *Atlantic* continued to profess a nationalistic editorial policy, their Americanism was less buoyant and doctrinaire than that of most of their predecessors. Whatever the limitations in critical sophistication these earlier magazines may have shared, they at least by their insistent campaign were a primary force in impelling the majority of ante-bellum authors to reflect upon their relation as writers to the national culture. The result was that through critical essay, correspondence, or formal discourse virtually every major and minor author between 1815 and 1860 felt obliged to expound some version of a national literature. Byrant, Emerson, Longfellow, Lowell, Simms, Cooper, and many another returned to the subject repeatedly; a few, such as Longfellow and Lowell, altered their views; some like Hawthorne and Irving, expressed their conclusions infrequently or obliquely.

It was in large measure the insistent campaign of the magazines that prepared authors and public alike for that "Declaration of Independence, in the Great Republic of Letters" which, as John Neal declared in 1828, would enable Americans "to feel like brothers of the same parentage—an elder and a younger—different in temper—but alike in family resemblance—and alike proud of our great ancestry, the English giants of older time." Neal was confident that such a declaration would be issued within a generation. It came, in fact, if Holmes's tribute to Emerson's "The American Scholar" is sound, within a decade.

Emerson was not, of course, the only author who aspired to proclaim definitively the independence of American letters. Minor poets like Solyman Brown and Daniel Bryan were as ardent, if not so convincing, as Emerson in exhorting their countrymen toward a "complete emancipation from literary thralldom" and from "mental bondage" in "taste and judgment." But within the vast chorus of authorial voices which deplored America's deference to England, none was clearer than that of Fenimore Cooper, for it proceeded from a comprehensive inquiry into the political and social contrasts between England and America. As Paulding had found this deference principally in the coastal cities, so Cooper concluded it to be an affliction chiefly of the so-called intelligent classes. So paralyzing did the effects of this cultural malady seem to him that he undertook, in the decade in which he became famous, to erect, as he said, "the foundation of the mental emancipation which alone can render the nation great, by raising its opinions to the level of its facts." Like Santayana a century later, Cooper was uncomfortably aware of the gulf between American art and American experience and principles. In fact, he maintained that unless a "manly, independent literature" in harmony with American facts were forthcoming, the very *"safety"* of the people and their institutions was in danger. It was mainly the uncritical absorption of English literature, he thought, that accounted for the "craven and dependent feeling which exists so sharply in what are called the better classes of America." As to prospects for subverting this "mental dependence" through a republican literature, he was not unduly sanguine, for he was convinced that "it is much easier to declare war, and gain victories in the field, and establish a political independence, than to emancipate the mind." Yet at the end of his life he must have known that he had attained the modest goal which he had set for himself twenty years earlier: "Her [America's] mental independence is my object, and if I can go down to the grave with the reflection that I have done a little towards it, I shall have the consolation of knowing that I have not been useless in my generation."

With Cooper's truculent republicanism, neither Lowell nor Poe was in accord; but both subscribed fully to his attempt to destroy deference to British critical opinion. "In Letters as in Government," Poe wrote in 1845, not merely a "Declaration of Independence" but rather a "Declaration of War" is required. With Cooper's further prescription of a political point of view for the national literature, however, he had no sympathy. The only proper Americanism seemed to him to be that "which defends our own literature, sustains our own men of letters, upholds our own dignity, and depends upon our own resources.

. . . Now if we *must* have nationality, let it be a nationality that will throw off this [British] yoke." Although Lowell was, to say the least, less stable than Poe in his attitude toward a national literature, he generally adhered to the creed of literary self-reliance expressed in Phoebus' jaunty admonition to American authors in *A Fable for Critics:*

> Forget Europe wholly, your veins throb with blood,
> To which the dull current in hers is but mud . . .
>
> . . . .
>
> To your own New-World instincts contrive to be true,
> Keep your ears open wide to the Future's first call,
> Be whatever you will, but yourselves first of all. . . .

So conscious of what Poe called "the sin of colonialism" were most ante-bellum authors that it frequently became a salient motif of their novels and romances. Sensitive characters like the historian Motley's Vassal Deane in *Morton's Hope* (1839), brooding over infant America's inability to wean herself from mother Europe, cried out that the "sin is, that we are not national." A decade later Mr. Churchill in Longfellow's *Kavanagh* argued somewhat sophistically through a chapter that since America's destiny was to fuse European racial strains, American literature was becoming increasingly national by becoming increasingly international! Hawthorne, however, unable to accept such easy verbal resolutions of the issue, pondered more incisively "the appearance of the great American writer," as he phrased it in his notebook, and concluded that such a writer might well "be discovered under some most unlikely form" and might even live and die unrecognized. In the story "A Select Party" which evolved from this germinal idea, he paid tribute to the unrecognized "Master Genius, for whom our country is looking anxiously into the mist of time, as destined to fulfil the great mission of creating an American literature, hewing it, as it were, out of the unwrought granite of our intellectual quarries." As the creator of "our first great original work," he seemed to Hawthorne a "worker of immortality," to whom Posterity must assign the highest honor in the great chair of state.

The great wave of national literary pride that swept across the country in the ante-bellum decades left no section untouched. In the pioneer society of the Ohio Valley the *Western Monthly Review* (1828) felt the impulse and proposed that a national university be founded in order to "Federalize . . . the mind of the whole American youth" and to assure the "real and permanent literary glory" of America. On the California frontier the *Golden Era* (1855), supposing that American literature languished because Eastern "literary snobs" had "exhausted their fount of nationality," proclaimed that the young writers of the Far West could provide the regenerative force. In the ante-bellum South as well, despite the growth of sectional consciousness, virtually every major author and editor protested the current deference to British critics and recognized a common cisatlantic obligation, as editor J. W. Simmons of the *Southern Literary Journal* (1836) phrased it, to "inculcate sentiments national in their tone, national in their tendency."

In this vast evangelism for a national literature ante-bellum authors were not unaware of the strength that would accrue to their cause from some man of letters who, as an exemplar of an indigenous tradition, might stand as a father-figure at the head of American literature much as Washington did in politics. In this attempt to find some sort of native literary ancestry few of them, apparently, were willing to join Melville in his half-jocular vow to stand by America's "Pop Emmons" and his *Fredoniad* (1827) and to swear that it was not far behind the *Iliad;* but many of them inclined to agree with Melville's contention that in establishing an independent literature America had better "first praise mediocrity even, in her children, before she praises . . . the best excellence in the children of any other land." Yet even by these standards that group who had first aspired to become the founding fathers of American literature, the Hartford Wits, could scarcely be so accepted by later generations. A more likely progenitor for a native literary tradition appeared in William Dunlap's *The Life of Charles Brockden Brown* (1815)—a work avowedly nationalistic in its aim, designed as it was to pay homage to a writer who had dared to throw "off the shackles of an absurd prejudice in favour of European opinions and writings" and who had perceived the "advantages of publications suited to a new state of manners and political economy." Even after Dunlap's tribute, however, young Longfellow felt that Brown's efforts in behalf of literary independence had not been properly honored, and from Bowdoin he wrote to his mother censuring America for "caressing the children of an exotick soil and fostering the offspring of another instead of her own." Although Brown's claim to the fatherhood of an indigenous literary tradition was further strengthened by Prescott's biography (1834), he became gradually superseded in the 1830's and 1840's by other figures. By mid-century any one of several authors—Cooper or Emerson or Bryant—was frequently praised, as Simms praised Paulding, as the first American man of letters who "never made any concessions to that foreign sway,—a relic of the old colonial tyranny." Even at the end of the century the identity of the "only begetter" of American literature had still not been established.

Whatever the progress toward a native American literature in the ante-bellum generation, even its most sanguine proponents could scarcely argue that the Master Genius, of whose appearance Hawthorne had written in "A Select Party," had arrived. In fact Hawthorne himself, attempting in 1854 to comply with Monckton Milnes's request for a half-dozen new American books which would be both good and original, felt obliged to write his publisher that he could "think of only three which would be likely to come under his description." And Hawthorne's younger contemporary Thomas Buchanan Read, returning from "foreign hills of song" and unable to discover any impressive stream of national poetry, prayed "for a cloud to oversweep the West,/ And with a deluge burst these deeper springs." As Hawthorne looked forward to the Master Genius, so Read at mid-century hopefully awaited the herald signs "Of him whose coming hath been stayed too long."

The Renunciation of Foreign Modes

The development of a national theory of letters in America was in a sense Hegelian: its principles were often cultivated antitheses of foreign modes rather than purely native growths sprung up in autochthonous isolation. Or, to change the figure: for three centuries after the founding of the New Zion American writers inclined to fix the direction of the national literature by simply steering away from the Old World. Always, of course, they professed New World destinations —destinations at first charted in Europe itself and then gradually modified by successive generations who discovered some passages to be blind but others, hitherto unsuspected, leading toward virgin land for the literary imagination.

Before much of the nineteenth century had passed, neoclassicism had been discovered to be the most patently blind of all the passages thus far explored. Loss of faith in the "rules" of Taste was of course not an exclusively cisatlantic phenomenon; but as Romantic critics in Europe protested the limited validity of neoclassicism for the imagination of mankind everywhere, American critics soon after the War of 1812 began to demonstrate its especial irrelevance for expressing the genius of the New World. The most influential of these early repudiations of taste came not from a Bohemian poet boasting of a hatred of culture and a love for the roughs, as did Whitman, but from Edward T. Channing, Professor of Rhetoric at Harvard and teacher of Thoreau and Emerson. Following the broad organic concepts of Romanticism to their nationalistic conclusions, Channing insisted that by adhering to "refined, artificial taste" a writer ignores the "differences of country, of habits, of institutions" and hence the rich variety of experience available to the imagination. Nor did he hesitate to apply this conclusion to the literary practices of his compatriots. Like Emerson and Whitman later, he reproached those who gave their days and nights to imitating so-called universal models, those who had allowed themselves to be turned into mere literary "confectioners" by the "mischief of learning," and those addicts of elegance and "foreign ornament" who employed "images, allusions, and a metaphorical language . . . unmeaning and sickly from abroad." To replace this servile correctness Channing boldly urged the charm of "nativeness" and of writing "from the heart." Convinced that the "most polished will be the dreariest ages of . . . [a nation's] literature," he attempted to save America from an Augustan era.

Fundamentally Channing's espousal of "nativeness" and his repudiation of polish marked the growing awareness on cisatlantic shores that the neoclassic "rules" were not genuine universals at all, but rather the belletristic corollaries of a particular cultural temper and epoch. For this historical insight with its nationalistic implications, American authors were especially indebted to the critical school represented by A. W. Schlegel, who taught them, as the Southern critic

J. W. Simmons testified, that "there is no monopoly of poetry for certain ages and nations, and consequently, that despotism in taste by which it is attempted to make those rules universal . . . is a pretence which ought not to be allowed." As a consequence, American critics began to assess literary works in a national context rather than by some "determinate standard of composition" from abroad. "Taste will be corrupted when the whole national character is corrupted," W. J. Spooner told the Phi Beta Kappa Society at Harvard in 1822; and as a corollary he added that there could "be no good literary history of a nation independent of its political history." With literary values tied thus firmly to the changing national milieu, the literary traveler Theodore Dwight, Jr., a decade later ventured to redefine the authority of the classics over American authors: "We are to imitate the style of the best ancient orators, poets, and historians . . . by saying what they would have said if they had been like us, and in our places." Literary emancipation from neoclassic "tyranny in taste" could scarcely proceed further!

If those ante-bellum writers who were charting the course of the national literature discovered Augustan taste to be a blind passage, they also not long thereafter found certain currents in the new Romanticism bearing them toward a literary landscape singularly alien to the New World. When they looked at their own nineteenth-century America they could but report, as did W. H. Gardiner in the *North American* (1822):

> Here are no gorgeous palaces and cloud-capped towers"; no monuments of Gothic pride, mouldering in solitary grandeur; no mysterious hiding places to cover deeds of darkness . . . ; no cloistered walls . . . ; no ravages of desolating conquests; no traces of the slow and wasteful hand of time.

This inventory of stock properties for the Gothic imagination was endlessly reiterated by ante-bellum critics as a point of departure for assessing native liabilities and assets; but as the century advanced, the absence of such properties evoked less and less despair. Rather, in an atmosphere of increasing confidence in indigenous themes Dunlap could count it only a gain that Brockden Brown had pointed the way toward abandoning "the hacknied machinery of castles, banditti, and ghosts," and Paulding could trust his Southern readers to recognize the irony of his remark that poetry could scarcely be expected of a region without a "good number of ruins, with subterranean passages and Donjon keeps." American literature, Paulding was certain, did not require "the agency of ghosts, fairies, goblins, and all that antiquated machinery which till lately was confined to the nursery."

In these Gothic literary properties the ante-bellum author perceived an Old World heritage which was not merely foreign to the American memory but also incompatible with American principles and prospects. He generally concluded that he could make a literature without them; but if not, he would readily forego the literature rather than the clear gains of a temperate republican society. The most notable statement of this position came in the Preface to *The Marble Faun* (1860), wherein Hawthorne counterpoised the simple well-being of his country and the price in "gloomy wrong" which Italy had paid for her romantic ground. But Hawthorne's statement had numerous precedents. Soon after the War of 1812 Bancroft on his return from Europe also looked "in vain for the land of romance"; but he, too, affirmed his preference for this unromantic refuge of pure religion, civil liberties, and domestic happiness over "all the high enjoyment of the fine arts" in Italy. Among the many foreshadowings of Hawthorne's famous Preface, however, it was Theodore Fay's Norman Leslie who most vividly expressed the "moral aspect of Italy" which at once fascinated the American as writer and revolted the American as republican:

> Oh, Italy! Who treads thy stricken and terrible domains, from the fresh and virgin dells of the new world, feels then . . . appalled that he is *man*. Beneath him every field has a voice, and a story . . . ; like AEneas, he shrinks, lest the very branch, as he plucks it, may shed drops of blood. War and hate, murder and superstition, have made themselves tokens that frown and bristle from every hill and dale. . . .

Thus cut off from the fertile subsoil of decadence out of which Romanticism seemed best to grow, the ante-bellum author was obliged to consider whether an adequate sustenance might be afforded the imagination by those "smiling aspects of life" which, Howells later was to say, were characteristic of America and therefore should define the tone of her literature. His problem was to reconcile the American idea, which he cherished the more, with the Romantic mode. He had to "venture to put our cheerful dwellings, and fruitful fields, and blooming gardens," as Catharine Sedgwick wrote in 1821, "against the ivy-mantled towers and blasted oaks of older regions, and busy hands and active minds against the 'spectres that sit and sigh' amid their ruins." Yet even such romantic pastoralism scarcely satisfied Paulding and Prescott, both of whom wished to replace the "machinery of ghosts, goblins, and fairies" with a sturdy rationalism and common sense which they judged would become increasingly characteristic of the American mind. If American literature cannot incorporate the "light of education" to replace the "shadows of a twilight age," wrote Prescott, "So much the worse for the poet and the novelist." And if necessary, young Bayard Taylor was equally ready to sacrifice romantic literature on the altar of republican progress:

> Ah! not the charm of silver-tongued romance,
> Born of the feudal time, nor whatsoe'er
> Of dying glory fills the golden realms
> Of perished song, where heaven-descended Art
> Still boasts her later triumphs, can compare
> With that one thought of liberty inherited—.

Yet American romance, having forsworn the Gothic as incompatible with a more cherished republicanism, did not easily find a promising or sunny alternative, as the durable and somber art of Hawthorne and Melville testified.

Beyond the threat of specific transatlantic modes and eras, however, lay the heavy incubus and the intimidating richness of British culture. Resistance to this culture was undoubtedly most intense in the early decades of the century during the "literary war," but even through the middle of the century major writers throughout the land reiterated Simms's charge that England maintained such a "pernicious influence . . . over our mental and moral character" that "we are emasculated and enslaved." In New York in the 1840's chagrin over this influence evidently reached a new peak. "The country is tired of being *be-Britished*," cried Willis and Morris's *New Mirror* in desperation over "having our thinking done in London, our imaginations fed only with food that is Londonish, and our matters of feeling illustrated and described only by London associations, tropes and similitudes." So intense did this native literary pride become that even the sober Bryant prophesied an imminent and crucial struggle not merely for literary independence but also for a decision as to "which power holds and governs the world—the mind of England, old and knit by years and wisdom into strength, or America, roused to new duties in its youth, and in the van with opinions born of the hour."

This literary resistance to the "mind of England" was sustained on several fronts. On the one hand, there was among native authors of a conservative or moralistic temper a disapproval of such Romantic contemporaries as Byron and Bulwer and Moore; on the other, radical equalitarians like Orestes Brownson preferred what they construed as the democracy of Byron and Bulwer to the feudalism of Scott. But in addition there was a broader attempt by all forces to clear American letters of the infiltration of imagery and symbol which had been absorbed from what Longfellow called the "whole body of English classical literature." Hence the full-scale campaign in the 1830's against the skylark and the nightingale. To be sure, there were those "smatterers," as William Tudor remarked, "who believed if the nightingale were out of the way, their own croaking would be music, and who therefore invoked patriotism to support what good taste condemned." Yet it was not merely the "smatterers" who, seeing in the cisatlantic use of the skylark and nightingale the most conspicuous example of the temptation to rely upon traditional rather than upon indigenous imagery, singled out these birds for literary slaughter. "Did you ever see such a bird?" wrote Cullen Bryant in 1832 to his brother John, who in Illinois had written lines on the skylark. "Let me counsel you to draw your images, in describing Nature, from what you observe around you. . . . The skylark is an English bird, and an American who has never visited Europe has no right to be in raptures about it." In almost identical words in the *North American* the same year, Longfellow advised American poets to write "from the influence of what they see around them, and not from any preconceived notion of what poetry ought to be. . . . This is peculiarly true in descriptions of natural scenery. In these let us have no more skylarks and nightingales. For us they only warble in books." A few years later at Harvard, Thoreau decided that American authors might well contemplate the babbling brook without "polluting its waters with a mill-wheel" and might well desist from singing of "skylarks and nightingales, perched on hedges, to the neglect of the homely robin-red-breast, and the straggling rail fence of their own native land." With the same suspicion of imported imagery, the New England essayist Leonard Withington argued that even "the screaking [*sic*] of the night-hawk's wings, as he stoops in our evening sky, should make better melody in our ears than the softest warblings of a foreign nightingale." In view of this concentrated effort during the 1830's to dislodge alien objects from American verse, it is impossible to justify Theodore Parker's sweeping assertion before several literary societies at mid-century that American poets, in their obsession with the lark and the nightingale, had never a thought for the brown thrasher and bobolink, and that "our American pine must be cut to the trim pattern of the English yew, though the pine bleed at every clip." Yet, unjust to his literary predecessors though he was, Parker in asserting the claims of the bobolink and the pine added his voice to the critical chorus of those who were convinced that the American imagination, both creative and receptive, would achieve the richer responses from symbols indigenous to American experience, however humble. Or, as the poet Brainard remarked, the traditional ivy and myrtle and bays could but be of less import to the American writer than "the vine that our forefathers planted."

For those literary nationalists who, like Cooper, distinguished between American and Old World literature by means of political rather than formal criteria, the voice of the nightingale seemed innocuous indeed when compared with that of Walter Scott. The feudalistic menace of the Waverley novels was in part atoned for, to be sure, by the fictional pattern they provided for an American romance. But there was less forbearance in the 1830's and 1840's toward the "load of trash" from other European pens contagiously imbued with the "*forms, usages,* and trappings [*sic*] of the old gothic monarchies," as Stephen Simpson phrased it in *The Working Man's Manual* (1831). In attacking this literature which seemed to have been "prepared with express reference to the diseased and perverted taste of the luxurious and aristocratic," spokesmen for the working class, the equalitarian West, and the Puritan tradition all joined. Whether from editor James Hall in Ohio, or from democratic Stephen Simpson in Baltimore, or from the historian J. G. Palfrey, the reformer Horace Mann, or the clergyman Leonard Bacon in New England, the indictment was essentially the same: this alien fiction and poetry emphasized birth rather than merit, it denigrated the common people as unprincipled, it placed wealth above virtue, it indulged in morbid fancies, and it encouraged the "uneducated and unthinking rich" in America to ape European fashions and luxuries, to imagine themselves a new aristocracy, and hence to "make themselves . . . ludicrously unhappy in this rough, Puritan, democratic world." Basically political and frequently chauvinistic, these denunciations of the antidemocratic tendencies of European fiction often approached such sweeping invective as that of the Philadelphia novelist George Lippard:

> "English novels" do more to corrupt the minds of American children than any sort of bad literature that ever cursed the world. They are filled with attacks upon American freedom. They sneer at what they do not comprehend in our government and grossly misstate facts where their comprehension is clear. . . . Written very often by authors who . . . cling to the whole list of British absurdities from absurdity A No. 1 of supporting a female Pope called a queen at the expense of the misery of a whole people to Z No. 99, of pouring all the life and blood of a people into that great funnel of degradation called the "Factory System," these "English novels" are the very worst class of books to put into the hands of an American boy or girl.

American resistance to the corrupting influence of foreign works was conceived, of course, not merely in a political and social but also in an ethical and literary context. Much of it was a kind of literary self-defense at a period when it seemed, as Stephen Simpson remarked, that "Nothing American . . . succeeds, not even with the Ladies, one English rake being equal to twenty Americans of pure morals." Despite the protests of cisatlantic authors, however, the "English rake" continued to taint the "wholesome atmosphere" of American society not only through fiction but also through the poetry and character of several of the Romanticists. Concerned over the Byronic vogue in America, George Bancroft remarked that such a literature of "profligacy and levity," if aped in America, would be the greatest evil with which the nation could be cursed; and Paulding, convinced that Scott and Moore were as dangerously alien as Byron, took occasion on the inauguration of the *Southern Literary Messenger* (1834) to plead with young authors to provide something "wholesome, natural, and national" to counteract "licentious love ditties, border legends, affected sorrows, and grumbling misanthropy." As mid-century approached, the American public turned to Continental as well as British sophistication. Througout the 1840's, owing in part to the lack of an adequate copyright law, what was variously called "crimson and yellow literature," "blue and yellow literature," and "yellow-covered literature," seemed to many an American man of letters to be "dispersed, like the seeds of a disease, everywhere." As a consequence, Bryant detected in New York the sapping of American character through the development of a taste akin to that born of the corruption of foreign cities; and in Virginia the novelist John Pendleton Kennedy disconsolately pondered the "very notable assimilation with foreign usages" of regional American manners and character. Although the denationalizing effects of sober Continental influences, such as German philosophy or German romantic legend, occasionally drew censure, the taste for the degenerate French romance which "rots and rots," as Catharine Sedgwick characterized it, caused the greater fear. America is "becoming rapidly Gallicized," the critic Charles Astor Bristed cried out in 1850; and in the same year the editor of the *Southern Literary Messenger,* John R. Thompson, observed that in the "alarming circulation of infamous books" from abroad the *feuilleton* was the worst. In fact, under the Gallic impact even the mother tongue in America had come to look to Thompson like "English oak o'er laid with French veneer."

Throughout the ante-bellum decades American writers were thus obliged by the influx of foreign books constantly to assess the relevance of dominant European practices to the American scene. Through this process they formulated, as it were, a kind of negative definition of American literature; through it they were able to see what American literature might be by perceiving, first of all, what it could not and should not be. Though some elements of European Romanticism were adjudged to be readily adaptable to cisatlantic conditions, Gothic horrors, mouldering castles, the nightingale, the idolatry of caste and leisure, and Byronic and Gallic sophistication were by almost unanimous consent discarded as modes and devices unsuitable for cultivation in the cultural soil of the New World. The next desideratum was to proceed beyond this negative definition and to discover American counterparts to which the imagination could legitimately respond.

Re-enforcements from Abroad

Despite their extensive rejection of Old World modes, proponents of a national literature in the ante-bellum decades were not blind to the fact that certain critical principles and literary developments currently dominant in Europe afforded a salient re-enforcement for their designs and aspirations. Between 1815 and 1820 Bancroft, Edward Everett, Frederic Henry Hedge, George Ticknor, and other young American students attending German universities were introduced to literary doctrines which were thoroughly congenial to the buoyant nationalism of America after the War of 1812 and which even afforded an apology for the mass of popular writing that accompanied the Jacksonian ascendancy in the 1820's. For in addition to the congenial doctrines which they found among the intellectuals, these students were impressed, as Ticknor enthusiastically reported, by the autochthonous expression of popular feelings in Germany and in Spain.

It was not necessary to go abroad, however, to feel the surge of the new currents of literary nationalism in Europe and especially in Germany; for both American and British magazines carried translations of the "new criticism" of the Schlegels. Even from the excerpts from A. W. Schlegel printed in the *Port Folio* in 1817, American readers could readily have deduced the central argument of the German school: Since the beautiful and grand can be comprehended only through the external and modifying particulars necessary to their existence, one may approximate a "universality of mind" only through an awareness of the peculiarities in the life and culture of other nations and other times; the attempt to erect the "rules" of any literary epoch into universals thus constitutes a "despotism in taste"; the making of poetry, in fact, is a gift shared even by barbarians; finally, great geniuses have proceeded "in a track of their own" and, following their spontaneous inclination rather than a specious duty to the learned, have become favorites of the people. Postulates more congenial to a young republican nation newly resolved on literary independence could scarcely have been hoped for; and throughout the ante-bellum generation, from J. W. Simmons in the South to the Young America group in New York, advocates of a national literature acknowledged their indebtedness to Schlegel's doctrines. It was not from A. W. but from Frederick Schlegel, however, that Longfellow derived his conception of literature as "the aggregate mass of symbols, in which the spirit of an age or the character of a nation is shadowed forth." And this conception Longfellow actively applied to the America of the 1830's by urging his literary compatriots to make their works "as original, characteristic, and national as possible."

If American authors owed much to the Schlegels for instructing them in what Prescott termed the new "science" of literary criticism and history, they owed even more to Madame de Staël. To her influence Prescott attributed his own repudiation of the neoclassic rules and his acceptance of national differences in taste as the "beautiful variety in the order of nature." On Edward Everett a similar influence during his student days in Germany may be reasonably inferred, for when he delivered his famous Phi Beta Kappa address at Harvard in 1824, he envisioned the future of American literature through the critical lenses, so to speak, which she had furnished. What could this literature properly be, he asked, except the product of our "state of society, its leading pursuits, and characteristic institutions" as they were in turn modified by the climate and topography? The precise belletristic features of this product Everett did not pretend to see; but he ventured to predict that a "strong peculiarity" in forms and modes of communication must and should issue from the unique nexus of a new political structure, of the excitement of American life, of the great homogeneous population speaking a single tongue, and of the westward movement. How steadily the German historical method of literary reckoning was superseding the neoclassic is suggested by Everett's conclusion that great authors "do not create, they obey the Spirit of the Age." In later decades under the sustained and acknowledged influence of Madame de Staël, critics as far apart as Samuel Gilman in Charleston and Margaret Fuller in New England felt that they could assume as "axiomatic" the principle that nations have an individual mental and moral character which should be reflected through a national literature. To the imaginative freedom afforded by this critical axiom the indigenous flowering of American literature in the ante-bellum decades was in no small measure due.

Despite the nationalistic impact of the German school, especially in New England, the doctrines of the Scottish rhetoricians continued until the Civil War to exert their more formal influence across the land. In the West of the 1820's students at Transylvania University were grounded in Blair's *Rhetoric* and Kames's *Elements of Criticism;* and as late as the 1850's, according to Timrod, among Southern scholars Blair continued to be an unquestioned authority, and Kames was still thumbed by learned professors and declamatory sophomores. Undoubtedly had the young poetess Lucretia Davidson pondered Madame de Staël instead of being a "fine scholar" in Kames, whose "ideal presence" she found congenial, she would have inclined more to national themes; and had not young James Brooks's compositions been so slavishly "written . . . after the manner of Dr. Blair and Allison [*sic*]," they would not have been rejected by editor John Neal as being "in a dead language." Yet it was not Alison's "manner" so much as his widely disseminated doctrine of the association of ideas that became a crucial issue in the quest for a national literature immediately after the War of 1812.

Alison's theory of taste, wrote the poet Richard Dabney about 1815, is "generally acknowledged to be the only correct one." This theory, as Dabney interpreted and paraphrased it, held that a "common occurrence or common scenery" becomes beautiful chiefly for "those who have poetic associations"; and hence it is the "faculty of association, acting under the influence of Memory and Imagination," which becomes the "messenger, from soul to thought," and bestows grace and grandeur on an otherwise barren scene. Before the vogue of Alison most American authors, assuming that beauty and sublimity lay intrinsically in the objects of nature, could confidently predict the grandest national poetry as an inevitable correlate of their country's unparalleled landscapes. But Alison, shifting the locus of the sublime and beautiful to the operation of memory and the subsequent trains of ideas, deprived American scenery per se of poetic significance. As a consequence, a salient feature of the campaign for a national literature throughout the 1820's and 1830's was the cumulative inventory of objects and scenes on which native writers might rely to "produce some simple emotion combined with a certain exercise of the imagination." The largest tally of national associations fell, not surprisingly, around the Revolution. But many writers who felt a further remoteness in the past to be necessary for a proper exercise of the imagination—and especially of the moral imagination—preferred Indian legends or antiquities. To those who sneered at America as "sterile in moral interest" Timothy Flint could reply from the new West that the Indian mounds not only were much older than the monuments of the Revolution along the seaboard but also afforded an ampler scope for "moral associations" than mouldering abbeys or dens of petty tyrants because they bespoke more impressively "the brief dream of human life." Such attempts to focus associations about the remains of another race, however, were virtually doomed to fail. Nor could the Revolution, as the literary history of the nineteenth century showed, yield quite the imaginative harvests which its early proponents prophesied for it. Only when the reservoir of national memory had been deepened by a more inclusive conflict or endeavor, such as the Civil War, was the native author to find a sufficient pressure of associations, so to speak, to induce the pervasive national response to the American scene which Alison's doctrine seemed to demand.

Like the doctrines of Alison, the achievement of Scott was regarded by literary nationalists with mixed feelings. Even before the War of 1812 Scott's poetry had become both the envy and the despair of those who were already thinking of the development of American literature as contingent on national associations; after the War the appearance of his fiction not only intensified the envy but also bred among radical republicans a new uneasiness. If the metrical narratives of the Wizard of the North had transposed Americans into monarchists who "bow to a pageant," as Paulding charged, his widely read historical romances clearly contained a more virulent feudal contagion. Yet, despite Scott's reactionary influence in the South, which Twain later deplored in *Life on the Mississippi,* his fiction seems generally to have been read from a nationalistic rather than a class bias. Indeed, his great vogue in the frontier West, John Hay testified, provided a national perspective whereby the frontiersmen could see their struggles as the necessary prelude to the future glory of America.

In a similar fashion American writers were disposed to discount the

feudal implications and to find reassuring analogies in the nationalistic tone and texture of Scott's fiction. "Why cannot I write a novel?"
asked twenty-one-year-old Lydia Maria Child, inspired by her reading
of *Waverley;* and within a year appeared her *Hobomok* (1824), a story
of early Salem. Yet in general Scott's rugged settings and action
seemed to point to inland rather than coastal America—to the struggles of the frontier or the Revolution. Coming to "the vicinity of
Pittsburgh," with its mountain scenery and its associations with "mar-
tial achievement," a devotee of the Waverley novels, like that Western
literary pioneer James Hall, could scarcely avoid prophesying that the
region one day would inspire "strains as national and as sweet as those
of Scott," and that the time would surely come when "the gallant men
who smoothed our path . . . [would] find a place . . . at least with
the Rodericks and Rob Roys of fiction." And when Audubon in 1826
was tremblingly awaiting his introduction to Scott, he reminded himself of how often he had already spoken to his idol in the forests of
the West:

> How many times have I longed for him to come to my beloved country,
> that he might describe, as no one else ever can, the stream, the swamp,
> the river, the mountain, for the sake of future ages. A century hence
> they will not be here as I see them. . . . Scarce a magnolia will Louis-
> iana possess, the timid Deer will exist nowhere, . . . the Eagle scarce
> ever alight, and these millions of lovely songsters be driven away or
> slain by man. Without Sir Walter Scott these beauties must perish un-
> known to the world.

Though Audubon's version of a national literature was apparently
simpler than that of the associationists, he joined many of them in
identifying a proper treatment of his country's unspoiled interior with
"the hand to which the world owes so much."

By the mid-1820's, especially after Scott's own venture into New
England in *Peveril of the Peak,* every week seemed to John Neal to
witness the publication of a novel written "after the Scotch fashion"
and set in Revolutionary times. By the early 1830's, American novelists
had become such "perfect literary resurrection-men" in imitating the
magician Scott's formula for raising the spirits of the national past, if
one may accept New York satirist William Cox's testimony, that
American historical novels had become all but a drug on the market.

Yet this "enchanter's spell," which Samuel Knapp also observed operating so "wonderfully upon our pin-feathered race of writers" that a thousand of them "started up at once," did not easily wane. As late as 1833 Rufus Choate proclaimed the need for a thousand Scotts to illustrate American history to the end of the Revolution so that this heroic age might "speak directly to the heart and affections and imagination of the whole people." In fact, neither the Civil War nor the rise of realism could entirely dispel the influence of the Wizard of the North; and even at the end of the century his historical romance, blended with sentimental and Victorian strains, burgeoned again with a new nationalistic flavor.

An American Romance

In the expansive decades after 1815 Scott's example, Alison's doctrines of association, and German nationalistic criticism continuously sowed the seeds of a varied transatlantic romanticism which took root in American soil. Sometimes, however, these influences were rather the nutriment for indigenous shoots which had germinated from American republicanism and individualism, from native traditions of idealism and religious sentiment.

Often the romanticism that flowered from foreign seed took on a distinctively fresh coloring from the cisatlantic soil and atmosphere; often the indigenous shoots were gradually shaped and pruned to accord with transatlantic patterns. In any of the ante-bellum romanticists—Hawthorne, Melville, Jones Very, Catharine Sedgwick, Poe, Simms—the indigenous blended with the alien in varying proportions. Native in theme and tone and temper, Melville did not entirely escape from Shakespeare and Carlyle; Simms could not avoid screening a Kentucky tragedy through the modes of Shakespeare and Scott; nor could Poe and Very deliver themselves from the climate of German romanticism. But whatever the inception or the debt, American authors between 1815 and 1860 felt impelled to frame a conception not merely of an American literature but of a romantic literature. Hence the countless stereotyped admissions of cisatlantic deficiencies—such as Joseph Rodman Drake's " 'Tis true, no fairies haunt our verdant meads,/ No grinning imps deform our blazing hearth"—were usually but the prelude to counterproposals for an American romance. For these proposals the genius of European romanticism furnished the imaginative ends; the problem for the American writer was to discover distinctive and appropriate instruments and agencies in the New World toward these ends.

In so far as romanticism implied shadows and distance and associations—and most ante-bellum authors supposed that it did—the crux of the problem lay in the obvious difficulty of finding such desiderata in a land which, as Prescott said, "wore a spick-and-span new aspect, and lay in the broad garish sunshine of everyday life." Many writers, like young Whittier, were confident that beyond this garish center of American life a "thousand associations of superstition and manly daring and romantic adventure" needed only to be "rescued" from rural byways and colonial legends. That a measure of such confidence was justified Whittier proved by his own New England ballads and tales. To those of the romantic persuasion who could not so readily discover the "thousand associations," however, it seemed that the individual imagination was charged with the obligation to diffuse an enchantment over a prosaic land. At Bowdoin Professor T. C. Upham spoke fervently of *creating* "splendid fictions" whereby America's valleys and forests would be transformed; and it was no doubt under the spell of Upham's teaching that Longfellow chose in his commencement oration, "Native Writers," to espouse a national poetry which would throw over America the veil of romance.

This transformation of America through a self-conscious diffusion of "enchantment" all too often compromised the indigenous in favor of the stock romantic. Bent upon redeeming their barren New England villages through romantic properties, sentimental female writers did not hesitate, as Catharine Sedgwick observed, to equip their milieu with "blasted pines" and "gnarled oaks" and to make a *"pilgrim* house . . . as prolific as haunted tower or ruined abbey." But even more than New England writers, the Knickerbockers, following not only Irving's example but also his dicta on the necessity of endowing American landscapes with associations, risked the importation of alien machinery. Even though Joseph Rodman Drake conceded that kelpies and gory vampires had been all but routed by reason from the New World mind, he ventured to suggest that Halleck might "Bid airy sprites in wild Niagara roar,/ And view in every field a fairy race." Of the impotence of such derived mythologies Drake's own major poem "The Culprit Fay" was sad proof.

The larger practice of ante-bellum authors, however, was not, as Drake had advocated, to try to "spread a train of nymphs on every shore." Scarcely trusting either alien mythologies or their own inventive fancies, they preferred in the manner of Scott to rely on whatever aura of suggestion might already be lurking in the slender shadows of American history and legend. Here, indeed, the American romancer might seem to have a certain advantage, as Joseph McCoy remarked in defending his version of primeval innocence in *The Frontier Maid; or, a Tale of Wyoming* (1819), for in the general absence of records there was little need to be troubled by historic fallacy. Hence the native writer, in treating, say, Indian and Quaker episodes in colonial history, might freely shape his materials toward what Rufus Choate called "The useful truth . . . only." By the very poverty of his country's recorded history, he could more boldly display the moral design of his romance. It was with a professed concern for this "general truthfulness" that Simms depreciated historical realism and rather sought to cast over the history of the Southern squatter, planter, Negro, hardy pioneer, and vigorous yeoman an "atmosphere from the realms of the ideal . . . [not] unfriendly to the great policies of human society." Yet, unrecorded and hence apparently pliable though America's past was, so much of it lay within recent memory, as Hawthorne discovered, that any romantic treatment of it was likely to be tried by realistic standards. Especially if one attempted a *Blithedale Romance* with the setting in the near past, he would be sharply reminded that America had no "Faery Land, so like the real world, that, in a suitable remoteness, one cannot well tell the difference, but with an atmosphere of strange enchantment beheld through which the inhabitants have a propriety of their own. This atmosphere is what the American romancer needs."

If America's thin past held no Fairy Land, not so her infinite future. What Duché and Crèvecoeur had affirmed in the 1770's, William Cox reaffirmed in the 1830's by remarking in his *Crayon Sketches* that "Hope must, in some degree, be to her [America's] poets what memory is to those of other lands." This view the Knickerbocker group for a time generally shared as the critical premise of a New World romance. To N. P. Willis as to Cox, it seemed that the American writer, deprived of ruins of a legendary past but endowed with a valley which sparkled with a civilization yet to be, "must feed his imagination on the *future.*" Here, no doubt, Willis was thinking of the Valley of the Mohawk as described by Cooper in *Notions of the Americans* (1828), where, as the admixture of civilization and forest, it is apostrophized as "completely an American scene" with as profound an associational meaning as the monuments of antiquity. The national imagination, Cooper said through his character Cadwallader, may be attached to and instructed by scenes which project one's thoughts into the mists of the future as well as into the mists of the past:

> The moral feeling with which a man of sentiment and knowledge looks upon the plains of your [Eastern] hemisphere, is connected with his recollections; here it should be mingled with his hopes. The same effort of the mind is as equal to the one as to the other. . . . But the speculator on moral things can enjoy a satisfaction here, that he who wanders over the plains of Greece will seek in vain. The pleasure of the latter, if he be wise and good, is unavoidably tinged with melancholy regrets; while here all that reason allows may be hoped for in behalf of man.

From the visible objects in the "bosom of that secluded valley" Cooper's friend, the painter Thomas Cole, projected a train of distinctively "American associations" with greater particularity than that found in *Notions of the Americans.* Far from accepting the common view that the simple serenity of rural American life was romantically inferior to the Old World, Cole gratefully contrasted the happy "spirits" of the valley with the darker intimations of transatlantic ruins. Nor did his associations stop with this Eastern valley. Allowing his "mind's eye" to roam "far into futurity," he could prophesy: "Where the wolf roams, the plough shall glisten; on the gray crag shall rise temple and tower— mighty deeds shall be done in the now pathless wilderness; and poets yet unborn shall sanctify the soil." Here, essentially, was the myth of the West submitted for imaginative synthesis; and it is not surprising that in the trans-Allegheny region this myth of the future should have been reiterated. In the Mississippi Valley Timothy Flint observed that American authors might evoke rich associations by using the Indian mounds as the background for a vision of "happy multitudes, that from these shores [of the Mississippi?] will contemplate this scenery in days to come." Perhaps it was not mere coincidence that soon after Flint made his suggestion, Bryant embodied the formula in "The Prairies" by proceeding from somber reflections on the fate of the aborigines to scenes of the happy future when advancing multitudes should have brought civilization to "these deserts." Several years earlier the author Edmund Flagg, floating down the Ohio, had also pondered the old charge that because America had nothing "to lead down the fancy into the shadowy realms of the past . . . [it] is steril [*sic*] in moral interest." His own feeling of romantic expansiveness in the West and the vistas that were opened to his imagination by a milieu where "All is NEW" were for him sufficient refutation of the charge. With his romantic commitment to the future, Flagg was confident that the steam engine and the axe were as rich in "moral interest" as castellated ruins and donjon keeps. Yet neither he nor most of his contemporaries could build a correlative American literature on the new critical foundation he had helped to lay. That superstructure, in fact, was largely to be erected a generation later by a carpenter named Whitman.

Though the Mohawk and the Mississippi had inspired a few New York and trans-Allegheny authors to project a new American romance embodying the vision of the future, the Hudson with its legends and its picturesqueness held the larger number within more traditional modes. So complete was the exploitation of its legendary past, in fact, that by 1840 Willis could conclude that "little of interest remained unsaid or unsketched." A decade later, however, the veins of romantic gold to be found in the adjacent Catskills and their streams seemed to Irving still all but inexhaustible. For him this "mountain zone" remained the great "rallying point for romance" not because it pointed toward the future but because it pointed away from it—because in its remote wildness it was "unburdened by commerce, unchecked by the mill-dam."

It was not only in the region of the Hudson, of course, that American romance continued to show the stamp of foreign design. Not only did numerous followers of Scott in the seaboard states exploit such associations as they could discover in colonial scenes and events; but also across the country workers in divers genres—Whittier, Cornelius Mathews, Timothy Flint, Schoolcraft, Longfellow, and a host of others —pushed further back through precept or literary example into what they supposed the more richly evocative shadows which lay about aboriginal relics and mythology. The Gothic tale had its conscious American counterparts, too; for, despite the progressive spirit of the age, there remained "in our secret soul," as Catharine Sedgwick said, some of the old "imaginative era of darkness." As Scott's pattern was readily adapted to the American scene, so the Gothic mode, Paulding thought, might find a cisatlantic embodiment through the imaginative use of phrenology and Mormonism! Yet the exploitation of what he called these new forms of superstition he was content to leave to writers like Brown and Poe, preferring for his own occult effects the descendants of the ancient elfin race whom he found naturalized in the New World in such creatures as the "little varmint women" who were credited with stealing Simeon Starkweather's game in Kentucky. Writers less committed to an urban and rationalistic position than Paulding, however, were scarcely willing to grant that "everything . . . marvelous amongst us," as Elizabeth Oakes Smith phrased it, is of "foreign origin." In the very vastness of the country, she perceived, there were the conditions of isolation and solitude which would foster an indigenous growth of "tales of the wild and marvelous." Both the lonely settlements in the forest and Puritan religious asperity seemed to her to have swelled the mystical element in the American mind into an indigenous fund of genuine credulity about the Unseen on which the writer could draw for more than superficial and traditional effects of terror and awe. But few ante-bellum authors save Hawthorne had both the imagination and the skill needed to transmute this credulity into a rich and native allusiveness.

As the Civil War approached, indeed, the romantic impulse tended either to be narrowed into sectional piety or to be transmuted into a zealous humanitarianism. By the 1840's regional romance had been pervasively established in New England by Hawthorne and Whittier, in the Hudson region by Irving and Cooper, and in the South by Simms and Kennedy. But for those minds which were committed to the New World vision of the future rather than to the Old World reflections on the past, an imaginative indulgence in sectional lore and legends was indefensible; and for this nationalistic and humanitarian vision Mrs. Stowe, in her ante-bellum years, was the clearest spokesman. That the South held "inexhaustible stores" for the traditional romancer she agreed. In fact, from the "merely artistic point of view," she said, "there is no ground, ancient or modern, whose vivid lights, gloomy shadows, and grotesque groupings, afford to the novelist so wide a scope for the exercise of his powers." In the South Mrs. Stowe perceived not a barren cisatlantic region but rather a complex of "institutions which carry us back to the twilight of the feudal ages" struggling with more progressive forces. Within this struggle it seemed to her that "a third race has risen, and the three are interlocked in wild and singular relations, that evolve every possible combination of romance." From the exploitation of this rich material on a romantic plane Mrs. Stowe conscientiously refrained lest she be guilty of compromising the "moral bearing" of literature for the sake of mere "cold art." That romance per se might have a moral relevance as a counteragent to the materialism and the "meddling intellect" of the age, as her contemporaries Timothy Flint and Henry Tuckerman respectively maintained, she would scarcely have been convinced. And that a century later these "gloomy shadows" and "grotesque groupings" in the South would provide William Faulkner indigenous patterns and symbols for an incisive revaluation of the national culture, she scarcely would have dreamed. Yet Hawthorne's ventures in an American romance should have told her that the mode need not be mere "cold art."

CHAPTER FOUR

The Sweep of Confidence:
Cisatlantic Impulses (1815-1860)

American Nationality. In the fusion of all its elements in a generous union under the influence of a noble National Literature lies the best (if not the *only*) hope of perpetuity for the American Confederacy.

CORNELIUS MATHEWS, 1846

Hence do we require of the American people, great power, stout original power; productions . . . indigenous to the country. . . . Give us a bad original . . . ; keep your good copy. . . .

JOHN NEAL, 1824

The Indigenous Counterbalance

The line at which the authority of foreign patterns fades and indigenous experience supersedes is all but impossible to fix. Certainly the ante-bellum writer in America, whatever his reliance on European modes, was so avowedly nationalistic that he habitually seized on those very transatlantic principles and practices that would allow him most fully to exploit the literary resources of his country. But his system of reckoning these resources was, of course, in large measure derived from abroad; and hence, for all his use of Choctaws and Niagaras for all his Revolutionary or Colonial themes, he was likely to find his literary directions through the chart that Scott or the associationists had furnished him. Or, like Simms, he was prone to write of Captain Porgy in Carolina with a heavier reliance on Falstaffian traits than on indigenous perspective and sentiment.

Yet Simms himself was not unaware that new imaginative data confronted the ante-bellum American writer with special problems of assimilation—that the world of wigwam and cabin, as the title of one of his collections of tales denominates it, did not easily yield itself to the enchantment which, by the terms of the romantic tradition, he was obliged to throw over the native scene. Simms continued, to be sure, to shape most of his work by the romantic design; but some of his contemporaries more boldly proposed to give American writing a distinctive flavor and configuration by allowing its emphases to be determined by an indigenous temper and substance. It was by no means left to the Transcendentalists to inform American authors that they had better begin with the modest data of their experience, "the meal in the firkin" and "the milk in the pan" and the stump speeches of the frontier politician, and achieve a form grown organically from impulses and stresses of familiar life across the continent. A decade before Emerson's "The American Scholar" gave memorable expression to this view, John Neal had avowedly dedicated his *Rachel Dyer* (1828) to the purpose of demonstrating to his countrymen that

> there are abundant and hidden sources of fertility in their own beautiful brave earth, waiting only to be broken up; and barren places to all outward appearance . . . where the plough-share that is driven through them with a strong arm, will come out laden with rich mineral and followed by running water.

To those literary compatriots who, under the spell of alien romantic formulas bewailed America's lack of millennial shadows, Neal replied with a prophecy that "he who shall first dare to grapple with the *present,* will triumph, in this country." In effect he was suggesting that the inherited romantic mode, whether directed toward the past or future, was obscuring the distinctive outlines of American experience and the reassessment of human values emerging from it. To "grapple with the *present"* was, in his view, to impel the writer's imagination toward the most unalloyed contact with the indigenous and therefore to provide the soundest base for a truly national literature.

Even though ante-bellum authors were not in complete agreement as to what this grappling with the present would ultimately reveal to the American mind, they increasingly concurred in the conviction that they must approach the "everyday of Life," as young W. W. Story said in his Phi Beta Kappa poem at Harvard, with a "brave sincerity." Evidently inspired by the Transcendentalists, Story before his expatriate days professed to hear all the magic tones of the Past in the native Present of the 1840's—in the mill wheel and forge, in the spindle and furnace. "Today is new, its tale was never told," he proclaimed; and in this tale he saw the "unblurred foot-prints of Divinity." This attempt in a romantic age to pull American literature away from "distant unsubstantial clime" and from "stale convention" reached even into Mississippi, where the essayist J. B. Cobb assured his fellow-townsmen in Columbus that if they would "only bring the imagination from its *wandering* flight" to their own homely scenes, they could "paint a miniature of the world."

The ante-bellum problem of grappling with the present, of telling the tale that had never been told before, of achieving a "wise passiveness" before American materials so that they would lead the imagination through a fresh cisatlantic route toward the macrocosm, was perhaps nowhere better exemplified than in the Indian. For over two centuries the aborigines had, for the most part, passed into the American imagination through a series of transatlantic categories ranging from diabolic antiheroes to noble savages. Within this range the conscientious literary nationalist could never be entirely at ease, for though he knew that the red men were his distinctive literary possession, he could scarcely give them an indigenous focus which would at once do justice to the cultures of the conquered and the conquerors. Not only Longfellow but also frontier writers like Caroline Kirkland, as her apology for an Anglo-Indian literature makes evident, generally inclined to view this "peculiar race" as "picturesque." Though the aborigines embodied for her the only "distinct and characteristic poetic material to which we, as Americans, have an unquestioned right," they seemed poetic to her because their lives were as "shadowy as those of the Ossianic heroes."

To this all but inevitable tendency to subsume the Indian under Old World modes may be traced, one suspects, the red man's persistent refusal to surrender himself unconditionally to the thousands of American pens which have sought to catch his identity. Dominant, perhaps, among these European modes in the ante-bellum period was the Homeric. On the frontier Mrs. Kirkland saw aboriginal life not only through Ossianic shadows; when she reflected on the Indians' legends, religious ceremonies, songs and chants and eloquence, she concluded that nothing was wanting "but a Homer to build our Iliad material into 'lofty rhyme,' or a Scott to weave it into border romance." To these ritualistic analogies such Eastern editors as William Tudor and John Neal added the Indians' wild and heroic warfare as a counterpart of the Greek heroic age; and in the South Simms proclaimed the Indian tribes not only to be a people whose wars and mythologies would be made immortal by some future Homer but also to be Greek-tragic victims whose melancholy history would afford a high theme for an American drama.

As the nineteenth-century march across the Mississippi Valley brought millions of Americans face to face with the Indian, however, the inherited fictions yielded to the continuous pressure of experience. Under this indigenous pressure the old categories of interpretation proved unstable and deceptive; the real Indian was seen to be neither Ossianic nor Homeric, nor was he quite the wild and intense Gothic character which young Robert Sands, the author of the long and popular aboriginal poem *Yamoyden* (1820), declared him to be. In the light of this experience there was justice, no doubt, in John Neal's complaint that nowhere in American fiction or poetry had the Indian been represented "accurately and worthily"; but there was also a growing conviction, especially among the writers in the West, that Neal's criticism involved a contradiction, since to represent "accurately" the red man whom they knew precluded representing him "worthily." Major Henry Whiting, author of the Indian poem *Sannillac* (1831), inclined to blame the lack of fidelity of which Neal spoke on the sheer ignorance of "literary pretenders" who, without traveling "beyond the march of fresh oysters," were content to "put a hatchet in his [the Indian's] hand, and stick a feather in his cap, and call him 'Nitche Nawba.'" Though these frontier writers were willing to concede that works set in the dim past of the race might legitimately indulge in romantic heightening, they also insisted that harsh reality would not permit them to accord the contemporary Indian either eulogy or sentimental lament. The Bostonian W. J. Snelling, despite the appealing tales he wrote of aboriginal life, after living for several years among the Indians could but confess that they are "barbarous, ignorant men," that their conversation is flat and commonplace, and their rare poetry, spoken in councils, is a studied effort "in which the speaker purposely obscures his meaning with parables and verbiage, often not understood by his brethren, and not always by himself." Among other Easterners of a romantic turn of mind doubts also arose concerning the poetry and heroism of Indian life. To write realistically of the "North American savage," the novelist Robert Montgomery Bird concluded, is to write of a "gentleman who wears a very dirty shirt."

It is not surprising that the impingement of this pervasive frontier experience upon the dictates of the romantic vogue should have been most acutely assessed by Henry Rowe Schoolcraft, who, after spending thirty years among the tribes, was himself made a member of the Mohicans. Though his first decade among the Indians convinced him that they were "susceptible of being handled by the Muses," he was equally certain that few treatments would be successful, for the American author must choose either to create a poetic Indian who would lack authenticity or to depict an authentic Indian who would be lacking in literary interest because he could have "no sustained eloquence, no continuous train of varying thought." To the numerous authors, like Irving and Mathews and Longfellow, who wished to make use of the aboriginal tales and legends which he had assembled, Schoolcraft replied that his collections were not "mere materials to be worked up by the literary loom." Through such a process, he wrote Irving, the "roughness, which gave them their characteristic originality and Doric truthfulness, would be smoothed and polished off to assume the shape of a sort of Indo-American series of tales; a cross between the Anglo-Saxon and the Algonquin." Jealous to the end of his life to preserve the authentic texture of the stories as the "only true, original American literature we have," he consistently discouraged efforts to "dress them up in English epithets," to "make them *English* tales or *German* tales," and thus to erect a dishonestly *"foreign fabric of fiction."* Certainly he must have felt that the adaptation of the legends in *Hiawatha* and in Mathews' *The Indian Fairy Book* a year later further compromised the indigenous through a reliance on preconceptions alien to both the actual character and art of the American Indian.

Frontier writers like Schoolcraft and Snelling were willing to concede that, whatever the imaginative limitations of the nineteenth-century Indian, the decline of a once mighty people constituted a most poetic theme; but there was little disposition in the progressive atmosphere of ante-bellum America to exalt this dim aboriginal past into a paradise of primitivism. No doubt Bird reflected the spirit of the age in remarking that while it is "right that poetry" should lament the decline of the Indians, "philosophy has no sigh for the change." Bird's "philosophy" was, in effect, that pragmatic commitment to Progress, which increasingly in the ante-bellum decades was dominating the national mind and dictating the national behavior. Yet this same progressive spirit of the age which declined to cast a nostalgic gaze toward the noble savage also involved a native humanitarianism which could not entirely ignore the suffering wrought by the white man's conquest. If American common sense precluded pictures of aboriginal Edens, American justice nevertheless demanded that at least something be told, as Robert Sands said in protest against Cotton Mather's denigration of the Indian, of the "dismal tale of foul oppressions borne." Thus the more secular ante-bellum writer revised the extreme Puritan version of the national epos as one in which the saints of Zion were divinely ordained conquerors of diabolical aborigines.

To be sure, some political men of letters like Rufus Choate still professed to believe that Providence appointed the Americans to sweep from the earth one of the primitive families, but they also insisted that their literary compatriots were obligated to preserve the mournful history of the conquered and to desist from such jests as those made by Hubbard and Mather on King Philip. Though it was possibly true, as Mrs. Kirkland charged, that at mid-century all too many Americans still regarded the Indian as a being without a soul and hence worthy of only nefarious roles in "Pirate Literature," many of the nation's men of letters concurred in her view that to see the Indian's true literary potentialities is to be reminded of neglected Christian duties. In this literary atonement for previous national injustice to the Indian, in this humane attempt to portray justly the Indians' motives and character, the Yale poet William Thompson Bacon insisted that American writers had "a theme to stir the soul of song,/ Give tongues to stocks, and fire the mountains dumb."

Out of this humanitarian literary soil in the ante-bellum generation developed Mary Eastman's long poem *Dacohtah* (1849) and such later apologies for the Indian as Mrs. Jackson's *Ramona* and Oliver La Farge's *Laughing Boy*. Whatever the limitations of such works, they represent more of an indigenous reading of the Indian theme than did the early attempts to construe the aborigines as figures out of Homer or Ossian or Rousseau. Dubious of old romantic perspectives and as yet uninitiated into naturalistic modes, the ante-bellum American writer moved, like Mrs. Stowe, away from "mere cold art" toward a "moral bearing" which would at once acknowledge the limitations of the minority race and the social consciousness of the dominant. In the course of writing the Leatherstocking Tales (1823–41) Cooper himself fascinated the Old World by providing in the aggregate a view of the Indian the like of which it had not seen.

Though the American's extensive experience with the Indian in the ante-bellum decades appreciably subverted the transatlantic categories under which the aborigines had been traditionally viewed, his extensive experience with the continental landscape scarcely afforded the same emancipation. Despite the fact that hundreds of rhapsodists continued to invoke a distinctive national utterance from Niagara and the Rockies, from the Alleghenies and the Mississippi, no such utterance was forthcoming. Indeed, poetic exhortations (like Drake's) "To sing the beauteous scenes of nature's loveliest land" far outnumbered the memorable nature lyrics; and one may suspect that the national pride which inspired such exhortations afforded a more genuine impulse to the literary imagination than the "beauteous scenes" themselves. The prospect of a seat "on Appalachia's brow" where he could scan the "glorious prospect" of "level glades" and "heaving hills" could inspire Drake to song, but his imagination was all but helpless before the actual scene; and similarly young Angus Umphraville, in introducing "The Alleganiad," wrested better poetry from his envy of European bards singing their mountains high than he did from the "Alleganies" which he had proposed to treat. Much of the sterility of this nature poetry may surely be traced to the fact that the traditional patterns and associations of Old World pastoral and nature poetry had not as yet been transmuted by that redemptive counterbalance of the indigenous which they were to receive from Whitman and Dickinson and Frost.

Though American nature, differing as it did in degree rather than kind from that of Europe, fell all too readily into literary stereotypes, that complex of conditions and forces known as the frontier required something of an indigenous shift of the imagination. Western nature in itself, of course, might afford multiple themes for the neoclassic sublime; but with the admixture of an aggressive and elemental society such a category became irrelevant. For the romancer the frontier lacked associations and antiquity; for the novelist of manners it lacked maturity and contrast. In view of the recalcitrance of the frontier to transatlantic modes, it is not surprising that one of Cooper's friends should have predicted that he would have such a difficult time in making the transition from "high life" in Europe to the uncultivated deserts of the West that the appearance of his projected novel *The Prairie* would be long delayed. Though Cooper himself frequently noted the belletristic limitations of the uncultivated native scene, in practice he exploited the frontier so often that at heart he must have concurred in the view of the popular novelist J. H. Ingraham: "The West is the legitimate empire of the American novelist; and when he shall be content to . . . unfold its wild traditions, his works will contain the true principle of life."

What this "principle of life" was, of course, constituted the crucial issue for the writer who ventured to deal with the frontier. In its simplest terms it was a "novelty of subject," as Paulding observed soon after the War of 1812, wherein a merely faithful portrayal of the life of the pioneers—the "wild and terrible peculiarities of their intercourse, their adventures, and their contests with the savages"—seemed rich and varied enough to satisfy the taste of a romantic era. Indeed, in the same backwoodsman whom Paulding commended for the "higher works of the imagination," Simms discovered a treasury of ravishing romance, just as in Daniel Boone's woodland adventures Bird perceived chapters "which, if they be not themselves poetry, are productive of all the effects of poetry on the minds of the dreamy and imaginative." Yet the expectations which Paulding, Simms, and Bird advanced all smacked of romantic preconceptions which ante-bellum residents on the frontier generally failed to discover inherent in life about them. Nor did such settlements as "Tinkerville, Montacute, and the Turnip" seem to Mrs. Kirkland during her residence in Michigan to contain any indigenous imaginative principle from which the native writer could proceed. These communities, she suspected, would yield a literature only through the perspective of an alien and civilized intelligence like that of Miss Mitford, just as the wild flowers of the region deserved a Shelley, a Lamb, or a Bulwer! But such alien treatments, whether satiric or lyric, Timothy Dwight had earlier pronounced inadequate. The white man's conversion of the wilderness, he had said, is not only a distinctive and inevitable theme for American writers, but one which demands an epic scope. In the defeat of savagery at the hands of Christianity, mild manners, and learning, the New England divine saw the boldest outlines of the New World design and hence the most valid counterbalance to Old World decadence. For the American writer to invert the pattern and to glorify the impact of the wilderness on the inheritance of mild manners and learning, for him to yield to what Fenno Hoffman called the "expansiveness" of frontier materials, would have been in Dwight's judgment to play the devil's disciple. Most of this indigenous impact was felt only after the Civil War in such writers as Mark Twain, Garland, and Dreiser. Meanwhile, in so far as American writers allowed New World values to shape their treatment of the West, Dwight's version of Christian-republican progress prevailed. Even Bird, who was able to see poetry in Boone's adventures and to catch in his own fiction something of the wild passions and strife of the West, professed to illustrate for the "reflective" the justly destined conquest of the common man over an inferior race and hence the "efficacy of the republican principle in enlarging the mind." The increasingly indigenous shape into which the frontier mind would be enlarged once the common man had made his conquest, however, neither Bird nor the other ante-bellum authors clearly envisioned.

Although the imagination of the American writer for two centuries was genetically bound to the literary perspectives of Europe, the very magnitude and assurance of the nation's growth during the ante-bellum decades impelled an increasingly indigenous point of view. Whereas in colonial days the cisatlantic scene had been a novelty to be interpreted by inherited aesthetic modes, by the time of the Civil

War the novelty itself had begun appreciably to determine these modes. American literature increasingly involved a distinctive temper to supplement distinctive materials. In the rise of cities, industries, and the West, in political experiments and in diversity of sectional cultures, both fresh points of reference and mutations in values emerged. Such sectional types as the Southern gentleman, the Eastern merchant, the Connecticut pedlar, and the Western pioneer became not merely picturesque aberrations from some transatlantic norm but rather the spokesmen of intranational attitudes which, in the aggregate, constituted the American mind. To these sectional types the growth of various metropolises at mid-century added, as Cornelius Mathews observed, a motley and infinitely diverse society on which the native writer could draw; and in the men of business of this new metropolitan world Orestes Brownson perceived the outlines of heroes as worthy of celebration as the old chivalric monarchs. Like "the steamboat and the rail car, the cornfield and the factory," which Lowell recommended for literary reinterpretation in the 1840's, the society which environed the romantic writer of the ante-bellum generation was likely to seem less distinctive and provocative than "the mountain and the rock, the forest and the red man." Yet in the turmoil of the ante-bellum years the texture of the American imagination was being inexorably altered by the stresses and values of what Cooper termed an "unadulterated provincial democracy."

The Impact of Democracy

Though the ante-bellum preoccupation with the more distant aspects of American history, such as the colonial wars and the aborigines, was by no means divorced from current nationalistic ideology and policy, its major impetus and nurture can be traced largely to Old World literary principles and practices. As a more authentically indigenous literary temper asserted itself, however, the movement in American letters increasingly tended toward the centripetal rather than the centrifugal in theme and accent; and, as a somewhat belated corollary of Jeffersonian and Jacksonian democracy, new critical emphases helped to shift the literary imagination away from the Indian and Niagara and the colonial past toward the popular tastes and issues of the day.

If American literature was not to be wholly the voice of the people, they were at least to be its most valid theme and its final arbiter.

American romanticists, to be sure, were not insensitive to popular taste and sentiments. Few of them would have demurred at Paulding's dictum that to be authentically national, American literature would need to reflect "the feelings, attachments, and associations" of the "people at large, who constitute the nation; who are the true depositories of its manners, habits, strength, and glory, preserve, and are fond of those original peculiarities, which give a national physiognomy, distinct in various features from every other." If American literature were to have a sharp and authentic national stamp, both Paulding and Cooper remarked, it could scarcely draw its main sustenance from "the higher, more refined" classes with their Anglophile bias and their susceptibility to foreign novelties. Yet as to whether, on the other hand, a worthy national utterance could be properly encouraged and sustained by the "people at large," by those masses who cared no more for a lord than for a woodchuck, Cooper expressed doubts. In theory, at least, he preferred to commit the national literature to the illustration of republican principles rather than to the expression of the popular impulse. But whatever his theory, his fiction both depicted and interested the "people at large"; and it was his achievement that impelled Francis Parkman at mid-century to define a national literature in thoroughly democratic terms: "With but few exceptions, the only books which reflect the national mind are those which emanate from, or are adapted to, the unschooled classes of people. . . ." Like Paulding, Parkman could see no vitality and distinctiveness in American literature apart from an organic reliance on the "vigorous life of the nation [which] springs from the deep rich soil at the bottom of society."

Attuned though the American author's imagination might be, however, to the "vigorous life of the nation," his critical faculties had generally been conditioned by canons of taste which permitted little recourse to the "bottom of society." The result was a bifurcation in American writing which by mid-century had become a matter of frequent concern. On the one hand, there were the reputable authors who aspired, however broadly national their themes, to please the discriminating and traditional taste of the cultivated few. On the other hand,

as Theodore Parker reluctantly observed, only the "transient" literature, only the political orations and periodical "productions, [which]
come directly from the people and go directly to them," had sufficient
fidelity to the popular mind to contain the "germ of a genuine nationality." Yet Parker's own literary loyalties were no less divided and
troubled than those of the reputable authors whose narrowed gentility
he disparaged. For they, too, were undoubtedly trying to embrace
those incompatible desiderata of refinement and authentic nationality
in their writing. Certainly they, like Parker, regretted that the "American pine must be cut to the trim pattern of the English yew" and yet
at the same time shuddered at the vulgarity and boldness which the
"transient" literature of the day, bearing as it did the uncensored impress of the national character, was free to reflect. In the terms of his
own figure: Parker did not wish the American pine to be trimmed,
but decidedly he did not approve of the shape of the pine.

In both the art of this popular literature and the integrity of the
national character which it reflected, young Orestes Brownson professed a greater faith. Indeed, for the mass of newspapers and journals
of America he claimed a more vigorous thought and a more genuine
eloquence than that to be found in many of the classics of England
and France. Nor did Brownson, in his early sanguine years, hesitate to
credit this journalistic vigor to the fundamental character of the American people at large. Inherently they were not vulgar and mercenary, he
insisted, but were possessed of a rich vein of poetry; and hence the
national literature could only be enriched if American "scholars"
would abandon their "lone reveries" and "scholastic asceticism" and
rather seek their inspiration in the "thronged mart" and "peopled
city," in the "really living, moving, toiling and sweating, joying and
sorrowing people around them." Thus nearly two decades before
Leaves of Grass Brownson proposed to invest American literature with
democratic sources of power, for to him as to Whitman the pre-eminent writer was "merely the glass which concentrates the rays of greatness scattered through the minds and hearts of the people. . . . To ob-
tain an elevated national literature, it is not necessary then to look to
great men, or to call for distinguished scholars; but to appeal to the
mass. . . ." The aesthetic poverty of his country in the 1830's he attributed to an infidelity to its political genius—to the fact that since most

American authors were not "true democrats in their hearts," they could not draw on the sustaining energy of the people.

Holding to this democratic literary postulate, Brownson and a number of his contemporaries concluded that the surest remedy for the nation's literary poverty lay in the elimination of the professional literary class. In a democracy, this group believed, all men may share the cultivation of the mind and may aspire to become writers; and, conversely, writers cannot be wisely exempted from the ordinary duties and experiences of practical life. The author in a democracy they viewed as merely a citizen who emphasizes a special verbal skill which depicts the life and values of the society of which he is an integral part. When genuinely *"American* authors" appear, Brownson prophesied, "they will form a most numerous class, or rather be *so numerous as not to form a class";* they will not resemble the present clan of dictatorial craftsmen who follow literary fashions and mock "sincerity's work-day dress," but they will rather utter "the *best* thoughts of *all."* In this attempt to democratize literature by eliminating the specialized literary class, the magazine *Brother Jonathan* became a salient medium in the early 1840's. In its pages one of the early champions of American literature, the aging Robert Walsh, from his consulship in Paris expressed doubts as to the benefits conferred on morals and taste "by professional authorship, stocked and exercised as it is in Europe"; and in the same journal it may well have been young Whitman who, having already heard all America singing, editorially proposed to excommunicate "purely literary men—apprenticed as such —devoted as such—practising as such"—from a republic which had "no room . . . for any such diploma pedants." The contagion of this movement to democratize the arts by construing them as an organic phase of everyday life reached, one may say, as far as the experiment at Brook Farm; and it also reached the poet Henry Tuckerman, who at mid-century sustained the argument that the best American poets were those who wrote from the context of extra-literary labors and did not, like professional authors of Europe, enlarge one power at the expense of others in an exclusive form of achievement. Although a prolific writer like Simms could scarcely subscribe to the elimination of professional authorship as a cure for the anemia of the national literature, his complaint that authors were writing *for* rather than *from* the American people pointed to a similar diagnosis of native literary ills. The "high and stimulating sense of nationality" which he desired for American letters involved above all a recourse to the heart and mind of the people, and he thought it to be a prime obligation of the American author "to endow them with a life and a name— to preserve them with a history forever."

On the shifting design for the national literature Jacksonian politics thus left its strong equalitarian imprint. Within two centuries American authors had all but ceased to expect that a distinctive New World utterance might be heard in the songs of the New Zion and had turned hopefully instead to *vox populi*. The ardent Jacksonian poet-journalist William Leggett, like many of his party, might refer to the "Republic of Letters" instead of the Democracy of Letters; but he made it clear in the 1830's that this Republic must "be upheld by *the people*" and "be composed *of* the people" as the constituency which could most positively counteract the influence of "the tawdry and sickening aristocracy which bedizens the pages of British novels and romances." And though Caleb Cushing as a Whig congressman referred to "the empire of the people" rather than to a popular democracy, he agreed with Leggett in insisting that America's minstrel voices must love and exalt this "empire" rather than "the pomp of courts" and "the largesses of the great." Even sometime Federalists like William Dunlap were not unaffected by the Jacksonian tide. Convinced in his last years that the future was to be and ought to be "democratic" and that "every source of knowledge should be opened to the governors, *the people*," he sought to place the "mighty engine" of a national theater in their hands through governmental patronage. If Dunlap's theater was not primarily the voice *of* the people, it was at least to exist *for* and *by* them.

The people themselves, however, were not always as confident of their central role in the republic of letters as their Jacksonian apologists. It was not merely Miss Edgeworth in England who had doubts about Cooper's literary propriety in venturing to place a pedlar hero at the center of *The Spy*. For it was to the plain American reader as well that the elder Richard Dana and Paulding evidently directed their defense of Cooper by asserting that the hero's occupation "matters not a farthing," that in this country kings and nobility are not necessary "to render our literature genteel," and that the criterion for vulgarity in American life and fiction should be moral, not social. Nor were such reassuring dicta on the literary implications of democracy pertinent only for readers in the Eastern states. On the frontier as well Timothy Flint realized that the taste of so many readers in the late 1820's would be biased against his backwoods hero George Mason that he thought it necessary to preface his story with an entreaty that they discard the enslaving notion which "for ages" had led even the humble to suppose that "the rich, the titled, and the distinguished . . . were the only persons who could display noble thinking and acting." And it was the prevalence of this same bias that led Senator Thomas Ewing a few years later to advise the Midwestern students of Miami University that, since hatred of the vulgar mob was incompatible with the spirit of the times, they should adjust their taste to a literature which finds its subjects in "the general mass of society," in the pursuits and affections and passions of the "simple unsophisticated man."

Despite the disinclination of the "general mass" to accept a title role for its members, American authors were to continue for over a century their attempts to establish and validate the claims of the humble hero and heroine. Their apologies took numerous turns. In the simple "domestic heroism" across the land young Paulding perceived an effective antidote for unwholesome Old World romance; and in his old age his espousal of normal American experience and of the country's "honest discreet women" as worthier themes than the adulterers and seducers of "high-seasoned dishes of foreign cookery" was avowedly a proposal for a "sunny realism" which anticipated Howells' efforts a generation later to turn American authors toward the American girl and toward the everyday "smiling aspects" of their country's life. With a greater emphasis on the masculine and vigorous, Bird elevated the common, unsophisticated American by interpreting his conquests on the frontier as an illustration of the unique power of republicanism to enlarge the mind and awaken the energies of the average man. Yet among all the literary apologists for the populace none was more reverent than Simms. No truly democratic author, he said, can so fail to sympathize with the gentler side of the people as to ridicule them; nor can mere partisan politics, however liberal, supply the insight which "walks among the people" alone can provide. "We

may not say what should constitute a national writer," he concluded,
"but this we do say, that he who shall succeed in illustrating the nation, must make his leading idea a full acknowledgement of the impetuous and intense earnestness of the people. . . ."

With this acknowledgement of the steady ascendancy of the people
as theme, audience, and resource in the ante-bellum decades, something of an American stamp was placed on literature not only through
materials and point of view but also through style. Paulding's dedication of *The Puritan and His Daughter* to "the Most High and Mighty
Sovereign, King People" in 1849 not only anticipated Mark Twain's
assertion to Andrew Lang a generation later that he wrote for the
ear of the masses rather than the privileged classes; it also echoed
Cotton Mather's recognition five generations earlier that the obligation
to suit one's discourse to the general understanding had even then
effected a distinctive mode of communication on the American strand.
Such a discourse rested on the assumption, as a minor essayist of the
1830's remarked, that a democratic country required "a popular literature of a peculiar kind; a literature deserving the name of American."
It is not surprising that under the swelling literary acclaim of "King
People" the old yearning for private patrons all but disappeared. A
Phi Beta Kappa orator at Harvard, John Gray, could now share with
the Westerners Caleb Atwater and James Hall a confidence that with
public education Americans would become "universally literary" and,
in wholesome contrast to older aristocratic states, would demand a
literature applicable not only to kings and warriors but to "every class
of society." Thus sustained and encouraged by the People, the American writer seemed destined to "far outshine . . . all the poets of
Greece and Rome."

Despite this zeal for a "popular literature" the democratic critics
all too often failed to make the distinctions which the term required:
Was such a literature to be primarily of and from the people, or was
it to be merely for them? Was it to proceed from and to accommodate
itself to popular impulse, or was it rather prophetically to espouse
issues in behalf of the people, whatever the lag in popular awareness?
The easy and general assumption was that the authentically democratic
writer could be identified through his adherence to a few basic themes
and attitudes. "The necessity and dignity of labor, . . . the native

nobility of an honest and brave heart; the futility of all conventional distinctions of rank and wealth . . . ; the brotherhood and equality of men . . . ," wrote the prominent critic W. A. Jones of the Young America group in New York—"these are the favorite topics of the Poet of the People." In this sense a democratic literature was conceived to be something of a monitor of the popular mind—directed toward it rather than proceeding from it. It was to be, as the influential New England divine Leonard Bacon supposed, a literature not written for elegant amusement and bound in satin covers for a noble class but rather composed for the preservation of manly republican principles among the common people who might read it at their kitchen fire. These republican principles involved the dignity of labor as opposed to the fashionable life of the Old World; they involved utility, justice, common rights and common sense. Informed by such values, America's popular literature seemed to Bacon to be sounder and worthier than that which glorified the old chivalric ideals of honor and loyalty and pride in founding a family.

These professions of literary faith in the people thus by no means implied a concurrence in Whitman's desire for an American literature which would be essentially an autochthonous utterance of the popular mind. Indeed, most ante-bellum critics seem rather to have been of the mind of Theodore Parker, whose faith in the people went only so far as to suppose them capable of being instructed, of being elevated through a high-minded literature written by "scholars" who had extra-popular sources of insight and who formed a vanguard of truth. Believing the popular mind to be amorphous rather than affirmatively creative, Parker assured his literary contemporaries that any American writer who arrives at truth could be sure of an audience not of scholars alone, as in Germany, but "of earnest, practical people"; for American literature had become "the daily meat of the multitude," and no native author had so far been "too high" for their comprehension. Yet he took care to add that the American "scholar" must be certain, in being "common," not to be "vulgar," that he must not merely reflect "the average thought of respectable men . . . and their average morality," as American writers were wont to do, but rather "represent the higher facts of human consciousness to the people." With his suspicion of the "average morality" of the American people, it is not surprising that

Parker sought in vain for an American literature which should on the one hand be "wholly indigenous and original" and on the other contain the "great idea of absolute right." Perhaps the very significance of the indigenous lay in its wariness of absolutes!

Critics and authors less confident than Parker of grasping the "absolute right" were willing to allow the popular imagination to measure the scholar rather than scholarly high-mindedness the people. What other final tribunal of literary excellence and of truth and fidelity can there be except enduring popular favor? asked Bancroft in the 1820's, already certain that this favor was a criterion over which the logic of the critics could not prevail and beyond which there was no valid appeal. It was to this tribunal that Seba Smith willingly submitted his *Powhatan* two decades later, for like Bancroft he felt that "the test by which the author desires to be tried, is the common taste of *common readers*. If *they* shall read it with pleasure, . . . he will care little for the rules by which critics may judge it, but will find satisfaction in the assurance that he has added something honorable to the literature of his country."

This willingness to abide by popular judgment, tinged as it was by national pride, increased throughout the mid-century. Not only Jacksonian Democrats like Whitman professed it; by the late 1850's such an erstwhile literary conservative as Donald G. Mitchell (Ik Marvel) had become convinced, as Howells was to be in the next generation, that the "more intimate alliance of all literary endeavor . . . with the wants of our everyday life" compelled American authors to recognize that the final test of their literary work would be its relevance to the experience of millions of readers: "Your book . . . has not found final judgment with respect to its fitness as an American document, till it has gone far out three thousand miles west of the sea, to the land of the new settlers, who lay your argument or your fancies, like a plummet, to the stature of their mental need; who test it by that much of hope, of fulness, of joy, it adds to their inner life."

When early nineteenth-century critics envisaged the popular reader, they generally thought of the small farmer or townsman "by the kitchen fire," as Leonard Bacon phrased it; but with the steady industrialization of the Eastern states multitudes of urban workers slowly began to claim their share in the designs of those who identified an American with a democratic literature. Yet there was little inclination to create for the laborer and tradesman a special class literature. Rather were the artisans, small merchants, and mechanics expected to help "form a national character for elegant literature," as that early and conspicuous champion of the literary rights of the working men, Stephen Simpson, remarked soon after the War of 1812. Simpson's neoclassic taste mingled oddly with an equalitarian impulse in a literary evangelism which sought to break down the barriers between the "unlettered mechanic" and the "classical dignitary." As the Jacksonian 1820's deepened his devotion to Liberty, Science, Justice, and Philanthropy, he concluded that his classless ideal could not be achieved unless a literature were created by liberty-loving *"American minds"* to counteract the "gothic" principles being imported in "loads of trash" from class-conscious Europe. This national literature was to be broadly humanistic and was in no sense to pander to proletarian tastes or economic interests; for Simpson—a sort of harbinger of the educational doctrines of Hutchins and Adler a century hence—believed that the same brand of humane literature and liberal education which in the past had narrowly served "a regal *society*" must now be allowed to confer on the American working man the kind of refinement "which renders social intercourse the charm of life." In Simpson's view the national literature should be designed to elevate the laborer by placing him on a cultural rather than an economic par with the "classical dignitary."

Among the few ante-bellum writers who moved toward an identification of American literature with proletarian interests, the most cogent and conspicuous was the young Orestes Brownson. A genuine American literature could arise, he believed in the late 1830's, only by becoming the indispensable instrument of some great humanitarian cause; and this cause he found in the current conflict between what he termed "the accumulator of wealth and the simple laborer who actually produces it." Out of this "struggle between MAN and MONEY," he prophesied, the "true American literature will be born," and when placed beside this national literature which champions the orthodox party of the People, all other extant writings will sink into insignificance. Yet few of Brownson's compatriots ventured into this Marxian atmosphere which was to sustain so much American literary effort a century later. Most of them who professed a devotion to the laboring classes supposed, as did Stephen Simpson and William Ellery Channing, that they had absolved their literary obligation to these classes by facilitating their access to those works which would develop their taste and moral sense. And since recent European literature was decadent, the argument went, a wholesome American literature must afford a proper standard. Such works could provide "that force of thought which the laborer is to seek as his true elevation," Channing remarked; and this "elevation" he construed as "the love and admiration of what is fair, and perfect, and lofty, in character and life!" Any assumption that American authors should achieve a People's literature by descending to a low average of popular interests and politics as their norm constituted a brand of literary democracy which before the Civil War had few adherents. Nevertheless, in these ante-bellum decades the American people had gone far toward establishing themselves as the arbiters and focus, though scarcely the creative matrix, of American letters.

The American Idea

"I am the first poet who has endeavored to express the American Idea, and I shall be popular by and by," wrote Lowell to C. F. Briggs in 1848. Whether this odd boast sprang from a mood of intense nationalism or from one of critical irony, it is difficult to say; but whatever its inception, it is misleading, for it dismisses the earnest efforts of two generations of Joel Barlow's literary descendants, who had quite explicitly accepted the expression of the American idea as the decisive factor in a national poetry. It slights, moreover, that most consistent proponent of republicanism in literature, Fenimore Cooper, who (though no poet, to be sure) early in his literary career asserted that the "only peculiarity that can, or ought to be expected" in the literature of Americans "is that which is connected with the promulgation of their distinctive political opinions." In fact, so confident was Cooper that national ideas and not national settings were the crucial desiderata in the creation of an American literature that he did not hesitate to use foreign settings in such novels as *The Bravo* (1831) and *The Headsman* (1833), with the avowed purpose of bringing "American opinion . . . to bear on European facts." Increasingly he moved in his later novels toward the substitution of "American *principles* for American *things*" as the best means of lending an unequivocal nationality to his work.

Such a concern as Cooper's for national ideas was a salient aspect of American romanticism; for though the movement frequently encouraged a pursuit of nationality through association or feeling, ante-bellum authors never abandoned entirely the neoclassic penchant for universals or the Puritan devotion to moral ideas, and hence many of them were wont to make the primary test of the Americanism of a work its degree of alignment with distinctive composites of New World principles. These composites were usually a blend of the political and social and ethical, such as Theodore Parker had in mind when he proposed to certify as truly national only that literature which was committed to "the great American idea" of "personal freedom, of the dignity and value of human nature, the superiority of a man to the accidents of a man," and of a government "of all the people, by all the people, for all the people." To illustrate such American principles —the "precedence of honest usefulness, incorruptible integrity, or superior genius" over wealth and manners—the *Knickerbocker* in New York agreed, is to become a truly national and not merely a native writer.

Though such broad identifications of individual worth with the American idea found reiterated assent, inevitably emphases and interpretations varied according to the party affiliation of the author. As a radical Democrat, young Brownson would call no scholar American if he failed to understand and practice the principle of the equal rights of all men; and the Jacksonian William Leggett, lamenting to Edwin Forrest that Shakespeare had so little "love of equal human liberty," longed for a little of the Bard's genius so that he might "assert the principles of democratic freedom" around the world. For the Whigs, however, individual achievement rather than equal human liberty was likely to be stressed as the crux of the American idea. If an author had instilled self-respect into his countrymen, his "American office" seemed to J. G. Palfrey to have been fulfilled; and John Pendleton Kennedy bespoke a similar emphasis when he defined "the proper tongue of this clime" as one which gave currency to America's characteristic belief in a society where merit is the only source of respect.

Though ante-bellum authors generally accepted the obligation "to carry republican progressiveness into Literature as well as into Life," as Melville expressed it, they not only gave the American idea diverse political constructions but religious implications as well. By Puritan precedent politics were subsumed under transcendental imperatives, and American literature accordingly became enlisted in the especial service of the eternal verities. It is not surprising, of course, that eminent clergymen, sustaining the old literary influence and interests of the theocrats, should have evangelistically identified the national with the religious view—that the prominent Yale divine, Leonard Bacon, should have been certain that American literature in manifesting the national character would *ipso facto* be enlivened by the Christian virtues dominant in the New World; that the Reverend Horace Bushnell should have prophesied before the Phi Beta Kappa Society at Harvard that "a new body of literature" reflecting a "pure intellectual love of God" would arise in America to supersede the literature of the "lower love"; and that, most influential of all, the Reverend Rufus Griswold, should have set the tone of American writing through numerous anthologies which by preface and editorial selection identified wholesomeness with the national genius. From the authority of such clergymen or their professional counterparts, students in American colleges were likely to accept moral elevation as a primary touchstone for American letters. A graduate of Harvard, young George Bancroft was not to be diverted by his subsequent student days in Germany from expecting his native land to produce a literature imbued "with a high moral purpose"; nor after his return could he countenance a Voltairean vein in American writing as compatible with the national character. And at Yale young Donald G. Mitchell (Ik Marvel) was no doubt but echoing his literary preceptors when he affirmed in his valedictory oration that the "only real nationality of American literature" lies in its "subordination to morality." Indeed, it was the very destiny of America, he prophesied, to consummate a union of "all that is pure in morals and all that is elegant in letters."

More narrowly, the Puritan vision of the New Zion was persistent enough until the Civil War to persuade many men of letters that the American idea, and hence American literature, must be identified not merely with morality but with Christianity itself. "The highest transcendent glory of the American Revolution was this—" wrote John Quincy Adams in 1837, "it connected, in one indissoluble bond, *the principles of civil government with the precepts of Christianity.*" Even the very American mind itself, the annalist W. B. Sprague told the Harvard Phi Beta Kappa Society a decade later, has been "baptized in the name of Protestant Christianity." The literary implications of this baptism seemed as inescapable to Sprague as they did to such varied critics as Charles Sumner at Harvard, Noah Porter and T. S. Grimké at Yale, Caleb Atwater in the West, and William Cooper Scott of the *Southern Literary Messenger:* American literature was to pursue its distinctive mission by abjuring any dependence upon the pagan primitivism of the classics and by committing itself to Christian humanitarianism. The degree of acceptance of this literary postulate among American writers at mid-century can scarcely be overestimated. That Mrs. Stowe had consciously accepted it before writing *Uncle Tom's Cabin* seems clear from her avowed concern, stated in the Preface to her famous novel, that all literary influences should achieve a "unison with the great master chord of Christianity, 'good-will to man.'" In a more nationalistic vein Herman Melville concluded during these same mid-century years that America could never be delivered from her "literary flunkeyism toward England" until proper recognition were given to "those writers who breathe that unshackled, democratic spirit of Christianity in all things." How integrally the American idea involved Christian humanitarianism even for political journals is suggested by the policy of the *Democratic Review,* whose editors in the early 1840's announced that they could approve only those pieces which both instilled in the reader a love of liberty and also strengthened the Christian character.

The Christianity with which such writers as Melville and Stowe identified American letters was Protestant; but Orestes Brownson felt equally "sure that true American literature will be the product, not of Protestant, but of Catholic America." The individualistic temper of such works as "The American Scholar" seemed to him to afford ample grounds for doubting that the major Protestant writers of his generation had been deeply enough imbued with the great social vision of the age to express the national genius. "The great American author will be he who lives out the American idea—the Christian— the Divine idea of *Brotherhood*," he declared; and for the comprehension of this idea he was convinced that the American imagination must be tutored primarily not by the Nature which Emerson had proffered but by the daily, common life of the country. By the mid-1840's Brownson's hopes for a Christian-democratic literature worthy of the Republic became narrowly contingent upon the growth of American Catholicism. The current literary reflection of the national character he dismissed as merely "provisional"—Protestant and infidel. Not until Catholicism should have fused the diversity of the nation into a unity of brotherhood, he prophesied, would have America fulfilled the indispensable conditions of an authentically national literature.

Though Brownson's later sectarian delimitation of the American idea had few literary disciples, his earlier insistence that God had selected the American people to point the way to universal freedom and American writers to embody this idea in their works met with no such indifference. As in the days of Mather and Sewall, American authors were to lift up the New Zion before all the world, so in the spirit of a later age they were to be, as the Yale poet James Hillhouse phrased it, the "left arm" of a nation whose mission it was to become the "Vicegerent of Eternal Justice" among all men. To *Brother Jonathan* (probably John Neal) they seemed "a *native militia*" offering the surest defense of republican usages and institutions; to Theodore Parker, a tribe of priests and scholars who would attract the "unconscious electricity" of justice in the nation and spread it as beauteous light around the world; to young W. W. Story, Phoenixes rising from the ashes of Old World art, singing the "austere song of Justice" and slaking their thirst in the well of Freedom. Confident of this quickening and elevating power of New World humanitarianism, dedicated writers like Mrs. Stowe became avowedly contemptuous of "mere cold art." The consequence was frequently a disparagement of the Old World imagination and an ingenuous calculation of the literary value of a work on a literal scale of its humanitarian intent. No Hamadryad or Pan was present when America was born, sang young

Bayard Taylor in what Emerson judged to be the finest Phi Beta Kappa poem ever delivered at Harvard, and with the greater legend of Freedom nestling in her heart, America has now no need of ancient mythologies. The American imagination would be sufficiently stirred, he affirmed, if at Freedom's "living springs/ Our bards should drink, and lave their dusty wings." In this evangelical ardor of the 1840's and 1850's the avowed abolitionist Whittier was not alone in being moved to lay his best gifts on the shrine of "holy liberty"; even the Southern mystic Holley Chivers apostrophized America as Freedom's Home, down whose aisles to all souls rolled "Man's eloquence in thunders!"

Probably no surer index to the tight mid-century involvement of American literature with the gospel of Humanity is to be found than the changing demands which the editorially astute Rufus Griswold made on American writers at the time. Instead of the commonplace remarks on a national literature which he had prefixed to his influential *The Poets and Poetry of America* in 1842, Griswold proffered in *The Prose Writers of America* (1847) an elaborate analysis of true and false Americanism in literature. During the five intervening years nature and the aborigines had faded in the strong light of humanitarian zeal; and "the recognition of the freedom and dignity of man" had become "the vital principle in our literature—its distinctive and diffusive element." Griswold's dictum that the Pyramids are as national a subject as Indian mounds, provided all the characters involved are regarded as equal in rights and privileges, was but one of many vanes which showed the winds of literary doctrine shifting from picturesque romanticism. An American literature, Griswold and a host of his compatriots now believed, "must teach that the interests of man are the highest concern of men." This was the "New Civilization of which our fathers were the apostles," and it must be "universally diffused" as a prelude to an era in which would arise "a literature of the world."

Thus with the approach of the Civil War both the spirit of the age and the impact of critical opinion veered American letters away from the romantically descriptive and associative toward the normative. The national literature was charged with the obligation to depict not what had been or might have been or even what was, but what ought to be. It was to become "intensely national," as Parker said, by reflecting "the higher consciousness of mankind." It was, in the words of the prominent Southern anthologist and critic A. B. Meek, "to rectify the erroneous spirit of history"; and toward this end American authors seemed to him to need ask but one question of their characters and situations: What have they done for human progress? In this strong current of humanitarian confidence even the aged Irving was sufficiently involved to declare that before the "rising tribunal" of the American press all previous history was to be rewritten and all past judgments were to be corrected and confirmed. Such was to be the literature of the American idea. In enlisting the services of American writers in the diffusion of this idea no one was more eloquently definitive than the "American Macaulay," the Boston critic E. P. Whipple:

> We want a poetry which shall speak in loud, clear tones to the people;
> . . . which shall give visible form and life to the abstract ideas of our
> written constitutions; . . . which shall disentangle freedom from cant
> and senseless hyperbole, and render it a thing of such loveliness and
> grandeur as to justify all self-sacrifice; . . . which shall force through
> the thin partitions of conventionalism and expediency . . . and speak
> out in the high language of men to a nation of men.

The American Temper

Though the literary proponents of the American idea did not prescribe merely a calculated and explicit embodiment of New World principles, they were prone to ignore the subtler manifestations of the national temper in both American life and letters. Conceiving literature to be largely the utterance of consciously held values, they slighted the mythic, symbolic, and more oblique processes of the imagination and hence also the distinctive idiom and image which issue ineluctably from the pen of an autochthonous writer. Yet as early as 1815 Paulding had suspected that "That which distinguishes the literature of one nation from that of another is not so much a difference of thought as of expression"; and increasingly during the ante-bellum decades other American authors shared in this implicit recognition of the undertones and overtones of the national genius which resist articulation except through literary texture and tone and figure. Involved in such a dictum was the Romantic conception of the national culture as an organic process. As the sculptor Horatio Greenough phrased it: civilization is a plant, springing from the ground, rooted in the bosoms and business of men, and blossoming in poetry and heroism. Under such an assumption the blossoms of American literature could derive a peculiar hue and flavor only from the indigenous impulses uniquely at work deep in the national soil.

As to what these organic forces and the consequent cast of the American imagination were, ante-bellum analysts were in general agreement. Though Timothy Flint admitted to his London readers in the 1830's that the separation of England and America had been too brief to produce marked differences in national character, he nevertheless felt that he could discern the emergence of an American type "probably more ardent, quicker in movement, more misled by his imagination, more figurative and impassioned in his diction, than the Briton." It was a similar composite of originality, force, and passion which the New York critic W. A. Jones, following Tocqueville, found in American society and demanded in American literature; and it was a similar composite of vigor, life, and movement which Poe pronounced to be "the qualities which, above all others, the fresh and vigorous intellect of America should and does esteem." The presence of these qualities proved to Poe the authentic nationality of the works of Simms, who in turn expressed his own conviction that the American people were "all enthusiasm, all impulse," and hence that any literary work pretending to be indigenous would have to reflect their earnest excitability.

To reflect such qualities was, in effect, to project through style and image the temper of youth. At the close of the Revolution Noah Webster had feared that the wrinkles of a decrepit Old World culture would remain stamped on the youthful brow of American literature, and many an ante-bellum author reiterated his concern. Like Santayana at a later day, Horatio Greenough reluctantly acknowledged that though "the country was young, yet the people were old"; and on American artists and writers he placed the obligation of evolving new structures and modes consonant with the real genius of the land. America was "a new country, with a new history," Bryant agreed, and hence her authentic literature would be inspired with impulses suited to her untried condition; her poetry especially should be a "newborn being," awkward and affected perhaps, but at least "full of youth and life" and not the cold embalmed body of imitation.

In invoking this youthful spirit for the national literature, antebellum authors were prone to resort to personifications and metaphors to suggest its more precise character. For some it was a wildness and self-reliance, for others a simplicity and wholesomeness. Irving, fearing the infectious decadence of the Old World imagination, prayed that American letters would not be "like some of those premature and aspiring whipsters, who become old men before they are young ones, and fancy they prove their manhood by their profligacy and their diseases." It was just this ill-advised attempt to reach a premature sophistication and to repress the faults natural to a "rude and lusty prime," Cornelius Mathews thought, that had transformed American literature by the 1840's into an "idiotic monster . . . [with] purposeless look and gaping mouth." Or, as the early *Knickerbocker* (1833) disconsolately remarked, as a young people Americans had renounced the "wildness and exuberance" that was their imaginative birthright for an inappropriately "cold reflection" of Old World literature. For restoring to imaginative health this "idiotic monster," which American literature by ignoring its youthful genius had become, John Neal had a remedy:

> Come forth naked, absolutely naked . . . though your muscles *be* rather too large . . . ; but . . . do not come forth in court equipage. . . . We had rather see the Belvidere Apollo in breeches; or, if that be much too "coarse," in "shorts," or "tights," or "inexpressibles."

Thus in the expansive ante-bellum decades youthful America seemed not far removed from giant America. Her literature, Father Knickerbocker prophesied, one day would reflect a "giant's might" in a "giant's form." When that day came the American Parnassus, as W. A. Jones pictured it, would cease to be a garden of exotics where only the rose and lily and mignonette languished; its virgin soil could better nurture the giant oak and elm. Even in the ante-bellum years it seemed to young Bayard Taylor that the "sapless bulk of Europe" was mouldering away, and that a mighty harp should be singing an America where "moves a larger life, to grander measures."

An American Medium

One of the major clogs which kept the national genius from soaring to its distinctive heights, ante-bellum like post-Revolutionary writers frequently suspected, was the weighty heritage of the English language. Such was the view in the 1820's of the historian Jared Sparks who, distinguishing like De Quincey between the literature of knowledge and the literature of power, conceded that a uniform language would doubtlessly facilitate growth in the abstract realm of ideas but added that a diversity of tongues is needed to reflect the peculiar tones and images with which nature has stamped the fancy of each country. Just as a universal Greek language would have precluded the appearance of great epic poets other than Homer, Sparks argued, so the alien vehicle of an inherited English tongue thwarted any cisatlantic Shakespeares who might even then be striving to give autochthonous utterance to the American imagination and heart. Postulating this tight organic bond between a national language and a national culture, many an early nineteenth-century literary patriot shared the author-physician Walter Channing's regret that the Revolution had not expelled English speech as well as English troops and thereby thrown America into a "confusion of tongues" from which the nation might evolve a language as precisely adapted to its incipient culture as the Indian language was adapted to American nature. The very existence of the national mind, the Southern editors Hugh Legaré and J. W. Simmons ventured to say, is contingent on the formation of a "*dialect of our own*—a language as American . . . as the principles and opinions which it shall embody." Even the omission of certain letters, they prophesied, would have effects "at once moral, political, and intellectual."

Yet for all these bold assertions about the need for an American dialect, native linguists generally conceded that a national language was likely to be the correlate rather than the genesis of a national character. Moreover, they were concerned that the emergent American language be an improvement and purification of the mother tongue and not a cisatlantic corruption. Hence John Pickering's insistence, in *A Vocabulary . . . Peculiar to the United States* (1816), that all native mutations be subjected to severe tests of utility and subsequently be labeled "noxious" or "innocent," lest a "wild luxuriance might overspread our literary soil, if left to its natural fertility"; and hence the aging Jefferson's profession that he was a friend to only a "judicious neology." Hence, too, Timothy Flint's later assurance to his English readers that many Americanisms were ephemeral, that the dialect of Jack Downing had had its day, and that this frontier patois was at least eight parts invention to two parts authentic popular speech. To later generations Flint's chagrin over the salt-river dialect may seem to betray an all too sensitive colonialism; yet his reluctance to sanction any usage beyond an American-English with "some new words and phrases" built on a broad base of Saxon and cognate languages is representative of the generally cautious advance toward linguistic divergence before the Civil War.

Compelled as they were to accept English as the broad base of any American language, ante-bellum authors were likewise forced to recognize that the superstructure of cisatlantic style and diction would be fashioned and erected not by some American linguistic academy but by indigenous forces at work in popular speech. It was in the camp meeting sermon and the Fourth of July oration, in the stump speech and the parlance of market-place, as Timothy Flint and many others noted, that an idiom *"sui generis"* and "purely and properly American" could most readily be found. To a taste formed on neo-classic models, as both Cooper and William Wirt testified, this idiom often seemed wanting in a proper simplicity. Yet even for this native turgidity, the less decorous John Neal discerned in the common speech of the people the surest antidote. In their colloquial idiom lay both a poetry and a directness, he thought, as did Mark Twain a half century later, which would displace both the "entangled sentence" of the patriotic orators and the "sleepy modulation" of the Addisonian essayists. "For my own part," he wrote in the late 1820's, ". . . I hope to God . . . I never shall write what is now worshipped under the name of *classical* English. . . . We have dead languages enough now; but the deadest language I ever met with or heard of, was that in use among the writers of Queen Anne's day." If American authors would but catch the tone and pattern of men as they "*do* talk, in our language, every day, in the street," one of Neal's characters in *Errata*

(1823) observed, they would avoid the "holy-day dress" of foreign cadence—both the Addisonian sentence, "daintily put together," and the Johnsonian sentence, "jointed and cramped with iron."

Neal's bold prescription for purifying and nationalizing American style by rejecting Augustan models and incorporating the idiom of everyday speech was virtually disregarded for a half century. Few ante-bellum men of letters were willing, with Samuel Woodworth, to risk clothing their thoughts in a "homespun uniform, coarse and inelegant," when the patterns of neoclassic elegance or romantic rhetoric could be had for the taking. Perhaps much of their hesitancy was rooted in a distrust of the basic temper and pace of American life from which they supposed the national idiom derived its peculiar character. The expensive industrial enterprise seemed even in these ante-bellum decades to the young New York poet J. G. Brooks to have left a disastrous stamp on American style: plays were becoming mechanical and bards were wielding sledge hammers in their ill-advised attempts to employ "such rough words as tariff, jobbing, cuts, stumpage, snags, sawyers," and the like in the delicate modes of verse. Though as a poet, Poe would surely have concurred in Brooks's displeasure over such diction, as a journalist he both accepted the "energetic, busy spirit of the age" and applauded the likelihood that this spirit would no longer tolerate the ponderous style of the Augustans, but would demand "the curt, the terse, the well-timed." And even more cordial to the impress of continental life on the native style was Edwin Forrest, who viewed America not as an industrialized machine but as a fresh and buoyant empire. The sweep of equalitarianism in the nation's life and creed, he predicted, would strip off the "tawdry trappings of superfluous ornament, and . . . the quaint conceits of cloistered rhetoricians, and their elaborate contortions of phrase," and in their stead would encourage the "simplicity of nature." Perhaps in Forrest's espousal of simplicity, in Poe's recognition of the terse, and in Woodworth's apology for the homespun there was present a common colloquial denominator from which, as Neal had prophesied, something of an indigenous American style might evolve.

If in diction and pace and tone American experience was beginning to mould an indigenous idiom, it was also enforcing new emphases in modes and genres. In a singular anticipation of Whitman, John Neal in the early 1820's proposed that American poetry absorb native cadences and sever its allegiance to the rigidities of rhyme and fixed meter. The "true home-bred man," he thought, would "talk in prose —with a sort of rhythm." Though Neal's proposals for a new native poetry to succeed what he called the old metrical acrostics were to be largely disregarded until Whitman illustrated their validity a generation later, his dictum that the epic belonged wholly to the past could be more readily accepted. To be sure, the remote frontier authors Genin in Ohio and Emmons in Kentucky toiled, respectively, at their *Napolead* and *Fredoniad*; and in Cuba one "Sylvia Occidentalis" tried to interest Cooper and Irving in her heroic poem. No major antebellum authors, however, were sufficiently inspired to respond to the lingering pleas for an American Homer. The epic impulse had been absorbed by the novel; and accordingly it was Mrs. Stowe rather than Barlow who most nearly approximated the Californian Edward Pollock's vision of a "sceptred minstrel" moved by a "sublime, national egotism" to "construct a moral hero, at war with wrong."

The most sensitive of all genres to the demands of ante-bellum as of post-Revolutionary American life and institutions was the oration. In the functioning of the most democratic of societies the art of persuasion was not only of paramount importance; it was also obliged to adapt itself topically to the changing temper and exigencies of the national life. It is not surprising, therefore, that Timothy Flint and N. P. Willis should have reported to their London readers in the 1830's that the American oration had achieved a "style *sui generis*" and that it afforded the best answer to the "great outcry for something national and peculiar." That American eloquence was frequently ornate and bombastic, Flint and many another were forced to concede. Nevertheless, as one obscure orator at Dartmouth remarked in an apology typical of the many given before college literary societies, eloquence seemed to reside in the very soil and air and institutions of America, and hence it was to "be cherished as the adopted agency of American mind."

On other literary types the distinctive national impress was less clear. To be sure, in such events as the Sharp-Beauchamp affair in Kentucky, Poe perceived the materials for American tragedy; and in New England legends Longfellow announced that he had found virgin themes for the national ballad. But the nationalization of these forms, as Poe and Longfellow conceived it, was to be accomplished through substance and idea rather than through such structural and tonal transmutations as Neal and Whitman proposed; and hence no distinctive American tragedy or ballad emerged. Nor was Simms more successful in his attempt to evolve in place of the old epic a distinctive American romance—a heroic poem with native materials but without rhyme. Perhaps Henry Tuckerman was more realistic in observing that neither a tragic nor an epic mutation but rather the lyric, with its refined and domestic sentiment, was best "adapted to our own busy and unimaginative country" in the ante-bellum years. At any rate, neither Simms nor his contemporary romancers succeeded in formulating and establishing a markedly indigenous type of fiction, and not until after the Civil War were critics and authors to engage in the long debate over the Great American Novel.

The Impulse to Realism

Although conscious efforts like that of Simms to foster distinctive American genres were gradually doomed to failure, the indigenous cultural forces that were shaping an American idiom in eloquence were also working in a somewhat different direction toward a native realism in fiction. Within the early fiction and poetry of the Republic, contingent though these modes were on the traditionally didactic or sentimental or Gothic, lay a substantial preoccupation with the proximate and the contemporary which, expanded and intensified through a century, issued in the conscious pictorial fidelity of Howells and Dreiser. If Dwight's *Greenfield Hill* (1794) did not afford an entirely faithful view of the New Canaan, neither did Lewis' *Main Street* (1920) of Sauk Center. At any rate, by the turn of the century Brockden Brown's *Arthur Mervyn,* Brackenridge's *Modern Chivalry,* William Hill Brown's *The Power of Sympathy,* and many another early work contained within the periphery of terror or satire or moralism solid centers of local detail in manners and familiar objects.

Yet of more import for the national literature than this early native substance was the evidence (and, at times, the awareness) of a native temper which was increasingly to impel that kind of attack upon the

American scene later to be known as realism or naturalism. Under the reiterated Romantic assumption that the imagination can best be nourished by the cumulative ruin of centuries, or under the neoclassic postulate that wit can have its play only in a society where social rituals and levels are stable, the early American writer inclined to lament the absence of ivied castles and social caste about him, and then to lay down his pen. Yet even the first American novelist, William Hill Brown, suspected that such Old World literary assumptions would inevitably be altered or abandoned in the pragmatic and progressive atmosphere of the New World. Enchanters and heathen mythology could not aid him in resolving his plot, he confessed in *Ira and Isabella* (1807); but the nonromantic structures and strategy which he perceived the American imagination to require, he felt unable to design. Nor a half century later, could the immigrant German novelist of the West, Charles Sealsfield, describe in any detail the distinctive literary "machinery" which, he also realized, was demanded by a people whose primary attention was so fixed on the useful sciences as almost to preclude American composition in the old tragic or "aesthetic" modes. It was this national bias and its literary corollaries that Hawthorne also seems to have had in mind when he observed, in the Preface to *The Blithedale Romance,* that the romancer's task in America was singularly difficult because the public inevitably tried his works by realistic standards, compelling his beings "to show themselves in the same category as actually living mortals."

However pronounced this realistic vein in the popular mind, its transposition into acceptable literary correlates and emphases had to wait, for the most part, until after the Civil War. For, paradoxically, the same reader whose realistic bent led him to test Hawthorne's characters by "actually living mortals" was scarcely able to accept into literary respectability these living mortals when they confronted him in the pages of an American work. "No attempt to delineate ordinary American life, either in drama or novel, has been rewarded with success," Cooper observed in 1837; and soon thereafter the popular novelist J. H. Ingraham, who could shrewdly count the romantic pulse of his public, more specifically traced the failure of such realistic ventures as F. W. Thomas' *Clinton Bradshaw* (1835) to a disproportionate reliance on everyday urban customs and manners. The American reader's "pretty nose is turned up, or the manly lip ejects a 'pshaw!' at meeting only plain misters, and colonels," Ingraham added. Indeed, the ante-bellum novelist who chose everyday life as his medium risked, if the testimony of *Graham's* can be trusted, being dismissed as an innovator who dealt with "base matter . . . that, while it is familiar as the aspect of the pavements and the air of the streets, seems also far fetched and remote, because it is narrated for the first time."

Thus, though a generation later Eggleston could confidently fuse backwoods social history and fiction, the earlier writer ventured only with diffidence and misgivings into an imaginative exploration of the unadorned world about him. In view of the romantic penchant of his public, it is not surprising that Longstreet should have prefaced his *Georgia Scenes* (1835) with an apology for the realistic coarseness of language and the minutely depicted manners and customs as elements which could be of interest only to some future historically minded reader. Though Longstreet's authentic accounts of the "low" elements of Southern frontier life scarcely met with the indifference which he had expected, William Gilmore Simms faced such positive disapproval for his descent from a lofty romanticism into the mores of squatter and Indian that he felt obliged to issue to offended sensibilities an apology for his shift in mode. It is easier to concoct a fairy tale than to depict man modified by circumstances, he reminded those who saw in his sally toward naturalism a decline in fictional art; and to those whose objection to realism was moral rather than aesthetic, he replied that if vice is to be made properly revolting, the historical novelist must paint it as it actually has existed.

Even before Simms found it necessary to defend his "Flemish freedom of touch," however, a few authors whose imagination had not been captivated by Mrs. Radcliffe or Scott were cautiously beginning to fashion and illustrate a principle of simple indigenous realism which was to find its fullest explication in Howells' *Criticism and Fiction* at the end of the century. Convinced that their new and unromantic country could have little authentic embodiment in styles and devices filched from the rich and established cultures of the Old World, these fledgling realists proposed a modest reorientation of the imagination proceeding from known and felt familiar objects. They were in effect subscribing to the jurist George S. Hillard's dictum that since life in the Western world is "too coarse to bear the embroidery of romance," American novelists must "hold the mirror up to every shape of life and every hue of opinion" about them. In the "broad sunshine" of American life, as the historian Prescott phrased it, they were consciously abandoning the "old credulity" on which the romanticist had depended, and committing themselves to the observable behavior of "poor human nature."

The "mere novelist" deals with the Present, but the Romancer dwells on the Past, wrote Paul Hamilton Hayne, observing an honorific distinction in favor of Romance which the major ante-bellum writers like Hawthorne and Simms inclined to accept in both theory and practice. In view of the inferior literary status of the "mere novelist," it is not surprising that in the main it was such lesser figures as F. W. Thomas and Theodore Fay and Cornelius Mathews who ventured toward a comprehensive realism. Though among them, as among most literary nationalists, the literary will exceeded the literary imagination, each illustrated to a respectable degree the potentialities for native fiction of a mode which Thomas, anticipating Howells by half a century, defined as the portrayal of such scenes, characters, and materials "as may fall under the observation of the generality of readers." Like Howells, Thomas not only explicitly rejected the "feudal bias" of Scott and pronounced "our own times" a better and wider field than the past; he also construed realism as the literary correlate of democracy, since "all . . . [could] *feel* the truth of the portraiture." As Howells was to say, it freed literary judgment from coteries and from dogma by placing the criteria for literary truth within the experience of the people.

Most of the early ante-bellum authors who consciously experimented with the realistic mode were, like Thomas, concerned as well with the nationalistic implications of their rejection of the romanticism dominant at the time. In the metropolitan East this native bent toward realism frequently was exhibited in comedies like *The Politicians* (1840) of Cornelius Mathews, who avowedly set out to provide a domestic satire which would "furnish countenance" to the cause of American literature and deliver the stage from the spate of stale English farces. That the motley society of expanding American cities in the 1840's could afford suggestive materials for the satiric realist is attested by the appearance of the volume *American Comedies* within the decade. Limited in comic thrust though the collection may be, it did constitute, in the words of one of the plays it contained, an index to a growing disposition of native writers to dispense with those romantic foreign vagabonds and lovers who had so often "overleap[ed] the barriers of nature" and landed in the "regions of impossibility."

While the urban East consciously moved toward native realism through comedy, the frontier West likewise began to suspect that, in the absence of that fund of historical associations currently adjudged requisite to romance, it had best make a virtue of necessity and commit its literary future to the everyday world. A half century before *Huckleberry Finn,* the Cincinnati jurist Isaac Jewett prophetically observed in the *Western Monthly* that among the most promising themes for an original literature in the region were the Mississippi boatmen and the "ludicrous anomalies" of avaricious pedlars swindling an unlettered people. Do not banish the novelist from the Real and Present, he pleaded, claiming for fiction not only local manners and dialect but also the larger cultural patterns inherent in the ceaseless push westward. It was these cultural patterns which the early Western literary arbiter Daniel Drake also had in mind when he remarked the inevitable emphasis on business and mechanic arts in a pioneer society. And though Drake expressed doubts that such arts would have sufficient leverage to elevate native literature to any considerable heights, he was convinced that they would enrich the resources of the novelist: they would generate new figures of speech to "tincture" his style, and in effect through their "fellowship" they would afford him "a power loom and steam press." Such Ohio writers as Jewett and Drake, devoted though they were in the main to traditional literary proprieties, were thus by no means blind to the possibility, as the lawyer-editor James H. Perkins of Cincinnati remarked, that a society which attended primarily to the concrete and practical would give a new turn to the literary imagination. That this new realistic mode should later have as its most zealous apologist a critic (Howells) whose mind was formed in the atmosphere of ante-bellum Ohio journalism is not surprising. The same cultural temper extended, however, into the South of Longstreet and Baldwin and veered them also toward a realism which would "illustrate the periods, the characters, and the phases of society." It also extended into the Michigan frontier and emancipated Caroline Kirkland's imagination sufficiently from the European Romantics whom she revered to enable her to picture with conscious fidelity the "very ordinary scenes" and the "fiddle-faddle" of *A New Home* (1839) and *Forest Life* (1842).

For the antiromantic American writer before the Civil War to whom the "ordinary scenes" of his unadorned land seemed unredeemable through any imaginative process, there was one last recourse: to turn inward. As early as the 1830's the novelist Theodore Fay had defended the literary propriety of American writers' copying "from the great world those 'infinite doings' of the mind and heart which make up the material of human existence." Yet he did not see, apparently, that some of his contemporaries (Hawthorne, Melville, and Poe) were in part impelled toward the "mind and heart" by the limitations of the external scene itself. It was left to Cornelius Mathews to observe in the early 1840's that the "very nakedness of our new condition . . . might be reasonably expected to drive us upon a profounder delineation of the inner life." Just before the Civil War Lowell sustained this view that America's lack of romantic associations and social contrasts might well be resolved into the richest of literary assets. It may well be, he concluded in the course of advising Mrs. Stowe to avoid what people commonly call the "Ideal," that unable to rely upon the external distinctions superinduced by older aristocratic systems, the American novelist will be compelled toward an intensive focus on the "collisions of innate character" and on "that element of universal humanity" which outside a social democracy would be all but closed to his imagination. Whatever the influence of Lowell's statement, it was at least prophetic of the increasing commitment to psychological realism to be made by American writers during the ensuing century.

An American Humor

By twentieth-century interpreters of American culture and literary history the hardy substratum of national humor has been frequently and appreciatively explored—notably by Miss Constance Rourke and Professor Walter Blair. How acutely it formed an evolving index to the national temper and values is now a familiar story which needs no retelling here. Moreover, how extensively it afforded substance and ironic perspective for such serious writers as Melville and Hawthorne is now at least partially clear. A century ago, however, native American humor was almost entirely disregarded as a germinal element in the growth of a distinctive and respectable American literature. In the thousands of pleas, analyses, and prophesies relating to a national literature, not one in a hundred before the Civil War even casually involved native humor. To be sure, the Transcendentalists perceived something of its autochthonous import and propriety, and by the end of the century its vulgarity had become picturesque enough to be countenanced by the national literary pride of many of the more refined men of letters—as will be seen in later chapters. But generally in the ante-bellum years the literary mores of virtually all American literary critics and even of the humorists themselves assigned the national humor and the national literature to discrete planes of utterance.

If the arbiters of ante-bellum literary taste found realism generally unpalatable, they were all the more unprepared to accept that phase of the mode which emerged in the 1830's in the vulgarity of Jack Downing and Davy Crockett. A generation before the Civil War the editor of the *North American,* William Tudor, was convinced that European clowns had their counterparts in America, and he foresaw a national comedy arising when native authors should embody "the nice shades of local peculiarities"; but even so genteel a rustic humor as that of the Connecticut Wits repelled him as boorish in its associations and "maukish [*sic*] to a correct taste." Soon thereafter William Dunlap more specifically found these "clowns of the New World" among the descendants of English, Low Dutch, and German settlers; but he was not so certain that "that compound monster which is found on our western frontiers" afforded equal comic possibilities. Unlike Tudor, however, he was not disturbed by the probability that the English type of humor exhibited in *Punch* was not suited to or relished by "our state of society," and that American conditions would evolve something other than mere adaptations of transatlantic types.

That this "compound monster" of the frontier and his uneducated, rural counterpart were able to claim even a humble place in the national literature was due to the concurrent support of an American public who relished his pungent humor and of a British public who felt that they at last had an answer to their pleas for something indigenously American. Those Americans who, like Tudor, affected a "correct taste" did not grant the "monster" a ready favor at home. In New England they admitted that Colonel Crockett might be amusing "where backwoods vernaculur [*sic*], and the anecdotes of the uncultivated son of nature" were preferred to scholarly or refined conversation; but Crockett on the printed page seemed to them as repulsive as the "atmosphere of a bar-room, on the morning succeeding a *feast* of whisky and cigars." Likewise, to Southern minds nurtured on the classics the Jim Crows and Jim Browns and sketches of the habits and manners of the "very dregs of society" seemed to have turned the native literary scene into "an Augean Stable." Anglophiles professed amazement and chagrin that odd fish like Crockett, Downing, and Sam Slick should continue to enjoy such a reputation in England that the eccentric and anomalous were becoming established as the *sine qua non* of an American literature. Even literary leaders of the Ohio Valley, supposing the dignity of their section to have been imperiled by a vulgar frontier buffoonery, deplored the vogue of new humor in the nation as a whole. As the *Western Monthly* summarily stated the case in 1835:

> The Jack Downing and David Crockett taste, which has been gaining favor even in polite circles, for several years past, is one which should not be encouraged; and we think it far from creditable to the nation, that it has so far been introduced into our literature, as to be spread through the newspapers and periodicals. There is neither wit nor meaning in the terms *Hoosier, Sucker, Corncracker,* and *Buckeye* . . . ; and it is not without mortification that we hear strangers inquiring into the origin and meaning of these names. They have in reality no meaning, but are mere slang, accidentally or arbitrarily introduced.

That the dialect humorists of the Downing-Crockett stamp had a great popular vogue in the generation before the Civil War is thus attested by the very critics who resented them. But that these humorists might well be forerunners of a respectable autochthonous literature was an assumption entertained by English more often than by American readers. Nor, apparently, did the humorists themselves regard their dialect compositions as contributions toward that end. Jack Downing's creater, Seba Smith, professing a desire to add "something honorable to the literature of his country," composed a metrical romance on Powhatan; but he wrote his Downing papers, he said, merely because he "couldn't help it." Like the Downing papers, the popular Mozis Addums letters of George W. Bagby in the South a generation later were no conscious part of a nationalistic literary design. Like Smith, Bagby saw his more pretentious literary efforts ignored, and as a consequence the name of Mozis Addums "for many years" made him "a little sick" whenever he heard it. In the decade of the 1860's Twain and Harte were also to express similar annoyance that the "public would have its way," perversely embracing as it did the subliterary clowns of its own soil in preference to either belles-lettres or humor based on alien circumstance and models.

The conscious efforts to create a national comedy, like those of Cornelius Mathews, met with less favor from both critics and public. Impatient with the succession of Lord Noddys and Lady Highdid-dlediddles on the American stage, Mathews attempted to nationalize the theater by substituting such New York political types as Brisk, Glib, and Joe Surge for satiric portrayal. Yet, despite his nationalistic purpose and his native materials, he could not altogether divest his satire of transatlantic categories and perspectives; and hence Griswold seems thoroughly justified and acutely prophetic in having observed in the late 1840's that not in Mathews' derived comic types but in the "originality and riant boldness" of the humor of the South and West lay the "abundant promise for the future . . . of an original and indigenous literature."

But only by such sporadic approbation did the new humor gain slow recognition as the most incisive and untrammeled expression of not only the "riant boldness" but also the shrewd adaptability and tough gumption of the American mind. It is not surprising, therefore, that in the light of its dubious status the indigenous humor of the South and Southwest should be sought not by the respectable magazines but by a sporting journal, W. T. Porter's *Spirit of the Times* (1831–58). Conscious of the unique Americanism and intrinsic vigor of the tall tales and hunting sketches from those regions, Porter not only published such writers as Audubon, G. W. Harris, J. J. Hooper, and Thomas Thorpe in his magazine but also included them in the five-volume *Library of Humorous American Writers,* which he edited for the publishers Carey and Hart. Such were the media which popularized Harris' prankish Sut Lovingood, Hooper's gambling Simon Suggs, and Thorpe's "The Big Bear of Arkansas." In the picaresque characters of the outdoor West and Southwest, Porter felt, much of the artifice in American literary themes and sentiment might find a wholesome counteragent. Popular though such characters were among the numerous readers of the *Spirit of the Times,* however, the native humor which they represented in the ante-bellum decades seemed to most of the cultivated public unworthy of any pretentions to an integral place in the national literature of which Americans had so long dreamed.

Publishers and Anthologists

Much of the stimulus to American writing before the War of 1812 came from the announced policy of such publishers as William Park, Isaiah Thomas, and Mathew Carey to favor native compositions and to provide a sympathetic critical atmosphere. With the marked increases in literacy and the subsequent expansion of the reading public in the early nineteenth century, however, the modest and patriotic publisher of earlier days was gradually transformed into the director of a complex financial venture where the desire for profit rather than national literary pride was likely to dictate the choice of literary material. As a consequence, the native author's need for copyright, which Paine, Hazard, and Webster had declared at the end of the Revolution to be the *sine qua non* of a national literature, became more insistently clear as the century advanced. Foreign reprints from the pens of established professionals to whom the American publisher was not legally obligated to pay royalties amassed for him easy profits; cisatlantic works, written by unknown amateurs, were likely to be distinct liabilities. It is not surprising, therefore, that the average publisher, as Theodore Dwight, Jr. reported in the 1830's, should have relapsed into the easygoing and evasive attitude that the encouragement of "solid literature and American authors is a good thing to talk about" and he would "like to practice it more and more."

Whether or not John Neal was substantially accurate in estimating that British authors received fifty to a hundred times as much for their literary labors as Americans, it was undoubtedly true that native literary energies were severely undernourished in a thin market and that, as a result, indigenous impulses in the national mind were aborted for lack of utterance and definition. This "piratical course" of American publishers, the novelist J. B. Jones observed, not only disheartened the American writer; more crucially it "promulgated" European fancies and sentiments. To Cooper it seemed equally clear that America would have no literature at all and hence American principles would be endangered so long as native talent could find larger rewards in other pursuits and had to contend with the "unpaid contributions" from established British writers. Cooper's view was reiterated hundreds of times by other authors in the ante-bellum decades. As the Southern author J. B. Cobb summarily stated the case at mid-century: we "owe all our literary discouragements to Anglo-American publishers."

No stage of the century-long campaign for the protection of both British and American authors was more fervently waged than that of the early 1840's. In 1837 an international copyright association had been organized by young George Palmer Putnam, who had begun even then to hope (as he was to hope for the rest of his life) that the "next year" Congress would take favorable action. Within a few years a host of New York authors, with some support from the South, became conspicuously active in behalf of protection. The climax to this major campaign came in February, 1842, upon the arrival of Dickens, who was also a proponent of copyright. Bryant, Hoffman, Griswold, Lewis G. Clark, Willis, Halleck, and nearly a score of other New York men of letters joined Irving and Dickens in petitioning Congress to remedy a system which they pronounced "fatally subversive of the interests of our youthful literature." At the dinner for Dickens on February 19, Cornelius Mathews, Corresponding Secretary of the American Copyright Club, bespoke the professional gloom of the time by describing American letters as a "state of desperate anarchy," as a barren field where foreign sowings had brought no native growths, and as a land where echoed the voice of neither "Allegany" [*sic*] nor the metropolis because of a lack of protection. With proper protection for English as well as American authors, he prophesied, "the two sections of Anglo-Saxon literature" would move "harmoniously onward."

Undoubtedly Dickens' presence further solidified the New York writers into a body for positive action on behalf of copyright, and their unremitting zeal persisted for several years before declining into a more temperate but sustained campaign. In the year after the dinner even the judicious Bryant was moved to make an especial address to his countrymen on both the rightness and expedience of strong protection, the crucial issue of which, he warned them, was whether American writers were to be free for a fair encounter with Old World authors for the ideological domination of the world. And a year later in a series of letters in the *Southern Literary Messenger* describing copyright as "the means, and the only means, of our perfect independence," Simms concurred in Bryant's recent statement on the desperate state of native letters: "American Literature is as suddenly silent as if it never had a voice. Its authors, if they have not ceased to write, have almost ceased to publish." To such expressions of nationalistic sentiment, moreover, Simms added analyses of the legalistic and economic aspects of the issue, with the result that his series of letters stands as one of the most cogent arguments for copyright before the Civil War. By the mid-1840's the bill of particulars had been fully drawn by Cooper, Mathews, Bryant, and Simms, and many another. Nevertheless, in the ensuing years such nationalistic critics as Griswold continued to protest the injury wrought to both Americanism and young American authors by "legalized piracy," and such patriotic scholars as George Ticknor continued to support protection as a means of excluding republication of trashy English books ("now so common") and of encouraging a larger number of American authors to write those books "wisely adapted to our wants" and to the "elevation of the national character."

Though most authors were avowed proponents of a copyright law, occasionally dissenting voices were heard—in general from the Republican-Democratic group. Whatever the motive of this dissent— whether the party's alignment against Hamiltonian tariffs, or a Jeffersonian confidence that the American mind would be enriched rather than betrayed by transatlantic ideas, or mere journalistic self-interest —it persisted from Stephen Simpson's *Portico* (1816) through John Neal's *Brother Jonathan* (1842–43). A restriction on literary importations, argued these journals, would stifle emulation; and they declared it not necessary to "put out the moon to let the stars shine." Neal's position occasionally wavered; but not that of the Jacksonian William Leggett, whose thoroughgoing democratic principles led him to insist in the 1830's that the whole principle of literary property be abrogated in order to prevent the emergence of a special literary class out of sympathy with popular interests. Moreover, this principle he construed as merely a legal privilege with no foundation in natural rights. With a Miltonic faith that Truth would emerge the victor over Error when both were freely expressed, he was convinced that American writers in his own century needed no more protection than they had had in the Revolution successfully to counteract "the tawdry and sickening aristocracy which bedizens the pages of British novels and romances."

While many an American publisher continued to allow his left hand to reap substantial profits from pirated British authors, at the same time he could in part satisfy the promptings of his nationalistic conscience by publishing with his right the domestic annuals, gift books, and anthologies which appealed to the popular taste, especially during the 1820's, 1830's, and 1840's. As rivals to British gift books, the American volumes consistently attempted to utilize not merely American themes and authors but also formats and engravings by native artists. Though the romantic temper of the time persuaded some compilers of the annuals to include tales and sketches saturated with that Arabian remoteness of which Emerson complained, yet the majority of such gift books, like *The Amaranth, The Magnolia, The Dewdrop, Our Country,* and *The Home Book of the Picturesque,* were avowedly dedicated to displaying American talent and indigenous materials. Editorially typical was N. P. Willis' hope that the "national character" of *The Legendary* (1828) would earn the publication good will, as was his plea for contributions of national ballads and articles on the Southern and Western states.

In these same Western states a year later James Hall similarly proposed to give the first gift book published in the section (*The Western Souvenir*) "an original character, by devoting its pages exclusively to our domestick literature." Undoubtedly the publishers Carey and Hart summarily bespoke the well-intentioned if not very incisive nationalism that commonly characterized the annuals when they pronounced *The Gift* (1843) "in every respect an American work. The contributions are by American authors—the illustrations by American artists."

That despite such nationalistic avowals, the contribution of the annuals toward a richly indigenous literature was dubious, astute critics soon perceived. Though "these little works" might be "especially suited to the instant genius of our land," as the *North American* (1829) phrased it, at best they were to be regarded as "the blossoms of a harvest to come" rather than as "the *twilight dawn* of American literature"; their service was perhaps scarcely more than to allow American writers to "keep their pens ready" and to afford a modest "habitation" for early American anecdote and legend. Even their Americanism was partial. In their sentiment and delicacy, in their propensity to the melancholy and macabre, they were undoubtedly authentic reflections of one aspect of the national mind; but to those authors who conceived of the national character in more virile terms, the annuals seemed unfortunately to commit American literature to what Whitman called the "highly-refined . . . and gilt-edged themes." They were likely to resemble *The Mayflower,* which Mrs. Elizabeth Oakes Smith launched in 1847, patriotically maintaining that it was no "piratical craft," no "exotic" bearing sweetness from the land of myrtle or tears from some Lady leaning from a balcony, but rather "a hardy native, indigenous to our own soil." Yet the America in which she believed and which she would wish to reflect, she made clear, was not that which lay in "the fiery eye, the great muscle, . . . the firm foot, the brute nationality; but in the subtle and changeful and beautiful filiments [*sic*] of thought which are in our midst."

In the numerous anthologies of American poetry and the rarer collections of American prose which appeared contemporaneously with the annuals, the same aspiration to exhibit and accelerate the nation's literary achievement prevailed. Though the titular epithet "American" served as a guarantee that only native authors were included, the concept of nationality implicit or explicit in the anthologies was usually as uncritically generous as that in the gift books. Like Samuel Kettell's three-volume *Specimens of American Poetry* (1829), the collections were consistently devoted to an "attempt to do something for the cause of American literature"; but like John Keese's *The Poets of America* a dozen years later, they generally found it difficult to define

the features of the Muse of the New World. Yet however undiscrimi-
nating in their sense of nationality both anthologists and the reading
public may have been, their interest and pride in native compositions
was impressive enough to convince Poe that among his countrymen
there was in American life no incompatibility between the utilitarian
and the poetical, that *"we are* a poetical people."* In the vogue of anthologies in the 1840's such poets as Bryant, George P. Morris, and
Thomas Buchanan Read edited their several volumes. But even more
ambitious series were planned by a few publishers, with the professed
"desire of aiding our native literature." Samuel Coleman, publishing
in 1839 a selection of Rufus Dawes's poems, counted it the first of a
series of uniform volumes that were to constitute a Library of American Poetry; and a few years later M. M. Noah projected *The National
Volume,* a work which he hoped to issue "in a style of suitable magnificence" representing every eminent author of the country. Neither of
these large compilations was completed; but the very fact that they
were planned affords a clue to the growing confidence in native literature in the 1840's.

It was Rufus Griswold, of course, who, by devoting volumes respectively to the poets, the female poets, and the prose writers of the
country, became all but the anthologist laureate of the decade. "A
national literature is ever the burden of his song," wrote the historian
J. T. Headley at mid-century; and this characterization Mrs. Elizabeth
Oakes Smith elaborated by reporting that at the mere mention of an
American author or book Griswold "smelt the battle afar off like the
war-horse" and "grew eloquent, dogmatized, and bore down all opposition. [¶] We have reason to be grateful to him, as Americans, for
what he did for literature." Undoubtedly Griswold through his collections did much to popularize American authors; but the brand of
literary nationalism issued from no sustained critical insight but vacil-
lated from anthology to anthology. In his early *The Poets and the
Poetry of America* (1842) he demanded no more than an independence of English opinions, a moral tone, or a romantic use of American
nature, history, and the Indian. A half decade later, in *The Prose Writers of America* (1847) he had only scorn for the "absurd notion abroad
that we are to create an entirely new literature," and that "Indian
chiefs or republican soldiers must be the characters of our works of

imagination, or that our gloomy forests, or sea-like prairies, or political committee rooms must be their scenes." With Cooper he had come to believe that the distinction of American letters could only be an ardent republicanism—the embodiment of the American Idea. But soon thereafter, finding it necessary to accommodate his principle of nationality to *The Female Poets of America* (1849), he conceded that originality might well come to American literature merely through an infusion of the domestic temper and spirit. By the time the 1851 edition of *The Poets and Poetry* appeared, he was looking forward to an international rather than a national literary order, in which American writers as the spokesmen of progress should represent the man of the future.

This instability in critical principle, this veering from a picturesque romanticism to universal humanitarianism, inevitably aroused the suspicion among Griswold's contemporaries that he was a literary opportunist, that he was confused or parasitic, that he was ignorant or dishonest. Especially censorious were those authors associated with the influential *Literary World,* which proclaimed itself "no equivocal supporter of true nationality." Within this group were E. A. and G. L. Duyckinck, and it was the appearance of their ambitious *Cyclopaedia of American Literature* in 1855 which signally challenged Griswold's dominant position as anthologist, custodian, and arbiter of the native literary tradition. Through detailed charges of errors, omissions, misconceptions and plagiarism in the *Cyclopaedia,* Griswold attempted to sustain his own critical authority; but for students of American literature in the ensuing century the compilation of the Duyckincks, despite its errors, proved to be a more judicious repository of American literary achievement than Griswold's somewhat erratic anthologies.

With all the vogue of anthologies and gift books devoted to native themes, the ante-bellum author was likely to receive little compensation for his contributions thereto; and in view of the limited returns to be expected from most American publishers, he sometimes found his only hope for financial reward to lie in the numerous literary prizes offered by wealthy proponents of a national literature. It is scarcely surprising that in this desperate atmosphere over two hundred plays should have been submitted to win the $20,000 which young Edwin

Forrest offered to advance what he termed his proudest wish, a National Drama. Perhaps such prizes unloosed a flood of composition in which, as William Cox sardonically observed, the aborigines were "hacked and tortured by all the poverty-stricken and unfledged poets in the country"; but at least they permitted the gifted as well as the "unfledged" to engage in serious literary endeavor with some hope of compensation for their efforts. Yet such stimulants, extended though they frequently were to various literary genres, were too sporadic and inconsequential to sustain a continental literature. A more nearly adequate sustenance was to come later in the century when a wider reading public and an array of prosperous magazines could provide an increasing assurance of liberal payment for native works.

The Organic Stamp of the Nation

Between the second war with Britain and the Civil War the conceptions of a national literature as expressed by the major writers and critics were essentially of a piece. Though neoclassical assumptions and phraseology lingered in the critical vocabulary here and there, and though during the succession of decades between the wars there were small tributary streams like realism, the main current in both concept and achievement flowed steadily forward within romantic channels toward an organic expression of the national mind. Such a group as the Transcendentalists could lend the strength of a metaphysic to the cause of an organic and independent literature; but the salient arguments of Emerson in "The American Scholar" essentially were a synthesis of what had been developed by scores of authors in the two preceding decades and what was to be reiterated by scores of authors in the two subsequent decades. For as during this period the concept of the nation as a balanced system of contracts yielded to the concept of the nation as an organism, so the neoclassical idea of national literature as the embellishment of orthodox political or ethical principles yielded to the romantic idea of a literature which would be an organic phase of the whole national life and which would derive its very style and tone from the state of the national health. "Nations are intelligent moral persons," Senator W. H. Seward told the Phi Beta Kappa Society at Yale in 1854, "existing for their own happiness and the improvement of mankind." American literature had at last ceased to be ephemeral, he thought, because it had actually begun to reflect the "principles and sentiments" which constituted the unique personality of the American nation.

For the authentic utterance of this "intelligent moral" person, the American nation, astute critics perceived that certain established assumptions about the literary imagination must be reassessed. Dominant among these troublesome assumptions, and present to a certain extent in both the neoclassic and romantic modes, was that of the incompatibility of belletristic interests with the expansive life of the nation. Clearly, if the real genius of America was to be expressed, this very intense and buoyant commitment to political and mercantile activity must be reconciled with serious literary endeavor.

The American writer, involved in and accountable to a nation whose brief past was unique and whose future character was still being formed, gradually realized that the creation of a national literature could not remain indefinitely in abeyance, contingent upon the arrival of either a new Augustan era or a romantic accumulation of moral associations. Convinced that the American milieu must be accepted as the ineluctable base of an organic national utterance, critics began soon after the War of 1812 to argue that the very mobility and tensions of American life were not the liabilities that transatlantic criticism would have them be, but were actually assets. Even William Tudor, for all his devotion to "correct taste," applauded in 1820 the peculiar mingling of men of learning and of affairs as conducive to the destruction of pedantry and the enrichment of literature; and two years later members of the Phi Beta Kappa Society of Harvard were assured by W. J. Spooner that the brightest polish was to be found in "those nations whose busy and agitated state of society would seem to leave the smallest room for literary pursuits."

To support their assertions that the highest literary utterance might be expected from "busy and agitated" societies like America, nationalistic critics were prone to rely partly on a romantic aesthetic, partly on the literary example of classical antiquity. If literature ultimately springs from the imagination and passions, Spooner argued, then commerce and the party spirit are not at all the impediments to belles-lettres in America which the neoclassic conception of a polite literature had tried to make them; they are, as the classics of Greece and Rome demonstrate, the very soil out of which the most memorable works have grown. "Literature thrives but in the midst of busy scenes," Bancroft summarily asserted in another critical defense of the expansive life of his country; and during succeeding decades many other critics, major and minor, elaborating this view, observed that since the greatest authors have often been responsible public figures, America's literature might well develop all the more richly from the common involvement of writers with the interests and exigencies of the enterprising life of the nation. Most conspicuous and cogent in propagating this apology were the two Everetts, Edward and Alexander. Statesmen, warriors, and poets are of one stock and proceed from the same excitement, said the former, anticipating the unified conception of Man that was to underlie "The American Scholar"; and more specifically Alexander listed some of the "abodes" of activity which the Genius of Poetry would inevitably love:

> Politics,—commerce and manufactures,—the bustle of business,—the din of crowded cities,—the clang of forge and shipyard,—the angry contests of the bar and the senate, present no obstacle to the successful cultivation of the elegant arts. The Muses are not a set of sentimental fine ladies who are frightened at the free and open face of real life. Real life . . . is the element in which they live and move, and have their being.

This attempt to construe America's energetic atmosphere as congenial to the literary imagination was, of course, but one of the major critical preparations and encouragements for an organic national literature— a literature in which "the whole tone of intellective action," to use Donald G. Mitchell's phrase, would faithfully show the imprint of American behavior, climate, institutions, and social values. Even by the 1830's this inclusive concept was so pervasive that few of the major authors and magazines of the country could long be content to define the national literature in terms of some single or narrow dogma. And it was the search for inclusive principles which, no doubt, accounts for many of the inconsistencies which one finds in critical pronouncements on American literature in Emerson, or Cooper, or Lowell, or Griswold.

Longfellow is also a case in point. In his commencement oration he wished native compositions to do little more than throw a veil of romance over America; but within a few years he called for a national literature in which not only "the state of society is shadowed forth" but also the very form of language is "ever flowing and filtering through the roots of national feeling." American literature, he instructed his compatriots, must be genuine and distinctive by receiving its features "from the spirit of a nation—from its scenery and climate, its historic recollections, its government, its various institutions—from all those national peculiarities which are the result of no positive institutions." What Longfellow envisaged in such a description was a literature which in the fullest sense would be an organic outgrowth of all that constituted American nationality—the same kind of literature which soon thereafter the *Knickerbocker* declared to be the consequence of the "impregnated character" and which Emerson termed "a generic result."

Thus, a generation before Taine proposed to anatomize a nation's "soul" through its literature and to correlate this soul with climate and epoch and race, American critics had projected their own national literature substantially on his postulates. Like Timothy Flint, some traced the already evident distinctions between American and English writing to "the great difference of climate, pursuits, geographical position, and physical circumstances." Others, like Prescott, emphasizing "epoch" and the changing constitution of society, maintained that the American imagination must proceed on new principles consistent with the spirit of the age. To most of these ante-bellum literary analysts race seemed less of a formative influence than geography or institutions. Yet to those who believed in the transmission of racial characteristics, the American melting pot held a promise of a literature of unparalleled richness; for, as Longfellow, George P. Marsh, and others supposed, through the inheritance and fusion of various national traits the American mind would most nearly approximate the universal and hence create a universal literature!

Yet for most authors this merging of the American into the universal mind seemed at best a distant prospect. Meanwhile they judged that their immediate task was to sensitize their art to the distinctive nuances and even the contradictions of national life—to make their work so comprehensively faithful, as Theodore Parker said, that any reader would know that they lived "and wrote in a republic—in a land full of new life, with great rivers and tall mountains, with maple and oak leaves that turn red in the autumn; amongst a people who hold town meetings, have free schools for everybody, read newspapers voraciously, who have lightning rods on their steeples . . . : who listen to the whippoorwill and the bobolink, who believe in slavery and the Declaration of Independence, in the devil and the five points of Calvinism." The ultimate dimension which such a richly autochthonous literature would require was perhaps that of myth. Though the mythical mode was rarely invoked by ante-bellum writers other than the Transcendentalists or Whitman, occasionally some prescient critic like the anonymous essayist in the *Western Monthly*—probably the young Cincinnati lawyer Joseph Reese Fry—could perceive that such a character as David Crockett was essentially a mythological figure in whom "private qualities are forgotten and merged in those of his class and age—of whom he is the allegory and personification." A new race of men, the critic remarked, require "some such metaphorical *person* to motto forth their peculiarities to the world—a nucleus around which the floating traits and individual anecdotes of the land may crystalize [*sic*]. . . ."

As this Western critic acutely discerned the wild life of the backwoodsman passing into the myth of Crockett and the mighty scale of Western nature issuing in extravagant idiom, the New York poet A. B. Street sensed that "the swart Steam Engine," as the common and necessary instrument of the country's industrial life, must also find its imaginative transposition. "We have the stern solidity of the iron/ Without the precious sparkle of the diamond," wrote Street of the national temper; and about the plain "Doric column" and "naked shaft" of American industry he hoped that a native poet might "twine some future garland bright." That the "naked shaft" might have an inherent beauty of its own which would be compromised by such a decorative poetic garland apparently was not a principle of Street's aesthetic, as it was of Horatio Greenough's. Though Greenough's concern for the "organic" expression of America was focused on architecture, though his chief censure fell on the erection of Gothic cathedrals and Greek temples in the cisatlantic scene, he recognized also the need of "a structure of our own" in literature. Nevertheless, toward a genuinely organic expression of their life American writers seemed to him to have made greater progress than other artists; and they also seemed to him to have made the most legitimate use of the classical masters: "We assimilate all of their principles . . . , and we learn of them to belong to our day and to our nation, as they to theirs." What sort of American writing would emerge when the imagination was fully "rooted in the bosoms and business" of men, however, Greenough did not state. The elaboration and illustration of his organic principle was soon to come, however, in *Leaves of Grass.*

CHAPTER FIVE

The Spur of Transcendentalism
(1820-1860)

> We too have eyes. To us the world and the soul and God are
> bared. We, as were the ancients, are in their presence. . . .
>
> AMOS BRONSON ALCOTT, 1838

The Critical Center

The Transcendentalists, said T. W. Higginson at the end of the century, are to be honored for having done "so much to emancipate and
nationalize American literature" through their recognition of the infinite value of the individual man. In offering his tribute Higginson
cited Emerson, Thoreau, Margaret Fuller and, strangely, Hawthorne;
but he might well have added Alcott, Parker, Hedge, Ripley, and
many another. For in that climate of expansive idealism in the New
England of the 1830's and 1840's, the circle of authors whose minds
were impregnated by some strain of the transcendental faith in the
divinity of all men was constantly widening.

Drawn occasionally into the circle, too, were tangential figures: Wil-
liam Ellery Channing, who indeed set the tone and premises of Tran-
scendental reflections on a national literature; E. T. Channing, whose
Harvard lectures provided dicta and conclusions which Emerson and
Thoreau assimilated into their own literary principles; and Theodore
Parker, who came late into the Transcendental orbit and ranged more
widely in his literary discourses than most of the group cared to do.
Yet there were also defections. Attracted in varying degrees of intensity

for a time, Brownson and G. W. Curtis and Hawthorne later became indifferent or hostile. Within these peripheral fluctuations, however, a stable center remained—the germinal cell of Emerson, Thoreau, Alcott, and Margaret Fuller, from whose manifold pronouncements emerges in substantial clarity the design that Transcendentalism traced for American letters.

Few of these young Transcendentalists in 1830, one may be sure, were unaware of or indifferent to Dr. Channing's eloquent essay of that year, "On National Literature." Few of them, too, escaped the critical dilemma which was implicit within its pages: whether the ultimate index to the national character is most surely found within the sentiments of popular majorities or within the refined reflection of the discriminating few. A national literature, Dr. Channing said innocuously enough, is the written expression of the mind and feelings of a people, and since the American soul is not that of Europe, "this new soil" will bear "new fruits" which in some ways will be "more precious" than those of olden days. Indeed, he affirmed as had many of his critical precursors for two centuries, he would have "no heart to encourage a native literature" were it not to be "instinct with a new spirit," a spirit which would repudiate the social artifices of Europe and would recognize the "worth and claims" of each individual as a man. Seeing all too little of this "new spirit" in the popular manifestations of the national mind, however, Dr. Channing was obliged to amend his initial plea for a literature broadly representative of American character. The only utterance which he could accept as properly national, he decided, was one, "refined and beautiful," in which the "higher minds were brought to bear upon the multitude" and in which truth was diffused "between the gifted few and the many." In effect, what Dr. Channing, like Theodore Parker, desired was not so much an autochthonous literature springing organically from American experience, but rather one which, emanating from the divine mind, should reveal the innate moral absolutes of the Infinite Spirit. The stump, the camp meeting, and the tariff could be but tenuously embraced, the Transcendentalists discovered, by a literature devoted to the "higher truths."

Throughout the early 1830's other exponents of the "new spirit," like the Boston reformer Amassa Walker and the liberal young clergyman James Freeman Clarke, continued to extol "a spirit of *mental independence*" and humanitarian nationalism. In the fall of 1836, however, with the organization of that symposium later called "The Transcendental Club," the literary implications of the "new spirit" were brought into sharper focus and more comprehensive formulation. That the creation of a worthy national literature was to the Transcendentalists a prime desideratum is attested by the fact that the first meeting of the club on October third was given over to a discussion of the topic: "American Genius—the Causes which Hinder its Growth, and give us no First-Rate Productions."

When Emerson selected the same theme for treatment the next year in his "The American Scholar," he was risking reiteration of prophetic clichés which for a generation had been the staple of numerous Phi Beta Kappa addresses or of such valedictory orations as that of his classmate, Robert Barnwell, who declared at their commencement exercises that Americans had already "broken from the mental thraldom" of Europe and would now live for themselves, turn to their own history, and "promote the establishment of a national literature." That "The American Scholar" contained a critical vigor and trenchancy which distinguished it from previous discourses of its kind was undoubtedly due in part to the probings of the theme by the Transcendental Club and especially by Alcott in conversations with Emerson during the preceding year. Months before the delivery of the oration, Alcott had perceived in Emerson a regenerating force in American letters and the precursor of a "race of more worthy artists [who] shall take the place of our present vulgar artisans." With his "honorable daring" and his "whip of small cords" Emerson would purify the "temple of literature," Alcott predicted in the pages of his journal; Emerson would turn up the "time-worn and vulgar associations thickly strewn over the soil of our land."

If to Alcott "The American Scholar" was largely a confirmation of previous judgments, to younger authors outside the Transcendental circle it was an arresting manifesto of national literary self-respect: to Lowell it seemed "an event without any former parallel in our literary annals, a scene to be always treasured . . . for its picturesqueness and its inspiration," because it helped "cut the cable" which "still socially and intellectually moored [us] to English thought"; to Holmes it seemed "our Declaration of Literary Independence"; and a half century later, according to G. W. Curtis, "the hearts of men who were young then still vibrate[d]" to the notes that Emerson had struck. But in the "crowded and breathless aisles," as Lowell said, there was not only the "enthusiasm of approval" but also the "grim silence of foregone dissent"; in fact, Orestes Brownson reported, responses among the auditors ranged "from kindling admiration to gaping wonder, shrewd cavilling, sneering doubt, and even offended dignity." As for Brownson himself, the address afforded reassurance that Emerson did not belong to that class of writers who merely watched the truths of eternity smiling through far space on a darkened world, but rather to a class which, expecting a brighter social life, wished literature to be its voice. Yet he feared, too, as he told Emerson and his friends soon after the occasion, that implicit in the address was the fallacious and ridiculous assumption that a national literature might be produced merely by deliberate resolution and calculated effort. Emerson might better advance American letters by convincing the educated that democracy is worthy of sincerest homage, Brownson suggested; for real scholars arise not in consequence of a prescribed discipline but from devotion to some end like justice, God, or country, to which all high art is ancillary.

On Emerson the strictures which Brownson proffered regarding attempts to create an American literature by prescription apparently were not without effect. When soon thereafter in a Master's oration at Harvard Robert Bartlett, who had attended the Transcendental Club, played variations on the theme of "The American Scholar," he received only a tardy snub from Emerson, who announced in 1843 that he had become impatient with those who in Harvard orations and elsewhere inquired for that great absentee, American literature, instead of recognizing it to be a generic result! Indeed, even earlier when Emerson wrote (with some collaboration with Margaret Fuller) the editorial prospectus for the first issue of the *Dial* (1840), he was careful to declare, as if in consideration of Brownson's reservations on his famous address, that the editors were obeying and not creating "the strong current of thought and feeling, which for a few years past, has led many sincere persons in New England to make new demands on literature." The *Dial* was to be for four years the Transcendental organ of this "new spirit" as interpreted by Emerson and also by Margaret Fuller. But Emerson, committed in the 1840's to American literature as a "generic result," and abjuring a criticism of "orderly propositions" for one which should be "poetic" and "unpredictable," ventured only the principle that the *Dial* would seek to emphasize the spirit of youth, to measure "no hours but those of sunshine," and to "be one rational voice amidst the din of mourners and polemics." This benign view of the "new spirit" was echoed a half century later in Howells' dictum that American literature should identify itself with "the more smiling aspects of life" because they were the "more American."

Before Transcendental theory made its major impact on American letters in the 1830's and 1840's, romantic authors like J. G. Percival had already conceived of Poetry as a manifestation of "the *mens divinior*" and had registered their confidence that "native sons of song" might be imbued with this "great animating power" in America as surely as in the Old World. Yet Emerson needed to go no further than the Harvard of the 1820's to find established the poles of divinity and autochthonism between which his own conception of American literature was to oscillate. His "early oracle," the Swedenborgian Sampson Reed, in an "Oration on Genius" at Harvard in 1821, projected the transcendental view that the arts have their source in the Divine and that the varied taste of nations and ages constitutes merely a modifying factor, an intermediate form which the mind "as it wanders from heaven" must use to "cover its nakedness." Though Emerson followed Reed in encouraging the "scholar" to utter the Over-soul immanent both in himself and in nature, he was less impatient than his oracle with the impurity of the temporal media to which utterance is bound; for in the lectures of E. T. Channing at Harvard he was reminded that though the writer may wish in a single leap to encompass the universal mind, he must be content to "pass through the discipline or instruction of particular facts" of his own age and country. To attain permanent literary fame, Channing taught Emerson and Thoreau, the writer must be "educated like other people, under influences which make him national, a representative of the period in which he lives," for the universal can only be approached through "home character and experience."

With the literary temper and aspirations manifested in the central

group at Concord and in "The American Scholar," the pronouncements of such tangential Transcendentalists as George Bancroft or
Cornelius Mathews or Lydia Maria Child had only a general con-
sonance. On the other hand, the Transcendental affirmation of literary
independence left strong and indubitable traces on many an author
who was identified but briefly, if at all, with the school. When
W. W. Story in his Phi Beta Kappa poem (1844) attested the "unblurred foot-prints of Divinity" in everyday American life and accordingly renounced the "Copyist and follower, thieving from the Past,"
his very imagery was an echo of Emerson; when he claimed all nature
and all passions for young America as well as for old Italy, and when
he concluded, "Who speaks his own truth, speaks the truth of all," the
thoughts of many of his audience could but have reverted to "The
American Scholar" and "Self-Reliance."

When Melville at mid-century hailed "men not very much inferior
to Shakespeare . . . this day being born on the banks of the Ohio"
and contended that it would not "at all do to say that the world is
getting grey and grizzled now," Emersonian overtones and cadences
sounded through his declaration of literary faith: "Not so. The world
is as young to-day as when it was created; and this Vermont morning
dew is as wet to my feet, as Eden's dew to Adam's." Furthermore, if
Lowell did not derive from the Transcendentalists his impatience with
blind adherence to "bygone manifestation of Divine Beauty," he at
least shared it with them, as he did the belief that "Truth manifests itself in some new form in every age." Under what influences Parke
Godwin came to believe that American authors must discover the "in-
estimable secret, that no object in the universe is unworthy of note,
. . . that every emotion in the meanest human soul is the emotion of
an infinite spirit," he did not say; but he might readily have reached
his position through Transcendental associates. And when young
Richard Henry Stoddard wondered why he should read books when
Nature was before him, when he arrived at the equation "My mind
the Universe, the Universe my Mind!" he would seem to have been
bent on becoming the ideal American scholar that Emerson two
decades earlier had described. Thus from the critical center at Concord, as Emerson might have phrased it, spread perennially widening
circles of Transcendental literary doctrine across the national mind.

The Metaphysical Context

Phrase for phrase, dictum for dictum, the Transcendentalists added surprisingly little to the stock of prophecies and prescriptions for American literature that had accumulated before the 1830's. A generation before "The American Scholar" so obscure a poet as Eaglesfield Smith could assure his literary compatriots with Emersonian eloquence that the sun shines as brightly in the New World as in Adam's garden; but his proclamation like many another was abortive because it was isolated, because its implications were shared and supported by no zealous group, because it was rooted apparently in no sustaining philosophical soil. What the Transcendental school contributed to the development of the national literature, therefore, was not an arresting inventory of novel themes and modes, but rather a sustained aesthetic based on a coherent metaphysical structure. By focusing attention on the metaphysical guarantees of a cisatlantic literature, the Transcendentalists undoubtedly at times turned the American imagination away from the rich body of native experience; but such a focus, enhancing the dignity of native media by infusing them with divinity, also expanded and deepened the current of nationality. If Emerson's "early oracle," Sampson Reed, yearning for a poetry "in exact agreement with the creative spirit of God," at times inclined American writers toward the rarefied air of universals, he also at other times brought them down into their own progressive age by reminding them that they no longer could find congenial the "gothic structure of the feudal ages," and that they were to advance a destined moral and political order free from the "haunts of dissipation and vice."

Though Emerson more fully than Reed inquired into the identity of the Genius of the New World, his inquiries also led at last to the Over-soul. To him, as to Reed, literature at last justified itself only as a report of "the inextinguishable soul of the universe." The poet, degenerated into the "decorous sayer of smooth things," Emerson said, was no longer the voice of the divine principles and majestic ideas from which the world proceeds: God, Freedom, Justice, Necessity. How lacking were the most eminent writers of his own land, Bryant, Cooper, and Irving, he exclaimed, in the "vital faith" and the sense of the ideal Beauty and Good of which the New World "sayers" should be the vehicle! How pathetically short such writers fell of becoming that "brood of Titans, . . . with the errand of genius and of love," whom the Old World had rightly expected from an America "when all feudal bandages and straps were snapped asunder"—a "brood" whom the novelist Sylvester Judd's heroine Margaret also explicitly endorsed in her transcendental vision of an American art and literature which should fuse Christianity, Aesthetics, and Heroism. Thus far, said Emerson in "The American Scholar," native authors had timorously declined to be "inspired by the Divine Soul which also inspires all men." If they would become true creators in whom the ephemeral and imitative in form and content would disappear, he counseled, let them strive for a brave sincerity of utterance which, casting "on God the responsibility of the facts," would become a proof of the divine presence.

The fresh utterance of America which the Transcendentalists so consistently espoused was therefore always posited on the more comprehensive expression of the Over-soul. "The great American author," wrote Brownson in his early Transcendental years, will draw his inspiration from "the universal reason which glows within and agitates the American heart, not less than the English heart"; he may gain a generous confidence from the conviction that "American human nature is as rich as English human nature; that the emotions and forms of speech natural to an American are as proper in themselves, as conformable to the laws of universal human nature, as those natural to an Englishman." In Robert Bartlett's Master's oration, Brownson's "universal reason" appeared as the "same All" which lies behind history, as the "one essence" of which great books and great deeds "are only so many outshapings." Hence the poet must never forget that his highest mission is not to "expound the established," Bartlett concluded; but to direct his eyes beyond this shadowy pageant toward the "divine darkness." Even Thoreau expressed this transcendental yearning for a poetry beyond mere intellectual fashions and fashioning, for a poetic "maker" who dwells "with Eternity alone" while "idle Time runs gadding by":

> Fame cannot tempt the bard
> Who's famous with his God,

> Nor laurel him reward
> Who hath his Maker's nod.

By such divine investiture the Transcendentalists thus delivered both the American author and his milieu from the taint of colonial debasement. Assured that the highest literature bespoke a pervasive Oversoul whose percipients they might pre-eminently be, American writers could attach a new dignity to their work. "What seems so fair and poetic in antiquity—almost fabulous—is realized, too, in Concord life," Thoreau affirmed in one of his rare encomiums on the village. For surer clues to the All, however, the disposition of the Transcendentalists was to rely not so much on the institutional life of village or city or nation as on those correlatives, Nature and the Soul. Literature is only "a heap of nouns and verbs enclosing an intuition or two," wrote Emerson turning to the soul within; but an equivalent purity of vision he promised the American scholar who should properly attend the undimmed revelations of Nature: "Do not believe the past. I give you the universe a virgin today." For literature seemed to him not only the testimony borne from within, as Alcott had implied, but also a report of "the inextinguishable soul of the universe" as revealed in the world outside the self:

> He, who doubts whether this age or this country can yield any contribution to the literature of the world, only betrays his own blindness to the necessities of the human soul. . . . The heart beats in this age as of old, and the passions are as busy as ever. Nature has not lost one ringlet of her beauty, one impulse of resistance and valor.

For this American nature of which Emerson spoke the Transcendentalists claimed both less and more than had the early American neo-classicists. To most eighteenth-century authors the grandeur of American landscapes had augured a national poetry of unprecedented sublimity. To the Transcendentalists, who regarded the minuscule as well as the grand phenomenon as an "emblem and sign of some fact in the soul," the magnitude of Niagara and the Rockies held little relevance for the imagination. All "natural imagery" illustrates truth, they believed with Sampson Reed, and mirrors Him who made the world. And in Reed's advice to the writer to "respect the smallest blade which grows and permit it to speak for itself" they found the cue for a poetic retreat from majesty to simplicity which was to extend eventually to the omnipresent divinity of *Leaves of Grass*.

Though the Transcendentalists conceived of Nature as "spirit out-laying herself," they could not so readily as Whitman permit leaves of grass to speak autonomously for themselves. Nature can only suggest and quicken, Robert Bartlett observed; it can never "prevail," since it is only a "remote type and copy of the soul, and so must not be copied by the soul." Indeed, nature at times becomes beautiful, he supposed with Emerson, only when linked to virtue. Hence America's rich skies and fair fields seemed to him scarcely absolute indices to the Over-soul; until they were "suffused with the immortal hues of the spirit, of beauteous act and thought," her authors could not make of them "something nobler than Salamis or Marathon."

Imagination, agreed Thoreau, is born of the "marriage of the soul with Nature"; yet Nature is nothing but as she draws man out and reflects him. True, looking at a fine New Hampshire range, he inclined to think mountains themselves great poets undoing a great deal of prose; and meditating on White Pond, he was chagrined to think that Shakespeare had made "dull, ugly England . . . amiable and enviable to all reading men" while New England grapes and orchards and cider mills had found no adequate native singer with a "chanting constitution." Yet in his later years, though he could indulge in apostrophes to America as a land of higher heavens, bluer skies, and brighter stars, he preferred to regard these natural facts as "symbolical of the height to which the philosophy and poetry and religion of her inhabitants may one day soar." Accepting a measure of climatic and topographical influence on the mind, he expressed the hope that, in contrast to the Old World, American thoughts would be fresher and clearer like native skies, that American understanding would be more comprehensive like native plains, that the American intellect would be on a grander scale like native mountains and rivers and forests, that the American heart would correspond in breadth and depth and grandeur to native inland seas. But finally Thoreau seems to have shared the Coleridgean conclusion that the imagination and not Nature is the primary agent, that the poet must impress the winds and streams into his service, that he must, indeed, create a new mythology.

The Amazon and Mississippi seemed to him to serve the poet not so much by shaping his mind as by yielding to his fables. Accordingly, the wonder which Thoreau increasingly found in the New England countryside was that of the old prophets and poets. This countryside he could not regard as merely America: "There is a truer account of it in mythology than in any history of America . . . that I have seen." The ultimate use of American nature which he commended to the native writer, therefore, was neither its discipline (on which Emerson discoursed in "Nature") nor its national associations. To Thoreau, as to Coleridge, Nature became the pliable stuff by which the imagination is enabled to create an image shadowing forth the most precious human perceptions.

Though occasionally Thoreau, like the other Transcendentalists, seemed disposed to deem the Over-soul more transparent in the unencumbered landscape of America than in that of any other country, the group generally followed the logic of their romantic postulates and attributed equal divinity to all phenomena. Such a view was of course not peculiarly American, but it notably served the national imagination by ascribing an immanent and absolute value to simple native scenes and objects long nullified by the associationists' aesthetics. By proclaiming the divinity of the commonplace and by espousing untutored genius, the Transcendentalists provided from the Romantic movement a coherent view of both literary theme and creator from which an American literature might as confidently proceed as any other. This literary elevation of the commonplace in American life, to be sure, also owed much of its development in the nineteenth century to the fondness with which the "female authors" treated the domestic milieu; but for the writer whose imagination required a firmer motivation than sentiment for attacking the vast unhallowed particularity of American life, the Transcendentalists provided a reassuring metaphysic.

When in the West the Transcendental poet Christopher P. Cranch read "The American Scholar," he concurred especially in Emerson's affirmation of the "great stride" which could be taken through embracing "the near, the low, the common." To supplant "the great, the remote, the romantic," Emerson had urged a comprehension of the familiar world which had been "negligently trodden under foot . . . :

The meal in the firkin; the milk in the pan; the ballad in the street; the news of the boat; the glance of the eye; the form and gait of the body." In these "suburbs and extremities of nature," he had argued, is lurking the highest spiritual cause, the design that unites and animates all creation, the polarity that ranges them on an eternal law. To such Transcendental convictions Emerson through the years gave reiterated expression: "rags and offal" were to become "hieroglyphics" for the Poet, who could suspect nothing more unclean about them than could the chemist; shops and a tradesman's dinner were "as good materials in a skilful hand for interest and art as palaces and revolutions"; "common household tasks," the subjects of "all the Greek gems," were "agreeable to the imagination"; the scent of an elder blow, or a timber yard, or the corporation works of a nest of pismires were emblems enough to a keen sensibility; indeed, why should the American poet travel when he could eternize his own woodhouse? It was this inclination toward the common and near that accounted for Emerson's pleasure in the great mass of household "verses of a ruder strain" in contemporary journals, for in them he saw some proof not only that the Muse had "found a voice in these cold Cisatlantic States" but also that poetry need ask "no aid of magnitude or number, of blood or crime," having "theatre enough in the first field or brookside, breadth and depth enough in the flow of its own thought."

For the average native author poetic overtones could be more readily detected hovering about domestic objects than about political and commercial structures. But Emerson saw no reason why "politics, economy, manufactures and stock-brokerages," when "placed in their true order," did not belong to the poet as much as did "sunsets and souls." More specifically, he did not see why "the vivid energies working at this hour in New York and Chicago and San Francisco" should not be converted into universal symbols. Why had there been no American genius "with tyrannous eye," he asked again, who could see "in the barbarism and materialism of the times, another carnival of the same gods whose picture he so much admires in Homer"? How timid had been American poets in failing to chant their banks and tariffs, Methodism and Unitarianism, their logrolling and stumps and politics, Negroes, Indians, Northern trade and Southern planting, Western clearings, Oregon, and Texas! Though Emerson was disposed to regard such raw activity as emblematic, as a daily bread which required a transubstantiation into holiest symbols, he was aware that on the other hand excessive moralists and abstractionists like Alcott's colonists at Fruitlands were prone to project their minds too far beyond "the poetry that is in man's life, the poorest pastoral clownish life; the light that shines on a man's hat, in a child's spoon, the sparkle on every wave and on every mote of dust." Yet at last the subject per se seemed to Emerson "absolutely indifferent." Write of hay, of cattle shows, of a ship, of Ellen, or Alcott, he admonished himself in his later journals, "if only you can be the fanatic of your subject, and find a fibre reaching from it to the core of your heart."

To Thoreau the subject was equally indifferent and the heart was equally the clue. "Give me simple, cheap, homely themes," he said to Ellery Channing, for "the theme is nothing, the life is everything." Like Emerson, he would deliberately eschew the extraordinary as a literary province for the workdays and barren fields which in America had seemed to many a romantic associationist too thin to yield a poetic harvest. As early as his college days he concluded that the homely robin redbreast and straggling rail fence afforded more for the native writer than did "skylarks and nightingales, perched on hedges." And later the music played by a New England west wind blowing through the telegraph wires he pronounced "a new Orpheus" which made "Greece and all antiquity seem poor in melody,"—"the first strain from the American lyre." His own locale seemed to him "luxuriously crowded without margin," and in it he judged that Herrick could have found nearly everything on which his imagination had been fed: a cherry, Julia's hair, Netterby's pimple, the hen Partlett. Like Emerson, he perceived the danger of the American author's overreaching himself through an ambitious focus on mighty abstractions like immortality. The poet had better improve the soil under his feet and harvest the crop which his experience yields; he had better dig than soar; a "bushel of woodashes" was preferable to "a cartload of mythology." The truest beauty, he observed in his last years, is that which surrounds us: "the forms and colors which adorn our daily life, not seen afar in the horizon, are our fairest jewelry." As Emerson had concluded that the only concern that a writer need have regarding a subject is that it have a fiber reaching to the heart, so Thoreau urged his literary compatriots to write not on "chosen themes" but on those which had kindled a flame in the mind: "The poet's relation to his theme is the relation of lovers. It is no more to be courted. Obey, report." The fortunes of American literature evidently did not seem to Thoreau to be contingent upon a milieu either endowed by romantic association or conspicuously emblematic of the Over-soul; the perspective of the neighborhood was wide and rich enough for the receptive imagination.

In the redemption of the American commonplace for literary uses the other Transcendentalists played a minor but consistent part. Like Emerson and Thoreau, Alcott was distressed that by the late 1850's no pastoral poet had arisen to sing the fields and streams, the garden and orchard, the youths and maidens, the homelife and occupations, and all "the genial sentiments and dear humanity of private life" in America. And Margaret Fuller, though generally concerned with more pretentious themes, traced the febrile and bodiless character of American drama to the fact that native playwrights had "no relish for the berries of our own woods, the roots of our own fields." It was probably Parker, however, who most indubitably echoed Emerson and Thoreau in pleading the dignity of familiar experience: "Common things are not . . . unclean. In plain New England life he [the native writer] finds his poetry, as magnets iron in the blacksmith's dust. . . . It is not for him to rave of Parnassus, while he knows it not, for the soul of song has a seat upon Monadnoc, Wachusett, or Katahdin, quite as high." Striving though they were to comprehend the All, the Transcendentalists pronounced each particular to be a fit vehicle for their quest, and accordingly conferred on the American scene an imaginative distinction which the doctrines of no previous group had been able to bestow.

Not content with dignifying all phenomena for the native poet, however, the Transcendentalists inclined to liberate him into an equal range of forms and modes. In a world pulsing with the Over-soul rather than fixed in a Newtonian order, they supposed, aesthetics must follow nature in conceding to each object its own unique embodiment. What authority, indeed, could inherited transatlantic genres hold for those who believed with Sampson Reed that "poetry can have but one essence, love, but one form, nature"? "The poet should be free and unshackled as the eagle," proclaimed Reed in *Observations on the Growth of the Mind* (1826), a volume which Emerson deemed one of the best he had ever seen; and he prophesied that eventually poetry would have tests more valid than those of "mere versification" and "the peculiar state of public taste." Though Reed's attack on rhyme as the detracting mask of art, as an artifice not grounded in the mind or paralleled in nature, was furthered by Whitman rather than by Emerson, the latter concurred with his "early oracle" to the extent of distrusting "the coil of rhythm and number" and of seeing America itself as a poem which would "not long wait for metres." Yet Emerson admitted he was not wise enough to envision the new forms, and hence he resigned the national literature to using "the old largeness a little longer."

The vision of a riper time when the national character should be expressed "in a thousand fresh and original forms" came also to Margaret Fuller; but, like Emerson, she hesitated to describe or exemplify them. Indeed, the Transcendental conception of free organic form all but precluded attempts at prosody. Believing genius to be above the canons of taste, the Transcendentalists could scarcely do more than urge the native poet, as did Thoreau, not to "adorn his deformities" but rather "cast them off by expansion, as a tree its bark." By such a process of growth from within he would no longer be a "scald," a mere "smoother and polisher of language"; he would become a Cincinnatus who "indifferently selects his rhymes, and with a liberal taste weaves into his verse the planet and the stubble."

A more fitting image of organic form seemed to James Freeman Clarke, however, to be the perfectly proportioned ships in Boston Bay whose beauty was achieved through a design adapted to their essential function. Similarly the living poem, he reasoned, must take its shape and tensions from the exigencies of the national life, for "Poetry, the flower of life, consorts with Thought and Deed." And thus, in implanting the authority of form within the unique American object and experience or within the Divine Idea to which all Nature aspires, the Transcendental doctrine helped to divert the concern of native authors from transatlantic literary modes and to fix it primarily and confidently on the fresh contours and substance and myths of a new world. As with the singers in the New Zion a century and a half earlier, the New World imagination was to be made self-reliant through an unencumbered recourse to the All.

The Genius of America

Though American nature could be convincingly exalted by the Transcendentalists as a permanent symbol of the All, the national culture was not so readily redeemable for the literary imagination. As to what degree the spirit and institutions of the age should be embraced and reflected in the national literature Emerson was notably vacillating; and the contemporary American writer trying to achieve a steady and proper aesthetic focus on his own society would surely have been considerably confused by Emersonian dicta. If society is a wave which in reality never advances, if his contemporaries were no wiser than Plutarch, as Emerson at times declared, then as a nonconformist individual the writer should abjure his age and strive to utter a truth beyond the shadow of national limitations. But if he listened to Emerson again, he could learn that his nation and era were culminations in the progressive revelation of Divinity through time, and that to ignore them was a craven disbelief in the Present, a timid regression to the dark inhumanity of feudalism.

Emerson himself as a young man, in fact, recognized the conflict between seer and autochthon when he heard in Everett's Phi Beta Kappa address (1824) a doctrine "the more disagreeable, that I have found some reason to think it true,—to wit, that geniuses are the organs, mouthpieces of their age; do not speak their own words, nor think their own thoughts." Throughout his life, indeed, he continued to resist this "disagreeable doctrine" which implied that the individual must be absorbed by the social nature, that the intuitively perceived moral law must yield, consciously or unconsciously, to the generalized expediency of the national mind. Thus in "The American Scholar" he assured the timorous writers in a new land that through individual recourse to the unchanging pattern of nature and the soul they might rival the ancients, and soon thereafter in the early *Dial* he pronounced literature to be only "in some sort a creature of Time." The oracular soul in its utterance takes precedence over "the low mediations of circumstance," he said, and Society in vain seeks to assign themes and modes to the writer.

Yet in these same years Emerson perceived also the hazards, if not the impossibility, of resisting one's age by an exclusive preoccupation with Nature and the Soul. The imagination, he conceded, was redeemed from thin abstraction by the sustenance of the body politic and the vital currents of an active society. "A literature is no man's private concern, but a secular and generic result," he retorted to such Cambridge orators as Robert Bartlett who had implied that by individual initiative a national literature could be acquired, "and is the affair of a power which works by a prodigality of life and force very dismaying to behold. . . ." Accordingly, for the author to rely upon his own dissociated faculties when the "very Time sees for us, thinks for us" could only be a "fatal prodigality." As to what the "very Time" would impress upon the native imagination and utter through native pens, Emerson was generally sanguine. Hence he dared to advise a literary integrity which would report the "barbarism and materialism" which were so obviously rife among his countrymen; for involved with these qualities he saw an incipient culture which was at once "the fruit toward which a whole past eternity has flowered and ripened, and . . . sprouting seed of all that shall ever be."

Emerson's dilemma over the concessions which the American writer should make to the forces of the age was not altogether resolved by the other figures in the Transcendental school. At times they inclined to concur in his Platonic view that throughout history the writer had been afforded an equal access to the Absolute, that the nineteenth-century American could perceive no larger truth than that vouchsafed to ancient Greece. Yet they were sons of the Enlightenment as well as of Plato, and through it they were persuaded that succeeding centuries brought a cumulative refinement to human relations and understanding; or, as Emerson had said, in their own country's progressive society they could well be witnessing the ripening of a fruit which all the past had nurtured.

This humane freedom the Transcendentalists tended to equate with the Genius of America; and to utter this Genius was, they supposed, to express the liberated soul of all mankind. Old institutions, creeds, and usages "which clog the ever flowing Present" are periodically swept away by the "flood tide of the soul," wrote Alcott, perceiving in the fresh vitality of American life a world being swept clean by such a tide. Americans seemed to him, as to Crèvecoeur, new men in a "situation . . . wholly new," men shaped by Nature in her own moulds and standing on the highest vantage point of history; and their writing could not be termed genuinely American unless it utilized this vantage point. In the Old World, Robert Bartlett explained in voicing this transcendental interpretation of a national literature, the belief is not in the soul but in the extraneous and traditional; but American history is "transcendent . . . for pure, homogeneous sublimity and beauty and richness," and when its high philosophy is diffused through the conduct of American society, it will be "outwritten" in a national poetry. This literature embodying the Genius of America, Frederick Hedge prophesied, would be "such as the ages have not known,—a literature commensurate with our idea, vast as our destiny and varied as our clime."

The new, democratic heroism needed to exemplify the Genius of America and to provide the redemption of letters from the sterile ethic and formalism of European literature many Transcendentalists found in the abolition movement. The moral warfare against slavery, wrote James Freeman Clarke, is the culmination of "every earnest thought, and act, and prayer/ Of former centuries," and treatment of this high, insistent theme will liberate the American poet from composing trivial closet verse on Dryads. Yet in the current writings of the abolitionists and in the narratives of fugitive slaves, Theodore Parker perceived already born a literature which expressed "most fully the sentiments and ideas of America." Uncouth in form though he conceded this exceptional literature to be, he predicted its survival because it respected "human nature above history"; and because it bespoke hope, aspiration for truth, justice, love, and piety, its authors seemed to him "American all through; so intensely national that they do not fear to tell the nation of the wrong it does." Such "writers of the newness" indeed exemplified his conception of the American scholar: they used the past only "to acquire the momentum of history"; they took their stand in the present and leaped into the future. Though Margaret Fuller did not so narrowly identify the national letters with abolition, she was convinced that "America, if awake to the design of Heaven . . . would become the principal exponent" of "that new Idea of republican liberty and justice which agitates the sleep of Europe." But it appeared to her that both America and her writers had thus far been false to the divine scheme made out at the nation's nativity; and hence she felt obliged to concur in Griswold's judgment that "Milton is more emphatically *American* than any author who has lived in the United States," for he had expressed more than any native writer the vitality of republican thought.

Yet the Genius of America clearly involved more than a political idea, as Emerson perceived; it involved also something of that "primitive vitality" which Margaret Fuller praised as an integral part of Milton's republicanism. To suggest this quality, Emerson resorted to metaphors which implied primal energies rather than mature ideologies. The Genius of America is a colossal youth whom Xenophon and Thucydides would have thought a worthier theme than ancient Greece or Persia, he wrote soon after his graduation. Conceding that the young country had as yet originated no great poems and histories, he was nevertheless confident of the imminent arrival of an indigenous literature; and especially before mid-century he continued through a series of figures to identify its genius with that of a colossal youth: it was to be the voice of a "brood of Titans"; it was to be as unmanageable as "the wild horse of Heaven"; it was to be Homeric in its "barbarism and materialism"; through its lines was to course the "strong black blood of the English race"; it was to be the "great breath of the New World, the voice of aboriginal nations opening new eras with hymns of lofty cheer." In these decades the very grace of Allston, Irving, Bryant, or Dana seemed to him an imported slur on the virile national temper. The work of these "abortive Homers" he dismissed as merely a "boulder of the European ledge"; it lacked "nerve and dagger." Even in the late 1850's he lamented that the "fireeyed child" had not yet been born, that the necessities of the New World had not evoked the "mystic Power," that he had not heard "the Choral Hymns of a new age & adequate to Nature." Yet in those current publications which he admitted to be most genuinely and vigorously indigenous, Emerson, like Parker, could take little satisfaction; he could but sneer at the gracelessness of "American writing . . . written at odd moments,—Unitarian writing, charlatan writing, Congress speeches, Railroad novels." As a "cruel critic" he demanded instead, as he declared to Cranch, "a devotion that seems hardly possible in our hasty, facile America." That haste and crudity should be inevitable correlatives of the autochthonous utterance of the "colossal youth" both Emerson and Parker were apparently loath to admit. The expression of the Genius of America they seem to have expected in a curious literary amalgam at once maturely reflective, zealously transcendental, and spontaneously expansive! The youthful literature which Parker professed to desire was one which should bear the "marks of a new, free, vigorous mind at work, looking at things from the American point of view"; that which he found, alas, seemed to him rather the stammering of big, raw boys in the presence of a schoolmaster: "timid, ungraceful, and weak."

Parker's and Emerson's impatience with the raw boyishness of American authors reflects the indifference of the Transcendentalists, despite all their invocations to the youthful Genius of America, to the emergence of an American Homer. Their construction of the national genius was, in fact, Platonic rather than Homeric. That the Genius of America was at best merely a way station on the Transcendental itinerary to the Over-soul they frequently remarked. With Dr. Channing they loved their "country much, but mankind more," and they enlisted in the campaign for a national literature principally as an operation in behalf of a new freedom which they judged to be more nearly in accord with universal truth. With Emerson they cherished American letters chiefly in the hope that their "emancipating quality" would lead beyond nationalism, "onward and upward,—to a Columbia of thought and art, which is the last and endless end of Columbus's adventure." For though Emerson granted every nation its distinguishing virtues, the "peculiar and legitimate advantages" of any nationalistic utterance he could sanction only to the degree that they benefited all humanity. On the plane of ideas, he concluded, such peculiarities disappear: "National traits stand no chance beside intellectual. . . . Our national traits may appear so long as we are drowsy . . . , but put me in good spirits, search me with thought, and all nations are men together."

This uneasiness of the Transcendentalists over the vulgarity of what Bartlett called "this shadowy pageant" undoubtedly tended to outweigh their concern for the "meal in the firkin, the milk in the pan"; and this anxiety to reflect "human nature above history," as Parker phrased it, clearly strained from American writing some of the full-bodied vigor which they professed at times to desire in native letters. It is hardly surprising that Emerson's complaint about Longfellow and Lowell was not that their poems were lacking "the meal in the firkin"; it was rather that they afforded him no "heavenly bread." The office of poetry is deifying or imparadising, he said; poetry should serve religion as the gay petal serves the flower. Accordingly to Carlyle he wrote: "what room for a poet—for any spiritualist—in this great, intelligent, sensual, and avaricious America." Unlike E. T. Channing, who admonished native authors to write for their own time and society if they wished to be cherished by posterity, Emerson encouraged poets to write not "to any person or moment, but to life generalized and perspective." Even Thoreau, dismissing for the moment that circumambient world of which he was so generally aware, could define the great poet as one who "speaks without reference to time or place."

More fastidious than Emerson in distrusting the vulgar currents in national experience, however, were the Brook Farmers. With them the office of literature became almost wholly normative. It must serve as an instrument for the solution of problems which agitate the soul, said their leader, George Ripley, and its redemptive element is the fearless search for truth. The Farmers held little hope for American writing, therefore, until it attained the perspective of absolute Justice; and they were concerned with the Genius of America only so far as it was a disguised universal. Native poetry will flourish only when the *"New Spirit* has . . . made its way among the gentler muses" and "when the *Poet* has once comprehended the Destiny of Man," wrote Charles A. Dana, editor of the organ of Brook Farm, the *Harbinger*. A national poetry can only "gush forth," and the creative power of American genius can only be liberated, agreed the Brook Farm music critic John Sullivan Dwight, when the social life of the nation embodies the beauty of its political principles. Yet to call the poetic realization of this spirit "peculiarly *American,"* Dwight added, would be paradoxical; for in expressing the spirit of American institutions such a poetry indeed would inevitably be human, wide, and universal—not national and patriotic: "It is not the love of country, but the love of man, and recognition of the spiritual equality of all men, which is the idea of our Constitution." For the colonists at Brook

Farm the poet could not bespeak the Genius of America by looking across the land; he must, in James Freeman Clarke's appropriately abstract phrasing, tower toward God and Truth and slay Lies and Fraud and Dogmas which as customs sit enthroned.

To subsume the treatment of American life under such moral absolutism was no doubt to lend intensity and direction to the national literature, but it was also to impose an exclusiveness which would preclude the appearance of American Homers and Shakespeares. It was so stringently to identify literary value with humanitarian progress—as Joel Barlow had done a half century earlier—that even Thoreau could ponder why John Brown's charge should not be celebrated more impressively than that at Balaklava, since the former had been undertaken in "obedience to an infinitely higher command," or why abolitionists should not provide richer themes than King Arthur, who never assailed a nation's peculiar institution or sin! It was to lead Ellery Channing in the 1840's to acclaim Emerson the ideal poet, not because he uttered the Genius of America but because he bespoke a time

. . . when the pure mind can sing,
When true philosophy is linked with verse,
And moral laws in rhymes themselves rehearse!

When the Genius of America involved taints of vulgarity, the Transcendentalist counseled a retreat into the purity of the Absolute. Hence the need for Whitman's inclusiveness in the Preface to *Leaves of Grass*.

If the Transcendentalists sustained Barlow's identification of the national literature with New World humanitarianism, they also reiterated the eighteenth-century concept of the westering cycle of civilization. Sometimes regarding the heartland of America as the beneficiary of the ages, sometimes regarding it as the book of God where men might again read the uncorrupted text and perceive their own divinity, the major figures in the Transcendental group perpetuated the century-old dream that the West would beget the most authentic expression of the national genius. Recalling Berkeley's famous words on the westward course of empire, Thoreau reckoned the backwoodsman to be as favorably situated as Adam; and he supposed the Mississippi, with its steamboats and rising cities, to be the manifestation of a new heroic age as grand as that which the Middle Ages had achieved along the Rhine. "I must walk toward Oregon, and not toward

Europe," he wrote. And though he adjudged the Atlantic a Lethean stream which happily allowed all Americans to forget Old World institutions, he confessed that he was tempted to follow that great Western pioneer, the sun, beyond the Alleghenies, since these mountains were barriers "which many species of folly, no doubt, do not cross." If the Atlantic and the mountains could not emancipate his countrymen from the mind of Europe, he said, the one chance that remained lay in the Lethe of the Pacific.

These reflections from Thoreau's last years were of a piece with the pattern of his thought since those Harvard days when he had wished that his countrymen might sink all sectional feelings and "rest satisfied with one mighty, all-embracing West, leaving the other three cardinal points to the Old World." Consistently in the intervening years he held to the opinion that Americans "must look to the West for the growth of new literature, manners, architecture, etc."; for he perceived "more language there than here which is the growth of the soil"— "ram-slang-like and colloquial" words which would become "genuine American and standard." In Western stump speeches, "untoward and rude" though they were, he discovered not only good "Greekish words . . . in abundance" but also "traits of genuine eloquence" which reminded him more than did "the Beauties of our Atlantic orators" of the masters of antiquity. At times, indeed, enraptured by the symbol of the West, Thoreau felt that "the way to heaven" itself wound through the defiles of the western hills and that "new dynasties of thought" were announced by the western gales.

To Emerson and Margaret Fuller, who traveled more widely in the section, the cultural prospects of the West were somewhat equivocal. As a young man Emerson feared that among the "off-scourings of civilized society" and the "ignorant and licentious people" who commonly settled the new land the "oracles of moral law and intellectual wisdom [would] . . . speak faintly and indistinctly"; and Margaret Fuller undertook a western journey with admitted distaste for the mushroom growth of the region. Both skeptics, however, were undoubtedly reassured by such sanguine adventurers from their circle as James Freeman Clarke, who had gone into the Ohio Valley in the early 1830's, had reported "Everything here . . . free, open, active," and had determined in initiating the *Western Messenger* that the magazine could not do better than to try to achieve a *"Western . . .* character." Hence Margaret Fuller set out resolved to "woo the mighty meaning of the scene," to "foresee the law by which a new order, a new poetry, is to be evoked from this chaos," and to find a compensation for sacrificed forests in "new intellectual growths." These growths, she hoped, would be aesthetic forms and modes "entirely new," emerging from the peculiar materials and needs of time and place. Yet in her travels she found little to sustain such hopes, for on the "lately peopled prairies" she encountered young people acting not a "drama, ready made to hand by the fortunes of Boon [*sic*], or the defeats of the Black Hawk" but "Tamerlane and the like . . . to the 'store keepers' and labourers of republican America."

A literature springing from and pertinent to the life of republican laborers and storekeepers Emerson supposed he had discovered, how- ever, in the 1840's in "Kentucky stump-oratory, the exploits of Boon [*sic*] and David Crockett, the journals of the western pioneers, agri- culturalists, and socialists." Unlike the majority of American critics of the decade, he did not deplore the avid welcome that such autoch- thonous works had received in Europe; for, like transatlantic readers, he preferred these "genuine growths" to more graceful imitations. Crude though such Western utterances might be, they seemed to him the rich subsoil indispensable for a new literature which increasingly would be directed to America rather than to the British Isles as the center of the English-speaking population shifted toward the New World. "Our eyes will be turned westward, and a newer and stronger tone in literature will be the result," he prophesied from Concord. A decade later, however, his travels in the section convinced him that this fresh native element which he had praised the West for intruding into American literature had belied its promise. There he found "no singing birds" and no thought distilled from all the life of the land and water. The workingmen of the Mississippi and prairie had no high thoughts, he complained to Carlyle; America was "a wild democ- racy, the riot of mediocrities" and gave no sign of sublimating into a genius, of ending in bard or hero.

So intractably gross did this Western life seem also to Alcott that he could conceive of its being used only in symbolic terms. Perhaps a "philosophical romance," comparable to Plato's *Republic,* he suggested, might be fashioned from various Utopian searches for an earthly paradise. Thus at mid-century, especially when confronting the fact rather than indulging in the dream of the expansive West, the Transcendentalist was all too apt to betray his innate distaste for the "genuine growths" from the soil of Boone and Crockett. For him the Genius of America became increasingly obscured by the national behavior through the decade after mid-century.

Literature and the People

Probably no group of critics in the nineteenth century more earnestly pondered the relation of the literary imagination to the massive energies at work in American life than did the Transcendentalists. Their general inclination, on the one hand, was to think of the poet as the heroic sayer of the Over-soul; on the other, they inclined, with Emerson, to suspect Society of being a vast stock company in conspiracy against each of its members, of being a wave whose substance never advances, of being a complex of low expediencies. In the popular mind they did not generally discern, as did Whitman, rich springs of perceptiveness and wholesome norms of conduct which needed only to be articulated and focused for the emergence of a truly national literature. The native author, they supposed, might reckon democracy an asset not because it afforded him wider resources of sensibility but because it afforded him a vast and susceptible audience. Accordingly, when young Emerson proclaimed that the Third Estate formed for the American Muse patrons superior to the frivolous dowager queen and the imbecile royal baby on which Old World literature depended, he also affirmed that this Third Estate must be instilled with "wholesome principles." And Dr. Channing likewise construed the benefit which republicanism conferred on a national literature to be the facility which the system afforded for the "higher minds" to "bear upon the multitude," for truth to be diffused "between the gifted few and the many." For most of the Transcendentalists this multitude constituted, as it did for Christopher Cranch, a "society [which] is stagnant, unspiritual, and corrupt."

In the early 1830's Margaret Fuller confessed the same "sometimes despairing, sometimes insolently contemptuous, feeling of incongeniality" with her time and place; yet she was somewhat more acutely aware than most of her Transcendental contemporaries of the hazardous effects of this "incongeniality" on the creative imagination. Moreover, she did not, with Cranch, place all the onus of "incongeniality" on American society. She conceded, rather, that all Americans who had been formed almost wholly, like herself, by the European tradition would have to unlearn and lay aside much if they would understand the emergent mind and character of their native land. To be sure, at the inauguration of the *Dial* she indulged in stock Transcendental laments on the paucity of higher sentiments in an American society dominated by a commercial aristocracy and a rationalistic religion. Yet subsequently she manifested more faith in the popular mind: she argued that the production of American literature need not be left merely to the literati; and she found reassurance for the national literature not only in coarse and homely little pictures of the American scene but also in that fusion of races which seemed to her so greatly to enrich America "with new blood from other stocks the most unlike that of our first descent" that the nation might hope to "develope [*sic*] a genius, wide and full as our rivers, flowery, luxuriant and impassioned as our vast prairies, rooted in strength as the rocks on which the Puritan fathers landed." This willingness to admit new, autochthonous points of view led to more generous literary perspectives. The spirit of the times demanded a genial rather than a perfectionist criticism, she concluded, lest the graceful literary plant nurtured by native soil be ignored as a weed, or lest American literature be considered merely the garden of the nation rather than "the growth of the entire region, with all its variety of mountain, forest, pasture, and tillage lands." The eye must range around as well as be lifted on high, she concluded in her attempt to respond "genially" to all indigenous compositions; the larger the literary wave, the more fish it sweeps along.

Even though the Transcendentalist might ordinarily contemn the low moral average of public opinion and suspect an aesthetic poverty in the popular Muse, he made at least a gesture toward democracy in an avowed confidence that the commonalty would be responsive to the "higher modes," to the "intellectual and moral best" of which Margaret Fuller spoke. The scholar may well reverence the "hard-handed

many" whom he serves as a new order of priest, wrote Robert Bartlett, for the "many seek truth" and "unphilosophic souls lie near to
the spontaneous and universal reason." It was "the leisurely, the educated, the purse-proud and aristocratic" who resisted the "higher
modes" of thought, he said, but the "great brave heart" of the toiling
masses, he was sure, afforded the likeliest home for truth and beauty.
In this Transcendental repudiation of that concept of polite letters
which assumed discrete literatures for the few and the many, however,
Frederick Henry Hedge ventured beyond most of his contemporaries
by affirming the mutual infusion of insight between author and populace. The "scholar," he declared, is to be "with and of the people, in
every genuine impulse of the popular mind"; he gains intellectually
and socially by "free and frequent intercourse with the people whose
instincts, in many things, anticipate his reflective wisdom." Hedge
had no patience with the fastidious aesthete who would "falsify his
nativity," who inclined to "coquet, in imagination, with the dowered
and titled institutions of the old world, and [to] feel it a mischance
which has matched him with a portionless Republic." The best acknowledgement which an author could make of his commitment to
American ideas and institutions seemed to Hedge to be a recognition
of the identity of what he called our common nature. In this view and
in his conception of the American "scholar" as exponent rather than
as priest of the people, he moved away from most of the Transcendentalists toward Whitman.

Had Hedge returned as often as did Emerson to ponder the relation
of "scholar" to society, perhaps his remarks would have taken at times
a less sanguine turn. For, though Emerson did not "coquet . . . with
dowered and titled institutions of the old world," his reservations regarding American society, especially in the 1850's, had become strong
enough for him to despair temporarily of "this empty America," whose
subserviency to the practical seemed all but to stifle a national poetry.
Chagrined by "the riot of mediocrities" across the land, he feared that
Nature herself had "only so much vital force, and must dilute it, if it
is to be multiplied into millions," and that among this multitude the
nation's "few fine persons are apt to die." Yet in the preceding decades
Emerson, like Hedge, had regarded the Third Estate as a regenerative

force which might happily expel imitativeness from the national literature:

> I suppose the evil of leaning on England may be cured by this rank rabble party, the Jacksonism of the country, heedless of English and of all literature— . . . they may root out the hollow dilettantism of our cultivation in the coarsest way, and the new-born may begin again to frame their own world with greater advantage.

Like Margaret Fuller, in the 1840's he hailed the new alloy which would issue from the melting pot of the nation, predicting that "the energy of Irish, Germans, Swedes, Poles, and Cossacks, and all other European tribes,—of Africans, and of the Polynesians,—will construct a new race, a new religion, a new state, a new literature, which will be as vigorous as the New Europe which came out of the smelting-pot of the Dark Ages." Even when the 1850's apparently dimmed his confidence in the popular mind, Emerson never entirely renounced his earlier faith that the riches, energies, and power of America would be transfused into poetry. Nor did the other Transcendentalists, despite all the expediency which they observed across the land at mid-century, abandon all hope that the populace would rise to the "higher modes" of imaginative perception. "California, with all its greed of gold, will become poetical," wrote Alcott. And Thoreau prophesied a similar transformation among the whole people: "Our native democrat, whose brains, boots, and bones are spent in composing a free republic and earning money, is growing up to the fine arts, even if at present utility sways the balance."

An American Style

If during the mid-century decades the Transcendentalists expressed frequent doubts concerning the soundness of the restive populace, they nevertheless consistently clung to the belief that in the speech of their plain countrymen resided a regenerative medium for the indigenous literature which they desired. Nature is the source of language, they supposed, and hence the "sayer" closest to her is likely to use most sensitively and authentically the verbal tools which man must shape ultimately from her phenomena. In expounding this assumption they developed the Scottish rhetoricians' earlier insight into the metaphorical genius of primitive peoples. From American nature, therefore, the Transcendentalists expected a varied and unique flow of indigenous metaphors which would lend to cisatlantic literature a distinctive flavor and communicative power. But language becomes a peculiar national instrument not only through the impress of nature, as Hedge observed; it is moulded also by "all the peculiarities, historical and organic, of the nation which uses it. . . . The English language is the English mind." Though Hedge followed his postulate to the general conclusion that the poetry or metaphysics of one nation can scarcely be expressed in the language of another, he applied his principle to American writing only so far as to urge the scholar to commingle with the people. Some of his Transcendental contemporaries, however, ventured further in identifying American literature with the speech which was taking indigenous shape from the activities and institutions peculiar to the expanding republic.

"Strong thinking makes strong language; correct thinking, correct speech," wrote Emerson in the early 1830's; and perceiving, as Whitman was to do later, an acute wisdom among the uneducated, he did not hesitate to claim for them the habit of using language with purity and force. Accordingly, for poetry he thought a discourse vibrant with this popular usage not merely admissible but imperative: "in English, only those sentences stand which are good both for the scholar and the cabman. . . ." Language with "life and meaning" likewise seemed to Alcott not to be shorn of woods, winds, and toil; and hence he preferred to study the "simple countryman amidst the scenes of nature, as dictionary of . . . [his] native tongue, [rather] than commune with citizen among his conventions, or read with professor in college or hall, the tomes of a library." Alcott could only regret that the outspoken buxomness and proud motions of Elizabethan English were rarely paralleled in the speech which he heard; and he put down as a proof of "the shallowness and indelicacy of our American authors that our rhetoric is so seldom drawn" from "the richest and raciest phrasebook," the human body.

In recognizing and accepting the alternative to what Alcott called the lack of "blood-warmth and the flesh-colours of nature" in American speech, however, Thoreau was characteristically more consistent than the other Transcendentalists. Venturing further than they, he vindicated for standard usage such "Greekish words" as "diggings" from the West, and he affirmed the rich communicative values of such phrases as "gone coon" from the "language of Tippecanoe and Tyler too." Preferable to artificial words like "judiciary," which refer to things "not fair and substantial," he wrote, are words "which are genuine and indigenous and have their roots in our natures, not made by scholars, and as well understood by the illiterate as others." To the end of his life Thoreau was impatient with that linguistic authoritarianism in America which, having scarcely any root in the soil, sought to impose alien symbols to the neglect of those which arose from the objects and phenomena of the American scene:

> All the true growth and experience, the living speech, they [American scholars] would fain reject as "Americanisms." It is an old error, which the church, the state, the school ever commit, choosing darkness rather than light, holding fast to the old and to tradition. A more intimate knowledge, a deeper experience, will surely originate a word. . . . What if there were a tariff on words, on language, for the encouragement of home manufactures? Have we not the genius to coin our own?

With avowed distaste, therefore, Thoreau felt himself compelled to describe the serpentine course of the Musketaquid by a word coined from a stream no older, the Meander. Indeed, the "wild nectar" that the gods continued to distill and pour down New England hills seemed so bountiful that at times he resolved not to taste the spring of Helicon again. For neither the impulse to song nor the acquisition of verbal symbols which are its medium did Thoreau admit the need of a primary reliance on the creative epochs of the ancient world. An American writer would honor the ancients more, he thought, by adopting the symbolic processes through which they had wrought a language from natural phenomena than by accepting their heritage per se: "It is too late to be studying Hebrew; it is more important to understand even the slang of today."

That their own reiterated identification of beauty of style with functional directness was rooted in colonial theory and practice the Transcendentalists were aware. Though the Pilgrim Fathers "Ne'er traced a tolerable line of verse," they were poetic in the "substantial basis of their minds," wrote James Freeman Clarke with that distrust of elegance and with that identification of Poetry and Divinity which characterized alike the seventeenth-century Puritan and the nineteenth-century Transcendentalist. The aesthetic link between the two centuries was most frequently attested by Thoreau, who was explicit in his admiration for the rugged vigor of the old chroniclers Josselyn and Wood. In his college essays he had already concluded that sublimity might be conveyed "in a plain and simple strain" and that the best style should omit all superfluous ornament. At mid-century he continued to regard such ornament as an enemy of the simple truth and as the mark of the belles-lettres and the beaux-arts, "which we can do without." He preferred an idiom which sprang directly from healthy senses and activity, which was "nervous and tough"; and, observing the sad contrast of "the weak and flimsy periods of the politician and literary man" with the force and precision in the utterance of the working man, he was persuaded that "plainness, and vigor, and sincerity . . . were better learned on the farm and in the workshop than in the schools." The artifice of the grammarians he feared as a "father tongue" which might displace the "mother tongue." The truest poetic sentence he characterized as being "as free and lawless as the lamb's bleat," and a good book as natural and as unaccountably fair as a wild flower. America was needed, he declared, to utter the "wild strain" which English literature had lacked.

Like Clarke and Thoreau, Emerson professed a more liberal doctrine of the poetical faculty and medium than the previous generation had allowed. The "democratical" literary tendencies which he saw about him he regarded as having a worth beyond "high finish" both in their honest spontaneity and also in their closeness to that colloquial idiom in which Thoreau found so much life. Indeed, literature is good to the degree that it approaches colloquy, Emerson and Alcott agreed in 1842: "The only true manner of writing the literature of a nation would be to convene the best heads in the community, set them talking, and then introduce stenographers to record what they say." The nearest approach to the colloquy, and hence the most authentic national utterance, Margaret Fuller found in the lyceum; and though she regarded this "entertainment" as a temporary growth, she esteemed it above the "dead form of traditional drama" because it arose from the spirit of the times and the national character. The dearest writers of America, she wrote in an attack on a "son of Europe," N. P. Willis, are those whose roots are in the soil and whose "complexion [is] given by its native air."

The Use of the Pas

Though Emerson, like Margaret Fuller, at times was disposed to test the verbal rhythms of native writing by the finer cadences of the fields which his eyes scanned, he nevertheless could become impatient with American authors whose forms had been too little disciplined by "the best existing standard" of Old World literature, past and present. So anarchic and callow, indeed, did the mass of American compositions seem to him in the early 1840's that he was forced to conclude that "a strict tribunal of writers, a graduated intellectual empire [must be] established in the land" so that its "writers . . . would begin where they now end their culture." In fact, for all his declarations of literary independence and his encomiums on the "meal in the firkin, the milk in the pan," as Holmes observed in *Over the Teacups,* Emerson "worked in Old World harness." And Holmes might have added that, despite all Emerson's fancy that the American bard should be the "wild steed of heaven," neither he nor the other Transcendentalists were quite willing to trust his nurture to the forage of native pastures alone.

The doctrine which underlay "The American Scholar" and later addresses like "Literary Ethics," to be sure, did not entirely discount the "tuitions" derivable from former masters; but it did relegate such disciplines to "idle times." As agents for enriching the imagination even Homer and Milton seemed to Emerson scarcely comparable to the infinite Reason which he supposed to be shining inexhaustibly every day through the dust and sand of his own cold America. Plato and Shakespeare and Milton, he said, are irrefragable facts, not absolute in form or idea; they are "glorious manifestations of the mind." Yet observed, approached, domesticated, brooded on though they should be, their best service is to set an example of literary self-reliance —to admonish the cisatlantic author not to dismiss hastily the visions which flash and sparkle across his own American sky. For two centuries, however, American genius seemed to Emerson to have distrusted such visions; it had been fatally intimidated by European achievements: "Pope and Shakespeare destroy all"; native writers, "timid, imitative, tame," had too long listened to the "courtly muses of Europe." Supreme possession of the present hour, he reiterated in the 1840's, must replace "false humility" and "complaisance to reigning schools or to the wisdom of antiquity"; the American did not come into the world "mortgaged to the opinions and usages of Europe, and Asia, and Egypt." Yet in this decade Emerson seems to have come to suspect that the poverty of American literature could not be charged primarily to the intimidation of Old World masters. So many "threatening" native authors had " 'delayed to strike' & finally never struck at all" that he had begun "to think our American subsoil must be lead or chalk or whatever represents in geology the phlegmatic." Perhaps no great Yankee writer could arise and speak untrammeled, he conceded, until he felt the authority of national power behind him—until "England kicks the beam" from the very weight of America's great expansion into the West. When America actually did begin at mid-century to "assert herself . . . to the imagination of her children," however, Emerson paradoxically prescribed more and more of the Old World discipline and grace which he had earlier contemned so unqualifiedly in Bryant and Dana and Irving. All young American poets should read Chaucer, Herrick, and Shakespeare, he insisted, in order to achieve an "objectiveness" which would counteract "what is almost a national quality, the inwardness or 'subjectiveness' . . . of our lyrics." America, he wrote again in 1857, had become "a vast know-nothing party, and we disparage books, and cry up intuition." But that this current inclination toward "un-learning and inspiration," might be traceable in some degree to his own pronouncements consigning books to "idle times" does not seem to have concerned him. In view of this reconciliation with the European Muse, it is not surprising that Emerson's earlier sneers at Bryant's alien grace should have been converted by 1860 into an acclaim for his long-established pre-eminence as a representatively national poet!

Implicit in Transcendentalism, therefore, lay the attitude toward the Old World literary past which Emerson promulgated in the 1830's and to which he generally adhered until mid-century: the old poets are a "splendid inheritance," but a colonial-mindedness has led to "a servile copying of what is capricious, as if it were permanent forms of nature"; for a proper national literature the American author is obliged to "write from facts" rather than "to state facts after the English manner"; he had better leave off being "secondary and mimetic" and trust "intuition and experience"; to be weaned from the enervating influence of "traditionary judgments," he may better proceed from Nature and the Soul than from "that barren season of discipline which young men spend with the Aikens . . . and Blairs." He who truly reverences the great dead, declared Robert Bartlett in the same transcendental vein, will least reverence "the particular dogmas and institutions and practices, in which that spirit [of the All] outshaped itself to them." The past, he agreed with Emerson, serves only to hearten the scholar, who, disdaining all "alien and superinduced thought," may trust his own intuition of the All.

Those Transcendentalists who had accommodated their literary doctrines to a steadier belief in humanitarian progress than had Emerson and Bartlett, could scarcely find in the literary past those heartening influences which the scholar might acknowledge with due homage. For Americans to avert their attention to the literary past to them seemed to endanger the signal progress that the New World had achieved in its march toward the beatific land of Truth. Alcott, indeed, testified that his own spiritual and intellectual growth had been impeded by his exposure to an English literature spawned "from the heart of moral disease." On such moral rather than on aesthetic grounds, Parker likewise rejected the courtly Muses of Europe, fearing that a veneration for English literature would perpetuate ideas of caste which were socially and ethically outmoded. And Emerson's transcendental friend, Charles King Newcomb, committed to the Hegelian principle that taste should be made commensurate with wisdom and that art should be associated with enlightenment, deemed a national preoccupation with "old reading" (Greek and Latin authors) equivalent to an adult's retrogression to the interests of childhood.

Whatever the variant strictures on "old reading" may have been among the Transcendentalists, there was a general consensus that the flood of Old World classics might sweep away the sprouts of literary confidence which were at last sending their roots down into the thin cultural soil of a new nation. Even Thoreau, with his reasoned admiration for the sinewy strength of Homer, was uneasy lest "the usurpation of the past, the great hoaxes of the Homers and Shakespeares" hinder the books and men of his own day; and as if to confirm his independence, he put Homer and Shakespeare aside to watch the battling ants. Shakespeare's "children should not hope to walk in his steps," agreed Margaret Fuller, admonishing her contemporaries that if they saw only with Shakespeare's eyes, they could not see with their own. That Young America took to heart such Transcendental admonitions is suggested by Hawthorne's Holgrave, who could see little hope for his country unless she were delivered from the Past which seemed to him to lie on the Present like a giant's body, compelling Americans to read in dead men's books and cry at dead men's pathos.

Perhaps the ardent Holgrave may be presumed to have read the Transcendental pleas for literary independence too literally. At any rate, the Transcendentalists themselves frequently betrayed beneath the bold assertions or in the implicit context or in their very habits of reading a substantial veneration for the giant Past. Emerson acknowledged his own debt to Greek art and poetry and berated him who benefits by such influence and then "like a fool, underpraises it in a sermon, because the worshippers are ignorant." The scholar who in some farmhouse "in this great, empty continent of ours" reads Homer, he wrote again, "adorns the land" and is "a subtle but unlimited benefactor." Even more comprehensive and acute were Thoreau's tributes to the Greeks, who "have carried their own serene and celestial atmosphere into all lands to protect them against the corrosion of time" and thus have become a "fit inheritance" for generations and nations. "We might as well omit to study Nature because she is old," he wrote in a neoclassic strain; for in such figures as Homer, Chaucer, Shakespeare, and Ossian he found the "noblest recorded thoughts of man," the "only oracles not decayed," and the "answers to the most modern inquiry." The New World, he concluded in his later years, needs Old World sand for her rich but unassimilated meadows.

Among the post-Renaissance Continental literatures the Transcendentalists generally pronounced the German more estimable than the English. In the former they discovered a texture and doctrine akin to the penchant of their own minds; in the latter they perceived more threatening temptations to literary servility and metaphysical thinness. Chaucer, Shakespeare, Milton, or Ossian, to be sure, were accorded varying degrees of praise from Transcendental pens; but later figures like Wordsworth and Coleridge could be esteemed, as they were by Alcott, not entirely in their own right but because they led to Herder, Schiller, and Goethe—to a literature where Imagination and Reason seemed most nearly to blend. To these generative minds of Germany Margaret Fuller insisted that the masters of Italian art and letters must be added as necessary stimuli to the maturation of the American character:

> It has been one great object of my life to introduce here the works of those great geniuses, the flower and fruit of a higher state of development, which might give the young who are soon to constitute the state, a higher standard in thought and action than would be demanded of them by their own Time.

Less confident than Emerson of the power of intuition and nature to form the American scholar, she counted more heavily on the "tuition" of the masters to raise her countrymen "above their native sphere" and thus to become its instructors rather than its slaves. In her last years in Italy, indeed, she renounced the aesthetic self-reliance of the American traveler who, like a "booby truant," supposed his own untutored judgment of Old World art, etiquette, and religion superior to that of the connoisseurs. The thoughtful American, she concluded, does not wish "one seed from the past to be lost. He is anxious to gather and carry back with him every plant that will bear a new climate and a new culture."

Through such volumes as *Specimens of Foreign Standard Literature* (1838–42), as well as by critical essays, George Ripley was as zealous as Margaret Fuller in seeking to elevate American literature above its native sphere and to liberate it from English domination by infusing into the national mind the germinal strains of Continental thought. Though other Transcendentalists such as James Freeman Clarke also bespoke the dangers of "sit[ting] exclusively at the feet of English Literature," none was more insistent on the indispensability of the Continental tradition than young George William Curtis. "Had foreign literature been cut off from us," he wrote in 1844 under the influence of Emerson, Brook Farm, and the *Dial,* "we should have had

few writers of poetry, and Mr. Griswold's book had been a . . . duo-
decimo and not a heavy octavo." Americans could not become artists,
he thought, without "the overshadowing of Time." Therefore he
urged his literary compatriots to suck the heart from the aesthetic
triumphs of the Old World in order to refine and adorn their native
land. Curtis conceded an inevitable national diversity in art—a diversity
which he defined as the "several ways that nations regard the same
thing." Hence he concluded that American literature could be "American only in respect of culture"; its core, however, would be "the same
thing" to be found in the European literary tradition. Like Margaret
Fuller, therefore, he was singularly impatient with that "shabby Americanism" which provincially defied the spirit and beauty and political
institutions of Europe, and he reminded his compatriots that they were
"born into the world with relations as men to men before . . . [they
were] citizens of a country with limited duties." Disciple of Emerson
though Curtis was, more than a decade seems to lie between the cultural self-reliance of "The American Scholar" and the younger Transcendentalist's dictum in 1847: "A noble cosmopolitanism is the brightest jewel in a man's crown."

The Hallmark of Americanism

Though the Transcendentalists made the final test of any native author
the degree to which he comprehended the All or the "common heart"
or "Highest Law," they also continually assessed the degree of his
Americanism. In employing "Americanism" as a critical referent, they
were at times pejoratively allowing for what they called the rind of
the visible and the finite enclosing the divine impulse; but more often
they seem to have been honorifically asserting the relative thinness of
this temporal rind in America in comparison with that in other epochs
and nations. At Harvard, Thoreau wrestled with the problem which
E. T. Channing had assigned him: "How it is that a Writer's Nationality and Individual Genius may be fully manifested in a . . . Literary Work, upon a Foreign or Ancient Subject,—and yet full Justice
be done to the Subject." Thoreau's answer came through a metaphor:
though it were desirable that an author see with the naked eye his subject, which is really universal man, "he must look through a national

glass." When due allowance is made for the quality of the lens, he said, "What is peculiar and national in the writer, by the side of what is real history and matter of fact in the description, will be made the more manifest by the contrast."

Undoubtedly Emerson expounded most comprehensively, though he may not have pondered most acutely, the specifications of the "national glass" through which the American author must view experience. Avowing that he was "not wise enough for a national criticism," he nevertheless frequently found occasion both to propound the elements of an autochthonous literature and also to censure the Bryants and Irvings and Danas who seemed to him to betray the indigenous impulse. Occasionally he doled out a cautious bit of praise for the sheer indigenousness of a Crockett, or a Jack Downing, or a Whitman, whose "nondescript monster" with its "terrible eyes and buffalo strength" he was willing to extol as "indisputably American," though soon afterward he might penitently long for an "exquisite" Tennyson or a "subtle" Browning rather than "wild Whitman, with real inspiration but choked by Titanic abdomen."

By the other Transcendentalists, however, Emerson himself was often adjudged to be the exemplary American author. "These I deem first fruits of a new literature," wrote Alcott in 1839 regarding a collection of Emerson's works which he had made. "They are indigenous. Like a plant uprooted from its native soil, the earth yet cleaves to the roots. . . . The images are American. The portrait is set in a frame of western oak." But as Emerson had second thoughts about the authenticity of Whitman, so Alcott within a decade also harbored doubts regarding the indigenousness of his Emersonian plant. Though he and Thoreau at first agreed in assigning Emerson the highest place among American authors in "pure thought and composition," they came to suspect that his works were a "swallow's flight," lacking the continuity and active energy and breadth of the old poets—that his "Natures" [*sic*] were never American or New English, "but some fancied realm, some Atlantides of this Columbia, very clearly discernible to him but not by us. . . ." Yet still at mid-century Parker, who was disposed to measure the nationality of his contemporaries by the degree of their adherence to the "American Idea," continued to regard Emerson as the "most American of our writers" because he espoused "personal freedom, . . . the dignity and value of human nature, the superiority of a man to the accidents of a man." And for Margaret Fuller, too, Emerson remained the "harbinger of the better day" which she prophesied for American literature.

As Alcott perceived the indigenous in Emerson beginning to pale, he found reassurance in Thoreau's *A Week on the Concord and Merrimac Rivers* as a book "purely American, fragrant with the lives of New England woods and streams, . . . [which] could have been written nowhere else." In it he recognized the "wild and mystic" of our brooksides and rivers, and in it he felt that "the sod and sap and flavour of New England have found at last a clear relation to the literature of other and classic lands." The persistence of Alcott's nationalistic criterion is attested when again at mid-century he adjudged Lowell "perhaps the most American" of the young authors and yet one who would feel most at home in England or Germany. When in turn Whitman appeared as a controversial figure, Alcott reckoned him a genius who would make his mark on Young America; and in the 1860's he apostrophized him as "great grand Walt. . . . Another American beside Thoreau and Emerson." Thoreau, in turn, as a young man resorted to the same nationalistic premise in order to measure the import of Brownson's *Boston Quarterly*: "It is high time that we knew where to look for the expression of *American* thoughts." And later, vying with Emerson's and Alcott's enthusiasm for Whitman's autochthonous voice, he acclaimed *Leaves of Grass* as "very brave and American, after whatever deductions"—"an alarum or trumpet-note ringing through the American camp."

And thus "American" became a recurrent epithet in the vocabulary of Transcendentalist criticism. To be sure, it did not for them signify the highest reaches of the native imagination. Yet they were generally agreed that any of their literary compatriots who remained ineligible for the term were also likely to fall short of adumbrating those further reaches of the Over-soul in and by which the visible world was sustained. For the author to disregard the spirit of the new age and the new nation was to reject at once the ever-flowing Present and the infusion of the ever-present All.

CHAPTER SIX

Questionings (1815-1860)

> I know very well it is said, that the war of 1812 liberated the
> American mind from its ancient thraldom, and for a time it
> did; so did the war of the revolution; but no sooner did things,
> in both instances, revert back to their ancient channels, than
> the habits of thought appear to have kept them company. We
> have gained a little, permanently, beyond a question.
>
> JAMES FENIMORE COOPER, c. 1837

A Natural Literature

With the ascendancy of the organic concept of the nation in the 1840's,
doctrinaire prescriptions for creating an American literature inspired
less and less confidence. In that decade most of the living major authors in the country affirmed their faith in the achievement of a distinctive national utterance, but they inclined more and more to concede that this utterance must be matured slowly and gradually defined
by the aggregate of indigenous forces. Like Lowell, by 1845 some of
them had become not a little weary with the "great babble [that] is
kept up concerning a national literature," though few of them voiced
his caustic conclusion that the country, "having delivered itself of the
ugly likeness of a paint-bedaubed, filthy savage, smilingly dandles the
rag-baby upon her maternal knee, as if it were veritable flesh and
blood, and would grow timely to bone and sinew." Yet the "rag-baby"
of conscious literary nationalism was not easily abandoned even by
Lowell, for a decade later he confessed to W. W. Story his pride in
his "country-breeding" and in his "Hosey Biglow experiences, as some-

thing real"; and he announced his intention of making "a poem out of them some day that shall be really American." Nevertheless, in general he was clearly of Orestes Brownson's mind that nothing could be "more ridiculous, than for the leading minds of a nation to set out consciously, gravely, deliberately, to produce a national literature."

This weariness with conscious nationality of which Lowell spoke and to which Brownson and others testified was in essence an attempt to redress what seemed to have been an ill-advised preoccupation with "originality" in the two previous literary generations. The term "original," in one sense or another, had become by the 1840's all but a shibboleth in the nationalistic critical vocabulary. For Noah Webster it had served to recall American authors to the mode of the ancient classics; to the philosophical American Romantic of the next generation it signified the value of the uniqueness and spontaneity of Genius as opposed to the disciplines of Taste. Out of this Romantic persuasion no doubt came Melville's conviction that "it is better to fail in originality, than to succeed in imitation." In the same vein Paulding envisioned some fearless genius who would become the "great original of a distinct . . . national literature"; and throughout the ante-bellum decades John Neal, Bryant, E. T. Channing, and many another critic shared and discussed, with varying degrees of modification, Paulding's position.

In this orthodox Romantic view originality was in essence a literary self-reliance which, as Channing phrased it, merely "takes its own view of things and makes its own use of them." Abhorring artifice and calculation, it eschewed mere eccentricity for a larger fidelity to an author's felt experience in nature and in society. But from this view Poe, though he also proclaimed originality the only respectable criterion of the national literature, conspicuously demurred. Like other Romantics, Poe scorned what he called the "beaten paths of imitation"; but he had little concern for that larger kind of originality which would involve the national as well as the individual mind, and which Emerson and Whitman sought to foster. The "true originality" with which he would have American letters endowed was, he explained, no "mere matter of impulse or inspiration. To originate, is carefully, patiently, and understandingly, to combine." If they would only subject Feeling and Taste to Reason, he assured American writ-

ers, they might burn the "old models." Thus, though "autorial originality" remained for Poe the chief desideratum for American journalism and American letters, it was a contrived novelty that he desired
rather than a fresh representation of universal or national themes. It
had little relation to that "innate perception and reflection of truth"
which, Hawthorne observed, "gives the only sort of originality that
does not finally grow intolerable."

With the rise of the organic concept of a national literature, a consciously fostered originality, whether that of Poe or of extreme literary
nationalists, became increasingly suspect. It was in summary impatience with such presumptuous tamperings with the imagination that
Emerson admonished American writers in 1843 that literature is "no
man's private concern, but a secular and generic result." Emerson's
conclusion, for all its Olympian air, had been anticipated or independently reached by other critics. A generation earlier one of the first editors of the *North American Review,* Willard Phillips, had compared
the zealous demands for a full-grown American literature to attempts
to mature a plant by "applying a mechanical power to force it up-
wards"; and John Neal, conscious of the dangers inherent in an undue
longing for novelty, advised American authors not to "think much of
originality" but to study and observe the world and then to write naturally.

It was Lowell, however, who most memorably sharpened the distinction between a synthetic and a natural literature. In the very
Introduction to his short-lived *Pioneer* (1843), he anticipated Emerson's remark on a "generic" literature by repudiating all species of
native writing which were not the "healthy natural growth" of the
American soil:

> We are the farthest from wishing to see what so many ardently pray
> for—namely a *National* literature. . . . But we do long for a *natural*
> literature. One green leaf, though of the veriest weed, is worth all the
> crape and wire flowers of the daintiest Paris milliners. For it is the
> glory of Nature that in her least part she gives us all. . . . We would
> no longer see the spirit of our people held up as a mirror to the OLD
> WORLD;—but rather lying like one of our own inland oceans, reflect-
> ing not only the mountain and the rock, the forest and the redman,
> but also the steamboat and the railcar, the cornfield and the factory.

The cumulative campaign for a national literature, Lowell feared, had been all too little concerned for a true mirror that would reflect the national scene and character and hence a portion of the universal. He did not wish the goddess of freedom to lose her "fresh country charm" by glancing into "Europe's cracked glass," as he asserted a few years later in *A Fable for Critics;* but neither did he desire the literary distortions which would be refracted from a narrow nationalism at home. Rigid historical and geographical prescriptions for American literature, he declared after reading Longfellow's assault on literary chauvinism in *Kavanagh* (1849), could only result in a "less narrow form of provincialism, a sublimer sort of clownishness and ill manners." That there was a "truth . . . wrapped up and concealed in the demand for nationality in literature" Lowell admitted; it was simply "that authors should use their own eyes and ears, and not those of other people." To demand more than this seemed to him to demand an unnatural literature.

Lowell's evangelism for a "natural" literature evidently did not lack converts. In the mid-1840's the poet-translator Charles T. Brooks, echoing Lowell's distinctions, judged that typesetters would be wise if they should always substitute "natural" for "national" in printing proposals for an American literature; and soon thereafter Rufus Griswold, with his usual alertness to critical trends, rebuked those writers who "in their anxiety to be national have merely ceased to be natural." At the end of the decade Longfellow used his schoolmaster Churchill in the novel *Kavanagh* to argue confidently the case of a "natural" utterance as opposed to stock nationalistic doctrines of the boorish Hathaway. Undoubtedly such conversions to the principle of a "natural" literature may be taken as indices of a growing reaction during the 1840's against a brash self-conscious nationalism—or perhaps at times of a disillusion with its literary results. Even the erstwhile nationalistic *Democratic Review,* surfeited at mid-century with plaintive articles demanding a national literature, brusquely reminded its readers that literature cannot be ordered like oysters in a restaurant. Clearly throughout the land the crest of a doctrinaire nationalism in literature was receding toward an unenforced naturalness whereby, as Horace Greeley said, American writers need only see through their own eyes, utter the honest impulses of their own hearts, and "speak and write as truth and love shall dictate."

The Barren Scene

Despite the simple reassurance of those critics who felt that American writers need only consult their own eyes and hearts to produce a national literature, the writers themselves frequently offered testimony to the contrary. The imagination, they had often discovered, requires a certain leverage from literary convention and the social milieu; and these requisites had not converged into a sufficient stability or richness in America in the ante-bellum decades. In the late 1830's the poet-editor Park Benjamin professed amazement that "Some asinine individual . . . has taken upon himself to remark, that there are few or no materials for romance in America." Yet during the two previous generations of the nation's existence almost every major author, whether working in the romantic or the neoclassical vein, had confessed the difficulty of wresting belletristic productions from the American soil; and in the two following generations Hawthorne and James were to add similar confessions to attest the persistence of the problem. Among the numerous ante-bellum statements on the intransigence of the American scene to the dominant transatlantic literary genres of the day, none was more devastatingly comprehensive than that of Cooper in *Notions of the Americans* (1828):

> There are no annals for the historian; no follies (beyond the most vulgar and commonplace) for the satirist; no manners for the dramatist; no obscure fictions for the writer of romance; no gross and hardy offences against decorum for the moralist; nor any of the rich artificial auxiliaries of poetry. . . . In short, it is not possible to conceive a state of society in which more of the attributes of plain good sense, or fewer of the artificial absurdities of life, are to be found, than here. There is no costume for the peasant, (there is scarcely a peasant at all,) no wig for the judge, no baton for the general, no diadem for the chief magistrate. The darkest ages of their history are illuminated by the light of truth; the utmost efforts of their chivalry are limited by the laws of God; and even the deeds of their sages and heroes are to

be sung in a language that would differ but little from a version of the ten commandments. However useful and respectable all this may be in actual life, it indicates but one direction to the man of genius.

To the ramifications of this problem of extracting literary "sweets from these wholesome, but scentless native plants," Cooper returned in such diverse works as *The Heidenmauer* and *The Water Witch* and *Home As Found*. Fundamentally he was wrestling with what became a disturbing literary axiom to so many ante-bellum American authors: that as a society approaches uniform well-being, the impulse to and the necessity for imaginative reconstructions of experience wither away. In such a state neither social satire nor romantic vision seemed to serve much purpose. Hence the very satisfaction with which many politically conscious writers like Bancroft and Hawthorne viewed humanitarian progress in the new nation involved *ipso facto* a skepticism regarding the future of American letters. In a land "where tranquillity flourishes under the law," as the Yale poet James Hillhouse phrased the issue, the "most ingenious fancy" could scarcely "naturalize" those vigorous passions necessary to epic and tragic poetry. And that same calm wholesomeness and common sense which Cooper attributed to American society seemed to George William Curtis to have infused even the American landscape itself and left only "space and mildness." Therefore in his native land, Curtis felt obliged to report in the 1850's, the American writer could find "few rivers of any romantic association, no quaint cities, no picturesque costume or customs, no pictures or buildings. . . . We have only vast and unimproved extent. . . ." In this mild land all but a few romancers felt the futility of any attempt not only to evoke a *genius loci* but also to acclimate the more sensational effects and properties of the Gothic genre. In American experience, the *Port Folio* observed in 1819, the "most terrible necromancer . . . is the sheriff, whose gates readily open on the exhibition of a piece of paper"; and, Cooper added a decade later, the vaulted passages of the Old World have been transformed into useful cellars in the New. To attempt to construct an interesting *Roman de Societé* from such a milieu, as Cooper testified, seemed indeed a desperate undertaking.

At the center of most of these numerous nineteenth-century laments over the deficiencies of American society for fiction and drama lay, of course, literary postulates born of a traditionally stratified society. Granted that tension and contrast are requisite to such genres, the antebellum writer, bound to and conditioned by the authority of transatlantic modes, all too readily supposed that external social or cultural stratification must furnish his reader the dominant clues to the underlying struggle of values in the fiction. Before the Civil War there was little exploration of what appropriate substitutes a democratic society could offer for such old indices of worth as rank, manners, and costume. Hence, given the leveling influence of political equality and the diffusion of property, given the shifting surfaces of American life, a host of authors found themselves at a loss for any stable value symbols in American social behavior. Unlike the transatlantic cultures mellowed and stabilized by time, the great new continent conceived time to be merely a beast of burden, N. P. Willis surmised in the 1830's; men were like steam engines, society itself was a great new machine, and hence the "whole character, history, and feelings" were "stripped of dramatic ornament."

To provide any touch of ornament or any enriching overtones to compensate for the stripped past and present of their national life, antebellum authors did not neglect even the smallest devices. Supposing their imaginations to be inhibited by the prosaic place names of the native scenes of which they felt obliged to write, some members of the Knickerbocker group proposed the substitution of "Alleghania" or "Appalachia" for "America" as a strategic step toward inspiring a national poetry. The sublimities of American landscape could never properly be sung, Irving prophesied, so long as unfortunate associations persisted through names inappropriately borrowed from the Old World or unimaginatively imposed upon the New. The Cow Bays and Cow Necks that dotted the country he hoped might be transmuted into Indian names, original and musical. Indeed, even into the 1850's Willis sustained this campaign to redeem the many scenes of natural beauty which had been desecrated through some "vile name" given them "by vulgar chance." An Indian legend or a national hero might supply a more "euphonious and poetical" name, he thought, for the beautiful mountain lake which, he learned, had been christened "Nigger Pond." Yet to those writers with a neoclassic ear, the admixture of aboriginal polysyllables with the mother tongue seemed to terminate in prosodic chaos rather than mellifluous associations. As a boy, Bancroft sardonically confessed his inability to envision the melodic resources of Indian names upon which Longfellow was to rely so heavily in *Hiawatha:*

> 'Tis said the Indians, tho' a barb'rous horde,
> Will noble subjects to our bards afford.
>
> .   .   .   .
>
> Cann-bat-cut, Caw-na-come, Qua-de-qui-na,
> Squan-to, Woo-sam-e-quen, and Menida,
> O pleasing sounds, melodious names like these,
> Would grace Pope's numbers and give Waller ease!

No mere transpositions in nomenclature, however, could quite supply a sufficient imaginative resonance to a land watered by rivers "deaf and dumb," to use Motley's phrase; nor could they quite satisfy what Hawthorne called "the yearning of the blood . . . for that from which it has been estranged." The fact that the yearning was confined to no one authorial temper or school suggests the degree of its involvement in the ante-bellum literary experience—the degree of a pressure that was after the Civil War to overflow into a deepening stream of expatriation. Such sentimental patriots as Catharine Sedgwick, traveling on the Rhine, could but confess that the beauty of the Hudson suffered by comparison with that of a stream where legends had "breathed a soul into every tumbling tower and crumbling wall." Such restive metaphysicians as Orestes Brownson, judging even American history to be "essentially prosaic," concluded that no one could set to music "the stern old Puritanism . . . , or surround with poetic associations a Congregational Meetinghouse." Such cosmopolitan minds as Oliver Wendell Holmes could confidently trace the poverty of their country's literature to the lack of a "sufficient flavor of humanity in the soil out of which we grow." And even before the Civil War the more renowned cosmopolitan, Henry James, Jr., had become aware of that "complex order" which was to draw him permanently to a Europe where "contrasts flared and flourished." What young James had so soon reckoned to be an "absence of tonic accent" in his native land, an earlier Southern poet, Richard Henry Wilde, had previously with a more sensitive regret assessed in his *Hesperia* as a commonplaceness which all but doomed the American imagination:

But the heart seeks, and has forever sought,
Something that man has suffered or enjoyed,
And without human action, passion, thought,
Nature, however beautiful, is void.

. . . .

Could we our country's scenery invest
With history, or legendary lore,
Give to each valley an immortal guest,
Repeople with the past the desert shore,

. . . .

We should—and then shall have—our poets too!

But now!—'tis true in this our day and land
All that is written perishes, alas!

For a time the Indian had seemed to afford American writers the fund of "legendary lore" which, as Wilde made clear, the literary imagination of the time was thought to require. Yet even by the 1830's, after hundreds of poems, dramas, and novels had tested the durability of the aboriginal theme, the limited role of the Indian in a representative and mature national literature was becoming evident. By that decade so sated was the market with variations on the theme that numerous critics, especially in New England, had become, as the poet Grenville Mellen expressed it, "stern unbelievers in Indian tales." From this current state of unbelief Margaret Fuller discovered that even a trip through the West could not deliver her, as she confessed in doggerel verse:

American romance is somewhat stale.
Talk of the hatchet, and the faces pale,
Wampum and calumets and forests dreary,
Once so attractive, now begins to weary.

By mid-century public antipathy toward the literary exploitation of the red man was so pronounced that the historian Motley felt obliged to assure prospective readers of his colonial romance, *Merry-Mount* (1849), that his narrative was not focused on that "dangerous wildfowl," the Indian. Most of these readers, Motley surely thought, shared the humorist Sam Slick's mistrust of "fancy sketches" wherein the red man ate dead horses and drank green swamp water, yet spoke in an idiom which was "half mist, foam, and cataract, and half sun, moon, and stars."

Even before public reaction against the spate of Indian tales and plays and poems had evidenced the limitations of such themes, critical reckonings in the 1820's had sounded some of the shallows that awaited those literary nationalists who were unreservedly committing American literature to aboriginal channels. In the previous century some of the Scottish rhetoricians had contended that a simple and primitive culture could not afford sufficient intellectual and imaginative depth for the literary needs of a progressive, modern society; and it was probably under the influence of their doctrines that the annalist John Bristed ventured to prophesy early in the century that "a novel describing these miserable barbarians, their squaws, and papooses, would not be very interesting to the present race of American readers." As a theme for poetry the aborigines seemed to Jared Sparks equally "barren," inasmuch as they had few large vices and virtues and so few delicate shades of character that any useful insight into human passions would have to be supplied by civilized man. For the American writer "to encircle the rude brow of a swarthy Indian, with a garland from Parnassus," the Southern editor-poet James W. Simmons summarily concluded, "is indeed like casting pearl to swine." To all these and many other critics it seemed increasingly clear that an unbridgeable cultural gulf separated the two races—that the white man had "commenced a new era," as Thoreau said, and hence for the valid commemoration of Indian deeds only an "Indian memory" would serve. Such observations, of course, did not signify the demise of the literary Indian, as *Hiawatha* was soon to prove; but they did cogently point to the fact that his role was to be a minor one in the next century of American letters.

At mid-century the American writer who assessed his country through traditional literary modes thus had reason to feel the imaginative limitations of both the contemporary scene and the distant past. In addition, he may well have been uncertain as to what established genre would best enable him to convey something of the peculiar texture of American life. Previous ventures toward an American epic had proved conspicuously futile; and by the 1840's Hawthorne judged that it was time to "break up and fling away" the moulds of the historical novel which had become excessively worn during the previous generation. Despite Hawthorne's and Melville's success in breaking the old fictional moulds, they scarcely succeeded in establishing a mode (such as the Waverley novels) which would help liberate the imagination of their literary compatriots. Not until the ascendancy of realism after the Civil War nurtured the aspiration for the Great American Novel did native authors of fiction feel the pervasive hope that Scott had inspired a half century earlier.

The Ominous Stage of Civilization

Although it is generally assumed that early American critics were in the main a provincial lot given to chauvinistic puffery, an examination of their principles obliges one appreciably to modify at least this article of condescension. Nationalistic though the majority of them were, they inclined more often than modern critics to appraise American literary trends within the larger context of Western civilization. Much of the eighteenth-century hope for American letters had been posited on the apparently ineluctable march of the arts from East to West through the centuries. America seemed destined to complete the circle; and still during the ante-bellum generation this Berkeleyan thesis echoed in Thomas Buchanan Read's "The Bards":

> Nor these alone—for through the growing present,
>> Westward the starry path of Poesy lies—
> Her glorious spirit, like the evening crescent,
>> Comes rounding up the skies.

Tangential to this line which projected the cumulative civilization of Europe into America, however, was the more controversial plotting of an arc of aesthetic maturity. Instructed by the Augustans or the Scottish rhetoricians or the German historical school, American critics felt obliged to fix nineteenth-century America in its proper stage of cultural development—in a period of infancy, youthfulness, or maturity (as the Romantic J. W. Simmons defined the stages), or in a period of imperfect taste, good taste, or decadent taste (as the somewhat neoclassical Alexander Everett preferred to say). For the immediate future of literature in America the broadly Romantic view, which supposed the early stages of a society more congenial to the imagination, held the larger hope. In the neoclassical view, these early stages seemed barbarous, and young America would need time to achieve what Everett called "correct forms" and "finished elegance." But that America had not yet (in 1815) "arrived at what may be called the manhood of a literary taste" Paulding was grateful, for such a stage, he feared, was the sure precursor not only of a decline of imaginative power but also of social decay. Numerous other authors—among them the poet Percival and Emerson—looking across the Atlantic at what they regarded as the moral and aesthetic decadence of the elder nations, shared Paulding's reading of America's position in the cultural cycle and happily accepted the unpolished vigor of the national literature as an inevitable correlate of a youthful society in its heroic age.

For those descendants of the Augustans, on the other hand, who valued taste rather than imagination, the youthfulness of America could but seem a liability. Poetry, declared N. P. Willis, "is the child of civilization"; and he reminded Englishmen who cried for a mature American literature that it is not the pioneer but the thoughtful clerk by his fireside that grows poetical. In the South the young novelist Philip Pendleton Cooke, pondering a literary career in an America where poetical composition seemed to gain a man no honor, disconsolately reached a similar conclusion that poetry is a product not merely of the individual but also of a stage in the national culture: "It is in the maturity of countries that the harp is listened to—or rather in the old age of countries, when energy has given way to ease & indulgence."

More acute cultural analysts, however, suspected that the character and course of American letters could scarcely be plotted by the old formulas of cycle or stage, since both American nationality and society were novel mutations in human history. Not only had the first modern nation been created by an unprecedented act of political will; but also, as the *Biblical Repository* observed at mid-century, for the first time practical thought had been given precedence over that imaginative faculty which the Scottish rhetoricians had found characteristic of other young societies. During the ante-bellum decades most American writers must have become thoroughly conversant with this argument from one or more of the numerous magazines in which it was sustained; and to the extent that they could accept it as valid they must have also realized that they could scarcely hope for either that simple stage of earlier cultures where poetic language is the communal norm, or that mature stage of a polite society which cherishes polish and elegance. If Americans are "a young nation" they are nevertheless "an old race," the critic Charles Astor Bristed wrote in summary comment on the issue: "They began with too much civilization for the heroic school of poetry: they have not yet attained enough cultivation for the philosophic."

Caught between these two stages in a sort of literary limbo, persuaded by positivistic doctrines that in America especially the era of poetry was beyond recall, or impressed by the inventive genius of the age, many American writers felt obliged to concede with the Boston jurist Franklin Dexter that "engineering" and "reasoning" afforded mankind his brightest prospects and hence eloquence and poetry "must give way before the progress of popular education, science, and the useful arts." Inasmuch as America was generally regarded as the prime national exemplar of the beneficent results of a commitment to the doctrine of Progress, the American writer could but feel especial estrangement from the drift of his national culture. To be sure, poets as diverse as Barlow and Whitman accepted as a part of their literary creed America's role as the pilot of a new rational and scientific age; but their confidence that a rich and influential national poetry could emerge from and could assimilate and propagate such a culture was not readily shared by many of their contemporaries, whose philosophy of history had led them to the positivist conclusion that the poetic imagination was little else than an embarrassment to Progress. From this premise the historian Prescott declared that nineteenth-century Americans could well afford to abandon poetry to the primitive races, and Gouverneur Morris advised the members of the New York Historical Society that "other fields" than poetry needed to be cultivated if America, as the "child of science, parent of useful arts," was to fulfill her destiny to lead in the amelioration of the condition of man. With more legitimate pride, he thought, America might boast that the first steamboat was launched on the Hudson than that her authors were rivaling Europeans in the production of hexameters. Though these apostles of Progress were usually willing to dismiss the literary imagination as a mere innocuous relic, Horace Mann actually feared it as an agent of the brutish propensities of mankind. In nineteenth-century America a writer could justify a place in society, he thought, only by "craniologizing" his literature—that is, by founding it on science. As a climactic argument Mann (who believed in the science of phrenology!) submitted the odd dictum that literature is "mainly conversant with the works of man, while science deals with the works of God."

Confronted by this disparagement of the literary imagination by conspicuous men of affairs and historians, some American authors themselves began to suspect that Progress had all but invalidated their role in society. "It is admitted we have none [no literature]," Emerson wrote in his Journal in 1824. "But we have what is better. We have a government and a national spirit that is better than poems or histories. . . . 'Tis no disgrace to tell Newton he is no poet, nor America even." Some years later N. P. Willis, reflecting on the demolition of the floating oyster shops near Faneuil Hall, seemed equally willing to forego an age of poetry for an "age of improvement." Yet the New York writer James G. Brooks clung to both worlds. America seemed to him not to have yielded her poetic birthright; she had merely transposed it to a new medium:

> Poetry, in fact, has left language, and is reigning in matter. Instead of an epic, it builds a railroad. Instead of the pen, it uses a pick-axe. . . . Enterprise, men call this spirit of the day,—but it is poetry, with all the soul of poetry. It acts on matter instead of mind. It speaks in works, instead of words.

Few ante-bellum writers, however, could accept such a generous view of the poetic character of Enterprise. The vast activity across the land generally seemed to them, as it had to the post-Revolutionary generation, to breed a materialistic complacence which increasingly calloused the national sensibilities. Subsumed under the national belief in Progress was an ardent commitment to the clearing of forests, to the benevolent manipulation of political interests, and to an acceleration of industry for the sake of profit and comfort. With this commitment, Simms thought, the American mind had become infused with a "feverish urgency" which was the enemy to the repose and stability necessary to the arts. One aspect of what Simms characterized as a "feverish urgency" Cooper deplored as a "rabid jealousy of the credit of American *things*." Against this "whirl of party" and this "spirit of gain" came an all but endless succession of indictments from authors of varying literary tempers and creeds—from Percival and Halleck, from the elder Richard Dana and Timothy Flint, from the aging Brownson and the aged Freneau, from T. W. Parsons and Henry Tuckerman. Those who had had a taste of European life frequently had little relish for returning to a literary struggle among countrymen who, as Parsons wrote, found "in business all their bliss" and who were spinning themselves to death with "speed, and speed, but never once God-speed!" In such an atmosphere the seeds of expatriation were already beginning to sprout.

Though the utilitarian threat to the imagination in ante-bellum America could scarcely be gainsaid, Progress was not altogether wanting in credits on the literary ledger. As it involved science, it involved thereby the widening of human perspectives; and as it involved easing man's physical lot, it involved humanitarian responsibility. Poe, to be sure, devoted a sonnet to castigating science as a vulture which had "driven the Hamadryad from the wood" and had torn "the Elfin from the green grass"; but Whittier, Bryant, and Whitman as well as many a minor writer were convinced that their art could come to terms with the scientific and humanitarian temper. Science, Bryant observed in a Wordsworthian vein, nurtures rather than stifles poetry because it enlarges the circle of mystery and doubt even with its conquests; and Whittier joined Bryant in declining to weep for the mythical lore of ancient times when the humanitarian struggles and achievements of the New World afforded themes of wider import and scope. Nevertheless, despite scores of similar reassurances, the ante-bellum American writer could but realize that his countrymen for the present trusted the resolution of their problems to Progress rather than to poetry. For such a society, wrote Melville in *Pierre,* Memnon's statue could no longer sound: "Fit emblem that of old, poetry was a consecration and an obsequy to all hapless modes of human life; but in a bantering, barren, and prosaic heartless age, Aurora's music-moan is lost among our drifting sands, which whelm alike the monument and the dirge."

Old World Aliment

In the early post-Revolutionary years of national existence a few writers professed to believe that America could within a few decades effect as severe a break with Old World literature as she had with transatlantic political power. By the mid-nineteenth century, however, any such hopes were seen to be patently illusory. Even the most persistent proponents of a national literature, such as Whitman, paid homage to the English language as the ineluctable base and hence in a measure the cultural determinant of any American utterance. In a more comprehensive perspective the American mind and myth were seen to be, as Whitman wrote in "A Passage to India," but the highest point of a cultural arc which had risen cumulatively out of the older civilizations. For the ante-bellum writer, therefore, the question of a thoroughgoing repudiation of other cultures was scarcely of moment; for by such isolation, as John Bristed recognized in a survey of American resources soon after the War of 1812, the very vigor of indigenous expression would be threatened:

> The most powerful mind is, in itself, but a barren soil, soon exhausted, if left to repeat often the periodical growth of its own native vegetation; a soil which will produce only a few scanty crops, unless continually fertilized with the abundant addition of foreign manure.

Granted, then, the necessity of foreign aliment to fertilize the American imagination, the controversial issue became the choice of that aliment which would supply the requisites peculiarly needed for the flowering of a New World literature. Moral and political distrust of recent European culture led many ante-bellum writers to Bancroft's somewhat paradoxical conclusion that a study of the ancient classics would provide "a means of preserving national literary independence." To be sure, critics of a Christian-humanitarian persuasion were never lacking to remark the perils of such pagan influences. Bancroft in effect replied that Homer was safer than Voltaire or Byron. But in a more positive vein the numerous apologists for the classics often pointed to the Greek and Roman orators, historians, and philosophers as the fountainhead of republicanism. Under the influence of these ancients, as the Southern editor Hugh Legaré wrote, the American writer would come to love liberty and his own free country all the more and would be delivered from that "slavish and nauseating subserviency to rank and title, with which all European literature is steeped through and through." Even by those who looked more critically at the anomalous character of liberty among the Romans, the classics could nevertheless be accepted as the choicest of foreign aliment because, as Jefferson said, of their "rational and chaste style." By the very fact that these models were far removed in language and time, they seemed the better suited to preclude slavish imitation, such as English writers generally inspired, and to serve rather as guides to what Bryant called the "original fountain" of Nature. Through a familiarity with such wholesome foreign literature, argued the Southern critic Samuel Gilman in a typical nationalistic apology for the classics, is the "taste rectified, and expression improved, and thought fired, and a nation's mind assisted to burst its old shell, and put on new wings."

Such attempts to nurture American letters with the aliment of the classics, however, could scarcely deflect the American writer's all but inevitable recourse to the literature of a country whose language and history were his more direct heritage. In the ante-bellum decades Howells' later construction of American literature as a "condition of English literature" was widely, though sometimes reluctantly, accepted. Even the nationalistic John Neal, in the last analysis, could not refuse to recognize the work of his countrymen as a phase of "English literature—that literature, which is put forth in the English language . . . on both sides of the water"; and the historian Prescott conceded that, in view of the common sources and disciplines of American and English writers, "our literature can only be a new variety of theirs." Alexander Everett felt obliged to make further concessions, admitting not only that England and America "must always, in a literary view, be regarded as one great community," but also that the "head-quarters of the common literature . . . for some time to come," would remain abroad.

Having acknowledged an obligation to English literature for "the greater part of our intellectual aliment," as Edward Everett phrased it, ante-bellum writers nevertheless acted to preserve their national distinctiveness and independence by frequently denigrating their literary contemporaries in England and exalting the Elizabethans and

Augustans. Indeed, much of the lag in cisatlantic romanticism, one suspects, may be traced to a nationalistic pride which bred an especial rivalry with and suspicion of post-Revolutionary British works. "The authors, previously [*sic*] to the revolution, are common property," Cooper declared in his *Notions of the Americans,* "and it is quite idle to say that the American has not just as good a right to claim Milton, and Shakespeare, and all the old masters of the language, for his countrymen, as an Englishman." In divers metaphors other authors concurred in this building on old foundations, in this mingling with the great English literary stream, in this willingness to derive literary vigor from the healthy old Anglo-Saxon root and stock. The English Romantic branch of this old stock, many American writers insisted, was for the most part rotting away. As late as the 1830's Wordsworth seemed to Longfellow an unsafe model, and Byron a poet who had done twice as much as any other author to corrupt taste and moral principles in America.

Though this distaste for many of the English Romantics did not necessarily involve a fixed attachment to English neoclassicism, it is nevertheless true that throughout the ante-bellum decades not a few American critics shared aging Noah Webster's view that literary aspirants in America should take as their models the dominant figures of the "most splendid era of English literature": Addison, Swift, and Pope. From this Augustan era Goldsmith's "graceful ease" also commanded the especial veneration of such diverse authors as the jurist Joseph Story, the novelist John Pendleton Kennedy, and Washington Irving; and John Quincy Adams was so impressed by the age that he thought not only that Gray was the greatest lyric poet of all time but also that nine such American poets as Bryant, Willis, and Percival would be required "to make a Tate"! Yet also among the ante-bellum writers there were many who felt that the only English literary stock on which the American branch could be safely grafted was the massive growth of pre-Restoration times.

With the development of the American stage Shakespeare grew in especial favor. Whitman's fears that the great tragedies and history plays would subvert the republican mind were the exception rather than the rule. More representatively the currently esteemed poet

Charles Sprague expressed a hope that this "Monarch-Bard" should bind anew to England the sons of Independence as they pushed their banners toward the West. Nor were the Bard's contemporaries overlooked. In contrast to the elegant and polished Augustans, these "old, manly, rugged writers," as General Albert Pike called them, seemed to be reassuringly akin to the temper of young America. There were of course those, like Whittier, who envied the gentler Elizabethans Sidney and Spenser rather than the more "rugged" Bacon or Browne. Moreover, as events of the ante-bellum years sharpened the issue of liberty, Whittier was not alone in turning from the Elizabethans to "mighty Milton" for ethical and imaginative direction. By mid-century, indeed, Milton had become the master for writers as varied as Griswold, Margaret Fuller, and Boker. Griswold went so far as to call him "the most American" of all writers and to claim for a paragraph of his "Areopagitica" more Americanism than could be found in a whole library of Irvings. It was not Milton's political creed, however, which led Boker to advise young R. H. Stoddard to study the poet. Read Chaucer, Spenser, and Shakespeare, wrote Boker, but for the purest English diction, read Milton's minor poems.

At mid-century, therefore, as American literature flowered into its first real renascence, it consciously sent its roots deep into the subsoil of the English tradition. As a consequence, it is not surprising that the poet Henry Tuckerman, in reviewing the Duyckincks' *Cyclopaedia of American Literature* (1855), should have concluded that the American literary mind was still "thoroughly and essentially English." In this decade, too, Hawthorne's character Middleton, in "The Ancestral Footstep," was discovering that an American's connections with England through history and literature, through memories and interests, were likely to be far more numerous than his disconnections, however much he might desire to let the past alone and seek not to renew it. Much of this bond the linguist George P. Marsh traced to the deep linkings in the recesses of our being wrought by the Anglo-Saxon element in the language common to both countries—to a "certain sensibility to the organic laws of our mother-tongue." That this organic bond was likely to be strengthened rather than weakened in the future seemed certain to N. P. Willis as he watched the coming of new modes of transportation and communication. *"In literature we are no longer a distinct nation,"* he said in an urbane apostrophe to the *Great Western* in 1840:

> Atlantic steam-navigation has driven the smaller drop into the larger, and London has become the centre. . . . Our themes, our resources, the disappearing savage, and the retiring wilderness, the free thought, and the action as free, the spirit of daring innovation, and the irreverent question of usage, the picturesque mixture of many nations in an equal home, the feeling of expanse, of unsubserviency, of distance from time-hallowed authority and prejudice—all the elements which were working gradually but gloriously together to make us a nation by ourselves, have, in this approximation of shores, either perished for our using, or slipped within the clutch of England. . . .

The *young* American author is the principal sufferer by the change. Perhaps the timidity and uncertainty that afflicted the literary generation immediately following the Civil War is the surest evidence of the soundness of Willis' observations.

Before the advent of the steamboat, however, a few proponents of a national literature who saw the need for Old World aliment and yet shared Simms's fear of the "pernicious influence" of England turned to the Continent. The writers of continental Europe, thought William Ellery Channing, were not so deficient in the "highest views" as those of contemporary England and hence would afford a proper stimulus for an American literature "instinct with a new spirit." It was Peter Du Ponceau of Philadelphia, however, who presented the most specific proposal for breaking America's mental dependence by forming foreign literary alliances. Already a successful "conspiracy" with Germany and France in the interchange of books and papers had been inaugurated, he reported in the 1830's, confident that American authors, like bees, could suck the flowers of continental literature and, by bringing their juices to cisatlantic hives, could produce the most delicious literary honey. Yet such deliberately nationalistic resort to the literature of Europe was apparently rare. To be sure, American students in German universities in the 1820's had their nationalistic predilections re-enforced by the literary and critical atmosphere abroad; but the later interest of Margaret Fuller and Henry Hedge in German literature seems to have had a more nearly transcendental motivation than that of Du Ponceau. At any rate, the recourse to Continental literature in the ante-bellum years, whatever its motivation, was evidence of a general recognition among American authors that a distinctively national literature could scarcely flourish without foreign aliment. Lowell was not speaking merely for himself when he recorded in his Commonplace book: "The constant study of our own literature is like breeding in and in. The breed degenerates. We must cross with other minds and modes of thought."

The Diversity of Design

In the ante-bellum attempt to raise an imposing structure of national literature there was clearly no master architect. No one spoke with the critical authority, say, of Howells in the 1890's. In this stage of the campaign for literary independence no man of letters commanded the unqualified respect to become, in response to N. P. Willis' plea, a "Washington among the critics." As mid-century approached, Cornelius Mathews lamented that American criticism was still "sceptreless"; and Poe went further to charge it with being clique-ridden and corrupt. Perhaps the "corruption" was for the most part little else than a literary self-interest such as Poe himself frequently manifested; but that there were cliques is unquestionable. Among those of which Poe felt himself the victim was the New England group, who seemed to him not always to judge the works of other American writers by those "eternal and unchanging laws of beauty" to which Lowell, at least, professed allegiance.

One of the cliques which in turn drew the ire not only of the Cambridge poets but also of Griswold was that of "Young America" in New York. Associated at times with the influential *Democratic Review* and the *Literary World,* its members included Cornelius Mathews, W. A. Jones, Parke Godwin, and the Duyckinck brothers. Its general design for the national literature in the 1840's resembled that of young Whitman: it was suspicious of Old World culture and judged the propagation of equalitarian principles to be the distinctive mission of American writers. During the very decade in which the academic critics at Cambridge were proposing that American literature should be "natural" rather than "national," the Young Americans placed the national literature in an impressive historical context of manifest destiny. Hence Longfellow's attack in *Graham's* (1842) on "Young America, which mocks the elder prophets" and follows the literary school of Young Germany. By the mid-1840's Rufus Griswold, who was often at odds with members of the group, had joined the attack on the "mob of 'Young Americans'" and especially on the "centurion of the sect," Cornelius Mathews, whom he accused of an ignorant "clamor about 'Americanism.'"

If Griswold and Longfellow felt the sound evolution of American literature threatened by the "mob of 'Young Americans,'" Hawthorne apparently judged it to be in greater danger from the "d—d mob of scribbling women" to whose "trash" he thought the public at mid-century wholly addicted. These were the female "Cacoethes Scribendi" whom Catharine Sedgwick had earlier observed "working up" the New England life about them for the literary annuals and gift books. In their preoccupation with the detail of their own narrow locales, these female writers undoubtedly contributed to an indigenous domestic realism; yet in their general concern for fashion and sentiment per se they also evolved what was frequently called a "milliner's literature" which found a ready and remunerative publication in such journals as *Godey's Lady's Book.* "What are called the lady's magazines, with plates of the fashions," wrote E. A. Duyckinck in 1846, "do not generally indeed enter into an estimate of a national literature." To such exclusion, however, the ladies would scarcely accede. Even in post-Revolutionary days Mrs. Rowson, Mrs. Morton, and Mrs. Murray had set the precedent for the claims of American women to help design a literature which should sustain the fresh moral tone of the New World. Chiefly concerned though they were to be "helmsmen in the mighty vessel of improvement," as fifteen-year-old poetess Lucretia Davidson phrased it, Mrs. Sigourney and other popular female writers of her stamp nevertheless usually reflected a national piety as well.

Probably the most vocal exponent of this brand of feminine nationalism was Mrs. Sigourney's associate in the editing of *Godey's Lady's Book,* Mrs. Sarah J. Hale, whose announced policy it was to provide an outlet for female "effusions" that would delineate American scenery, characters, and manners and counteract the influence of "European manners, fashions, and vices." When in her early editorial days she had assumed charge of the *Ladies Magazine* (1828) she had proclaimed her national bias by prefixing *American* to the title, and soon thereafter she culled from its pages a collection of sketches which she thought worthy of the title *Traits of American Life.* Even in editing a book of flowers, *Flora's Interpreter,* she did not neglect to infuse "American sentiments" throughout by using native poets to express in a native idiom the thought that the flower was intended to convey. And when she put aside the editor's pen to attempt a tragedy, she was careful that this work should be "imbued with American principles and feelings." In intent, at least, the work of most of the other antebellum "scribbling women" was much the same. There were variations in sentiment and learning and taste, to be sure, among Catharine Sedgwick, Alice Cary, Caroline Kirkland, and Mrs. Stowe; but in both pronouncement and practice they did not deviate in their Americanism far from the norm established by the influential Mrs. Hale. With all their moralistic emphasis, their fidelity to "the passing character and manners of the present time and place," as Catharine Sedgwick remarked in *Redwood* (1824), was a conscious part of their endeavor toward a native literature. Their realistic scope was, of course, limited by their point of view; for when like Mrs. Elizabeth Oakes Smith they ventured toward such distinctively fresh subjects as the American newsboys, they were likely to insist on construing them as "little flower[s] of Innocence" in order to displace the "great ugly burdocks" of literature. It was no doubt this feminine preoccupation with Innocence that led the satiric poet Lambert Wilmer to echo Hawthorne by including the scribbling women in *The Quacks of Helicon* (1841):

> Alas! what sad decisions must we find
> When gentle woman rules the realms of mind.

In the long campaign for a national literature it was inevitable, of course, that such diverse groups and such diversity of principle should exist. This very literary factionalism, however, was in effect evidence of an all but unanimous acceptance among native writers of the principle of a distinctive American utterance. It proceeded from a central impulse toward nationality in much the same way that contentious political parties evolve from a common matrix of nationalism and religious sects from a common scripture. When Lowell in 1845 uttered his famous dictum that ". . . before we have an American literature, we must have an American criticism," he surely cannot have intended any national critical orthodoxy. At any rate, what was required and in part achieved during the ante-bellum decades was a manifold and cumulative reassessment of the European literary tradition as it was modified or outmoded by a new milieu and society. On the degree and pace of independence permissible to the American imagination the Young Americans, the scribbling women, the Transcendentalists, the Knickerbockers, the romancers and the incipient realists all in a measure disagreed. Yet for all their separate and at times incompatible strategies, and for all their disorganized sallies, the various groups moved zealously or cautiously toward a single objective, a literature consonant with what they conceived to be America's peculiar destiny. Using the same critical instruments and maps, so to speak, they formed one massive ante-bellum attack on the issue of a national literature.

CHAPTER SEVEN

A Half Century of Whitman (1842-1892)

> The prophet and the bard,
> Shall yet maintain themselves, in higher stages yet,
> Shall mediate to the Modern, to Democracy, interpret yet to
> them,
> God and eidólons.
>
> WALT WHITMAN, *Eidólons,* 1876

Incubation

Just as Whitman conceived of an American literature which would embrace the Old World heritage in developing its distinctive character, so his own prescriptions for a new "literatus order" were at first but consolidations and echoes of earlier American critics. His early critical ventures, undertaken in the decade of the 1840's when the campaign for a national literature was reaching its crest, reflected in the main the equalitarianism of William Leggett and the Jacksonian element in the Democratic Party, of which he was at the time a zealous adherent. As early as 1842 he had begun to define the American writer in terms not unfamiliar to the readers of the *Democratic Review:* one whose work tends "to destroy those old land-marks which pride and fashion have set up, making impassable distinctions between the brethren of the Great Family . . . one whose lines are imbued, from preface to finis, with that philosophy which teaches to pull down the high and bring up the low." The daintiness of the "literary fop," Whitman had already concluded, must be supplanted in a democracy by a more vigorous disclosure of "the thousand distortions engrafted by custom upon our notion of what justice is."

As editor of the Brooklyn *Daily Eagle* in 1846–47 Whitman, following his own dicta, not only consistently advocated legislation to counteract the "thousand distortions" of justice, but he also defended the expansive policies which underlay the Mexican War. Yet in these years reflection upon the essays of some of the major proponents of an indigenous literature was also projecting his vision of American writing beyond that of the simple equalitarianism which had marked his earliest criticism. Among his most esteemed critical oracles in the 1840's was undoubtedly Margaret Fuller, though her influence was by no means so exclusively formative as some critics of Whitman's "pose" have assumed. Before he reviewed her *Papers on Literature and Art* for the *Eagle* (November 9, 1846), he had already voiced the same distaste for both the "cast-off literary fashions" and the feudal implications of many Old World books which the *Papers* expressed. That her Transcendental plea for a literary manifestation of the Idea underlying American life made a marked impression on Whitman's mind, however, is suggested not only by the enriched nationalism of his famous 1855 Preface but also by his explicit references in later years to her prospectus for an American literature. Found among his papers after his death was an article entitled "Criticism" (probably written by Whitman sometime after the first edition of *Leaves of Grass*), the opening sentence of which reflects his debt to her essay. And in his last years, he once more reverted to her words when he wished to remind his countrymen that the mere mass of cisatlantic publications did not per se confirm the arrival of a truly American literature.

Yet Whitman in the 1840's was alert to all clues which might help him define a national literature; and in this decade the clues were numerous. Two which he especially valued, in addition to Margaret Fuller's essay, he preserved as clippings throughout his life: one was Simms's review of the writings of Cornelius Mathews, which Whitman annotated, "Very Fine"; the other was an anonymous magazine article, "Nationality in Literature," dated March, 1847—no doubt the first portion of an essay in the March and April issues of the *Democratic Review*, apparently from the pen of W. A. Jones, one of the Young America group of New York. In Jones's article Whitman found a cogent statement of his own belief that America still lacked a literature which authentically reflected her physical, moral, and intellectual character, and especially the republican spirit, and that all great peoples have achieved a nationalistic utterance to commemorate their era. As for Simms's essay, Whitman undoubtedly cherished it as "Very Fine" because it admonished American writers not only to beware of foreign models but also to adopt as a "leading idea . . . the impetuous and intense earnestness of the people." Indeed, Simms's insistence that genuine national attitudes are to be derived not so much from partisan politics as from "walks among the people" became one of Whitman's cardinal prescriptions for the American literatus.

As a young Democrat, seeking at mid-century a proper image of a people's author wherever he might find it, Whitman may well have been also attracted to and inspired by the portraits of literary and humanitarian artisans in such novels of George Sand's as *The Countess of Rudolstadt, Consuelo, The Mosaic Workers,* and *The Gentleman-Joiner.* But later and larger than his debt to Sand, Margaret Fuller, Jones, and Simms for the fund of his critical principles was that to Emerson. Whitman's own inclination in later years to minimize the debt somewhat obscures both its beginnings and its magnitude. From an interview with Whitman in Boston in 1860 John T. Trowbridge recalled the poet's statement that in 1854 Emerson's essays, carried along with the dinner pail to carpentry work in Brooklyn, helped him find himself—that when he was "simmering" they brought him "to a boil." He would have come to himself without Emerson, he told Trowbridge, but it would have taken longer. Not only the strong tribute of disciple to "Master" in the second edition of *Leaves* but also the recurrent verbal echoes in the 1855 Preface and poems attest the strength of the Emersonian impact. Yet Whitman may well have begun writing *Leaves of Grass* before he read Emerson, as he told Kennedy in 1887; and he was certainly justified in declaring that the *"common concrete"* genesis of his poems was "certainly *not* Emersonian." If in his last years he construed his early reverence as a youthful phase of "Emerson-on-the-brain," if he suspected that Emerson's admiration of power was only a "gentleman's admiration," he was scarcely more guilty of ungracious repudiation than Thoreau and Alcott, who arrived at similar reservations. Perhaps his ultimate attitude toward his Master is to be found in his words to Traubel in 1888: despite the varying opinions he had had about Emerson, he said, he

was "always loyal at last." And as for his growth beyond an early
discipleship: "But I got my roots stronger in the earth—master would
not do any more: no, not then. . . ."

Under such varied critical influences Whitman developed and bespoke in the decade before *Leaves of Grass* a conception of American
literature which transcended the narrow chauvinism which he is at
times accused of fostering. Indeed, his prospectus for an indigenous
utterance contained few specifications not favored by the most judicious American critics of the 1840's. As editor of the *Eagle* he was
explicit in condemning "a bigotted [*sic*] misnamed nationality" which
insisted on applauding only compositions of native birth and on disparaging the treasury of English letters. Like Poe, he saw American
writers imperiled between the extremes of an intimidation by British
reviews on the one hand and, on the other, a provincial puffery of
"writing that is merely American because it is not written abroad."
With much critical justice he laid the insipidity of native drama to its
reliance on outmoded theatrical formulas and themes appropriate to
English society but irrelevant to "American opinions and American
institutions." Like Poe, too, he felt that at the heart of the intelligent
masses lay a propensity toward the original which would welcome and
nurture fresh, indigenous compositions. But, unlike Poe, he also
wished American literature to use its independence of foreign modes
in order to sustain the humanitarian temper of the New World as
well as the "good taste" of the Old. A genuine native drama, he
argued, might be "the mouthpiece of freedom, refinement, liberal
philanthropy, beautiful love for all our brethren, polished manners and
an elevated good taste." Like Emerson, he was convinced that a lofty
national literature would be born if American authors would be true
to the thoughts that God had given them; for he supposed that the
absence of corrupting social institutions had permitted the "American
mind [to attain] powers of analysis and acuteness superior to those
possessed by any other nation on earth." Whitman's literary nationalism in the 1840's, indeed, was catholic enough to permit an apology
for Longfellow as an unrecognized master in his treatment of "com-
monest occurrences" and as "an honor and glory . . . to the American
name." Just as his later praise for the Cambridge poet in the 1880's is
a projection of his early estimate, so does his final vision of a national

literature square with the outlines he sketched as editor of the *Eagle*. The intervening generation of literary and social experience of course induced elaborations here and reconsiderations there; but, in accord with his own faith in the organic processes of the mind, his early critical assumptions became the seedlings which, nurtured by time and the imagination, matured into the more impressive critical passages of later Prefaces and poems.

An Expression Transcendent and New

Though Whitman's concern for a memorable expression of the republican stage of human culture echoes frequently the antecedent voice of Joel Barlow, two generations of Romantic criticism had instructed him in functions of the imagination of which the earlier poet was unaware. By 1855 neither the affirmative political epigram nor the pastoral or heroic depiction of national well-being could serve as an adequate vehicle of a mobile and expansive democracy. Hence, noting in his first Preface the complexity and variety of the national life, Whitman also submitted that the "essences of American things" could never be comprehended through the pastoral or heroic modes of works like *Greenfield Hill* or *The Fredoniad*: "For such [experiences] the expression of the American poet is to be transcendent and new. It is to be indirect and not direct or descriptive or epic. Its quality goes through these to much more."

To achieve this indirect and yet transcendent expression, to sing this "great psalm of the republic," Whitman supposed, the native bard must first commit himself to a kind of wise passiveness in order to absorb the poetry with which the American scene was instinct. For the States themselves seemed to him the "amplest poem"—a "teeming Nation of nations" where moved "magnificent masses." In the common people—in their candor and freshness, their attachment to freedom, their blend of self-esteem and sympathy, their fluent speech—he found "unrhymed poetry." This inherent poetry filling the nation's veins, he predicted, would in turn "embouchure" into the receptive imagination which, needing only to respond to his country's spirit, would be moved to frame the grand autochthonous poem that had been impressed upon it. Thus would the poet "incarnate" his country's geography; he would "tally" the blue breadth of its inland seas; he would "stretch" with the long coast lines; to him would "enter" the essences of real things. His songs, therefore, would not be the elegant contrivances of polite literature; they would rather be projections of the "varied carols" which could be heard issuing spontaneously from the shops and farms of the land.

As a corollary of this espousal of the autochthonous as against the contrived, Whitman felt obliged also to denounce the presence of a literary class in America as a forced product which encouraged "mostly critical and querulous men" and hence an artificial and devitalized literature. "We should not have professional art in a republic," he told Traubel: "it seems anti to the people." More expressive of the rude democratic spirit, he thought, were the thousands of newspapers and presses; these, he wrote Emerson, are "the stairs by which giants shall mount." In view of Emerson's earlier expectation that American bards would be a "brood of Titans," Whitman no doubt supposed that his "Master" would welcome his denunciation of those inbred literary fops who favored "mental expressions . . . in sneaking defiance of the popular substratums of the States. . . . Poets here, literats here, are to rest on organic different bases from other countries. . . ."

This organic different base, therefore, on which Whitman wished to establish "an expression transcendent and new" was a culture arising from and consonant with the normal sentiments and activities of the people—that "best culture . . . of the manly and courageous instincts, and loving perceptions, and of self-respect." Yet such a view also adumbrated a national literature as myth. Seeing the old sectarian priests depart, Whitman envisioned each future democrat becoming his own priest and the great poet becoming the oracle of composite Man. All past days, he asserted, "were what they must have been," and those days had their myths, gods, and demigods and hence their bibles. Today and America consequently seemed to him what they are destined to be, and the fully autochthonous American poem will be as mythically reflective of the Personalism of the New World as the Old World bibles have been of their respective cultures. "Largely considered, great and true poetic expression is a growth (and a signifying portrait also)," declared an article apparently written by Whitman but designed for the *Nation* under Burroughs' name, "of clime, age, culture, race—even of species and crises, and politics."

For Whitman, therefore, the supreme American poem could never be merely an explicit utterance or a versified sequence of democratic ideas and sentiments. The great cultural epochs, he perceived, had achieved their literary monuments by a much more subtle hold in the recesses of the imagination. Yet he was equally convinced that these monuments, however rich their aesthetic interest, in turn were never ideologically innocent but always involved *"their point of view."* The "actual living light" of such literature does not shine by a mere literary luminosity, he concluded, but is "always curiously from elsewhere and is lunar and relative at the best." Just as the luminosity of the Old World classics had derived from "long trains of presuppositions," so American works, if they are to acquire such a powerful and distinctive light, will involve a "tallying" of the democratic structures of the New World. But for imaginative uses the democratic idea must not merely be conceived, Whitman emphasized; it must be realized or felt through the American author's associating "freely with powerful uneducated persons"; it must be transmuted into a correlative spirit and mood out of which the author would contemplate Humanity and Nature afresh. Like early republicans such as Barlow, Whitman was confident that American poets, drawing on a more humane stage of social evolution—a stage "consistent with the Hegelian formulas"—might form a "higher class" than Old World singers by reason of the evolved richness of their presuppositions; but he did not so naïvely reckon the mere statement of an indubitably progressive point of view the decisive factor in achieving an adequate national literature. At last, he knew, only "the image-making faculty" could breathe into literature the breath of life. Such a faculty could enhance democracy as the literature of chivalry had enhanced the feudal system, by transfusing it into "the conscious and unconscious blood, breed, belief, and intuitions of men."

This conversion of democratic ideology into democratic sensibility through manly experience Whitman saw as "the new esthetics of our Future." The exemplar of such aesthetics, having absorbed the national life into his very blood, would in turn be absorbed almost unconsciously into the popular mind. His style would be "new-born and red"; and his rhythms and forms, conceived in the fresh matrix of the New World, would emerge with the quintessential beauty of lilacs on a bush. In the movements of his verses he would catch the "sweeping movement of great currents of living people." In the expansive and organic poetry of the States, Whitman prophesied, traditional ornaments and rhymes would yield to larger and more flexible modes consonant with the prairies and with the whole people and with the free play of passions and emotions that belong to them. Thus, with Greenough and Emerson, he supposed that American forms might achieve genuine beauty only if they were linked to function—only if they were in honest alignment with "natural models" and with the "presuppositions" underlying the current and active life of the nation. As Crèvecoeur a century earlier had concluded that American writing must assimilate and convey the native flavor of the wild cherry, so Whitman lamented to Hamlin Garland that the national literature, with persistent suspicion of its indigenous aliment, still lacked the distinctive tang of "a wild strawberry, a wild grape." American writers timorously renounced their autochthonous character in a mass of adjustments, he said in *Democratic Vistas,* and hence their writing was clipped away like the bordering of box in a garden; it should be full-bodied like "the tumbling gorgeousness of the clouds."

As Whitman postulated a national literature related both in inception and effect to the very marrow of American life, so he perceived that the prime requisite for his "expression transcendent and new" would be the vitality of its language. Repudiating the static implications of a set poetic diction, he conceived of language as a growth, as a living organism whose character formed a most delicate index to the innermost life of nations and eras. As the "universal absorber," language seemed to him to comprehend in the subtlest fashion the history of Nature and civilization. Hence the American writer as the expositor of the furthest social revolution of the race would most sensitively embrace "a cosmopolitan range of self-expression."

Yet, as the language of the Old World masterpieces was organically involved with the myths and presuppositions of former cultures, Whitman argued, a new tongue would be required to reflect the cultural mutations of the New World. Of this new tongue the autochthonous

American writer would be the most alert and sensitive agent; his works would be perforce, like *Leaves of Grass,* bold experiments in language tallying the new vistas opening to man. The new "iron architecture" and new rugged characters and new political facts of America were all bursting the old formal linguistic bonds, Whitman thought, to form the Real Dictionary and Real Grammar consonant with the feelings and the "adjectival facts" by which the American imagination was being nourished. These new forces of spoken and written language beyond "pedagogue forms," he said in concluding *Democratic Vistas,* permit a communication breathing Nature itself and one which "tallies life and character, and seldomer tells a thing than suggests or necessitates it." To venture toward this sensitive utterance through the use of these new linguistic forces would require "supple and athletic minds," Whitman admitted; but such a venture he adjudged "the sole course open to these States" and, indeed, one entirely befitting an athletic democracy.

Though Whitman thus proposed in effect an evolving American language as the distinctive medium of a native literature "electric, fresh, lusty," he also recognized and repeatedly honored the English substratum as a mighty inheritance. The American writer, in fact, he said in his 1855 Preface, could have received in no other tongue so generous a linguistic legacy. For it was brawny and flexible enough for the "grand American expression," it was the achievement of a tough stock who had endowed it with a rich terminology in a long march toward liberty, and it was the dialect of common sense. Yet its especial merit seemed to him to be that "it favors growth as the skin does," that it is "grandly lawless"—or rather that it is so "instinct with that which underlies laws" that it fosters infinite enrichment within its structure. Accordingly, as the "most fluent and melodious voiced people in the world—and the most perfect users of words," Americans would enlarge and renovate their mother tongue and add "Kosmos words," he predicted, so that it would serve larger purposes than the "etiquette of saloons." American writers may use "the same old font of type," he remarked in the West in his later years, but what they "will set up will never have been set up before."

The American accretions to the "most capacious vital tongue of all," Whitman conjectured, might come from such diverse sources as science and Indian legend. Already he observed enrichment from the large imperatives of "new occasions, new facts, new politics, new combinations" in these States. Like Thoreau and especially Emerson, to whose theories of linguistic origins and development he is clearly indebted, he approvingly watched an expanding nation "sprout in hundreds and hundreds of words, . . . all having texture and beauty." Like the Transcendentalists, he supposed the farmer and the artisan capable of a richer discourse than the scholar because their utterance kept faith with the concrete origins of language in manual toil. As Thoreau applauded the stump slang of the West, so Whitman welcomed words like "shyster" and "doughface." The coarseness and directness of such words seemed to him to be the stock ingredients of popular speech. They signified for him the "attempt of common humanity to escape from bald literalism"; and since this fermentative and essentially poetic process was prevalent across the nation, it might well be, transmuted and refined, an indispensable element in the creation of a national literature. To the manly instincts of the People the rude beautiful words are ever welcome and understood, Whitman insisted, and if American writers would only employ the "ten thousand native idiomatic words . . . already grown," they could convey "that taste of identity and locality which is so dear in literature."

Cognizant though Whitman was of the copious heritage of the English tongue, he reckoned of peculiar value for imaginative uses the fund of words by which America had been uniquely endowed through her Indian and African strains. Like Irving and the Knickerbockers, he thought that to neglect the thousands of peculiarly indigenous aboriginal names was to impoverish the American tongue. "Names are magic," he wrote. "One word can pour such a flood through the soul. . . . I say America, too, shall be commemorated—shall stand rooted in the ground in names—and shall flow in the water in names and be diffused in time, in days, . . . in their names." That ultramarine names could not be dispensed with overnight, Whitman conceded; yet he judged that no country could have its own poetry without its own names, for in them lay not only national identity but a "test of the esthetic and spirituality" as well. California cities named for saints and Eastern cities named for lords (Baltimore) could better serve the American imagination, he argued, with aboriginal nomenclature, whose descriptive aptness would permit the writer to tie his work to the earth. Through the Negro, moreover, the writer could gain additional music. Indeed, such modifications in American speech seemed to Whitman to have been effected through "nigger dialect," with its "old English instinct for wide open pronunciations," that a native grand opera might be born.

In the vigorous linguistic currents flowing through Indian, Negro, and popular usage, therefore, Whitman found the surest counteragent to that constriction and triviality of style which, imitated from the salons of the Old World, he regarded as perverting the utterance of the Genius of these States. Sounder the poet who partakes of the "common idioms, manners, the earth, the rude visage of animals and trees, and what is vulgar," he said, than he who, isolated from common life and its verities, aims at only literary literature. What had such literary confections, with their "lady-words" and "gloved gentleman-words," he asked, to do with the liberty and brawn of these States? On these virtual importations he poured through four decades his sustained contempt: they were "piano music," played with "tinkling rhymes" and filled with the "thin sentiment of parlors"; they were "copious dribble" and "perpetual, pistareen, paste-pot work." Of such work the authors, shamefully indifferent to the sane and heroic life at the center of the nation, merely copied surfaces and pandered to an effete taste. The artifice of these literary fops, "cowardly, fractional, dyspeptic, subdued to other men's or nation's models," Whitman predicted, could but fall dead on the American soul. Far beyond this gilded coterie art the genius of American poetry seemed to him to lie sleeping in some Western idiom or repartee or stump speech, or perhaps in the songs and allusions of miner or mechanic or farmer. There, he was certain, common humanity would at last not suffer humiliation.

Among his contemporaries, Whitman, like the Transcendentalists, could find none who consistently exemplified "an expression transcendent and new." Joaquin Miller's "wild-horse business," he perceived, was not an authentic utterance of American breadth so much as a mere grafting of novel Western subjects on the stock of Byronism. As more representative of the temper of democracy he continued to value, as he had in the 1840's, the evocation of the poetic quality of everyday objects which he found in Longfellow. *Hiawatha,* with "all sorts of things" imported into its meters and attitudes, he admitted, was not so racily and vigorously indigenous as Cooper's Leatherstocking novels. Yet at Longfellow's death, dissociating himself from Margaret Fuller's earlier strictures on the Cambridge poet, he declared that America should be "thankful for any such singing-bird," especially when his songs more than any others had served to counteract the materialistic tendencies in American society. Above Longfellow in sounding the antifeudal note, however, Whitman placed in ascending order Whittier, Emerson, and Bryant. Loyal though he continued to profess himself to be to Emerson, in his last years he accorded to Bryant the tribute of being "our first man" and "thoroughly American." More than any other American he seemed to Whitman to have had the power "to suck in the air of spring, . . . to breathe it forth again— . . . the new entrance to life." Yet not even Bryant had quite achieved "an expression transcendent and new."

Presuppositions of Democracy

If American authors are to match the imaginative heritage of feudalism, Whitman declared, they must transpose the democratic concept "far beyond Politics, into the regions of taste." Though Whitman thus conceived of literature as a discourse richer than ideological statement, he also judged its entire texture and values to be conditioned by the nature of its political axioms. An integral factor in the imagination, therefore, would be the political creed which nurtured it, even though the explicit verbal respect paid to such a creed might be small indeed. As out of the feudalism had filtered the aesthetic tones and stresses of chivalric literature, so in republican America an indigenous utterance could not evade the aesthetic realignment implicit in its new ideological base.

It was on this assumption that Whitman reiterated his concern for a "school of live writing . . . consistent with the free spirit of this age, and with the American truths of politics." Such a school, he believed with Barlow and Irving and Higginson, would involve such revaluations as that of the traditional concepts of glory; it would involve reporting "all heroism from an American point of view." Indeed, almost everything that had been written in other lands, Whitman said in *Democratic Vistas,* "needs to be rewritten, re-sung, re-stated, in terms consistent with the institution of these States, and to come in range and obedient uniformity with them." From all the social and political worlds which history had evolved, the "democratic personality" seemed to him the finest flower, and, tried by its standards, all ultramarine forerunners seemed to be as dead ashes. Yet this revaluation of history by the standard of the "democratic personality" would be best achieved, he apparently thought, by indirection. The poet is no moralizer, the 1855 Preface declared, but "knows the soul." To become the oracle of the democratic genius the poet must employ, above all, those simple, uncalculated strokes for which his experience in a democratic society had uniquely equipped his pen.

Whitman did not entirely commit the American poet, however, to such uncalculated strokes. The core of the American author's presuppositions, he repeatedly declared, is the "great Idea" or the "tremendous Idea" of democratic equality; and of this Idea the sacerdotal poet is to be the avowed exponent. Out of "adherence to the good old cause," to that which "promulges liberty, justice, the cause of the people as against infidels and tyrants," Whitman said again, is born that imaginative vigor which should characterize the American literatus. From this premise he reflected in his earlier writings the equalitarianism of the radical wing of the Democratic Party of the 1840's. As the Idea led him on into the Free Soil Party and through the hospitals of the Federal armies, it inevitably took on the richer associations which the trial of experience brings to concept: it evolved from hatred of tyranny into a more positive definition of democratic freedom. To the literary masters, he declared in the 1855 Preface, the "grand idea" of liberty had been indispensable; they had been its voice and had sustained it. In *Democratic Vistas* a decade and a half later, however, he interpreted the idea not so much in terms of revolutionary struggle as of Personalism—a recognition of "that Something a man is, . . . standing apart from all else, divine in his own right . . . , sole and untouchable by any canons of authority." Accordingly he enlarged the American poet's function beyond that of "cheering slaves"; they were to illustrate the doctrine of "perfect individualism," of "independent separatism," which holds that "man, properly train'd in sanest, highest freedom, may and must become a law, and series of laws, unto himself." This Personalism came to be for Whitman the "high façade" of the democratic structure which the work of the autochthonous bard must at least implicitly support.

In the rise of democracy and in the upward spiral of human welfare Whitman also counted Science a prime agent, and hence he supposed that the American literatus must acknowledge its method and achievements among his "presuppositions"—indeed that the "true use for the imaginative faculty of modern times is to give ultimate vivification to facts, to science, and to common lives, endowing them with glows and glories and final illustriousness which belong to every real thing." For was not the American imagination, he asked, an integral factor in the New World brain whose obligation it was to "formulate the Modern"? In the "demonstrable," he argued, is to be found all the beauty hitherto attributed to the "mythical," and hence the laws of exact science afford encouragement to rather than a check on the imagination and, indeed, underlie the structure of all perfect poems.

With this insistence on the presupposition of the demonstrable and real, Whitman in effect was charging the American poet to become, somewhat parodoxically, the mythmaker of positivism. For him as for his young contemporary Charles Godfrey Leland, science and democracy and the real formed a trinity more worthy of reverence than that worshipped by the Puritans. Hence, though he retained the Puritan vision of America as the nation which betokens man's most blissful estate, he modulated the Song of Zion to the joyous exaltation of "the present and the real." The science which had dispelled the indigenous gloom of Puritanism from the national literature seemed to him also to have displaced the militaristic and amorous stereotypes of the old romance. Abjuring both Puritanism and romance, Whitman's poet of the modern would celebrate a sane comradeship which, at first exemplified in America, would at last unite all humanity. That the Muse would migrate from Old World romance to this "fresher, busier sphere" of the real, Whitman, like many of his eighteenth-century predecessors, had no doubt; but more particularized than theirs was his vision of this "illustrious emigre" in the cisatlantic scene, "install'd amid the kitchen ware" and undismayed by shrill steam whistles and gasometers and artificial fertilizers. The Muse of the Modern, he was prompted to remark by the Exposition of 1871, with richer themes than those of the past, would "teach the average man the glory of his daily walk and trade"—a walk in the real world made more humane by the twin-forces of democracy and science.

Since Whitman thought that the poet of the Modern would supplant the priest, he attempted to convey the veneration due this oracle of science and democracy by resorting to established religious terminology and imagery. In this vocabulary the American poet becomes the "divine literatus," the "sacerdotal bard"; he "withholds by his steady faith" the "time straying toward infidelity"; he is the son begotten by the "fatherstuff" of science, and his greatness is "the exuding of the greatness of the father"; he will "write the evangel-poem of comrades and of love"; he will recognize "the divinity of sex." Now that appropriate political and material foundations had been established under these States, Whitman declared in *Democratic Vistas,* the third stage had arrived: that of "a sublime and serious Religious Democracy" which, promulgated by a genuine national utterance, would reconstruct society.

Though Whitman found little evidence of this Religious Democracy in the literature of the post-bellum years, he continued to believe that American poetry must serve a religious function, and that, in order to project the presuppositions of Science and Democracy even beyond the realm of taste into the "unconscious blood," it must like the classic epics discover its appropriate symbols and myths. At times he thought the most inclusive personification of the New World genius might be a figure like Emerson's "colossal youth." America often impressed him as an "athletic Democracy" whose future poets—if scarcely "a brood of Titans," as Emerson had hoped—would at least be "a new brood, native, athletic, continental." Their autochthonous utterance would be "an athletic and defiant literature," replete with "gristle and beards, and broad breasts, and space and ruggedness and nonchalance that the souls of the people love." Of this muscular and creative America Whitman could find no fitter emblem than the broad-axe, the instrument which, unlike the headman's axe of the Old World, bequeathed not death but rather the manifold structures of an expansive yet peaceful culture.

As the poet of woman as well as of man, as the proponent of her equal place in Democracy, however, Whitman conjoined (and indeed superseded) the athletic image of the national genius with the maternal. In his own attempts to set the pattern for "one modern, native all-surrounding song," his notes show, he early resolved to "bring in the idea of Mother—the idea of the mother with numerous children— all great and small, old and young, equal in her eyes—as the identity of America." But the Mother in these years was more than a mere unifying political symbol: "What the mother, our continent, in reference to humanity, finally means . . . is *Individuality* strong and superb, for broadest average use. . . ." In the ante-bellum decade Whitman thought of this federal Mother as majestic, "seated with more than antique grace, calm, just, indulgent to her brood of children." Yet after the Civil War she recurrently became for him the "dread" Mother; evolving into a transcendent figure, she became the symbol of a "mystical Union" which adumbrated "immortal reality" itself; she loomed as the matrix of the "giant babes" who would create the "freer, vast, electric world, to be constructed here." Incessant within her Whitman could foresee bibles and saviours. As "Protectress absolute" in the 1870's she appeared to him as "generous as God": in her all goods are owned, and without her nothing is secure.

With such associations as those attaching to the "dread Mother" did Whitman seek to transpose the presuppositions of the transcendental Union into an imaginative correlative. Conceiving the grandest office of the literary imagination to be thus mythical and sacerdotal and hence unifying, Whitman was consistently cool to the partial designs and restricted focus of local color. The American bard shall "not be for the eastern states more than the western or the northern states more than the southern," he declared in his 1855 Preface. When the vogue of local color captured the interest of most American writers a generation later, he continued to accord precedence to the national over the *genius loci*. This literary fashion, he feared, had a "deplorable tendency toward the *outré*"; it inclined to treat "the exceptional, the diseased," neglecting the generous and heroic quality central in the national character, and hence was "not true, not American in the deep sense at all." The Good-Nature, Decorum, and Intelligence which seemed to him uniquely dominant in American manhood he could not find appropriately represented in tales which stressed regional peculiarities. For the element most needed in America and hence in American writing of his day, he concluded, was a "moral identity" which would fuse all races and far localities into the completest democracy through its hold on men's hearts and beliefs. Fear of "conflicting and irreconcilable interiors" haunted him, he confessed, even after the Union victory. Accordingly "the tap-root of National Literature" became for him the imaginative fusion of the American people into a moral and religious unity—into what he called "Ensemble."

For all his dicta regarding sectional impartiality in national literature, however, and for all his insistence that the poet effuse "what is universal, native, common to all," Whitman could not divest himself of the long-established tradition of looking to the West as the index to the future national character. Like Thoreau, he saw the great Idea impelling America to become "one all-embracing West." Though he told Traubel that "the country out there is my own country," his affection for it was more than personal; and though in his last Western trip he extolled it to trans-Allegheny audiences, his tributes were grounded in considerations more solid than that of satisfying the provincial pride of his listeners. Like the Transcendentalists, he saw in Western expansiveness the antidote to the cramped and servile literary habits that had enervated American writing and betrayed the genius of the New World. Accordingly, indifferent to mere local color quaintness in the region, he remarked instead the phenomena which would symbolically serve the great Idea. The matchless prairies, he thought, might be "fused in the alembic of a perfect poem . . . entirely western, fresh and limitless—altogether our own, without a trace or taste of Europe's soil, reminiscence, technical letter or spirit." It was they which, above all, presaged the character of future Americans—of "vast-spread average men" like Lincoln and Grant, who combined the practical and the ideal in a New World heroism. Farther west in the "elemental abandon" of chasm, gorge, and misty peaks he felt that he had found the law of his own poems and hence of a large, autochthonous American utterance. Instinct with more terror and beauty than Old World ruins, the "non-utilitarian piles" of the Rockies seemed to him to offer primal nurture not only for the poetry and painting and oratory but even for the metaphysics and music suitable to the New World.

Thus by construing the West symbolically and by defining American literature in terms of attitudes and presuppositions rather than of milieu, Whitman aligned himself with the native critical tradition of Barlow and Cooper. Hence so long as the democratic presuppositions were sound, the setting and theme seemed to him of little consequence. If American objects and occupations and locales abound in his poems and his critical dicta, they do so as counterparts and correlatives of the great Idea. His long catalogues comprehending the behavior and habits of artisans were designed, he told Traubel, "to give them [American laborers] a voice in literature." Perhaps in his 1855 Preface he stated once and for all his concern that American literature transmit the "moral identity" of the nation rather than the mere beauty and wonder of its natural phenomena:

> The land and sea, the animals fishes and birds, the sky of heaven and the orbs, the forests mountains and rivers, are not small themes . . . but folks expect of the poet to indicate more than the beauty and dignity which always attach to dumb real objects . . . they expect him to indicate the path between reality and their souls.

Beyond Chauvinism

To isolate Whitman's proposals for a national literature without considering his qualified concept of nationality is to conclude, as many have done, that the half century of his critical endeavor was little more than a naïve and protracted demand for a chauvinistic utterance of the rawest spread-eagle democracy. Yet Whitman was increasingly careful to explore and define the implications of his nationalistic dicta; and indeed the reservations and delimitations by which he sought to discourage immature nationalism both in life and letters constitute as cogent a phase of his criticism as his more positive doctrines. A confirmed Hegelian, he regarded his country as a stage of cultural evolution and not as a perfected society; and since evolution seemed to him the rule in verse as in nature, he never doubted that the future would give birth to a literature more nearly reflecting the Ideal than that of his own democratic America. Like E. T. Channing, he assumed that the universal could be perceived only through the particu-

lar, that indigenous lights and shades uniquely derived from epoch
and milieu must serve at once as the medium and the veil to the All.
Out of these mutable materials of nationality the literary imagination
was obliged to "glean eidólons," which, he thought, accumulating and
narrowing through the centuries into "higher pinnacles," would point
to the ultimate reality.

The America which Whitman wished the divine literatus to comprehend was not a static terminus but a moment of cultural force, as
it were, at once the fullest repository of the past and the most acute
index to the eidólons "Sweeping the present to the infinite future." As
to the veneration he held for all that antecedent cultures had "wafted
hither" Whitman left no doubt, for throughout a half century he reiterated in varied figures the debt of the New World to the "infinite
greatness" of the past: America is the "heir ship and heiress ship of
the world"; hence the American poet will "enclose old and new."
Could there not be a poet in America, he asked, who, reflecting *"this
age,* and so all ages," would thus enclose more than had either Homer
or Shakespeare?

Lavish in tributes to the greatness of past masters in their own right,
Whitman further acknowledged that in stamping this age the American literatus could no more separate himself from the Old World
"language-shapers" than a son from the father. The New World writer
is to follow and obey as well as lead and command, he wrote in the
"Song of the Exposition"; he is "not to create only, or found only,/
But to bring perhaps from afar what is already founded." Clearly
Whitman was never an exponent of that Know Nothing nationalism
which, placing a tariff on cultural commerce, would repudiate America's debts to other lands and other peoples; and of these "many debts
incalculable" the chiefest he pronounced to be that to "old poems."
Nor would he align himself with those narrow nationalists who so
frequently in the ante-bellum decades sought to restrict American writers to cisatlantic landscapes and persons and situations. The "true use
of precedents," he wrote Emerson, would involve the use of foreign-
born as well as home-born materials—all to be pertinent to the bodies
and souls of men everywhere. Indeed, Whitman's work in its full
context attests his own adherence to the principle which he set down

for himself in his early notes: *"Caution*—Not to blaart constantly for *Native American* models, literature, etc., and bluster out 'nothing foreign.'"

Inevitably from the "great shadowy groups gathering around" from the past Whitman adjudged some to be more consonant than others with the genius of America. Nourished in his critical principles, like the Transcendentalists, by the liberating romanticism of recent German philosophy, he supposed that Hegel, Fichte, Schelling, and Kant had bolstered Democracy by the soundest postulates and hence were the most congenial aliment for the American mind. Hegel's doctrine of the unfoldings of "Creative thought" through history, he explained in *Specimen Days* and in *Democratic Vistas,* is an especially fitting presupposition for the American literatus. Likewise, the "huge English flow, so sweet, so undeniable, has done incalculable good here," he wrote Emerson; but, with all his generous praise, he could but observe that by reason of the power of kindred race and language the "flow" had frequently engulfed the small, clear stream of cisatlantic letters. Especially perilous to the American imagination seemed Shakespeare, "luxuriant as the sun" though he was. To be sure, Whitman could discover in the comedies and histories democratic points of view emerging, but the passing decades scarcely tempered his fear that the republican mind would absorb and transmit the feudal temper of many of the Shakespearean heroes.

If Whitman read Scott, too, on a level too exclusively political, he accepted his influence in America far more equably than did Mark Twain. Indeed, Scott had permeated him through and through and was at the roots of *Leaves of Grass,* he admitted to Traubel. Equally ambivalent in influence was Tennyson, in whom he found intermingling a sophistication and sweetness that represented the worst and best of England. Reflecting or reading at times with a less literal mind, however, he perceived that even in the old Greek and Roman sources lay the "seed stuff of our American liberty," that in the Elizabethan period could be heard the "proud modern definitions of democracy." Preluding America, acting as her "entrance porch," he wrote, are the "old chants": the Biblic books, Hindu and Homeric epics, and many "singing birds." From Egyptian priests through Tennyson—Whitman, despite frequent misgivings, besought America "with courteous hand" to accept them all.

Yet Whitman was more concerned over the destination than the origins of this America which, culturally considered, seemed to him to be but the movement of "a projectile form'd, impell'd, passing a certain line." Following a well-established critical tradition inaugurated by Duché and Crèvecoeur in the 1770's, he found more substance for American letters in the happy prospect than in "the dark unfathom'd retrospect." Asia and Europe, he declared, have sung of man as he has been; America is to sing of man as he is and is to be. Cultural repository of the past though the New World might be, it seemed to him to hold even greater purport as the instrument through which creative thought would unfold the future: "For the scheme's culmination, its thought and its reality,/ For these (not for thyself) thou hast arrived./ . . . thou too by pathways broad and new,/ To the ideal tendest." The America of his time seemed to him "the promise and reliance of the future," as in each historic period he thought one land is destined to be. Thus, fusing the nineteenth-century conviction of Manifest Destiny and the eighteenth-century concept of America as the crown of civilization, Whitman charged the native literatus to pass "in compassion and determination around the whole earth" and to give his "salut au monde."

In celebrating the present, the American bard might best sing of science and the modern, Whitman thought, and of Identity, of "One's Self—a simple, separate person." But for the "grander future," the poet must suggest a more harmonious state when the promise of the whole human race would be fulfilled. Two centuries earlier the Puritans had envisioned American saints singing the songs of the New Zion and uniting all nations in God. Whitman, under the more secular influence of the Transcendentalists, substituted Nature for Zion as the ultimate condition and measure of blessedness. He saw the "genius of the modern, child of the real and ideal,/ Clearing the ground for broad humanity" and ushering in a "new society . . . proportionate to Nature." To "tally" this Nature, Whitman both invoked and chanted "Adamic songs" appropriate to "the new garden of the West" —a garden scarcely consonant with the Eden of Puritan tradition. For here unharassed by a sense of sin, the new race would be blessed by an inner harmony as serene as their garden home and would find mere living a sufficient end in itself. But in his more comprehensive idea of Nature Whitman progressed beyond this innocent hedonism to the "towering superaddition" of conscience and intuition, which Emerson described in "Nature" as Spirit. Only on the spiritual heights of such an estimate of Nature, Whitman concluded in *Democratic Vistas,* is to be found the tonic atmosphere requisite to invigorate and sustain the prophetic voice of the New World:

> In the prophetic literature of these States . . . Nature, true Nature, and the true idea of Nature, long absent, must, above all, become fully restored, enlarged, and must furnish the pervading atmosphere to poems, and the test of all high literary and esthetic compositions.

In his prophetic design for an American literature Whitman thus invoked not merely the modes and assumptions of the Enlightenment and of Positivism but those of cultural primitivism, Transcendentalism, and the New Zion as well. Indeed, beyond science and democracy, whose priests he so often declared the ideal New World literats to be, he postulated a transcendent and primal Being to the comprehension of which "the Modern" could be but instrumental. His own chants were undertaken, he wrote, so that his comrades might share with him "two greatnesses, and a third one rising inclusive and more resplendent,/ The greatness of Love and Democracy, and the greatness of Religion." To feed worthily the soul of man, Whitman concluded, "immenser" poets must arise in America and "make great poems of death" so that man could confront time and space without fear. The highest dedication of native poets was therefore to be made to the transcendent—to the expression and support of the eternal rather than the temporal. Moreover, as democratic Personalism may be translated into this Religiousness, so the Mother (symbol of the Union on the political plane) is at last transformed by him who chants the Square Deific into "Santa Spirita, breather, life,/ Beyond the light, lighter than light." As the Mother bound together by affection her equal brood of States, so the Santa Spirita would in a larger mystical union bind all humanity into one.

Nationality was clearly, therefore, not the ultimate determinant and end in Whitman's literary principles or practice; and if its image at

times seems dominant in his prescriptions, it is only that he felt
obliged to linger over certain neglected native resources rather than
to reiterate the more inclusive critical doctrines, which he supposed
to be so well established as to need little amplification from his pen.
The diversities of nations he saw finally converging in one human
family; and it was the universal rather than the contingent trait, he
wrote to Emerson, that must be the ultimate focus of American writing. "All must have reference to the ensemble of the world, and the
compact truth of the world," he asserted in enumerating tests for the
"perfect literats for America." And these tests, he explained further in
his unpublished essay "Criticism," lie beyond the rules of literary
fashions; they reside rather in ocean, daylight, and simple human passions.

Even the autochthonous opening tones of the 1855 Preface are resolved in its concluding paragraphs on a universal note. The greatest
poet must "flood himself with the immediate age" and "attract his
own land body and soul to himself," Whitman said; but through these
floods and attractions, he added, was to be "opened the eternity which
gives similitude to all periods and locations . . . and which is the bond
of time." The very paradoxical instinct of American standards, he
concluded, was among other questions to ask of the literary work: does
it answer universal needs? With consistent if not conscious projection
of this principle he later conceived of the bardic Answerer, who with
a moral imagination which reaches beyond his own time and place,
"settles justice, reality, immortality." And closely affined to the Answerer as Whitman's supreme literatus is the Mystic Trumpeter, whose
highest strains are "Hymns to the universal God from universal man—
all joy!"

The Contemporary Appraisal

Of the long and heated controversy over Whitman's right to be called
a man of letters there are numerous records and analyses. Among the
many issues of that controversy only one aspect is here relevant: the
contemporary appraisal of Whitman's Americanism. For not only as
an arch-proponent of a New World literature but also as an avowed
exemplar of poets to come, Whitman more than any other American

literary figure of his century compelled emphatic assents and demur-
rers; and in this flood of comment the crosscurrents of nationalistic
literary sentiment may be discerned with especial clarity. Such crosscurrents may be most readily detected in those among his critics who
before the appearance of the *Leaves* had advocated some principle of
national literature, or who judged him not primarily by aesthetic criteria but in relation to some concept of America.

Neither adherents nor detractors came predictably from well-defined
classes or sections. As to his stature not only was New England divided, but members of coteries therein displayed among themselves
varied degrees of cordiality toward him; in the so-called genteel tradition outside New England he was both acclaimed and derided; ecclesi-
astical critics both hailed and damned him; and in Southern and
Western journals he appeared as both barbarian and prophet. His pretentions to interpret the national character and destiny produced the
greatest dismay and the bitterest antagonism, however, among those
who inclined to accept Lowell's as the orthodox literary creed for
American letters. American writers, Lowell had reiterated in the 1840's,
should aspire toward a "natural" rather than a national literature; but
from the record of his specific appraisals of native works this "natural"
literature oddly emerged as one pervaded by a New England ethos
and temper and aligned with the accepted forms of English literary
tradition. It is not surprising, therefore, that Lowell in Trowbridge's
presence should have compared Whitman to a grocery "with very
common goods inside," or that he should have attempted to chill
young Norton's admiration for and imitation of *Leaves of Grass* by
writing him that "the kind of thing you describe won't do. When a
man aims at originality he acknowledges himself consciously *un*original."

It was perhaps T. W. Higginson, however, who in the generation
after the Civil War most persistently tried Whitman's brand of nationality by the New England tradition and pronounced it a fraud.
Higginson's explicit standards were "taste" and "absolute righteousness." Holding that the laws of art were above time and nations, he advocated a national literature which should marry universal form (to be
derived from foreign models) to a "sublimated Puritanism"! Whitman's renunciation of both aesthetic and Puritan absolutes, therefore,

could issue only in Higginson's curt dismissal: "It is no discredit to Walt Whitman that he wrote *Leaves of Grass,* only that he did not burn it afterwards." Whitman does not combine the "cosmopolitan culture and indigenous strength" required in American letters, Higginson declared in a series of letters to Burroughs in 1868. Moreover, in looking to the West for the expression of the American Genius, Whitman seemed to him to be relying on a "retarded" region whose uncouthness would not permit that union of "native force and high polish" which he insistently demanded of American works. In the light of such premises it is not surprising that Higginson should have been able to see in Whitman nothing more than a vocal Buffalo Bill whose democracy was as trite as Fourth of July orations. In Higginson's *The New World and the New Book* (1891) Whitman had no place!

More vehement than Higginson in attacking Whitman's refusal to accept the Puritan ethic as the foundation of the national character was Josiah Gilbert Holland, whose poems Lowell praised as being replete with New England flavor. As editor of *Scribner's Monthly* and as a major arbiter of American literary taste in the 1870's, Holland foresaw a day when Whittier, Holmes, and Stowe would constitute the fountainhead of a national literature and when America "will have ceased discussing Poe and Thoreau and Walt Whitman." "It is at least pure" and free from the "fleshly element," he said of the work of these "hearty and homely singers of this blessed early time." In contrast, Whitman appeared to him to be a mere literary eccentric who should not have and would not have for long either readers or disciples. To support such judgments Holland found a strong critical ally in the currently esteemed E. P. Whipple, who also with New England piety traced the central impulse in American literature to Lowell, Whittier, Julia Ward Howe, and Holmes by reason of "the sure emphasis they all lay on the ethical sentiment." Like Holland, Whipple relegated Thoreau to a limbo of eccentricity and judged Whitman to be nothing more than an innovator who would soon pay the penalty of unfounded revolt. Such measured terms of disapproval, however, could scarcely satisfy Holland's animus against Whitman, whose poetry seemed to him to be "a monster or a bastard . . . [which] will have no progeny."

Unable to share this New England moralistic repudiation of Whitman, other post-bellum critics rather challenged his claim to be the authentic voice of popular sentiments and manners. Across the country many authors concurred in Aldrich's charge that Whitman was by no means a poet "for the *People*" but rather a charlatan whose affectations could be pleasing only to a minority in his own day and could become only a museum curiosity in the years to come. Even in the rugged West the *Overland* professed itself unable to accept as national poetry the work of an indolent outsider who ignored the most vitally characteristic elements of middle-class life and who touched "no note that penetrated to the heart of American feeling." And here, too, the Eastern-born novelist and dramatist Edgar Fawcett branded Whitman's "chaotic lawlessness" as spurious Americanism and spurious democracy, the affectation and masquerade of a Westerner robed like a British harper and chanting eloquent passages of Carlyle and Emerson.

Conspicuous in these attacks on the authenticity of Whitman's Americanism was the charge that in effect he had betrayed his countrymen by giving substance to the European predisposition to view Americans as barbarians. The unwillingness of the English in particular to look for " 'The real American' among those who have made America what it is . . . , and who are the product of generations of American breeding," formed one of the main themes of Richard Grant White's *The Fate of Mansfield Humphreys* (1884). To his fictional Lord Toppingham and Lady Verifier, who long for a literature "peculiarly American" and accordingly praise "dear Walt Whitman" as voicing the aspirations of the people, White's rejoinder is that "dear Walt" is contemned by the plain people and is cherished only by dilettanti and "literary *bric-a-brac* hunters of the intellectual world."

The premise on which such critics as Fawcett and White pretended to repudiate Whitman as a national spokesman was that he had severed the tradition of English culture on which they supposed America, as a dominantly Anglo-Saxon country, must rely for sustenance in both manners and art. What they might better have conceded was that their critical postulates derived not so much from the broad scope of English tradition as from an Augustan predisposition toward polite society and hence toward polite literature. If these cisatlantic Augustans had no admiration for Whitman, they had scarcely more for Chaucer, Scott, or Coleridge—or, for that matter, for Thoreau, who so frequently appears linked to Whitman as an "eccentric." What they actually renounced in Whitman was not his revolt against tradition but his extension of tradition to include all the "old chants" and his extension of "culture" to include the myths of all peoples and the primary discipline of Nature as well as the secondary discipline of art. The America to which they claimed Whitman to be false was, in fact, the indoor America of "sublimated Puritanism" on the one hand or of social gentility on the other. Tested by the American out-of-doors, this culture of "saloons" (the eighteenth-century salons) seemed to Whitman to be compounded of an ennui, persiflage, and doubt not consonant with the national mind or the cultivation of Personalism. He could not believe that either the Puritan code or Augustan cosmopolitanism embraced the great humane tradition and prospect which he aspired to express.

It was as the disciple of such a cosmopolitan standard of civilization, however, that young Henry James admonished Whitman that if he wished to be "adopted as a national poet," he had better "respect the public . . . for it has taste. . . . This democratic, liberty-loving, American populace, this stern and war-tried people, is a great civilizer. It is devoted to refinement." To James in 1865 Whitman seemed to misrepresent the national ideal by being "careless, inelegant, and ignorant" and to be too much preoccupied with himself rather than to be wholly possessed by the idea of his country's greatness, as the genuinely national poet must be. Soon after James's words were written, young Howells also, with an aversion to Romanticism which allowed him to assign pre-eminence to the "divine Jane" Austen over Shakespeare, Scott, Thackeray, and Hawthorne, confessed himself "tired . . . of the whole Whitman business" and remarked that he and James had just settled the "true principles of literary art." These principles James later expanded sufficiently, if Edith Wharton's testimony can be trusted, to permit him to pronounce Whitman the greatest of American poets; but Howells at the end of Whitman's life was still berating those English critics who considered Whitman the exemplar of that peculiar American literature which they had long awaited. America can have no distinctive literature because at "this stage" all the forms have been invented, Howells retorted, and Whitman is only exhausting the resources of formlessness! Yet he conceded that Whitman might represent America in one of its aspects—its youthful vigor and independence—though he reckoned Longfellow equally representative of a country whose people in general seemed to him averse to having a spade in the parlor.

A similar dismay at the pleasure of Old World critics in "the most lawless freaks of New World literature" and a similar preference for an American literature which should depict the parlor rather than the factory and fields also lay behind Holmes's final estimate of Whitman in *Over the Teacups* (1891). Admitting that through his new idiom and his uncompromising democracy Whitman had a better claim than Emerson to be "considered as the creator of a truly American, self-governed, self-centered, absolutely independent style of thinking and writing," Holmes nevertheless feared that such a literary ideal would yield the nation at last a host of literary pretenders like the freakish merchant "Lord" Timothy Dexter. If literary independence "means dispensing with punctuation, coining words at will, self-revelation unrestrained by a sense of what is decorous, declamations in which everything is glorified without being idealized," Holmes confessed, then "I shrink from a lawless independence to which all the virile energy and trampling audacity of Mr. Whitman fail to reconcile me."

More inclined than Holmes and Howells to accept an expansive romanticism in American letters, Bayard Taylor for a time regarded with less apprehension than they the indecorous extremes to which Whitman's nationalism might lead. Among the literary types of mid-century New York which he depicted in *John Godfrey's Fortunes* (1864), Taylor created one Smithers, whose prescription for native themes was evidently intended as a burlesque of Whitman: "Take the fireman, in his red flannel shirt, . . . the clam-fisher, . . . the wood-chopper,—the street-sweeper: where will you find anything more heroic? . . . A strong-backed long-shore-man, with his hairy and sunburnt arms, and the tobacco-juice in the corners of his mouth, is worth all your saints!" Moreover, Smithers had exemplified his Whitmanian literary doctrines in *"Edda of the Present,* an heroic, muscular poem, in irregular metre." Such amiable if pointed strictures Taylor voiced again in *The Echo Club,* papers based on the meetings of a small literary group in New York in the 1850's—a group whose members no doubt had actually debated whether Whitman were "half-bowery-boy, half-Emersonian," and whether he needed "a truer sense of art." Whatever Taylor's precise position may have been on such questions, the recurrent zest of his jibes at Whitman points to his growing doubt that the author of *Leaves of Grass* was the model or prophet of a worthy national literature.

Though "sublimated Puritanism" and aesthetic decorum thus formed major bases of opposition to Whitman, the categories of approval are not so readily fixed. Sentimental Fanny Fern, provincial Joel Chandler Harris, pious Moncure Conway, and individualistic Henry Thoreau, diverse though they were in principles and temper, could at least with Emerson express a common measure of gratitude for something "indisputably American." In the ante-bellum years Whitman found his most substantial encouragement among the Transcendentalists. Though their early enthusiasm somewhat paled in the ensuing years, they never lost sight of his broadly indigenous quality merely through narrow canons of Puritanism or taste. During the Civil War Emerson recorded his gratitude for Whitman's "service to American literature in the Appalachian enlargement of his outline and treatment"; and a few years later in Boston he added a special tribute to the prose, asserting that he and Alcott were among the many who looked to Whitman "to speak the profounder message of our democracy." In these years Whitman seemed to Alcott "Great grand Walt. . . . Another American beside Thoreau and Emerson." In the 1880's Alcott suspected, however, that Whitman was too representative—too brawny and broad to be high or deep enough to become "the Bard"; yet he still found him majestic.

Among the perplexities which had always confronted the aspirants for a native literature, none perhaps was more troublesome than that of achieving a style and form which would reconcile autochthonous qualities and established aesthetic principles. To a number of his literary compatriots Whitman seemed for the first time to have pointed the imagination to an idiom commensurate with the New World temper yet not radically disjoined from that of the old chants and fables—or, as the journalist William Swinton said in introducing the poet to Sumner, to have given "America something genuinely her own

—something that is robust while full of feeling and idiomatic while universal." For such authors Whitman became, in Trowbridge's words, a "great original force in our literature" by using Nature's freedom as a release from artificial and irrelevant forms. Thus Lanier, through "sober comparison," found *Leaves of Grass* "worth at least a million of Among My Books and Atalanta in Calydon" because in the latter two he "could not find anything which has not been much better said before; but Leaves of Grass was a real refreshment to me,— like rude salt spray in your face." This native "refreshment," indeed, could be felt by authors as diverse as the restless expatriate Lafcadio Hearn and the earnest moralist Sam Walter Foss. Hearing in Whitman's "Titanic voice" the tones of future singers, Hearn besought honor for his priesthood in the cause of poetical liberty. And in Foss's opinion the *Leaves* marked "a new era in American literature, and is to stand out more and more prominently, as time advances, as the distinctively American book."

It was Whitman's reflection of hitherto neglected patterns of American folkways and attitudes, however, that brought him an even larger measure of acceptance as the prophet of an autochthonous literature. Charles Eliot Norton was impressed by that "mixture of Yankee transcendentalism and New York rowdyism" which seemed to stamp the *Leaves of Grass* as indubitably American, though he confided to Lowell that within its "great stretches of imagination" there were passages so coarse that he could not sanction it as a national literary model. Yet whatever Whitman's countrymen might feel about his iconoclasm and coarseness, argued Stedman in his influential evaluation of American poetry in 1881, his minute knowledge and healthy treatment of outdoor nature and American landscape had given him claims to a major position among those who had caught the distinctive flavor of the national scene. His poetry has, whatever else, the *"American* note," he added in 1888 in sending his "love and constant honor to the grand old bard."

Whitman's emphasis on the "tremendous Idea" of democracy, however, more than any other aspect of his work not only caught the imagination of young progressives but also tended to cancel out the moral and aesthetic reservations of many who inclined toward conservatism. "Democracy had at length its epic," the humanitarian

Moncure Conway ecstatically concluded on reading one of the first copies of the *Leaves*. The little book seemed to him "prophetic of the good time coming when the vulgar herd should be transformed into noblemen"; indeed, he added later, in terms that must have pleased Whitman, it seemed "the Genesis of an American Bible."

In the Midwest young Edgar Lee Masters felt the religious sweep of Whitman's "conception of America as the field of a new art and music in which the people would be celebrated instead of kings; and the liberty of Jefferson should be sung until it permeated the entire popular heart." Through Whitman, he asserted in his later years, he had looked forward "to a republic in which equality and fraternity should bind all hearts with a culture of that profound nature which enabled an Athenian audience to . . . follow with appreciative delight a tragedy by Sophocles. In that America Whitman would be the Hesiod and someone yet to arise the Homer." Farther west in California the critic William Sloane Kennedy had already found similar Greek analogies expressive of his own veneration for Whitman as a democratic poet: "We are Greek-Hindoo in genius," he said of Americans, "and Whitman and Emerson are our two Greek-Hindoo poets." New World poetry, he explained, would reproduce many of the naïve traits of the morning-time of the Old World; and indeed the American milieu seemed already to be producing "a race of spiritualized Athenians—an ethereal, volatile, laughter-loving people." Of this new race Whitman was the voice, said Kennedy; for scores of democracies he would be the textbook.

It was John Burroughs, however, who during Whitman's lifetime most sensitively perceived and expounded the direction and scope of the poet's Americanism. The extent of Burroughs' affinity is perhaps best suggested by the fact that occasionally his name was subscribed to Whitman's own material when the strategy of publication seemed to demand it. With a mind already shaped by the prior influence of Transcendentalism, Burroughs saw in Whitman not so much a prophetic nationalist as a seer of that Nature by which, in turn, America was to be measured. "I consider that America is illustrated in him," Burroughs wrote in 1867, perhaps with Whitman's aid; "and that Democracy, as now launched forth upon its many-vortexed experiment . . . is embodied, and for the first time in Poetry . . . in him." Yet the first impact of the *Leaves* on him in 1861, he adds, was not nationalistic: it made the same impression on his "moral consciousness" as did actual Nature. Hence the inexorable standard for judging Whitman must be "absolute Nature," and the critical question for American letters is not whether Whitman "can stand the test of the academy, but whether the academy can stand his tests."

From these premises, firmly aligned as they were with the structure of Whitman's criticism, Burroughs undertook numerous sorties against the entrenched debilities of the national literature as Whitman had described them. Neither America nor her literature, he asserted, could graft on "hardy Western stock the sickly and decayed standards of the expiring feudal world." The pursuit of beauty as an end in itself, the unwillingness to "enter into them [subjects] through their blood, their sexuality, and manliness," seemed to Burroughs, as to Whitman, to have made of American authors "a class of jugglers" and "swarms of poetlings"—a sickly breed given over to "smartness" in sad contrast with the simple manhood which characterized the "shaggy old antique masters." Genius and culture were not enough, said Burroughs; "Literature dies with the decay of the *un*-literary element." Beauty in America must be conceived, he said with Emerson and Whitman, as "the flower of necessity. . . . Woe to any artist who disengages beauty from the wide background of rudeness, darkness, and strength—and disengages her from absolute Nature."

Because Whitman did not attempt to create "beauty without the lion" and to divest it of its antecedents in the necessary and homely life of the States, because he did not flinch from reflecting a "sane sensuality," Burroughs honored him as the autochthonous and prophetic voice of the New World. Whitman seemed to him to be the needed counteragent to the "calcerous" tendencies in American life— to that deposit of flint accumulating in the national veins and arteries and hastening the death of the spontaneous and intuitive man. Whitman was not lacking in culture, Burroughs argued in a series of letters to Higginson, but had "the broader culture of real life and things" which had always produced rather than elegant *litterateurs* the "grand, primary bards upon whom a nation can build." By virtue of this culture, embodied in his criticism as well as in his poems, the author of the *Leaves* stood for Burroughs as the first of "a new race of intellectual American law-givers" who might redeem both the manners and the aesthetic perception of the nation from their current vulgarity. In him Burroughs heard the voice of the "time spirit out of which America grew," uttering almost alone "something commensurate with the hopes and prospects of the New World." In *Democratic Vistas* as in the poems he saw a fullness of utterance for his age that Whitman never quite claimed for himself; for here, he wrote to Emma Lazarus, is "the Democratic Spirit fully grown & master of itself & of its environment, . . . & the equal of the towering spirit that made the splendor of the old feudal world."

CHAPTER EIGHT

Nationality Through Region and Locale (1815-1892)

> We have so much country that we have no country at all; and I feel the want of one, every day of my life. This is a sad thing.
>
> NATHANIEL HAWTHORNE, 1854

> 'The North' is a political phrase, 'the Northwest' a technical one; 'the West' is one that means a civilization and an empire, as do (or perhaps I should say rather did) that of 'New England' and 'the South'—to be, I hope, the gainer by the excellencies and the defects of both.
>
> NATHAN SHEPPARD, 1869

The Regional Impulse: Ante-Bellum

At first glance the regional or local impulse in American letters might seem antithetical to the national. Yet most nineteenth-century American authors did not so construe it. During the vogue of romanticism before the Civil War Simms championed a national literature, but he was explicit in pronouncing sectional materials and themes to be the indispensable media for achieving a national utterance. Irving, Hawthorne, and many another who exploited regional legends and lore presumably worked from the same principle in which the narrower focus for the imagination was regarded as the surest guarantee of a cisatlantic flavor. After the war Howells, Garland, Eggleston, Riley and the host of local colorists similarly found no incompatibility in holding at once to a national literary end and local means. Since America's vastness precludes a representative imaginative grasp in one work, they argued, American literature can be national only in the aggregate of distinctive localized works. Against this reconciliation of regional and national literature the decades of the 1850's and the 1890's saw sharp reactions. In the ante-bellum decade regional literature inevitably turned divisive and threatened national unity; in the final decade of the century it was adjudged to have understated the national genius. Whatever its failures, the local or regional principle was so intimately involved with the quest for nationality in American literature that its varied course in the ante-bellum and post-bellum eras and in the major sections of the country must be briefly traced.

The futility of Noah Webster's hope of federalizing the language and literature and, as a consequence, the mind of the new republic, became increasingly patent as the nineteenth century progressed. For though politically a nation, culturally America was a blend of colonialism and indigenous regional diversity. Below the surface of political conviction and economic self-interest which coalesced into the unity of the Constitution lay the variegated stratum of regional manners, traditions, folkways, and sentiments from which the native literary imagination derived most of its themes and stimuli. Two centuries of divergent influences in climate and economy and colonization had issued not only in subnational cultural communities outlined in geographical sections but also in subsectional communities within the boundaries of a state. Even as early as *Greenfield Hill* (1794) Timothy Dwight noted three sets of uniform manners already established in the new nation—those of Virginia, of South Carolina, and of New England; and an obscure contemporary of Dwight's in Savannah observed that the inhabitants of almost every state were distinguished by some peculiarity in speech or behavior and were accordingly stigmatized by such appellations as Yankee and Cracker. Thus not only was Southerner contrasted with New Englander; the Connecticut Yankee could also be distinguished from his Yankee neighbor in Maine as could the Virginian from his Southern neighbor in Georgia. Indeed, during the first half of the century an American seeking a homogeneous culture was likely to turn to the state rather than to the larger section. It was Hawthorne's experience, at least, that he had so much country that he had no country at all, and that in the attempt to make a land with "no limits and no oneness . . . a matter of the heart, everything falls away except one's native State."

To denote these subnational cultural communities which could be made "a matter of the heart" (and of the imagination as well) the terminology in the 1820's and 1830's was varied. For Timothy Flint in Ohio an instinctive affection for some limited portion of the country invested with the associations of home constituted "nationality"; and this *"amor patriae"* he thought Yankees and Southerners possessed to an enviable degree. Something of this "nationality" which Flint assigned to the Southern character John Pendleton Kennedy attributed more narrowly to the Virginian, whose "once peculiar . . . cast of manners" he termed an "old nationalism" worthy of a faithful portrayal before it yielded to "foreign usages." In the Mississippi Valley Benjamin Drake perceived a "region" embodying the same kind of homogeneity that Kennedy called "nationalism." This Valley, he thought, required "the coronal of Backwood's literature"—an utterance which would be distinct from "the lighter and more superficial productions of other regions," and which would be "the result of the political, moral and physical conditions of things by which we are surrounded."

So long as this regional literature, under whatever terminology, involved chiefly the picturesque or humorous depiction of folkways and manners in the mode of Paulding's *The Dutchman's Fireside* (1831) or Kennedy's *Swallow Barn* (1832), it could be accepted as an innocuous and consistent part of the more pretentious designs for a literature expressing the mission and temper of the nation as a whole. But as the ante-bellum decades increasingly revealed a dissident South and an expansive West, fears arose among those of strong nationalistic convictions that the growth of such literature would foster sectional attachments at the expense of loyalty to the federal government. As a consequence, Flint, Kennedy, and other advocates of regional themes and sentiments in the 1830's and 1840's generally felt obliged to offer as a basic premise the assurance that what they proposed was in no sense politically divisive. Undoubtedly "Remarks" like those of the Western literary arbiter Daniel Drake on the "Importance of Promoting Literary and Social Concert, in the Valley of the Mississippi"

(1833) could easily have been construed as a plea for a sectional literature subserving a Western Confederacy had not Drake been careful to explain that such a literary "communion" would help perpetuate the Union by giving it a sound center. Nevertheless, Drake did seek to "encourage western writers . . . and create a western heart"; and in the same decade Daniel Whitaker as editor of the *Southern Rose* likewise espoused for his section a literature which would "breathe a Southern spirit, and sustain a strictly Southern character." Yet the achievement of this "peculiar tone" would not be antithetical to the larger design of American letters, he characteristically added; it was rather the sole and inevitable mode by which Southerners might compose an American literature, for "in a country so extensive as ours" a literature can be indigenous only through themes of a "local character" which reflect the distinctive experience and temper of a section. Southerners especially were anxious that their attempts to create a Southern literature should not be regarded as subversive, and toward this end they introduced the confederate principle, as it were, into the republic of letters. American literature, the Southern *Magnolia* explained in 1841, might be compared to the bow of the covenant and regional literatures to the varying colors of the spectrum which compose the bow and contribute to the harmonious perfection of the whole. Compositions representing the distinctive color of Southern culture, the *Magnolia* emphasized, "do not . . . constitute *sectional* literature, that, [*sic*] is based on prejudice." Simms likewise eschewed a literature "based on prejudice," but he had no fear of the word "sectional." Only works of a distinctive character can form a national literature, he argued, and this character can come only from the *genius loci*. "If we do not make *our* work national," he admonished Southern authors, "it will be because we shall fail in making it *sectional*." For Simms, as for Paul Hamilton Hayne and the Western anthologist W. T. Coggeshall, American literature seemed most appropriately regarded as a "republic of letters"—as a "confederacy of individualities" in which each section would have its equal and distinctive representation.

Most of such ante-bellum apologies for a regional or sectional literature came from those areas in the South and West where a firm literary tradition was still to be established. There was little pleading for a New England literature or for a Hudson River literature, perhaps because the writers of these regions supposed that their work transcended such a limited category and bespoke the dominant national temper. Though they might use local materials, they preferred to think of their work as having to do, as Hawthorne said in *The House of the Seven Gables,* rather "with the clouds over head than with any portion of the actual soil" about them. But not only in the coastal South and in the Mississippi Valley but also in the Southwest and the Far West, literary pride became vocal almost as soon as the region had dimly become an entity. As early as the 1840's Alabama, Mississippi, and Louisiana had coalesced into a "Far South-west" which, the Alabama author Alexander Meek proclaimed, offered high and unique incentives to the poet and novelist. A decade later California journals, conscious of the distinctive society being spawned by the gold rush and impatient with the Eastern habit of lumping all people west of the Alleghenies "into one generality," called for a Pacific literature to catch the unique temper of the Far West. Thus not only a country but even a region like the West might become too vast or heterogeneous to be made, as Hawthorne said, "a matter of the heart."

As the century advanced, the regional units tended to become smaller; and each region in the name of literary independence adapted to its own uses the major arguments which had been used for over a half century in behalf of an American as opposed to an English literature. To the South and West the literary dicta of New York and Boston were likely to seem as autocratic as those of London and the *Edinburgh Review* had seemed to early nationalist critics. But mere literary independence was not the only end in view. To be considered as well were the "Social and Moral Advantages of the Cultivation of Local Literature," as the anthologist W. T. Coggeshall reminded an Ohio audience just before the Civil War. The development of local literature and the individual character of a people, he maintained, were interdependent. Cicero and Milton, in fact, were "sectionalists"!

Despite the insistent attempts to reconcile the sectional with the national in literary interest and principle, sectional literature inevitably became a divisive agent. For if, as Simms remarked, a genuine literature "asserts the character of its people, speaks to their wants and represents their honorable interests," the representative works of a locality or region cannot remain politically innocent when the regional wants and interests are to be resolved through political action. By mid-century it was becoming clear that even to portray the struggle for existence on a rocky New England farm, or the sedate order of a Carolina plantation, or the inflationary atmosphere of the Far West was to sharpen sectional economic issues and struggles. More explicitly by the 1840's Lowell's *Biglow Papers* and Whittier's "Massachusetts to Virginia" were proclaiming the moral superiority of the New England character and polity, and Southern editors were demanding sectional works of their own to counteract the "smuggled literature" which was slipping into Southern firesides from the "incendiary madmen" across the Potomac. As sectional principles intensified into sectional aggressiveness, editorial policies of magazines could scarcely remain uncolored by the bias of the section in which they were formulated. The *Atlantic Monthly,* inaugurated in 1857 as an "exponent of what its conductors believe to be the American idea," was by editorial intention "the new literary and anti-slavery magazine"—an intention which was readily noted and countered in the South. It might well have been American literature as well as political institutions to which Rufus Choate was referring in 1858 when he remarked that "there is an element of regions antagonistic to nationality."

The Regional Impulse: Post-Bellum

The regional impulse which just before the Civil War inclined toward proud and thoroughgoing expressions of sectional cultures was diverted after the conflict toward local color. For this mutation toward the narrow and the picturesque two factors were chiefly responsible: the Union victory and the rise of realism. With the Union victory and the reaffirmation of federal authority, the inclusive utterance of the total mind and interests of a section might well be suspect as an unwarranted resurrection of issues already painfully resolved. To fix on a politically impotent Maine fishing village or New Orleans Creoles or a Tennessee mountain community was the less hazardous literary course. This discreet political temper affianced to the vogue of realism bred local color. Works that had sprung from long immersion in and loyalty to characteristic sectional values (like those of Simms or Hawthorne) yielded to more detached exploitations of provincial novelties. The nation, having painfully won a new political unity, was ready for a relaxed excursion into the quaint and lesser-known corners of the land.

Especially sensitive to possible charges of sectional bias were most of the writers of the New South. Looking back on the efforts of Simms, Hayne, and other ante-bellum writers to create a literature that would breathe a Southern spirit, Joel Chandler Harris pronounced the intrusion of sectionalism to be a "fatality that has pursued and overtaken and destroyed literary effort in the South. The truth might as well be told. We have no Southern literature worthy of the name, because an attempt has been made to give it the peculiarities of sectionalism rather than to impart to it the flavor of localism." The untouched and original materials which he found throughout the South Harris therefore proposed to treat from the "artistic standpoint," by which he meant, presumably, the exclusion of the larger cultural context of the section in favor of the politically neutral world of Br'er Rabbit, where the local and the universal might be happily combined in animal fables. For portraying the Tennessee mountain region Mary Murfree (Charles Egbert Craddock) adopted substantially the same principle. Her stories were "local" and aimed at the delineation of a unique society, she wrote Thomas Bailey Aldrich; they had no political bias and no "sectional purpose to serve."

In repudiating the ante-bellum doctrines of a national or a sectional literature which called for an inclusive reflection of the whole culture, such Southern localists as Harris and Murfree found literary allies among the new realists and regionalists whose literary origins were, for the most part, in the Midwest. In the common principles of their mode they supposed that they had at last found the only valid clue to Americanism in literature. "You are the only verse-builder within my knowledge who has caught the true American spirit and flavor," Harris wrote James Whitcomb Riley, after reading such verses as "The Old Swimmin'-Hole"; and Riley confidently replied that "we are at last coming upon the proper spirit of this voice ['the right scream of the Eagle'] in literature." Many of the figures who dominated American literature in the closing decades of the century—Howells, Eggleston, Garland, Taylor—tended to be of Riley's mind on the "proper spirit" of the American voice: it was to be the atonal strains of disparate provincial and local utterances. These "varying accents," Howells thought, bespoke a much sounder "growth of our literature in Americanism" than the pretentious attempts to write the Great American Novel. Like Hawthorne, Howells remarked the insuperable problem that the "very vastness" of America presented to the literary imagination that would comprehend it; but whereas Hawthorne supposed that he could at least fall back on his native state as an imaginative and cultural whole, Howells encouraged the American writer to retreat further "into provincialism of the narrowest kind." Nothing could be uniformly American about our literature, he concluded, except the "general taste." The sole genius of American literature thus became for Howells the *genius loci*.

In this conviction that the national literature must commit itself to a "provincialism of the narrowest kind," Hamlin Garland concurred through his doctrine of "veritism," which was essentially local realism. When Garland first visited Howells in the late 1880's, the two agreed that Eggleston, Cable, Harris, Jewett, Wilkins, and Harte were all advancing American literature by "working (without knowing it) in accordance with . . . [this] great principle." In assuming that these local realists were working naïvely, however, Garland was surely in error. Not only did Harris discourse extensively on the superiority of the provincial point of view; but Eggleston also was so concerned with the method of his own backwoods localism that he traced its genesis to the combined influence of Lowell's *Biglow Papers,* the Flemish realists, and the environmental doctrines of Taine. In *The Hoosier Schoolmaster* and the other "Western back-country" narratives that followed, his primary aim, he said, was to portray "correctly certain forms of American life and manners" and thereby contribute something toward the history of American civilization. So close, indeed, was Eggleston's explicit doctrine of an American literature to that of Howells, Garland, and Harris that much of his 1892 Preface to *The Hoosier Schoolmaster* might have come from the pen of any or all of them:

> The taking up of life in this regional way has made our literature really national by the only process possible. The Federal nation has at

length manifested a consciousness of the continental diversity of its forms of life. The "great American novel" . . . is appearing in sections.

Whether or not this localism or regionalism was the only valid process of nationalizing American literature, Eggleston was undoubtedly justified in remarking the pervasiveness of the mode in the decades after the Civil War not only in the Midwest but across the land. Its finest flowering came before the end of the century in the work of Sarah Orne Jewett and Mary E. Wilkins. But even before the publication of *The Hoosier Schoolmaster* (1871), Mrs. Stowe had detailed many facets of the life of the Maine coast in *The Pearl of Orr's Island* (1862); and her brother Henry Ward Beecher a few years later consciously employed a similar local detail in *Norwood; or, Village Life in New England.* In California Bret Harte had avowedly sought to give a freshness to his stories by showing the Far West to be a region like no other place on earth. Yet among the pioneers of localism in the 1860's none was more conscientious than Bayard Taylor, who anticipated Eggleston's method by resolving in *The Story of Kennett* (1866) to reproduce the pastoral landscape of Pennsylvania "field for field, and tree for tree" as well as the "common dialect" of the region as he had heard it. Like other localists and regionalists, Taylor had become convinced that no single literary work could be properly representative of the "complex national being," and therefore his Pennsylvania community, he readily conceded, was "incorrect of American life, in its broader sense." His narrative had sufficient justification, he thought, if it were "locally true."

At times, however, the regionalists felt that to call their work "locally true" was scarcely the ultimate and most impressive defense of their mode. Cognizant of the charge that their provincial pictures were not representatively national, they replied, in effect, that though their sketches were indigenously and distinctively American the focus was directed beyond the national—to the universal. To involve the imagination with national issues and institutions, they argued, is to commit it to unstable and limited themes; to focus it on the local is to disclose the elemental and hence the unchanging nature of man. To this belief in the local as a microcosm most of the regionalists testified at one time or another; and for this principle Howells claimed a sound national genesis in Emerson's prescription of "the meal in the firkin, the milk in the pan." In Atchison, Kansas, the author of *The Story of a Country Town,* Edgar W. Howe, was convinced that the local history of his or any other town in America contained the same strange incidents of which Tolstoi and Daudet had made use to show how much alike the "human story is . . . in every clime and every age." In Georgia among his rural neighbors Harris detected "the human nature that underlies all types of life," and in New Orleans Lafcadio Hearn agreed with Harris that American authors would find "the natural blossoms of human life" amid the "wild plants" of the common people rather than in the "hothouse growth of fashionable intellectuality." All this testimony Garland summed up by remarking that Americans were coming to see "that something heroic is not incompatible with flippancy and vulgarity, and that a local scene or character if painted faithfully becomes universal."

This provincial realism, with its tendency to ignore the dominant social and political forces of the national life in a single leap from the local to the universal, was nevertheless a consequence of these very forces. With political stability assured by the Union victory, as Horace Scudder observed, cultural and social diversity flourished in an atmosphere of national confidence. To catch this heterogeneity, the native writer was inevitably impelled toward two modes: dialect and the short story. A century earlier, proponents of a national literature had thought of this literature as an expression of the American mind in an American language, distinct and standardized. But with the cultural diversity of the post-bellum period, linguistic diversity was also at a premium. Eggleston, Harris, Thomas Nelson Page, Twain, and Riley all regarded provincial idiom and pronunciation as such salient ingredients of literary interest and value that they expended the most painstaking care toward making them authentic. Upon this precision in dialect Howells placed his authoritative critical approval by calling it a refreshing contribution to American literature and an evidence of a healthy decentralization. As wide indulgence in diverse dialects afforded linguistic evidence of a decline in popular concern for an inclusive national culture, so the preference of the local colorists for the short story was a corollary of the same phenomenon. For the small, disparate units of American life which they sought to portray, the short tale with an abundance of dialect seemed an adequate vehicle.

In this relaxation of national consciousness of which the mode of localism was a correlate, in this withdrawal of the "artistic" (to use Harris' term) from the total national mind, proponents of a more responsible and organic American literature found cause for uneasiness. Since this American provincialism had in it the "germ of nationality," Lowell was willing to give it temporary approval as a phase of the development of American literature. An even more provisional acceptance came from the poet-critic E. C. Stedman for what he called "our genre literature," with its novelty of structure, theme, and dialect. For this emphasis on the local, he was convinced, represented an unfortunate "lagging behind full nationality," a failure of the American imagination to grasp and interpret "our political enlargement," a deficient expression of the "tone" of the American character and the "dominant popular moods" of American society. To this picturesque localism Walt Whitman, however, could not grant even a provisional admittance to the plane of a genuinely national literature. For in their superficial reading of American life, in their "deplorable tendency toward the *outré*," Whitman told Garland, the local colorists under the guise of the real had misrepresented the national character and hence were not "American in the deep sense at all." For such writers as Lowell and Stedman and Whitman, who for all their dissimilarity inclined to measure American literature by its tone and genius rather than by its materials, by its representative rather than by its novel character, the national literary whole must be greater than the sum of its parts.

By the 1880's not only the inadequate nationality but also the aesthetic thinness of the localist vein was becoming evident. In California the poet Sill, satiated by the "straining after local flavor" through the endless use of Spanish missions, gamblers, and red-shirted miners, concluded that Bret Harte had initiated a literary fashion that was dying in intellectual poverty, provincialism, insincerity, and triteness. Consequently, near the end of the century, when the romantic mode began to reassert itself, Maurice Thompson and James Lane Allen tried to add a new dimension to regionalism in their narratives of Indiana and

Kentucky life. Convinced that dialect stories depicting what Whitman called the *outré* had had their day and had failed to "secure an American flavor," the two authors supposed that they could achieve a literature at once regional and national by turning to the broad wholesome stratum of American character as it existed outside the metropolitan centers. Allen especially wished to redress what he regarded as the exploitation and the misrepresentation of the South in the odd and freakish portrayals which Cable, Harris, and Craddock had irresponsibly supplied for urban taste. Yet by the 1880's urban taste, too, was becoming weary and suspicious of the picturesque. No enduring novel of a metropolis like New York could be written, the critic James L. Ford observed, by one who was content to apply to Chinatown, the Jewish old-clothing quarter, and the Irish political districts a "thin coating of that literary varnish known as 'local color.'" Like Allen and Thompson, Ford was certain that the only genuine expression of a region or locale can come from a native who is so imbued with his subject and so sympathetic with his characters and the forces shaping their lives that his local color would be in his blood and bones.

Whatever the shortcomings of Allen's and Thompson's romantic regionalism, it proceeded from the valid premise that the constriction of the regional impulse toward the quaintly local in dialect and manners had become so excessive that the American imagination was failing to catch the common pulse of the national life. The romantic reaction at the end of the century thus stimulated a dilation of local literature toward that more comprehensive sectional utterance which in ante-bellum days had attempted to embrace the political, moral, and physical character of a homogeneous region. It also served as a prelude for the richer regionalism of the twentieth century in that it proposed to reinstate as literary material the normal experience of those whose life and values lent the region its characteristic temper. When in 1892 Richard Hovey, in an essay entitled "On the Threshold," predicted an approaching renascence in American literature, he was certain that it would not be nurtured in local color (which "threatens to become a fetish") or in the literary creed that "to be American is to be local." Hovey, like Julian Hawthorne, looked toward an American literature which would be not merely the aggregate of local transcriptions but would rather adumbrate the large unity of a stalwart national mind: "We shall be quite American enough if we take the world for our heritage and use it with American hearts."

The New England Center

For the fact that in the generation before the Civil War there was in New England no such strenuous movement toward a sectional literature as in the South and West, an explanation is not difficult to find: with the two centuries of literary pre-eminence that the section had achieved, regional themes had already been abundantly used, and in addition her writers might reasonably assume that New England literature and American literature were all but synonymous. No doubt Margaret Fuller bespoke the conviction of most ante-bellum New England authors when in 1844 she wrote that New England was not a section of the New World but "a chief mental focus"—the brain of the body politic, the other portions of the country serving merely as the lungs, the heart, and other less sensitive but withal necessary organs. The same conviction Mrs. Stowe echoed a generation later when, tracing the character of ante-bellum New England in *Oldtown Folks,* she conjectured that the section was the seedbed of the Republic and of "all that is likely to come of it."

Although a few New England writers may have felt with Hawthorne that in the vastness of America only one's native state could be made a "matter of the heart," the majority of them embraced rather the firm homogeneity of the section as a whole as the definitive center of the national culture. From the New Zion of colonial days numerous ante-bellum orators and historians traced the gradual crystallization of a New England community with its own system of manners, speech, opinions, and government; and from this cisatlantic school of intelligence and virtue, as the religious historian W. B. Sprague phrased it, New England writers generally expected American literature to take its cue and to become the "sister of Freedom and Religion." If, as Margaret Fuller said, New England were the brain of America and the other sections merely the grosser organs, it was futile to entertain hopes for the inception of a worthy national literature west of the Hudson. In this view other Transcendentalists, despite their enthusiasm for the idea of the West, seem frequently to have concurred. It was Emerson's wholesome writings, Alcott said in 1865, that measured the "present expansion of the American mind" and best answered its needs, and these works "could have been written only in New England." Although Alcott afterward somewhat modified this close identification of the New England with the American mind, still near the end of his life he continued to credit the Transcendental school with producing "a literature indigenous and American" and to see in Concord "a rural cradle for the fresher literature."

In this conviction that the New England mind was the New World mind, that New England literature was not a sectional utterance but a national archetype, the writers of the section consistently foresaw the alignment of the rest of the country with their culture. In the settlement of the West Edward Everett envisioned New England's children standing dominant as a "kindred people"; and Ellery Channing, protégé of Emerson and friend of Thoreau, saw his "country" (New England) not only lighting "her fire/ In every Prairie's midst" but even standing guardian in the South. "New England's will/ Beats in each artery and each small part/ Of this great Continent," he wrote in the 1840's. So culturally dependent on New England did the great continent seem to the poet T. W. Parsons that he foresaw the "little Charles" becoming for the new territories a "consecrated stream"! Yet in these characteristic prophecies of the veneration to be accorded the mother-section by the West, the prophets had apparently forgotten the lesson that America's insistent campaign for literary independence from the mother country should have taught them. Proposals such as Lyman Beecher's that New England principles were required in the West as the *"leaven* in the loaf" pricked the sectional pride of ante-bellum Western literary leaders like James Hall, who replied that such patronizing attitudes toward the South and West were endangering the vigor and originality of American literature. Holding that American principles were not the possession of a "self-exalted few," Hall decried "the meanness and dishonesty . . . that would degrade *America* to elevate New-England. . . ." As successive centers of Western thought evolved across the nation in Chicago and in the Far West, each in turn reiterated both this protest against New England's cultural evangelism and also this concern for a more inclusive national idea than the mother-section had conceived.

On the older regions of the Middle Atlantic states and the South, New England could scarcely exercise the same maternal claims as over the West; yet from their more nearly co-ordinate cultural status they also protested a *"New Englandism"* which, in the words of the Young American W. A. Jones of New York, had made American authors "imitative, constrained, tasteful, and timid." The South, of course, had the most cogent reasons for resenting what seemed to be a "Yankee literature, which ever assumes to itself the title of American." But it was not merely the "malignant humanitarianism of Boston" which led Southern literary men in both ante-bellum and Reconstruction days to refuse to acknowledge New England writers as the curators of American principles. Even so temperate a critic as Lafcadio Hearn felt as late as the 1880's that New England novels which professed to be "peculiarly American" were in fact projections of "preconceived Boston sentiment," and that their authors had "no idea whatever of studying American life from a standpoint not New English."

That the kind of national literature that New England had developed was not representatively American but merely New English Howells had already observed during his early career in Boston in the late 1860's. Two centuries of persistent pride in the landscape and principles and traditions of a homogeneous region had found a characteristic and distinctive utterance, he felt, and it would "probably be centuries yet before the life of the whole country, the American life as distinguished from the New England life, shall have anything so like a national literature." In this utterance almost every aspect of the entity which was New England had been brought into focus by the regional imagination. The landscapes and legends had found romantic treatment in Whittier, Brainard, Hawthorne, and a host of others. The example of Scott had furnished a pattern for scores of fictional recreations of the historical conflicts of the region. New England moral and religious values had had such varied interpreters as the Mathers, Catharine Sedgwick, Louisa Alcott, Stowe, Emerson, and Thoreau— all in varying literary forms. Perhaps something of an index to the temper of this New England "nationality" was furnished by the poet Henry Tuckerman when, in an introduction to an anthology of local selections called *The Boston Book* (1836), he remarked that the literary taste of the Bostonians was marked by a fondness for the useful and vigorous, by an absence of humor, by an "antipathy to 'vanities,'" and by a deep interest in humanity. At any rate, it was through the dissemination of some such regional complex of values that Margaret Fuller and her associates on the *Dial* hoped to redeem a national culture which, they thought, had made the American people superficial, irreverent, and anxious merely to live rather than to live mentally and morally.

As the Civil War approached and the weight of both South and West exerted a heavy counterbalance in national affairs, the *amor patriae* of New England authors in turn became increasingly self-conscious and appeared in recurrent references to the section as a land, a race, a people, or a country whose character was worthy of a special literature. It was, indeed, not for the development of an American but of a New England literature that Ellery Channing reminded the writers of his "country" of the inherent poetry of the woolen frock and homely tools, of the fireplace and paling fence, and, above all, of their "plain, strong race, deep-rooted as a tree."

In such themes Thoreau, too, professed to find regional inspiration; and, when inspired by the draughts of "wild nectar" which the gods distilled and poured down "every hill/ For their New England men," he felt no impulse to "taste the spring/ Of Helicon again." For the bark of any literary adventurers among "New England men" who, less loyal than he, were enticed to alien themes, he predicted that as a kind of sectional nemesis "New England's worm her hulk shall bore,/ And sink her in the Indian seas." It was out of this sectional consciousness that Thoreau himself gave, as Alcott said, "the sod and sap and fibre and flavour of New England . . . a clear relation to the literature of other and classic lands." It was a faith in the "purely New English" that led Lowell to suppose that Dr. Josiah Gilbert Holland's poetry was of a high order, and that also impelled him to turn the *Atlantic Monthly,* as Howells observed, into a New England rather than a national magazine. And it was the conviction that New England was the safest place in the world that led Hawthorne on one occasion to indulge the hope that New England might become not merely in cultural homogeneity but also in political fact a separate nation. Yet among all the writers who both in ante-bellum and post-bellum days represented the New England national literature which Howells discovered upon coming to Boston, probably none was more consistently and persuasively devoted than Mrs. Stowe. For her—as for many of the New England poets of the 1840's—the radiance of the Italian sky or the odor of the Orient or the gayety of France held no such imaginative lure as the sturdy integrity of her section:

> No; let me turn to my own land—my own New England; the land
> of bright fires and strong hearts; the land of *deeds,* and not of words;
> the land of fruits, and not of flowers; the land often spoken against,
> yet always respected; 'the latchet of whose shoes the nations of the
> earth are not worthy to unloose.'

To portray the texture of New England life in such books as *The Minister's Wooing* seemed, indeed, to Mrs. Stowe like a fearful searching of the map of the Infinite, for it was an attempt to comprehend a "mode of thought, energetic, original, and sublime."

In the post-bellum years New England thus gradually abandoned its earlier pretenses to speak for the nation as a whole. Like that of the postwar South, her literature inclined toward the elegiac and nostalgic in a host of tales of village life on the pattern of Mrs. Stowe's *Oldtown Folks* (1869). In pastoral poetry, too, Daniel Ricketson expressed a piety toward the traditional character and institutions of his "land" which pointed, as Howells said, to the decline of New England as a "nation." Moreover, as Howells observed to Garland toward the end of the century, the old literary pride in native plainness gradually weakened, and the New England "country" became a "literary province whereon successive waves of European culture beat"—French impressionism, Russian veritism, Ibsen's realism. Yet, whatever the decline, for over two centuries New England had not only stood preeminent in American letters but also in the process created something of a national literature of her own.

An American Literature at the South

During the first fifty years of the Republic, writers in the South were much more concerned for an American than for a Southern literature, and even during the three decades preceding the War Between the States they spent much of their critical effort in trying to reconcile the sectional and the national literary principle. If before the 1830's they placed a premium on the use of Southern themes, they did so not so much to enhance their section as to give authenticity to its literary work. Even when the *Southern Review* (1828) appeared, it was acclaimed not as a sectional instrument but as a medium of literary interchange with all sections "of our happy country"; and when a few years later the major literary organ of the section, the *Southern Literary Messenger* (1834), was inaugurated, its editor James E. Heath bespoke the literary aid of his "northern and eastern brethren" and assured them that the appearance of his journal did not presuppose "any unkind feelings" toward Southern literature on the part of "the aristarchy [*sic*] of the north and east." Indeed some editors, like W. C. Richards of the *Orion,* even in the 1840's were so alert to the misunderstandings implicit in the term "Southern literature" that they preferred to use the phrase "literature in the South," or frequently "a literature at the South." But whatever the terminology, Southern editors until mid-century were generally explicit in their policy of delivering the South from literary "vassalage" and, at the same time, keeping it an integral part of the national literary design.

As mid-century approached, this editorial profession of loyalty to the cause of both an American and a Southern literature was sustained by the two most prominent writers of the section, Poe and Simms. Poe wished a Southern literary independence from the North as he wished an American literary independence from England only in order to free the individual author to follow his own course toward "originality." "We are embarked in the cause of *Southern* Literature," he wrote on behalf of the *Messenger* in 1836, "and (with perfect amity to all sections) wish to claim especially as a friend and co-operator, every *Southern* Journal." Poe's own "amity" with most of the New England writers was, of course, short-lived; but the several breaches with Lowell, Longfellow, and the Transcendentalists were usually personal rather than sectional in origin; and when they did at times involve Southern literature as a whole, they rarely related to the political aspects of Southern literature. When he attacked Margaret Fuller's essay on American literature as "a silly and conceited piece of Transcendentalism," and when he accused Lowell and his "set" of affecting a belief that there was *"no such thing* as Southern Literature," he was not advancing a Southern point of view but rather protesting what he regarded to be the impingement of a zealous and arrogant sectionalism on the privileges of the American imagination.

Simms, like Poe, sought an American literature free from British domination and a Southern literature independent of New England critical doctrines. But with this independence, Simms thought, both a national and sectional literature were responsible for reflecting the "moral aims" and "political achievements" of the area from which they sprang. Hence Simms became the ardent exponent of both an organic American and an organic Southern literature, and he reconciled the two on the principle of a literary confederacy. Subsumed under the broad scope of universal values were the distinctive cultural modes of nations, he supposed, and subsumed in turn under the American national character were the peculiar emphases of the several sections. As distinctive national cultures were the channels toward the universal, so the aggregate of the sections constituted the national. When, in the decade before the Civil War, Simms judged Southern interests to be short-weighted in the national scale, he became the proponent of a Southern literature wherein the moral and political aims were not merely distinct from but also antithetic to those of other sections. Yet most of his long editorial and critical career was spent on behalf of an American rather than a Southern literature, and in his sustained effort for a national literature he attacked British criticism, encouraged native writers, suggested native themes, campaigned for a copyright law, and through a varied fiction exemplified his own theory of an American romance. In this double allegiance to a sectional and national literature, many of his prominent compatriots joined. Simms's editorial associate, James W. Simmons, the editor of the *Southern Review,* Hugh Legaré, and the mid-century editor of the *Messenger,* John R. Thompson, for all their sectional loyalty, were for the most part concerned that the South not fail to contribute her share to a national utterance distinctively American.

Within the framework of this inclusive interest in American literature as a whole, the campaign for a Southern literature recapitulated on a smaller scale the stages of the campaign for a national literature begun after the Revolution. Southerners with a lingering neoclassic taste desired only a Southern Dryden or Pope to sing of Nature and

Reason; and the sectionalism of the women's magazines such as the *Southern Ladies' Book* went scarcely further than the hope that the moral sentiments might be cultivated through "homebred instrumentalities." Indeed, in the early decades of the century Southern literature generally implied merely a literature produced or published in the South, embracing Nature if the author were of neoclassic temper and embracing the Ideal if he were romantic.

As the vogue of Romanticism swept into the South, however, sharper definitions and more elaborate designs for a Southern literature succeeded the generalized encouragement of "native productions." Certain aspects of the South, to be sure, did not conspicuously lend themselves to the romantic mode. The scenery of the region, as Simms himself conceded in *Guy Rivers* and *Southward Ho,* could not claim the majesty of the Hudson or the Rockies, though a *genius loci* could be found, he thought, in a thousand quiet spots or in the gloomy wastes of pine and swamp. Yet richer veins of literary ore, Southern writers were aware, lay in Southern history and tradition than in Southern nature. Simms, once more, by critical essays and by narrative example provided the surest prospectus of a historical fiction which would exploit the events and figures of the section's past. In *The Partisan* (1835), in *The Yemassee* (1835), in the tales of *The Wigwam and the Cabin* (1845), and in many another work he avowedly sought to suggest the fictional resources available in Southern history and legends, and in such regional characters as the squatter, planter, Indian, Negro, hardy pioneer and vigorous yeomen. Despite the skepticism of some of his friends as to the literary value of themes so close at hand, Simms continued, as he said in *Katharine Walton* (1851), to invoke "the muse of local History—the traditions of our own home— the chronicles of our own section—the deeds of our own native heroes —the recollections of our own noble ancestry." Writers in other regions, he hoped, would adopt the same literary creed and thereby build a national literature by the only valid process, the use of the cultural milieu by which their imaginations had been formed.

At what point in ante-bellum literary history of the South this Muse of local history became divisively antifederal by an implicit allegiance to the supremacy of the states, it is difficult to say. Certainly George Tucker and Kennedy, for all their Virginian piety and their fictional explorations of the earlier history of the Old Dominion in the 1820's and 1830's, thought of themselves as contributing to a national literature free from British domination. The ante-bellum evocations of the Virginian past by the brothers Philip Pendleton and John Esten Cooke were apparently undertaken in the same spirit. Philip, under the influence of Froissart, had at first been satisfied to compose medieval ballads; but in his early thirties, awakened to the imaginative resources of his native region, he commenced a series of tales through which he hoped "to dramatize the whole life and manners, history and all, of Virginia and her people." Philip never completed his ambitious project; but his brother John Esten in *The Virginia Comedians* (1854) and other romances tried to point the way to some future master who would comprehend "the noble past of his native land" and of a "great race—the worthies of Virginia" before they slipped "deeper and deeper into the mist." In this profession of literary faith was not Cooke merely concurring in Hawthorne's admission, made in the year in which *The Virginia Comedians* appeared, that we have so much country that for the heart everything falls away except one's native state?

Simms's prescription for a national literature wrought from local themes had by mid-century been adopted by the Deep South. Across the realistic warp of Longstreet's *Georgia Scenes* (1835) or J. B. Cobb's *Mississippi Scenes* (1851) stretched the romantic woof of Cobb's *The Creole* (1850), with its re-creation of New Orleans life during the second war with Britain. And for any aspiring writers of the Delta region who might suppose the lower Mississippi barren of imaginative interest, the historian Charles Gayarré furnished in his lectures on colonial Louisiana the "faint outlines" for numerous compositions which, he said, might encircle the waist of his native land "with the magic zone of Romance." Yet all such regional narratives and sketches, whether realistic or romantic, Timrod asserted just before the war, could not be reckoned a genuinely Southern literature unless the Southern mind were to be found "in the tone and bearings of the thought, in the drapery, the colouring, and those thousand nameless touches, which are to be felt rather than expressed." In insisting that a sectional (or national) literature was to be defined not through its subject "but in the management of the subject," Timrod was applying to Southern compositions the same basic test that Cooper and Whitman had proposed for compositions which pretended to be American. Like Simms and Hawthorne, Timrod evidently felt that an American literature of any depth would inevitably reflect most vividly particular regional colors rather than the whole continental spectrum.

Though even by the 1830's the South had become for many of her writers not merely a geographical but also a cultural entity, the inclusive character of this entity remained ill defined in Southern literature until the impending conflict forced a sharper definition of the sectional values at issue. It seemed enough for a time for Southern poets to apostrophize the "soul of the sunny South," as did the Georgian poet Holley Chivers, or for editors to promise that Southern journals would "breathe a Southern spirit" and reflect the "general tone of thinking" of the section, as did Daniel Whitaker of the *Southern Literary Journal*. With the Southern economy and social structure actively threatened after mid-century, however, to reflect the "general tone" of the South was not enough, and the imperative increasingly placed on Southern literature was not merely that of reflecting regional life but also that of defending Southern interests and institutions. For the preservation of "that liberty, which is *our* peculiar boast" editor P. C. Pendleton of the *Magnolia* even in the 1840's had looked to the "infant literature" of the section; and to counteract the "fanatical blue" of Northern papers, editor John R. Thompson of the *Messenger* told Southern authors at mid-century, they were responsible for furnishing a "home literature" which would be "informed with the conservative spirit, the love of order and justice, that constitutes the most striking characteristic of the Southern mind." In order to provide the people as well as the writers of the South a more comprehensive and definitive analysis of their distinctive society and values, *Russell's Magazine* in its first volume (1857) inaugurated a series of articles on "Southern Civilization," the conclusion of which stressed the concept of a "hierarchy of races."

The literary harvest of such exhortations and analyses is difficult to estimate; but it was no doubt in part owing to this critical preparation of the literary soil that *De Bow's* could report in 1858 that "Southern books are beginning to be better reflexes of Southern thought, Southern feeling, Southern manners, customs, and peculiarities, and, in short, to be more 'racy of the soil' than formerly. All literature which has any value is instinct with nationalism, the more the better." Though Hinton Helper in his diatribe against a "purely Southern literature" in *The Impending Crisis of the South* (1857) could scarcely applaud such a development as *De Bow's* described, he was forced to concede that the "crisis" had supplied a rich if noxious fertilization to the hitherto thin literary growth of the section: ". . . Southern novelists bore us *ad infinitum* with pictures of the beatitudes of plantation life . . . ; Southern verse-wrights drone out their drowsy dactyls or grow ventricous with their turgid heroes, all in defense of slavery. . . ."

By the late 1850's the movement for a Southern literature, as Helper recognized, had proceeded far beyond Simms's original doctrine of the sectional as a component of a national literary harmony and had become a concerted effort toward an autonomous sectional culture which would interrelate the section's economy, education, politics, and arts. To implement this sectional ideal, delegates met in a series of conventions in various cities during the decade before the Civil War. Among the resolutions of the Richmond congress of 1854 was one declaring that "a just self-respect requires that Southern literature in all its branches, should meet with the hearty support of all Southern men"; and at the more famous Savannah convention two years later such prominent Southerners as Charles Gayarré and A. B. Longstreet were among the members of a committee appointed to "select and prepare" a series of textbooks, ranging from the "earliest primer to the highest grade of literature and science," which would inculcate the Southern point of view. So fearful, indeed, did the South become of ideas which might subvert its culture that the *Messenger* called not only for a Southern fiction to counteract Mrs. Stowe but also for a withdrawal of patronage from Northern colleges and pedagogues. To this all-inclusive Southern nationalism Simms eventually gave his support, holding that an "intimate sympathy" exists between the labors and morals and arts of a people, and that the mechanic and fine arts thrive together. An agrarian South therefore must remain culturally sterile, he concluded, so long as it derives its moral and aesthetic creed from an industrial North; and he could only characterize as "softheads" those obtuse Southerners who deferred to everything Northern from travel and watering places to books and opinions.

The coming of the war itself by no means signalized the end of the movement for a distinctive Southern literature. In fact, evidence supports Timrod's assertion in 1864 that the war had effected a large measure of that creative and critical independence for which the authors of the section had been striving with cumulative desperation during the preceding decades. Denied access to the popular Northern magazines, the Southern public of necessity diverted its patronage to Southern journals new and old, and as a consequence the journals were, at least for a time, prosperous enough to encourage contributions from native talent. Nor did Appomattox signalize a literary peace with the North. Estranged during the Reconstruction years from the rest of an expansive nation, Southerners were thrown back upon resources which consisted in large part of pride in the ante-bellum traditions and character of their section. Commercially and agriculturally impoverished, they began to find some financial succor from the pen to which in ante-bellum years they had been indifferent, and their all but inevitable subject became the brighter days of the past. Almost in inverse proportion to the narrow and meager scale of life during the Reconstruction years, the retrospect of the Old South broadened into a heroic tradition which, in meeting a moral and social need among a defeated people, suggested a more valid list of themes for Southern writers than Simms and Gayarré had been able to compile a generation earlier. Almost immediately after Lee's surrender, the literary triumph of the Lost Cause had its paradoxical inception.

"If we could not gain our *political,* let us establish at least our *mental* independence," R. H. Crozier's *The Confederate Spy* pleaded a year after the war. Even more apprehensive than during the ante-bellum years that thousands of tales would descend from the "vile den of New England" and that the *"yellow* and the red-backed trash of the North" would caricature and ridicule the defeated South before the world, numerous literary arbiters in the section echoed Crozier's words and reaffirmed the need of a literature to vindicate the Southern character. Nor was this desire for a literature of the Lost Cause confined to Confederate extremists. Even the judicious *Southern Presbyterian Review* joined in the call for publications in the section to counteract the "wretched stuff from the North"; and by the 1870's the *New Eclectic* of Baltimore, the *Nineteenth Century* of Charleston, and Bledsoe's *Southern Review* were all consistently following such a militant pro-Southern policy. Among these Southern periodicals the *New Eclectic* (which became the *Southern Magazine* in 1871) maintained over many years not only the most consistent assault on the "weak and trashy" productions which passed for American literature "at the North," but also the most substantial prospectus for a Southern literature which would disseminate those ideas which "our fathers gave us."

The Southern men of letters who embraced the Lost Cause as a major theme were in the main those authors whose earlier work antedated the Civil War. It is not surprising that among their number should have been John Esten Cooke, whose ante-bellum veneration for the old Virginian society was further intensified by the war to the point that he felt that a historical novelist would find it "almost impossible to over-color" its remarkable qualities. In similar terms Paul Hamilton Hayne paid tribute to the whole of Southern civilization as a life so nearly perfect that a faithful portrayal of its "mind and *morale*" would be adjudged an "extravagant idealism" by those unfamiliar with it—especially by Northerners who, he thought, were as ignorant of the actual life of the Old South as though it were a province in central Africa. Yet more pernicious than this Northern ignorance in Hayne's view was the "Fungous School" of writers springing up in the South with their repudiation of the values and codes of the ante-bellum culture and their attempts to depict realistically the New South as an integral part of the national scene.

This conviction on the part of Cooke and Hayne that the civilization of the Old South must constitute the substratum of the literature of the section was to be expected as but the projection of the views which they had held before the war. But the even more unqualified reverence for the Southern past expressed by a former editor of the *Messenger*, George W. Bagby, could have scarcely been predicted; for his policy in the 1850's had been to encourage Southern writers to treat the here and now in works that smacked of the soil rather than wear their literary spectacles on the back of their heads, as he accused John Esten Cooke and other romancers of doing. Converted, however, by the experiences of the war and Reconstruction to a belief that the spirit of the Southern past must be carried into the future, Bagby eventually proposed to test all writers of the section by their ability to vindicate Southern history. In the Virginian tradition especially he saw a civilization unequaled since that of Greece; and the beauty, simplicity, uprightness, warmth, and grace of its old country life he pronounced to be worthy of commemoration in "such prose and verse as has not been written since John Milton laid down his pen."

In this effort of the post-bellum years to resist integration with the current national culture and to foster a literature which would sustain the older Southern civilization, scores of minor authors, of course, were also active, and among them were the literary ladies of the section. Yet two anthologies, *Southland Writers* (1870) and its revision *The Living Female Writers of the South* (1872), scarcely augured the renascence of Southern poetry which the editors prophesied, nor did they manifest the rich civilization to which Cooke and Hayne and Bagby had paid tribute. Within a decade after Appomattox, in fact, the zealous cultivation of a literature of apology for the Old South began to lag. Yet within that decade the foundations had been firmly laid for a literary structure which would glorify a "peculiar order of civilization" with its "bead-roll of battlefields," its chivalric tradition, and its appeal to Constitutional rights. Though this structure of fiction and poetry could scarcely bear the weight of pro-Southern argument that the most exacting of the section's unreconstructed critics wished to impose upon it, in the course of succeeding decades it did serve as the medium for an alluring "myth," the essence of which Lafcadio Hearn devotedly described in the 1870's:

> It is the picturesqueness of the South, the poetry, the traditions, the legends, the superstitions, the quaint faiths, the family prides, the luxuriousness, the splendid indolence and the splendid sins of the old social system which have passed, or which are now passing, away forever. . . . The new South will be less magnificent, though wealthier; . . . less poetical, though more cultured.

The writers who came of literary age in the 1860's and 1870's for the most part breathed the atmosphere and expressed the temper of what Hearn called the "new South." From an inclusive Southern civilization they retreated to picturesque diversity; for the glory of the Southern past they substituted the glow of Southern progress; from Simms's romantic Muse of history they shifted their allegiance to the realistic Muse of local color. Disclaiming sectional piety, the writers of the new generation were persuaded by Harris' literary counsel to "depict life in the South as it really was and is." This creed was accepted not only by the ex-Confederate novelist Cable but also by the ex-Confederate poet Lanier, who wrote Hayne of his conviction that the section would not be enhanced by "blindly plastering . . . with absurd praises" either the South or those works which purported to depict its pre-eminent glory and honor. Viewing the post-bellum Union as a beneficent fact, he accounted the "habit of regarding our literature as *Southern* literature, our poetry as *Southern* poetry" an insidious evil because "art will have nothing to do with hate." It was all but inevitable that this view should have been curtly reiterated by the author of that famous oration "The New South," Henry W. Grady, who dismissed "all the talk about a distinctive Southern literature" as "silly in the extreme."

Thus did the literary South pass from an innocuous regionalism through an autonomous sectionalism and finally into at least a partial reinstatement with the dominant cultural trends in the nation as a whole. In the twentieth century the values of both the Old and the New South received their most searching reappraisal in Faulkner's portrayal of the Old Southern Sartoris and Compson families, of the New Southern Snopeses, and of the Negroes Dilsey, Joe Christmas, and Lucas Beauchamp. In the fullest sense Simms's dream of a Southern literature which should be national by being authentically sectional was finally realized.

The Promise of the West

For a century after America became a nation, nationalistic writers in the East viewed the West not merely as a geographical section but also as the scene of the literary millennium. In the light of the Berkeleyan principle whereby empire and the arts ever circled to the westward, the region beyond the Alleghenies seemed destined to complete the cycle long ago begun in the Orient. Almost every American school of critics—whether neoclassic or romantic, Transcendental or Christian-humanitarian—emerged with some version of this principle whereby the West was to become the crown of civilization. Nearly a generation before the Revolutionary victory opened the trans-Allegheny territory to the first wave of pioneers, the almanac-maker Nathaniel Ames, Jr., convinced "that the Progress of Humane Literature (like the Sun) is from the East to the West," could hear the "music of Orpheus" supplanting the howl of beasts in a region which, stretching to the "Western Ocean," was to be "the Garden of the World." In the atmosphere of exultant nationalism after the Revolution, commencement orators generously indulged in visions of a new Helicon and Parnassus amid the hills of the West. Even before the end of the eighteenth century, indeed, the republican poet James Elliot, journeying to a little settlement in Kentucky, reported his discovery of an Arcadian life of simple equalitarianism worthy of "a Virgil, a Milton, a Thomson, or a Shenstone!"

Elliot's feat of reconciling the actual and the millennial West was rare. For as the frontier pushed across the continent, the region where the arts were to be perfected was also consistently projected anew to some virgin territory beyond the settlements. To the fancy of various eighteenth-century authors on the Eastern seaboard, the "mazy waters" or "broad flood" or "deepening tide" of the Ohio seemed the likeliest place for the Hellenic-Christian tradition to find its ultimate expression. But within a generation after villages began to appear in the Ohio Valley, it was evident that "polish'd Culture" was, after all, to have her seat in some region still farther west. For a time thereafter Schoolcraft and the poet Charles Mead ventured to hope that the pilgrimage of man from Eden's gates and the long wandering of the Muse might be terminated in the valley of the Mississippi; but here, too, expectations died amid a rude society and few scenes to excite the imagination. By mid-century the site of the Western Eden had been moved by Bayard Taylor even to the continent's edge, for it was in California, he thought, that Art and Science would enable man at last to realize his Arcadian dreams.

As successive prospects of a New Eden faded across the West, romantic authors like Paulding, Bird, and Hall exchanged a visionary future for themes in the hardihood and courage of the pioneer past. So, too, in his Californian ballads Bayard Taylor turned to sing of a Far West distinguished not by a triumphant Art and Science but by legendary incidents more marvellous than those in the Arabian Nights and by characters as wild and picturesque as the Bedouins. For the literary imagination, Taylor discovered, the "sublime desolation" and "semi-civilized people" of the Southwest held a greater interest than the Pacific Eden which he had first envisioned.

But as the real character and influence of the West gradually emerged during the nineteenth century, many of the major writers in New York and New England reckoned the importance of the section for the American imagination to lie neither in millennial perfection nor in the picturesqueness which Taylor had glimpsed and which Bret Harte later exploited. In the West, they came to feel, lay the genius of America. In the "great internal states," Irving declared after returning from his long sojourn in Europe, lay the "heart of our giant Republic"; and to this heartland he thought the country as a whole must "look for the growth of a real freeborn, homebred, *national character,* of which our posterity may be proud." In the same heartland the Transcendentalists, too, persistently found a symbol of their hopes for the future character of American life and letters: to this "promised land" Emerson looked for a bolder and manlier action appropriate to the American genius; Thoreau wished that America might "rest satisfied with one mighty, all-embracing West, leaving the other three cardinal points to the Old World"; and Alcott, suspecting after the Civil War that New England was merely "England on this side of the Atlantic," conceded that only the West could claim to be American.

With a sharper sense of the topography of the West, Whitman and Burroughs found in the region the most suitable objective correlative for the American imagination. For the beneficent equalitarianism of American society the prairies seemed to Whitman the fittest symbol, and their vast expanse he hoped to see fused in the alembic of a perfect poem "entirely Western, fresh and limitless—altogether our own, without a trace or taste of Europe's soil." Whitman's disciple, John Burroughs, felt in the "strong unbreathed air of mountain or prairie" something of the tonic "nerve and heartiness" needed by American literature if it were to be cured of its sickly feudal standards. Only in the valley of the Mississippi or on the slopes of the Pacific, he believed, could the saner national literature expressing the "veritable Adamic man" be currently received and justified.

This identification of authentic New World literature with the West which had been formulated by several generations of Eastern writers was, of course, zealously perpetuated in the West itself as the section began to develop its own authors and literary centers. Even as late as 1892 the young Negro poet Paul Laurence Dunbar, speaking before the Western Association of Writers in Dayton, still found it appropriate to reiterate and amplify Berkeley's famous lines on the westward course of civilization. Thus the literature of the West, especially in ante-bellum days, was likely to be conceived as the flowering of an American culture which was in turn the triumphant culmination of the human quest for the good society. For the focal principle of his own regional literature, therefore, the early Western writer inclined to take his cue from New England rather than from the South, for Southern authors rarely claimed to be the appointed oracles either of America or of a new Eden. The West, however, saw in the Appalachians the same protective barrier against the impurities of the Old World that New England had for a time found in the Atlantic. Here at last, it seemed, the New World and the happy prospect of mankind might have at once their perfect utterance.

The energetic group of Ohio Valley writers who made Cincinnati the most substantial literary center of the ante-bellum West were, in the main, New England emigrants who were as zealous as their forebears in designing a distinctive literature of the New World. In the fresh transmontane atmosphere they supposed that they had found a milieu even more conducive to such a literature than Cotton Mather had reported a century earlier in Massachusetts. When the American ventures into the wilderness, James Hall wrote in his *Letters from the West* (1828), he is far removed from the aristocratic influences of British culture and he finds fewer citizens of English parentage than in other sections; hence his *"national character* will burst the chains of local habit." To other authors in the group the West seemed the "central arch of a great national superstructure" or the "heart of the Republic"; and that this "arch" or "heart" must be the most American because the farthest removed from vitiating foreign influences virtually every literary leader of early Ohio—Daniel Drake, W. D. Gallagher, W. T. Coggeshall, James H. Perkins—was convinced. Indeed, Drake told the students of Miami University in the 1830's, the literature of the West must inevitably be peculiarly imbued with the spirit of American institutions because in the heart of the continent "all that lives and moves is American."

As the frontier moved decade by decade toward the Pacific, minor but ambitious literary pioneers continuously sustained the assumption of the early Ohio authors that in the West lay the clue to a national character and literature. Even at the end of the Civil War Chicago was ambitious to become the "Sovereign City" from which would emanate a literature neither Yankee nor Virginian but American; and Minnesota, too, in these years aspired to serve as the "cradle" of a national literature for which the " 'Great West' must become the very nursery." But it was in California, of course, that the cultural mission of the "Great West" had its climactic proclamation. Not unaware of the old principle of the westward movement of the arts and empire, California writers stood ready to complete the cycle of human civilization by giving the American spirit itself the purest utterance. The more extensive analysis and confident prophecy of this "New Civilization" came from the numerous volumes of the historian Hubert Bancroft. "For centuries to come . . . ," he wrote, "the tendency of culture will be to concentrate on this Pacific seaboard, the terminal of the great Aryan march. . . ." Already California writers seemed to him to be giving a prophetically new direction to fancy and feeling—to be achieving "a certain democratic leveling and an irruption on puritanic soberness." As New York had come to overshadow Boston, so in turn San Francisco would be a "seat of letters," he predicted, not only for the nation but also for the world.

So convinced were some of the Californian authors of the terminal role of the Far West in the history of civilization that they ventured to revive proposals for the great American epic. In expeditions like those of Lewis and Clark they could see impressive Homeric parallels; and even in the Gold Rush Bret Harte found "an era replete with a certain heroic Greek poetry." The depiction of this era in *The Luck of Roaring Camp, and Other Stories* he regarded as a collection of "materials for the Iliad that is yet to be sung"; and in the early 1870's he himself dreamed of doing something "more worthy" than his successful stories of the previous decade, as he wrote Howells—"say . . . that great epic poem as truly American literature for which the world is anxiously waiting." Yet, convinced that the "New Civilization" far transcended the primitive impulses of the ancient Greeks, the Californian poet Edward Pollock reminded American authors that the "New Epic" could not have military glory as its theme; for the only war worthy of epic tribute in the new age was the war for "liberty and change." The singer of this "New Epic," Pollock concluded, would consider "our mighty country as the first and last upon the whole earth . . . and . . . would receive no inspirations, be swayed by no impulses from sources beyond the sea." For this transcendent epic of the New World, another critic asked, where could "our Homer" be bred except in the Far West "where Nature in her nakedness is seen, and where Fancy has room to spread her wing, and Mind expand huge as a Prairie"?

Consistently aware though most of them were of the national and historical implications that should inform their work, Western writers by no means ignored the probability that these large ends must be approached through regional means. Moreover, like the ante-bellum South, the West had its literary aspirations for equality with New England and New York. To be sure, Western authors proclaimed that in trying to advance the cause of Western letters they were " 'American system' men"—that in encouraging the home manufacture of literature they were striving to build up literary self-reliance rather than to awaken sectional feelings. At any rate, the term "Western literature" became a common one in the early decades of the century, and increasingly it came to signify not merely literature written in the West but rather an utterance peculiar to the region. Indeed, this literature was to be an integral part of a whole distinctive Western culture.

Just as Noah Webster had designed his *Grammatical Institute* to accelerate the separation of American from British literature, so Samuel Wilson in the early 1800's signalized the Western desire to be culturally independent of the East by issuing a *Kentucky English Grammar* and by projecting *The Polyanthus; or Kentucky Elegant Selections*. A generation later James Hall's *The Western Souvenir* (1829) and *The Western Reader* (1833) marked further stages in the effort to foster a "domestick literature"; and during these years Western authors met at Lexington and Columbus to form "a solemn league and compact to beat their eastern rivals," as Hall half jestingly admitted, or to achieve a "Literary and Social Concert" which would include "an uniform system of manners and customs," as Daniel Drake more soberly described the aims of Western cultural leaders. Such efforts to escape the domination primarily of Eastern culture continued for the rest of the century through such organizations as the Western Association of Authors, which was especially active in Indiana in the 1880's. But how slowly the literature of the region achieved an indigenous Western flavor before the Civil War is all too evident in the traditionalism of form, sentiment, and theme in Gallagher's *Selections from the Poetical Literature of the West* (1841) and Coggeshall's *The Poets and Poetry of the West* (1860).

Like the authors and editors of the South, those in the successive literary centers of the West felt themselves the victims of a colonial-minded public who preferred "second-hand wares" from the East to equally meritorious works from their own region. In ante-bellum Cincinnati alone over a score of attempts to sustain magazines with indigenous flavor and Western contributions failed, as Coggeshall sadly reported; and in the latter half of the century Chicago and San Francisco periodicals perished as abruptly. Nor was it merely an unskilled use of domestic themes to which the Western public was indifferent. Experimenting with local materials in the "very enthusiastic belief" that he might demonstrate the possibility of "a peculiarly characteristic Western American literature," Bret Harte published "The Luck of Roaring Camp" in the *Overland,* only to find Far Western readers so thoroughly "imbued with Eastern or New England habits and literary traditions," as he said, that they withheld approval of the story until Atlantic tribunals had emphatically recognized its art. Perhaps this literary colonialism would have diminished more rapidly had it not been for the transcontinental railroads which began to link East and West after the Civil War. Just as N. P. Willis attributed America's renewed deference to English culture in the 1840's to the coming of the steamboat, so a generation later both Eggleston and Bancroft attributed to the transcontinental railroad the decline of Western literary pride. With literary intercourse between the sections facilitated, the East not only "swallowed that incipient literature" and "even obliterated the memory of it," as Eggleston reported, but also fixed the ambitions of Far Western authors on Atlantic publications, as Bancroft observed, and lured eastward the "brightest lights." In fact, before the end of the century Eggleston himself, having done his bit in *The Hoosier Schoolmaster* to write a dialect novel "quite beyond New England influence," joined the procession of Harte, Garland, and other Western stalwarts toward the East. Joseph Kirkland and other writers who remained in the West could only continue to report a perennial discussion of the "building up of a Western literature" and a perennial scarcity of "Western readers of Western writers."

In devising its distinctive literature, the new West, like the rest of the nation, was obliged to proceed not merely from the indigenous impulses of the section but also from the prevailing literary modes of the day. Inasmuch as the settlement of the Mississippi Valley largely coincided with the crest of the Romantic tide, the distinctive assets of the section were usually construed in Romantic terms: its equalitarian "genius," its picturesque characters, its awe-inspiring nature, its aboriginal remains. In fact, to the characteristic romantic demands of the ante-bellum imagination the trans-Allegheny territory seemed to lend itself with a completeness that suggested a kind of manifest destiny for the future of American literature. Even in the early 1820's these Romantic ingredients appeared when the Cincinnati poet Thomas Peirce, enumerating the "grand and fruitful themes" for the Western bard, included the vast landscapes and the Mississippi, the Indian legends and mounds, the flora and fauna and caves peculiar to the region, the pioneers and the benign civilization of peace and reason which they brought. Yet from all these themes it is not surprising that the ante-bellum writers in the section should have most often fixed on the omnipresent pioneer as the epitome of both the romantic and the Western spirit. In *The Life and Adventures of Arthur Clenning* (1828) Timothy Flint provided, as he said, only a glimpse of the "thousand stranger histories" which were "hidden among our forests" in lives full of "incidents so marvellous" that anyone who had learned of them could thereafter consider nothing else "strange, or incredible." But to the pioneer as romantic adventurer Flint added the portrait of the pioneer as romantic democrat in *George Mason, the Young Backwoodsman* (1829) by explicitly pointing his narrative toward an illustration of the frontier belief that "in a log cabin in the forests of the Mississippi" the "actings of the heart are sincere, simple, and single," and hence as full of "solemn interest" as the lives of "the rich, the titled, and the distinguished." Yet among all the portrayals and pro-spective portrayals of the backwoodsman, it was *Colonel Crockett's Exploits,* as the *Western Monthly* perceived, which most fully pro-jected the myth of the West; for here the literary imagination, how-ever crude, had taken an indigenous stance to limn not an "actual man" but rather a "metaphorical *person*" required by a new race "to motto forth their peculiarities to the world"—a "nucleus" for the "float-ing traits and anecdotes" of the region. Such a wild frontier divinity as Crockett, however, was not quite what the more respectable James Hall and Timothy Flint had in mind in proffering the backwoods-man as a theme for Western authors.

But it was not the backwoodsman nor was it the Indian (to whom the nineteenth-century Western author paid perhaps less attention than did his Eastern contemporaries and predecessors) that was to provide the most distinctive literary figure of the region. With a surer prophetic sense James Hall, Isaac Jewett, and Benjamin Drake all remarked the fresh themes that awaited the imagination in the pica-resque life and characters along the great rivers. When Hall first traveled down the Ohio, he was not certain that the Muses would "honour a keel-boat with their presence"; but after hearing such songs of the boatmen as "It's oh! as I was walking out,/ One morning in July," he was convinced that the Muse of song, at least, was a "good republican" and would dispense her "smiles . . . upon the lowly as upon the great." Not the poetic Muse, however, but the realistic pen of Twain was to delineate the successors of Mike Fink and Pete Featherton in just such a colorful portrayal of Mississippi Valley life as Drake predicted could be wrought from the hardy exploits and ex-pansive characters of the boatmen. Nor did Twain neglect the pica-resque elements which Jewett perceived a generation before the Civil War in the fraudulent and avaricious pedlars who preyed upon the unlettered people of the Mississippi Valley. In the Far West, too, this interest in the picaresque continued, especially with the ascendancy of realism in the post-bellum decade. Indeed, within the sentimental formula which served as a framework for Harte's stories lay the prag-matic center of shrewdness which could be observed in the characters of the gamblers, the miners, and even the young girls of the Gold Rush era.

Though attention was paid to the sober aspects and characters of the West in such works as Eggleston's *The Circuit Rider,* Alice Cary's *Clovernook,* and Garland's *Main-Travelled Roads,* the Western "soul" that most of the writers wished the regional works to express was of a more sanguine cast. Whether in ante-bellum Ohio or post-bellum Chicago, they tended to attribute to the distinctive Western mind such traits as "vigor," "manliness," "breadth," and "fearlessness"; and these traits they conceived to be the salient qualities of a national American character which was directed toward the future rather than the past. Hence the Western author could scarcely find himself concerned with retrospective meditations on the Indian mounds or with prolonged veneration for the static grandeur of the regional landscape. By the very temper of the region he was impelled, as Isaac Jewett soon perceived, toward the Real and Present and toward a reflection of the ceaseless motion of his Western society. This focus of the literary imagination on the changing Present had its more comprehensive apology at the end of the century in the critical volumes as well as in the fictional narratives of the two Westerners, Howells and Garland. But meanwhile, something of an organic medium of this regional temper was suggested by Timothy Flint, who supposed that the venturesome life of the West had fostered a new mode of thinking which could be adequately conveyed only through such distinctive images as those "drawn from great distances on long rivers, . . . long absence from home, . . . and the habit of looking death in the face." Eastern taste could not act as a valid judge, he thought, of an authentic Western style displaying "a vigor, an energy, a recklessness of manner and form, . . . a racy freshness of matter, which smacks strongly of our peculiar character and position." With this concern for the Real and the Present and the active, Western literature would inevitably be drawn into a "fellowship" with business and mechanics, Daniel Drake thought—a "fellowship" which would diversify its themes and enrich its resources as well as "generate strange words and phrases" and "suggest novel modes of illustration."

Though the work of Western authors in the post-bellum era and also in the twentieth century did reflect some of the influences on theme and style which these ante-bellum critics had envisaged, it scarcely converged into the organic regional entity for which they had hoped. To be sure, the imagery of the long rivers appeared in Twain and Anderson, the "fellowship" of the world of commerce in Dreiser and Norris, the vigor and the raciness in Sandburg, and the "habit of looking death in the face" in Hemingway. But all these phases were disjunctive; they were never wholly fused into a Western mind and idiom. The West, in fact, like the South, after the Civil War yielded to the centrifugal forces of the time, with the result that there were many Western styles and tempers. Riley in Indiana, Fuller in Chicago, Howe in Kansas, and Bierce in California certainly had too little in common to be called a "Western school."

For all its thrusts toward a distinctive and independent literature, the West never really either abandoned or outgrew a concern for the literary proprieties inherited from the English tradition. For all their commitments to the future, the settlers on the moving frontier were dependent, as Lowell wrote, on a "screen of tradition and legend" and on a "landscape draped with some kind of memory." Hence nine-teenth-century Western writers, major and minor, were constantly invoking Apollo or Shenstone or Scott; or they were aspiring to be-come the Dickens of the Far West, as did Bret Harte; or they looked to *Don Quixote* and Goldsmith's *Citizen of the World* as the "*beau* [*sic*] *ideals* of fine writing," as did young Samuel Clemens. Within a generation after the riotous days of the Gold Rush, the influential *Overland* pleaded not only that a "generous margin" of literary in-debtedness to the past be permitted Far Western authors but also that this indebtedness be incurred to such "a Christian gentleman of scholarly tastes" as Tennyson rather than to the "naughty Swinburne." Thus as the West developed, it nurtured *ipso facto* a literary taste which could be satisfied only by a back-trailing toward eastern literary centers where literary standards were more firmly established and bel-letristic values were in higher repute. By the 1860's the young Ohioan William Dean Howells had decided that "there is no place quite so good as Boston" and had written to Lowell that most Western poets had blindly and futilely "delved and dug about in fields, that would never have yielded anything but weeds, whether upon the Ohio or the Charles."

By the end of the century Western authors who were well versed in the traditional literary modes had little but contempt for domestic literary aspirations. In fact, Ambrose Bierce sardonically confessed that he did not know whether he read the local poets of California before despising them or vice versa; and in Chicago Eugene Field judged such local effusions as "Hope; or, The Milkman's Dream" to be on about the same ridiculous level as the popular farm ballads of Will Carleton. Yet this *fin de siècle* acquiescence in the traditional canons of taste was temporary. After the turn of the century in Chicago and in the Far West and in subregional literary centers Western literary pride asserted itself again not only in critical manifestoes but also in the achievement of Dreiser, Anderson, Jeffers, Steinbeck, and many another who wrote avowedly with a regional consciousness. But this consciousness embraced a national literary ideal as well, as it had consistently done in the West. As New Englanders before the Civil War inclined to regard their literature as the utterance of the American genius, so Western writers for over a century have inclined to write from the assumption that "America is West." To reflect the mind and temper of the heartland, they have believed, is to come as close as possible to a representatively national literature.

CHAPTER NINE

The New Union: Literary Dislocation and Recovery (1861-1892)

> . . . the long darkness succeeding the war is about passing away, and literary interests—always the last to revive—will gradually improve. Our best age is yet to come.
>
> BAYARD TAYLOR, 1870

> Since the war our novitiate has ended.
>
> E. C. STEDMAN, 1885

The Impediment of War

The campaign for a national literature, having attained its greatest momentum in the 1840's, inevitably subsided under the pressure of graver political issues in the following decade. "It is a bad time for literature . . .," wrote Charles Eliot Norton on the eve of the conflict; and his comment was justified not only by the curtailment of publishing but also by the national tensions which militated against literary work in both a critical and an imaginative vein. After the beginning of hostilities, of course, most American writers of an analytical temper turned from a consideration of the character of the national literature to the graver and more elemental issue of the national structure: Union or Confederacy. On the rare occasions when some noncombatant author ventured to proffer a comprehensive design for American letters, he could do so only with the uneasy awareness, expressed by Charles Godfrey Leland in issuing *Sunshine in Thought*

(1862), that many would "object that a book of this kind is out of place during such a fearful and serious struggle." During the fearful struggle, indeed, most of the younger writers were obliged, as Lowell said in the Harvard "Ode," to seek Truth in "squadron-strophes" and lines of "steel and fire"; and most of the older writers must have shared the aging Halleck's feeling that the times were "too sternly sad to inspire a native minstrel." Among the few who supposed that American authors might keep to their accustomed literary paths in order to provide an antidote to the pervading sadness was, strangely enough, Mrs. Stowe. "It is not wise that all our literature should run in a rut cut through our hearts and red with our blood," she concluded in 1864; and to keep from thinking of things that made one dizzy and blind, she confessed her preference for pieces imbued with gentle merriment and the commonplace.

Much of the literary effort of the war years was, as Mrs. Stowe implied, devoted to bloody issues and events. In the ardor for the Union cause critics as diverse as Charles Eliot Norton and Emerson could unite in regarding Lowell, by virtue of his *Biglow Papers* and the Harvard "Ode," as an exemplary nationalistic poet; and accepting a similar obligation to express nationalistic sentiments, poets as diverse as Whittier and Whitman dedicated their pens to what they conceived to be the aims of the conflict. In this fervent atmosphere even the romantic George H. Boker was moved to turn his verse to admonish other American poets that the time had come "To strike aloud the sounding lyre,/ To touch the heroes of our holy cause/ Heart-deep with ancient fire." By such exhortations, however, Longfellow was not persuaded to yield to the sentiments of the hour. A genuine poetry could never result, he wrote during the war, from mere patriotic conformity to the current decree, "Go to, let us make a national song."

Although the intensification of national feeling may have in a measure accounted for some of Whitman's and Lowell's finest poetry, it probably thwarted more memorable works than it nurtured. As Richard Grant White remarked editorially in issuing the collection *Poetry . . . of the Civil War* (1866), the great body of occasional verse served at best to mark the course of popular feeling. Both for sustaining the hardy strain of native literature which had flowered at mid-century and also for directing its future course, the literary mind of the 1860's was rendered less than adequate not only by the tensions of the War and Reconstruction but also by a cultural vacuum which developed between a doctrinaire humanitarianism and vulgar materialism as major forces in American society.

The New Nationality

Even before the "long darkness" of the 1860's passed, however, the Union cause and victory, with attendant shifts in economic power and social values, had begun to alter the direction and tone of the literary quest for nationality. In both atmosphere and design the literary nationalism of the post-bellum generation was notably unlike that which preceded and followed. Its uncertainty in the 1860's, its change of pace in the 1870's, its modulation from a romantic to a realistic mode and temper and hence its aversion to strenuous affirmation in the 1880's—all these served to give post-bellum nationality an amorphous character decidedly erratic in outline when compared with the zealous and focused campaign for a national literature in the 1840's. Indeed, so far as nationality in literature was concerned, the era was not a markedly speculative one. "Let us cease to wonder whether there will ever be an American poem, an American symphony, or an American Novum Organon," wrote the reformer John Weiss in 1862, counting such literary speculations excrescent on a period of great national deeds. While men of letters did not entirely "cease to wonder" about the indigenous flavor of their writing, there was among them much less disposition to probe philosophically the national character and destiny and to assess native writing in such a context. The persistent nationalistic concern of Neal, Bancroft, Parker, Emerson, Simms, Longfellow, Cooper, Whitman and a host of other younger writers of the previous generation had little echo in Aldrich, Gilder, Taylor, or Twain. Perhaps Leland and Garland came closest to the earnest temper of the manifestoes and pronouncements of ante-bellum literary nationalism.

For this relaxed literary nationalism the Union victory itself was primarily responsible. In the first place, as John Weiss declared, the character and destiny of the nation seemed to have been given a definitive stamp by force of arms: in the triumphant strength of the New

Union there was an apparent assurance of direction which no mere verbal query or Emersonian declaration could challenge. In the second place, as the previous chapter on the rise of regionalism and local color has shown, with the Federal power firmly established and political unity assured, cultural diversity was not only permissive but even sanctioned. Thus, paradoxically, the dominant post-bellum concept of American literature was that it could be national only by being local. Hence the devoutly expressed hope of the Union General John W. Ames in the 1870's: "May the American novel never be penned and American social life never constitute the villain of romance." In this skepticism (if not in the hope) regarding an achieved nationality in American life and a consequent nationality in American literature, Garland, Howells, De Forest, and Eggleston largely concurred. The genius of American literature lay in the absence of an American genius!

Although the major explanations for the less sharply focused literary nationalism of the post-bellum period lay in the implications of the Union victory and other native factors, the lack of a supporting nationalistic critical doctrine from abroad also played a part. Whereas the ante-bellum proponents of nationality could draw convincingly from the theories of Madame de Staël and the German historical school, the later generation looked chiefly to Taine. Virtually all the major authors acknowledged the impact of his doctrine of literature as the expression of race, milieu, and epoch—Whitman, James, Garland, Clemens, Stedman, and, to some degree, Howells. But though Taine's famous study of the English soul through the application of his formula to English literature might be expected to have set a new pattern for the correlation of American literature with the national character, it tended instead to further the regional as opposed to the broadly continental approach. For if to write memorably is to write always of the milieu which one has experienced, Garland and other disciples of Taine argued, the American author should not venture beyond his own locale. With explicit adherence to this literary principle of Taine's, Eggleston wrote *The Hoosier Schoolmaster* as a genre painting of backwoods society. With a similar acknowledgement of Taine's influence the *Californian* in its first issue (1880) resolved to reflect Pacific culture by being Western in character, local in flavor, and vigorous in style; and a few years later the Chicago *Dial* also invoked Taine in an effort to stimulate a literature consonant with the "electric atmosphere" of the area. There were regional "souls" for some future Taine to deduce from nineteenth-century American literature, these editors and critics believed, but scarcely a national one.

Amidst this wide acceptance of cultural heterogeneity in the postbellum years as the essence of American nationality, however, one trait of the national character seemed to many authors sufficiently pervasive to form the central impulse of any literature which should aspire to embrace the national mind and heart: this was the humanitarian spirit which writers like Lowell and Whittier identified with the American Idea and with the Northern cause. Now that the Union victory had guaranteed that Idea, so the argument went, the utterance of the new nation would ineluctably reflect it. Once again American pens were to be dedicated to the New Zion, though a Zion of a dominantly humanitarian cast.

Even in the early part of the war, the young American authors Theodore Winthrop and Charles Godfrey Leland, confident that Progress had chosen America for her proving ground, made their separate pleas for what they called the spirit of the present as the generative factor in American writing. Faith in the present meant for Winthrop an "American view of history," and only from such a view, in which the past is continually on trial, he asserted shortly before his death in battle, can a vigorous national art emerge. In almost identical language Leland's literary manifesto *Sunshine in Thought* (1862) elaborated the argument that American authors must "Forget the spirit of the past, live in the present." To believe in the present, he explained with an optimism that is reminiscent of Melville's Confidence-man, involved the disavowal of Sorrow as an outmoded irrelevance and the recognition of the current age as a "turning-point" wherein "Right has at length virtually triumphed." Under the jurisdiction of Right the postwar era seemed to Leland to be one in which science and labor and management would work in harmony to establish the first humane civilization, and in this new society the arts would be dedicated to the service of "real wants." In an America on the verge of this happy humanitarian era under auspices of the Northern cause, he argued, the nation's authors could no longer indite "Psalms of Life" or pine for "lost Edens and buried Lenores."

Although the faith in Progress to which Leland and Winthrop wished to commit post-bellum American literature was almost wholly secular, a strong Christian strain was introduced by other exponents of the humanitarian view. For these writers the Civil War was a religious struggle; its all-embracing motive was the determination of the Union forces to establish social justice in accord with Christian principles. Probably no one traced the literary implications of this view so insistently as Dr. Josiah Gilbert Holland, whose influence was so strong in the post-bellum decade that one of his critics bitterly conceded that the period should be known as "the Holland age of letters." Underlying all of Dr. Holland's literary judgments was his conviction that "In Art, as in Nature, Beauty has a subordinate mission." The prime mission of the national literature, he therefore concluded, was to inculcate the spirit and values of the purest civilization of all time— that of the Northern states. By its commitment to a righteous war this civilization seemed to him to have achieved a "burning life, molten in Christian love." To try to cast this life "into the old molds of pagan art and life—outgrown, outlived, outlawed," would be a sacrilege indeed. Perhaps it was generalizations such as this that led the New York critic James L. Ford to charge that the Holland school had done more than Italian banditti and haunted castles to keep the facts of American life out of the national literature.

If to view the war as mankind's most courageous demonstration of the religion of humanity was to belong to the Holland school, however, its roll of literary adherents was large and respectable. No less a figure than Emerson professed his certainty that the war had converted America into the site of the battle for Humanity and that the sacrifices of the conflict were being "overpaid" by the vistas of Eternal Law which it opened. The war itself, indeed, he declared to be a poem which would inspire some master in the next age. Conclusions equally promising for the literary imagination were drawn by the poet Boker in his assurances to the Phi Beta Kappa Society at Harvard at the end of the war that no story since Adam rivaled that of the Northern cause—that in the light of their own "heroic days" the old

Grecian, Roman, and Arthurian themes were pale indeed. The elder Henry James found his country's "abstract manhood" no less stirring than Boker and likewise turned a disparaging literary glance toward the Old World, though not toward the ancient themes but rather toward Dickens and other "literary louts and flunkies" and "purblind piddling mercenaries of literature" who seemed to him to be unable to understand that the Civil War was the birth struggle of a new era of social righteousness.

The signal though narrow benefit that the war conferred for a time on the literary imagination was thus a tonic moral atmosphere. Its essence was remarked by Melville soon after the conflict when he expressed hope for the fulfillment of "those expectations which kindle the bards of Progress and Humanity." In the heat of civil struggle the minds of Holland, Emerson, Henry James, Sr., Boker and many another were indeed "kindled" into what Holland called "burning life," and this fervor they credited to Christian love, the religion of humanity, and confidence in the future. This tonic atmosphere T. W. Higginson preferred to call the "oxygen of liberty," and he had as few doubts as most other Northern men of letters that American literature, having breathed it, was about to enter its most vigorous era. By the centennial year of the Republic, however, it was clear that the "oxygen of liberty" had become all too heady for America's politicians and entrepreneurs, though scarcely a stimulus for her literary men. In "The National Ode" Bayard Taylor chose not to echo the disillusioned tone of Lowell's Centennial Ode; yet if in this public utterance he paid tribute to "Liberty's latest daughter [America]" whose future was to be made bright by the "oak of Toil, the rose of Art," in private he wrote in the same year to Hayne that these "are dismal days for all literary men." Taylor professed a faith that better days were coming; yet in the final decade of the century those critics and editors who had identified American literature with an intensive utterance of a pure and lofty humanitarianism had not seen their goal attained. In *The New World and the New Book* (1891) T. W. Higginson, who a generation earlier had supposed the "oxygen of liberty" about to effect a renascence in American letters, felt obliged to concede that the doctrine of individual worth and the equality of man had not yet had their proper expression in the great body of the national literature.

The Tide of Vulgarity

Beneath the bright, reassuring declaration of post-bellum humanitarianism flowed a strong undertow of materialism of which, it was soon evident, Dr. Holland and his school had taken too little account. If the Union victory was in a measure the triumph of Light over Darkness, it was also the triumph of an industrial power which seemed to the majority of Americans to promise a more satisfying future than did an era of righteousness and manhood such as Dr. Holland and the elder Henry James thought to be inaugurated by the war. Even within two years after Appomattox the public indifference to "intellectual aims" was so inescapable that Higginson cried out that "Our brains lie chiefly in our machine shops." By the end of the 1860's the earlier confidence of Boker and Leland in the regenerative influence of the war had been dissipated into a "melancholy view" over the prospects of poetry in "this practical, soulless, Gradgrind age," and from Joaquin Miller on the Pacific coast came a similar lament that he should be "pierced with intolerable pain/ Of poesy" in a land of greed and gold.

Within a decade after the war Leland's hope that only a literature serving "real wants" should survive in America was thus being realized with a vengeance. For the "real wants" had been construed by much of the postwar society in such a way as to make them synonymous with what Emerson described as the "great sensualism" of the postwar period, in which idleness, luxury, and selfishness were the conspicuous marks of national behavior. In fact, the devotion of the national intelligence to almost wholly material ends seemed so pervasive to the philosopher John Fiske that he charged America with having entered in the postwar years a barbarous stage in which the culture of the whole man was more deficient than that of all other nations. In the processes of the literary imagination, of course, such a society found little pertinence. Its financial overlords, in Helen Hunt Jackson's estimate, had eight-tenths contempt, one-tenth pity, and one-tenth respect for the literary man. The same fractional respect, no doubt, was allotted by the public.

Within this plutocratic climate the American author found his crea-

tive impulses all but paralyzed. He could not become the autochthonous voice of a culture in which he did not believe; he could not
gain an audience for his values in a society which did not believe in
him. "Even Longfellow, optimistic as he is," wrote Charles Eliot
Norton in 1873, "complains of the decline in taste for literary culture,
and of interest in literary pursuits. . . ." And Norton himself could
but characterize the post-bellum generation as one which, having
given itself over to making and spending money, had lost the capacity
for thought. Whether or not it had lost this capacity, it had clearly declined in its poetic sensibility. So "fettered and bound" in the prose of
utilitarianism did it seem to Christopher Cranch that he supposed the
American poet might best abandon all hope of touching the national
mind and retire to Parnassus to sing as he pleased. This mood of
defeatism at the hands of Philistia in the postwar years apparently lay
most heavily on Bayard Taylor, though it also became all but obsessive
with such friends and correspondents of his as Boker, Aldrich, Hayne,
and, at times, Stedman. Between the extremes of public taste represented by Josh Billings and J. G. Holland, between the vogue of
Western vulgarity and moralistic sentimentalism, Taylor could find no
substantial area of matured sensibility toward which the American
man of letters might point his work. To cater to the "vicious public
taste" of this "very dismal transition period" would be ruinous to any
author, he wrote Hayne in 1871. Five years later he seems to have
reached the nadir of despair over the futile attempts which he and
his literary acquaintances had made to maintain their self-respect and
at the same time reach the national mind. The summer of America's
centennial year he characterized as the "blackest period ever known
since we began to have a literature."

The group for whose sense of literary paralysis Taylor acted as a
spokesman may be charged, with some justice, as being too rigidly
derivative in taste. For the most part their imaginations lacked those
deep tones of indigenous coloring and that acute sense of nationality
which gave depth to the work of, say, Hawthorne or Melville or Whitman. No doubt they kept their attention too subserviently fixed on the
"age's craving for a novel thing," to use Boker's words, in an effort to
"find the trick to suit" it. It would seem that an almost obsessive concern over the "muddy tide" of vulgarity, bathos, and buffoonery led

Stedman to cry out against "the wretched, immediate *fashion* of this demoralized American period," and led Aldrich to shudder at masses who relished "abominations like Josh Billingsgate" and favored J. G. Holland twenty times more than Lowell. Yet the feeling of degeneracy in popular taste was not confined to Taylor's fastidious group. In the postwar years Whitman found the vistas of democracy clouded and Emerson was conscious, too, of a "sick public [who] want what is secondary, conventional, and imitations of imitations"; and from abroad young Henry James, appalled by the "incredible lack of *culture*" which his countrymen betrayed, wrote his mother that he could find but one word to describe them: "vulgar, vulgar, vulgar."

This estrangement from the popular will and taste, felt so keenly by American authors in the 1870's, was appreciably modified in the last decades of the century. Something of an index to the reconciliation is afforded by Stedman, who in the 1880's was disposed to lodge a deeper hope in the public mind which he had previously reviled. "If, then, the people care little for current poetry," he asked, "is it not because that poetry cares little for the people and fails to assume its vantage-ground?" The provincial humor which a decade earlier had seemed to him so degenerate, he now accepted as "not necessarily 'a poor thing,' although our 'own.'" Sharing this renewal of faith in the popular and indigenous, so conservative an editor as Robert Underwood Johnson reassured Joel Chandler Harris with the startling dictum: "The best American fiction is the outcome of what you call 'lack of culture.'" This rebirth of literary confidence apparently was effected not merely by less fastidious demands on the part of American authors but also by a less Philistine temper within the American public. Indeed, in the early 1890's H. C. Bunner could testify to an intellectual and artistic "improvement in the whole people" which in the past fifteen years excelled that of the whole preceding half century.

The Flight from Vulgarity: Ideality and Europe

In the deep gulf which in the postwar years separated the man of sensibility from popular taste and behavior there was bred a host of incipient or arrested expatriates. Unable to discover imaginative overtones or substantial values in the American past or present and lacking Henry James's freedom to escape to a more congenial transatlantic atmosphere, they were able to endure the callowness of their homeland only by flights into a rarified aestheticism or by proclaiming their allegiance to some established foreign culture. They were attempting, in Burroughs' arresting phrase, to achieve "beauty without the lion"—to cherish its form and flower while disowning its vulgar matrix. The literary consequence of this attempt to disown rather than sublimate the raw, coarse native scene was, as Burroughs perceived, also to strain from American writing its "blood or viscera." To this class such writers as Boker and Taylor essentially belonged; for they were self-confessed exiles in their own land—aware that they were "lost" because a "strain of distant and dead generations" had made them "other than these [neighbors] are."

Though Boker pursued a distilled art which, as he said, might belong to "all ages, every clime," some of his literary compatriots found a sufficient antidote to American vulgarity in the recent culture of Western Europe, especially that of England. The multiplication of American fortunes after the Civil War had encouraged an acquaintance with Europe which, as Henry Cabot Lodge noted in the 1880's, had "revived the dying spirit of colonialism" and had bred, especially in Eastern cities, coteries of young men who despised everything American and admired everything English. The literary ambition of these professed "cosmopolitans" seemed to Lodge not to go beyond that of writing clever fiction based on those aspects of American life which impress foreigners unpleasantly. These coteries were conspicuous and vocal enough for Henry Holt to fear that the Emersonian tradition of literary independence was being threatened "by an outbreak of Anglomania"; and even the sanguine T. W. Higginson was compelled to admit that "during the last few years" (the late 1880's) there had been "a curious relapse into something of the old colonial and apologetic attitude."

Of more import to American letters than this *fin de siècle* outbreak among the obscure young cosmopolitans, of course, was the lingering abasement before English culture among a few established authors. After the war the aging Fitz-Greene Halleck still punctiliously referred to the literary work of his compatriots as "American specimens of English literature" because, he insisted, he had never been able to define what *"American Literature* means." Although he thought that the " 'waters of the well of English undefiled' " could be drunk in America in all their purity, he supposed that these waters could only be imported in English bottles from London, which was the "court and capital" of the English language. Halleck considered the bond holding English and American culture indissolubly together to be a linguistic one; but with the late nineteenth-century emphasis on racial inheritance, other Anglophile authors found an additional argument for supposing that American literature must undeviatingly remain within the English orbit. The most conspicuous proponent of this view in the post-bellum period was Richard Grant White. Virtually ignoring the influence of milieu and epoch, to speak in Taine's terms, White insisted that America's ethnical as well as her linguistic ties with England would compel her best authors to "write good English words, and think good English thoughts." An acceptable American literature, he argued through the course of his novel *The Fate of Mansfield Humphreys* (1884), can come only from pure English racial stock uncontaminated by alien European races—from those "thoroughbred" Americans who are indistinguishable in taste, manners, and speech from cultivated Englishmen. Those Americans who wish a literature that smacks of the soil, the novel implies, must go to Sitting Bull and Squatting Bear. Convinced like Matthew Arnold that America was deteriorating through increased democracy and immigration, White sought to save American literature from the contamination of indigenous forces by confining it within the English tradition of polite letters.

The uncompromising Anglophile purism of Halleck and White was the exception rather than the rule among the major authors who remained in America after the war. Occasionally avowed "intellectual colonists," like Ambrose Bierce and Edgar Fawcett on the West coast, might lament that they could hear in their native land only a "faint and shimmering echo" of the English civilization from which everything worthy in the American mind seemed to them to have come. But the majority inclined, like Howells, to mingle a veneration for certain English masters with a recognition of both Continental and indigenous literary values. With Higginson they gladly took account of the "extra drop of nervous fluid" which the American milieu had added to the English stock.

The imagination of some authors, however, restive under both the traditional English and the nascent American modes, sought a purely transcendent and universal focus. Like the poet Charles De Kay, they abjured "national-nonsense" as a wall across the pathway of letters and would claim only the wide world as a Fatherland. Attempting to follow Bliss Carman's prescription that poetry should echo the joy of the whole earth, they were impelled toward symbols and images contrived from tradition for an abstract posterity rather than derived from impure but felt experience. Much of the emptiness of post-bellum American literature must surely be traced to this almost obsessive commitment to universal beauty on the part of sensitive authors repelled by the vulgar Philistinism and rude provincialism of American life. Their logic was essentially that of Christopher Cranch: since the people in the valley depend upon science for their light and on traffic for their pleasures, the poet can only retreat to Parnassus, sing as a voice in the wilderness, and consider Art as its own reward. Toward this Parnassus Sidney Lanier evidently hoped to move through what he called the "process of etherealizing," in which the poet would free himself from time and space—through a "spiritualisation" which was defined as a Tennysonian freedom from the "material accessories" that defaced the poetry of Milton. Although Taylor apparently made a more judicious effort than Lanier to discern the line which "Wavers between the Human and Divine," he too was ultimately driven by the "active air" of America into a devotion to Proportion and Repose and to "the Soul supreme whence they arose." Convinced that there are "eternal laws in literary art," he vowed to build of blocks hewn "from the everlasting quarries," to bring nearer to his countrymen that beauty which lies in the "dateless distance," and through an hour of perfect Song to feel the "Sunshine of the Gods." It could well have been such a poet as Taylor that W. W. Story had in mind when he wrote of the contrast between the older classical author and the modern who "dares not be simple and bold,/ But refines and refines and refines." For as Taylor had recorded his search for the line between Human and Divine, so Story described the current Brahmin poet as one who, sitting apart and brooding over the rude and offensive passions of the world about him, was hung between earth and sky, "to neither wed." Though White, Taylor, Aldrich, Gilder, Boker, and Lanier were scarcely Brahmins, they were hesitant to allow their art to spring from the American earth and as a consequence, ironically, they were unable to soar very far above it.

While the incipient expatriate remained at home and sang of Ideality, some of his literary compatriots crossed the Atlantic and committed themselves to what Taylor called the "myth of Europe." Many of them, unlike Taylor, decided once and for all that only the "splendid atmosphere" of the Old World could satisfy an imagination which their native land had starved. Increasingly during the century those who subscribed to this myth were able to test its validity by residence abroad. Often the very plutocracy which so many of them found intolerable provided, ironically, the resources which enabled them to linger indefinitely on foreign shores and denounce the crassness from which they had escaped.

The expatriated temper is as old, of course, as cisatlantic society; and it has been vocal since the days when Dennie longed to live under the patronage of an English monarchy and Freneau compared the plight of American poets to that of barbers in a country where there are no beards. Yet during the first part of the century, when few writers were sufficiently wealthy or sufficiently repelled by the native scene to remain abroad, perhaps the most conspicuous exemplar of this temper was the youth whom a brief sojourn in European capitals had rendered unduly critical of the arts and institutions of his homeland. As early as 1785, indeed, these denationalized sophisticates had been contemptuously dismissed by Timothy Dwight in a couplet: "Of all the plagues, that rise in human shape,/ Good Heaven, preserve us from the travell'd Ape!" Additional satirical portraits of the pretentious young *"cognoscenti"* came from the pens of Paulding, Theodore Fay, and other literary nationalists in the next generation.

With Cooper's and Irving's more extended residence abroad, however, the issue of expatriation took a more momentous turn. Over their alleged defection from American literary self-sufficiency popular indignation ran high enough to oblige both authors and their friends to offer reassurances and apologies. In much the same manner that Howells later came to the defense of James, the currently "acknowledged patriarch of American literature" in the 1830's, editor Robert Walsh, argued that Irving's literary achievement abroad had most effectively demonstrated that American men of letters were the peers of their British contemporaries, and hence it would be "sound policy" to send a hundred such authors abroad, even if they never returned. Meanwhile Irving himself had assured his friends not only that his life in Europe had not estranged him from America but also (as James was to say later in *The American Scene* of his own experience) that the coloring once given by his imagination to Europe was now gathering about the scenes of his native land. He could never forget, he wrote his brother after a dozen years abroad, the importance and the duty of producing some writings "of a decidedly national character" both to gratify his own feelings and to sustain his own literary character at home.

Though Cooper was not the object of so extensive a patriotic resentment, he was characteristically more forthright than Irving in meeting the criticism of his residence abroad. If any man is excusable for deserting his country, it is the American artist, he wrote from Europe in the 1820's, for there is little to gratify his taste in his native land, and his compatriots have little relish for poetry or music. A temporary sojourn in Paris, he had no hesitancy in saying, would do much to counteract that provincialism to which the American mind was so deplorably prone. But of the hazards of permanent exile he was well aware. "I cannot forget that I was born an American gentleman," he wrote Dunlap in 1832. "The idea of becoming a hack writer in a foreign land is not to my humour."

At mid-century it was not Northern Europe but Italy that afforded the strongest lure to expatriation among a new generation of American artists and writers. In Florence Thomas Buchanan Read contrasted the legendary shores of the Arno with his own Susquehanna, and not far away T. W. Parsons observed the aesthetic superiority of Ravenna's forests over the unstoried woods of his native land. In Rome Margaret Fuller concluded that her country, for all its political achievements, was still but a colony in literature and the arts; and she confessed that her joy in Italy was like that of a colonist returning home. The American who could remain unmoved in such an atmosphere seemed to her but a "booby truant."

Despite all the warm and classic charm of Italy, however, these ante-bellum artists and writers could never entirely renounce their homeland. To most of them the critic Augustine Duganne's current castigation of "bards who've 'crossed the water,'/ And think their native land earth's meanest quarter" could scarcely with justice be applied. Even such a confirmed expatriate as W. W. Story, who had written Lowell from Italy that he could never endure again the bondage of Boston and who had charged his countrymen with being too "scabbed over with pretenses" to sustain a worthy art or literature, could not push from his mind New England "dear, for all its prose" and "Hazed with poetic hues by childhood's dreams." And in the midst of the olive and the vine Buchanan Read longed for a leaf or bird or flower to be wafted from the "western strand" to breathe into one happy hour the "freshness" of his native land. It did not take him long to perceive that the dews which had at first bathed his "sandal-shoon . . . on foreign hills of song" were becoming dry. Like many another incipient expatriate and like James's Roderick Hudson, he had discovered that an imagination nurtured in the New World could not easily acclimate itself to the richer atmosphere of the Old. During these same years Hawthorne, drawing on his own experience and that of the sculptor Powers, pondered the hazards that attend prolonged absence from one's own country. The lingering expatriate, he concluded, is likely to fall between two stools and to discover that he is able to become a part of one country or another only by laying his bones in its soil.

Perhaps it was some such conviction as Hawthorne voiced that led most of the temporary exiles of the ante-bellum generation to return to America more staunchly if more judiciously nationalistic. "The American in Europe, if a thinking mind, can only become more American," Margaret Fuller decided; and young Taylor affirmed that his life abroad had sharpened his sense of the familiar aspects and the worth of his country more than any "American education" could have done. At times this intensified nationality was apparently little more than a feeling for the picturesque such as Henry Tuckerman found surrounding his "native spot" when viewed from a transatlantic distance. But generally it involved a more deliberate weighing of the whole culture of the Old World and the New, with an eventual incli-

nation toward the latter. Such was the nature of Hawthorne's preference expressed in the Preface to *The Marble Faun,* and such was
Ellery Channing's in the lines "On Leaving Rome":

> The truth that I had felt before,
>
> I now can paint with clearer eye,
>
> .   .   .   .
>
> My native land, the proud and strong
>
> Stands stronger matched with thy [Rome's] decline,
>
> I learn from thee that hate is wrong,
>
> And loving-kindness most divine.

During the mid-century years this assessment of the literary expatriate
became the recurrent burden not merely of essays and poems but also
of correspondence and fiction. Many of the letters that passed between
Lowell and Story or between Curtis and Cranch were, in effect, run-
ning discourses on the relative wisdom of taking one's literary chances
in Boston or in the kindlier air of Europe where, Lowell suspected,
the enchantment was always mixed with "humbug." One of the most
sustained ante-bellum arguments against expatriation came, oddly
enough, from the cosmopolitan Nathaniel Parker Willis in the novel
Paul Fane (1857). The artist Paul Fane returns to his homeland because he has come to subscribe to an organic theory of art. The imagination, he feels, is healthy only in the cultural climate to which the
formative years have conditioned it:

> But, very deliberately . . . I think my own country is *my mind's* na-
> tive air. After trying its lungs in the perfumed atmospheres of Europe
> . . . I find my American soul and brain, as well as my American
> heart, taste, and temper, pining for America to breathe in.

The air of despotism (for which the Southern poet Hayne was even
then desperately sighing) was, in Fane's estimate, "to republican lungs
. . . quite unbreathable." A few years later Robert Byng, in Theodore
Winthrop's novel *Cecil Dreeme* (1861), echoes Fane's republican creed
in arriving at his decision to return to a country where, his confirmed
expatriate friends assert, "there is no past, no yesterday, and if no yesterday, no to-day worth having,—but life one indefinitely adjourned
to-morrow." But it is only "the notion of Europe, and Europe-tainted
America," Byng insists, that his country is dull, prosaic, and tame. He
finds it quite otherwise because it is dedicated to the spirit of the pres-

ent and future rather than to that of the past; and he feels that the
art of the New World must proceed from the premise that the present
must try the past rather than be tried by it. Life itself can create
a fitting background, he avers, when acted on a new stage, and art
can survive "without antiquated stuff to curtain it."

After the Civil War Europe became the place where, as the temporary exile Charles Godfrey Leland remarked, "the majority of Americans who know anything or have read anything, go." Impatient with
a cisatlantic public who could respond to nothing in his art except the
humor of the Breitmann ballads, Leland himself resorted to the Old
World in search of an atmosphere which might allow him "to base a
reputation on the truly Beautiful." Moved by a similar aesthetic res-
tiveness, authors from all sections in the postwar decades journeyed to
Europe in the hope of meeting a kinder literary fate. For a time in the
1870's even the doughty Joaquin Miller found a cultural climate so
much richer than that of the "half-aware land" of his birth that he
was tempted to "rest on the plains of Lombardy for aye" and revel
in a world of old creeds and quaint old tongues. And in Florence a
few years later Constance Fenimore Woolson began a fifteen-year
sojourn by a similar immersion in "that old-world feeling," which
she described as "a sort of enthusiasm made up of history, mythology,
old churches, pictures, . . . the whole having, I think, taken me
pretty well off my feet." For many such writers, as for the young
Chicago novelist Henry B. Fuller, the greatest of life's longings had
become to "know the Old World through and through."

Yet among most American writers of stature this Old World intoxi-
cation was not indefinitely sustained. Miller soon conceded that Italia
was not his land, and Fuller returned to Chicago to portray in fiction
the commercial life which he had formerly despised. If Constance
Woolson remained longer abroad, she did so with increasing thought
of her homeland and of the relation of her art to it. "An American
who has lived so long abroad that he is almost denationalized, and
conscious of it fully," she observed in her notebook, would become an
"original figure" for fiction. Reading Cranch's poems in Europe, she
could not help responding to their American texture and becoming
homesick for the scenes they described. At any rate, through homesick-
ness or through a sense of literary expectations unfulfilled or through a

rebirth of faith in the American future, Leland, Constance Woolson, and most of the other exiles returned. Many of them, indeed, construed the alternatives in the simple terms of future versus past. Like Henry James's sister Alice, they might revert to America fully aware of "all that the ugly, raw emptiness of the land stands for, . . . undraped by the illusions and mystery of a moss-grown, cobwebby past." Or after seeing many peoples and lands, they might return with gratitude, as did Thomas Sergeant Perry, that Providence made them Americans. "These fellows over here have a magnificent past all around them," Perry wrote from Venice in 1889, "but what a present! And, apparently, what a future!"

The Jamesian Resolution

The notable dissenter from such sentiments was, of course, Henry James. Yet to suppose that his point of view was merely that of the American colonist in Paris "who has learned to be ashamed of his origin," as the novelist H. H. Boyesen charged in the 1880's, is to ignore much that James said and did. Moreover, the same ambiguity that marked his fiction also characterized his reflections on the artist in America. In the 1860's he felt both the intense glow of patriotism that attended the Civil War and also the vulgarity and gracelessness that were dominant in the American mind and scene. Although in the next decade he decided that his own literary career would best be served in Europe, he nevertheless exhibited in *Roderick Hudson* (1876) the hazards that confront the American artist who immerses himself in an alien culture. Surely through the judicious Rowland Mallet of the novel James voiced an argument that echoed the frequent misgivings in his own mind:

> It's a wretched business, this virtual quarrel of ours with our own country, this everlasting impatience that so many of us have to get out of it. Can there be no battle then, and is one's only safety in flight? This is an American day, an American landscape, an American atmosphere. It certainly has its merits, and some day when I'm shivering with ague in classic Italy I shall accuse myself of having slighted them.

Yet James had even stronger misgivings about Roderick's naïve nationalism, which assumed that a "typical, original, *aboriginal*" American art might be born by flinging Imitation overboard and fixing one's eyes on the National Individuality. In view of Roderick's later disintegration, both moral and aesthetic, amid the riches of Italian art, the novel scarcely encourages expatriation; nor does its action quite support the view that in America there was "beauty sufficient for an artist not to starve upon it."

Yet if America were somewhat lacking in "beauty" for James, it certainly did not seem to him to be lacking in characters and themes of interest to the novelist. The poverty that was likely to beset the writer in America, he apparently felt, was not so much that of materials as of perspective. Lacking a rich tradition, neither the American writer nor his readers had a lofty vantage point from which to comprehend their world. To the fastidious Charles Eliot Norton, who seemed to him to be "taking America rather hard," James expressed his belief that the face of both American nature and civilization were "to a certain point a very sufficient literary field," but that it would "yield its secrets only to a really *grasping* imagination. . . . To write well and worthily of American things one needs even more than elsewhere to be a *master*. But unfortunately one is less!" Hence, though he could but admit that to one who had been happy in Europe, even "Cambridge the Brilliant" was not an easy place in which to live, he nevertheless eagerly seized the locale for a novel (*The Bostonians*), which he determined to make as national as possible in order to prove that he could write "a very *American* tale." To be sure, James counted American materials sufficient only "to a point." The New York streets he felt obliged to abandon in one tale because they seemed "fatal to the imagination"; and he was skeptical enough of the appearance of an American Balzac or Thackeray to promise Howells that he would lie flat on his stomach when such a writer arrived. And though toward the end of the century his submission to what he called the Londonizing process led to extended periods when America faded for him and when he declined to trust America because he felt she had never trusted him, he never wholly reneged from the assurance given in the 1870's to his brother William: "I know what I am about, and I have always my eyes on my native land."

After the turn of the century James's mingled appreciation of and

strictures on the cultural changes in his native land were elaborated
in *The American Scene*. If in his later fiction he all but abandoned
America as too thin a setting, he neither abandoned the American
character nor failed to honor it. The three major figures of *The Golden
Bowl* (1904) he conceived of as "intensely American," and among
them was that type of sensitive American girl whom he recurrently
portrayed, as he said, as "the heiress of all the ages." For him the
woman of the New World, as he remarked in his Notebooks in 1892,
had paradoxically emerged as the worthiest exemplar of "the idea of
attachment to the past, of romance, of history, continuity and conservatism":

> She represents it from a fresh sense, from an individual conviction.
> . . . In other words, she, intensely American in temperament—with
> her freedoms, her immunity from traditions . . . represents the con-
> servative element among a cluster of persons . . . already in course
> of being demoralized, vulgarized, and (from their own point of view),
> Americanized. She "steps in" . . . with a certain beautiful beneficence
> and passion.

Moreover, lest the nationalistic lines of his "heiress" be blurred, he
admonished himself to represent the "unmistakableness and individuality of her American character." These are scarcely the words of
one who, as Boyesen charged, has become ashamed of his origin.

Through this paradox of the New World heiress who in the Old
World uniquely incarnated the flowering of Western civilization,
James apparently found his own solution for an old problem: the
absence in America of a settled culture which would allow the novelist
a suitably firm frame of reference. Not only was he one of those
spirits, of whom he had spoken in *Roderick Hudson,* with a "deep
relish for the element of accumulation in the human picture"; he also
supposed, he said in writing of Hawthorne, that the flower of art
blooms only where the soil is deep, that it takes a great deal of history
to produce a little literature, and that a complex social machinery is
needed to set a writer in motion. "It is on manners, customs, usages,
habits, forms, upon all these things, matured and established, that a
novelist lives . . . ," he wrote Howells; and it was the poverty of
"manners" in America that led him to fear that he would lie panting
on her bleak shores like a landed fish. The famous list of traditional

institutions which he listed in his *Hawthorne* as requisites for the novelist, Howells could dismiss as "dreary and worn-out parapher-nalia"; but to James they represented "an enormous quantity" of human life. Significantly enough, however, the *Hawthorne* passage appears in the Notebooks not as a personal tenet but as what "some-one says" in a story:

> Oh yes, the United States—a country without a sovereign, without a court, without a nobility, without an army, without a church or a clergy, . . . without a picturesque peasantry, without palaces or castles, or country seats, or ruins, without a literature, without novels, without an Oxford or a Cambridge, without cathedrals or ivied churches, with-out latticed cottages or village ale-houses, without political society, without . . . fox-hunting or country gentlemen, without an Epsom or an Ascot, an Eton or a Rugby . . . ! !

Since James believed that we know a man imperfectly until we know his society, the absence of such indices in the mobile life of America must have dictated in part his abandonment of his native country as the primary setting of his fiction. Every American writer, he con-cluded, must deal at least by implication with Europe; but a writer in Europe could be complete during the nineteenth century without America. Yet not only did James predict a reversal whereby in a half century or so European writers must be cognizant of America; he also suggested that Hawthorne and a few other Americans possessed the secret of literary triumph without the "paraphernalia" which he had specified. That they did so was in itself a measure of the magnitude of their achievement. A work like *The Scarlet Letter,* James affirmed, was not only exquisite in quality; "the best of it was that the thing was absolutely American; it belonged to the soil, to the air; it came out of the very heart of New England." To his friend Howells, too, James paid tribute as a great American naturalist who had quite properly deserted the Italian for his native scene; and to Constance Fenimore Woolson he accorded high praise for the "local tone" of her stories of the South. Living though they did in a great unendowed and un-furnished continent, such writers as these, James conceded, might "turn out something handsome from the very heart of simple human nature."

That James had either reached the most judicious conclusions or followed the wisest course for the American writer many of his friendliest contemporaries doubted. Even his brother William, whose national pride had been "tickled . . . not a little" by the presence of "some real American mental quality" in the early fiction, was increasingly distressed by a preciosity of style in the later novels which seemed to signify an interrelated decline in nationality and in art. The concern over national tone that William James intermittently voiced in his letters to Henry, Brooks Adams and Henry Cabot Lodge elaborated into a general principle: "Art, to be worthy of the name, must be the natural fruit of the soil from which it springs." Adams willingly conceded the superior richness of European backgrounds, but he counted it a stubborn fact that these rich fields were virtually closed to the American artist abroad because all "the wit, the fancy, the poetry, the knowledge of human nature" that mark great literature "must come from home." Despite such dicta, however, aspiring young writers continued to find themselves unable to convert what Henry James called the "tremendously positive" temper of American life into a fictional or poetic correlative. In the later decades of the century some of them, like Lafcadio Hearn, turned to the Orient rather than to Europe as the surest guarantee of the aesthetic values which they sought. America was a land for persons with great wills and energies, Hearn concluded; it was a land where publishers rather than authors succeeded. In the ensuing years many another author was to reach a similar conclusion and to follow Hearn's course of permanent expatriation.

The Counterpoise of National Humor

The antithesis of the expatriate movement in nineteenth-century America was a casual provincialism which bred an indigenous humor. The ante-bellum appearance of Downing, Mozis Addums, John Phoenix, and a score of other homely characters prepared for the comic provincials of Ward, Nasby, and Twain after the war. Whereas the expatriates turned a nostalgic gaze toward the past, these humorists fixed a pragmatic eye on the present; whereas the expatriates strenuously aspired to embrace the scope of European tradition, the humorists played on local minutiae with grotesque exaggeration; whereas the expatriates indulged in elevated tributes to legended scenes, the humorists with local dialect and idiom brought their compatriots down to an unstoried common-sense world.

With its journalistic origins and topical emphasis, such humor scarcely pretended to literary or aesthetic consideration; and until after the Civil War few American men of letters would accord it even a provisional place in the national literature. Even the post-bellum humorists themselves made few claims for it. Like many of their forerunners, such as Seba Smith and George Bagby, they inclined to disown their humorous sketches in favor of their more serious belletristic efforts. As a young author in California, Mark Twain expressed repeated anxiety about writing too "low"; and to his mother he professed annoyance that "those New York people" had ignored his better articles and "single[d] out a villainous backwoods sketch" ("The Jumping Frog") as the basis of his literary reputation. A few years later the vogue of "Little Breeches" brought constant embarrassment to John Hay, who hastened to explain that the composition of his Pike County ballads was a brief and amusing literary aberration which represented no part of his real self. And with a similar aspiration toward the "truly Beautiful," Charles Godfrey Leland depreciated the linguistic clowning of his own Breitmann ballads and claimed a special understanding of Artemus Ward's appeal to his son not to become "a great American humorist." Indeed, among humorists and belletristic writers alike, the prevailing attitude seems to have been that of the editor of *Puck,* H. C. Bunner, who cried out in protest against writing an article on American Humorists for the *Century*: "What do I care for Am. Hum.s! they interfere with literature."

Among the group of American jesters after the Civil War, Bret Harte seems to have given the most sustained appraisal of the nationalistic implications of the dialect humor of the period. Like Hay and Leland, he professed to be embarrassed by the popularity of his dialect verse. His worthier works were ignored, he thought, while "that cussed Chinaman" of "The Heathen Chinee" was always being "hoisted up aloft." Yet he could perceive the national overtones in the work of other Western humorists. In his early California days he acclaimed Ward for having caught the essence of fun overlying the surface of American life; and the "audacious exaggeration" and "perfect lawlessness" of this humor he explained as the indigenous product of a country of "boundless prairies, limitless rivers." As Harte settled into his life in Europe, however, he apparently became so chagrined over the crudities of Western humor that he began to disclaim its national character. The true humorist of the country, more serious and original than Twain, he insisted was yet to come. Confronted in his later years with the frequent English judgment that American humor constituted the only distinctive American literature, he begged to add that it was consciously devised as a kind of art and hence it could not be read as merely a "reflex of our life."

Despite the general condescension toward the humorists, however, respectable voices were increasingly raised in their defense in the post-bellum decades. As Emerson and Thoreau had earlier welcomed the indigenous raciness of Crockett and Downing, so Lowell saw at work in their successors a "genetic principle" which he thought an indispensable factor in the highest literature. They seemed to him exemplars, even though in a rudimentary stage, of the "natural" literature which he had espoused since the 1840's; for their work, and especially that of Twain, reflected an "Americanism which is there because we cannot help it, not put there because it is expected of us." Moreover, in the Introduction to his Second Series of *The Biglow Papers* (1867), Lowell paid tribute to dialect humor as a redemptive force in American style. Without a constant infusion of such racy popular idiom, he thought, the English mother-tongue would become a dead language; and the extravagance and exaggeration prevalent in native humor he adjudged symptoms of a vigorous imaginative faculty happily at work across a nation whose "ordinary talk" was fuller of "lively images" than that of any other people. Although Lowell's apology was buttressed chiefly by Yankee instances, he could also include "that genuine and delightful humorist," Petroleum V. Nasby, from the West.

In the revaluation of dialect humor that appeared in *Harper's, Putnam's,* the *Overland,* and other major magazines, especially in the 1870's, the nationalistic note was dominant. By virtue of its vernacular raciness and localism it was credited with an honesty which reflected the idiosyncracies of American life and provided American writers with the clues for a distinctive imaginative approach to their materials. By virtue of its searching irreverence, its impact was compared to that of Cervantes and Rabelais, and it was accorded a cisatlantic mission of "laughing aristocracy and old-worldism away." Even by 1870 pride in its indigenous flavor and point of view was sufficient to initiate a movement toward an American comic journal which would be devoted to the nation's unique group of jesters. In the tall tales and metaphorical bent of these jesters a vigorous young nation seemed to Horace Greeley to have found at last a literary idiom authentically expressive of its temper; and for this "keynote . . . of freshness and joy" as opposed to the pathos of declining races, Stedman at last expressed a similar gratitude. Though Stedman had at first lamented the horrible degeneracy of a public taste that could applaud Billings, he in the end acknowledged a debt to those foreign critics who had taught him and many of his literary countrymen the worth of purely American productions, "even our sectional humor, so as to bring about our discovery that it was not necessarily 'a poor thing,' although our 'own.'"

That adherents of the genteel traditions should have deplored the vulgarity and earthiness of Ward, Billings, Nasby, and other such characters was inevitable. But especial resistance to the humorists as spokesmen for the national temper came also from the Christian-humanitarians. Orthodox Christian critics found the Western clowns full of "sardonic blasphemy"; and the liberal editor of the *Nation* and critic of frontier influences, E. L. Godkin, charged that too often the humorists had vented their irreverence on the friends of liberty and progress and thus imperiled national ideals. It is not surprising, therefore, that in *The New World and the New Book* (1891) that eminent humanitarian T. W. Higginson should have dismissed the humorists as nationally subversive: they were promoted by English readers, derivative from English traits, and dangerous to the American character! It was not with this doctrinaire verdict, however, that the following century was to agree, but rather with the Emersonian insight that accorded the unpretentious native focus of the humorists the generative principle of an independent literature.

The Barren Scene Transformed

Although the humorists even before the Civil War had begun to point toward a fresh approach to the American scene consonant with native idiom and the pragmatic turn of the national mind, the lingering romantic doctrine of association still bred occasional doubts as to whether the country were not too callow for high literary use. Moreover, regardless of the achievements of Hawthorne, Melville, Simms, Cooper, Irving, and many lesser writers in the romantic mode itself, the old laments over the imaginative sterility of nature and society in the new land were still to be heard now and then in the post-bellum generation. Despite the changes wrought by a century of westward expansion, there were still those to echo Cooper's suspicion that the national society was too uniform to afford salient contrasts for the novelist and dramatist; despite the exploitation of Indian and slave, there were still those who concurred in Hawthorne's suspicion that America lacked depth for the moral imagination because the national conscience was weighted with no "gloomy wrong"; despite the aboriginal and colonial past and the conquest of a continent, there were still those who failed to discover any heroic interest in native history and legend. Soon after the war Dr. T. M. Coan, who a generation hence was to nurture the aspirations of Edwin Arlington Robinson, compared the fate of poetic sensibilities in America to that of "choice seedlings transplanted to a nursery where the soil is poor, the sunlight or the rain insufficient." And a decade later Henry James annotated Coan's figure, in effect, by marveling at Hawthorne's ability to wrest literary art from a milieu which lacked imaginative interest because it lacked aristocracy, peasantry, castles, country seats, and ruins. For both novelist and poet, for both realist and romancer, the thin current of the American past seemed to have deposited all too little of that rich soil of tradition out of which, as James phrased it, the flower of art blooms.

It is not surprising, therefore, that a frustrated author like Taylor should have blamed his failures not only on a Philistine public but also on "the destiny that placed us on this soil" and "robbed us of the magic of tradition, the wealth of romance, the suggestions of history, the sentiment of inherited homes and customs, and left us, shorn of our lisping childhood, to create a poetic literature for ourselves." When he attempted to create this literature in a home pastoral, he confessed himself thwarted by a rural life in which the old cheer of taverns and husking parties had given way to lectures on temperance and the rights of women; and he found little comfort in the possibility that two centuries hence milk-weed and mulleins might become "classic" and the juice of his country's foxy grapes, "Mellowed by time, . . . [might] grow to be sweet on the palates of others." Just as Taylor was convinced that "fancy's tenderest tendrils" withered for want of a past to cling to, so Boker in *Königsmark* (1869) bemoaned the plight of the imagination in a land in which there were no spoils of history:

All bare of legendary lore,
　Our grandest regions stretch away;
　These are the pictured scenes, no more;
　These are the scenery, not the play.

Such metaphorical expressions of despair came even from the aging Holmes, who wrote disconsolately of "this shallow soil of memory on which we live," and who counted it worth a year of his life to be able to walk once more under the high-groined arches of Westminster. In this climate of envy for the imaginative riches that Time had bestowed upon the Old World, Charles Eliot Norton came to feel Nature herself to be a kind of malicious accomplice, since she seemed to have expended all her "poetic imagination" in constructing the "exquisite elegance" of Europe and to have left America "very much in the rough." In such a view even Mark Twain, despite his apostrophes to the Mississippi and the lakes of the West, at times concurred. "There are mountains and mountains and mountains in this world—," he wrote Twichell after viewing the Alps, "but only these take you by the heart-strings." These had a soul and a voice, he conceded, which resounded in his memory with a glory and solemnity and pathos which those of his own native land could not evoke.

As the century moved toward its close, however, the old chorus of lamentation over the American scene grew fainter, dimmed in part by the very volume of literary works inspired by the native milieu. Of picturesqueness and diversity in the national life the mass of local color afforded substantial proof; and with the ascendance of the realistic mode the ante-bellum distress over the poverty of romantic associations became less keen. Moreover, for those whose imaginations could respond only to a locale already well infused with a *genius loci,* the nearly three centuries of American effort to build a nation had cumulatively amassed a fund of tradition and legend. In the islands off the New England coast, with their haunted gorges and caverns, Lucy Larcom professed to find the "genuine metal" for poetic wealth, even though it was still "somewhat in the ore." Yet the New England writer searching for romance seemed to Sarah Orne Jewett not to need haunted gorges; he could better find it in the "trivialities and commonplaces" of everyday life such as she had discovered in the country of the pointed firs. Nor was this sense of the romance inherent in the American scene confined to the feminine mind along the older coastal areas. There was a continental romance of a sturdier sort, John Burroughs thought, in the "heroic element" which clustered about the vast railways and mighty engines. The "proud spectacle" of a moving train or the "fast mail" seemed to him to have a mighty eloquence which was "as good as a page of Homer"; and in the crescendo of the mowing machine he heard a richer music than in scythe and whetstone. Yet Burroughs did not find a national poetry only in the hum of recent inventions. The mocking bird of the South, he contended, undoubtedly excelled the nightingale "in the variety and compass of its powers"; and the poetic uses of the hermit thrush he supposed adequately demonstrated by Whitman. In the Ohio Valley the poets Cawein and Riley had also discovered, as the former said, that America had so many sources of wild beauty that her writers need not trudge like mendicant friars to beg among the misty abodes of Europe. If American authors would but "Waken to/ The pipings here at hand," Riley contended in one of his poems, they might hear the clear halloo of truant-voices and the water's roundelay.

In these apologies for the imaginative sufficiency of American life and nature it was Jewett and Burroughs rather than Larcom and Riley who presaged the literary course of the next half century toward realism. What they were saying in effect was that their countrymen, through generations of struggle and achievement in a new land, had invested their immediate world with those overtones which had formerly been induced by romance. In Sarah Orne Jewett's world these overtones might be heard in a family reunion or the solitary life of a shepherdess off the Maine coast; in Burroughs' they might arise from the detailed tracing of the behavior of familiar American fauna or from the sense of national power and plenty implicit in American industry. In the last decades of the century, however, most American writers must have taken the views of Jewett and Burroughs essentially for granted, for apologies such as theirs for the American scene as a whole were much rarer than they had been a generation earlier. Only in the Midwest and Far West did there seem to be a continuing need for assaying the worth of the literary veins beneath the native surface. Howells, Twain, Cable, James, and Whitman, among others, were rendering apologies superfluous by showing numerous aspects of contemporary life viable for the writer seeking to mirror the human condition.

The Ascendance of Indigenous Realism

In developing their postulates for a national literature, American critics and authors always inclined to keep indigenous tendencies attuned to the prevailing literary modes, though not to the political and moral ideas, of Europe. When in the ante-bellum decades romance was dominant, they happily found the cisatlantic scene much more adaptable to the new mode than to neoclassicism: they adduced an aboriginal past, the adventures of colonization and frontier, a republican war, a beneficent future, and a milieu where the voices of both nature and the heart could most readily be heard. With the advent of realism at mid-century American writers professed to find a mode even more congenial to the national temper and background. Before the Civil War, as has been shown, indigenous impulses were already pushing American literature toward realism. The Union victory crystallized these tendencies and furnished a national climate for which the realistic mode was the most appropriate utterance. Its chief protagonists were Northerners who were firm Union men or counter-Confederates like Twain, Cable, and Harris. Sensitive to the large social and economic interests and values represented by the Union cause, it increasingly attuned itself to the rising industrial rather than the fading agrarian forces in the national life. Had the Confederacy triumphed, surely American literature would have taken a radically different turn.

In the rise of realism the victorious North found a mode consonant with the complex of qualities which it represented, and under its dominance the national literature veered toward the urban, optimistic, prudential, and pragmatic. Hence the new realism tended to discount the past, remote associations, and large ethical concepts in favor of the more narrowly defined social issue and a practical humanitarianism. When in its local color phase it turned toward the provincial, it constantly risked a romantic reversal by indulging the nostalgic, the sentimental, and the picturesque at the expense of the topical, progressive, and rational. The realistic literary corollaries of the Union cause and victory were most cogently expounded in two books which, in effect, embraced the realistic impulse of the period: at the beginning Charles Godfrey Leland's *Sunshine in Thought* (1862) appeared as a vigorous manifesto for a "whirling realism" proper to a new industrial civilization; at the end Howells' *Criticism and Fiction* (1891), holding to Leland's main postulates, sustained more temperately but no less positively the argument for realism as the mode most consonant with the common sense of American character and the humane progress of American society.

The "sunshine" by which Leland prefigured the next stage in American culture was more than a sentimental metaphor; it was the same image by which Hawthorne, Theodore Winthrop, and other contemporaries signified the mental climate of republican America as opposed to the shadows of Old World society. The Romantic thesis which precluded art from the sunshine and made it contingent on the accretion of "gloomy wrong" Leland rejected as historically naïve. The "sadness" on which Hawthorne and Poe inclined to posit the deepest probings of the imagination he relegated to an outmoded phase of Christianity which had fostered chivalric literature. Superseding this phase, he predicted, a new age born of Industry and Science and permeated with "an infinitely higher feeling" was at hand. This was the age of *Utilitaria*, a "tremendous incarnate Buddha, bent on redeeming the world," and of this new age industrial America was to be the prime exemplar and prophetic voice. Its literary medium Leland pronounced to be Realism; for the Romanticism which had long been nurtured by social decadence was being dissipated by a "Northern breeze" of emancipation and free labor. "Let us wash away the old romantic film from our eyes," he cried, "and put on new garments, and leave to the past its past."

Leland's proposals for a new realism thus rested on an optimistic positivism, on a faith that Science, destined "to conquer even literature," would usher in a new spirit. The Science which in his view was to redeem the age from specious beauty, however, was no abstraction; it was rather the technology with which Americans, especially in the North and East, had pragmatically identified it. This "steam wheel age" of science was in Leland's estimate not only making life more comfortable; it was also making art "practical, material, and natural," and it was leading America "to the highest forms of beauty." The American poet of the future, therefore, could no longer be one of the "sweet singers of sorrow," whose sober art was appropriate only to the less fortunate past; he was obligated rather to "fall in with the realizing tendency of the age, with its practical onward march." To his buoyant and self-reliant utterance, Leland predicted, the popular response would be a feeling of power and pride appropriate to the character and destiny of a "young, brave-hearted race." American authors could find a literary integrity, he insisted, only through a "steam-engine whirling realism" and a "brave naturalism" correlative with the utilitarian temper of the new civilization to which their nation pointed:

Young writer, . . . whoever you be, I pray you go to work in this roaring, toiling, machine-clanking, sunny, stormy, terrible, joyful, commonplace, vulgar, tremendous world in *downright earnest*. . . . I swear it . . . ; . . . you will find your most splendid successes not in cultivating the worn-out romantic, but in *loving* the growing Actual of life. Master the past if you will, but only that you may the more completely forget it in the present. He or she is best and bravest among you who gives us the freshest draughts of reality and of Nature. It lies all around you—in the foul smoke and smell of the factory, amid the crash and slip of heavy wheels on muddy stones, in the blank-gilt glare of the steamboat saloon, by the rattling chips of the faro table, in the quiet, gentle family circle, in the opera, in the sixpenny concert, the hotel, the watering-place, on the prairie, in the prison. Not as . . . the manufacturers of Magdalen elegies and mock-moral and mock-philanthropical tales skim them, but in their truth and freshness as facts. . . . Heavens! is not LIFE . . . as well worth the fierce grapple of GENIUS, here and *now* . . . as it ever was under the cedars of Italy . . . ? . . . and if you watch the time, you may see that it is the warm truth from real life, which is most eagerly read and which goes most directly to the hearts of all. . . . Be bold and seize it with a strong hand.

In his confident evangelism for an American literature consonant with Science and Nature, Leland had strong affinities with Whitman; and in his insistence on a literary tone of "serenity and cheerfulness" he anticipated Howells' famous words on the obligation of the native author to emphasize the "smiling aspects of life" because they are the "more American." Yet either because its zealous positivism facilely misrepresented and simplified the national temper, or because its issues seemed of little moment in the midst of the Civil War, *Sunshine in Thought* made no such impact on American writers as did Whitman's Preface to *Leaves of Grass* and Howells' *Criticism and Fiction*. No other nineteenth-century American author except Howells, however, so earnestly and cogently related realism to the post-bellum American culture. Garland, to be sure, under the influence of Taine and with a Spencerian faith in Progress, began in the 1880's to formulate his doctrine of Veritism, a somewhat pretentious and naïve version of realism which he later elaborated in *Crumbling Idols* (1894). And, like Leland and Howells, he made nationalistic claims for the mode. "Realism or veritism (or Americanism, at bottom these words mean practically the same thing) is on the increase," he reported. Veritism is American, he seems to have reasoned, not merely because it is faithful to the "stern facts" of American life; it also, by committing itself to the depiction of these facts, becomes the instrument of that social progress for which America pre-eminently stands. This identification of realism with the national devotion to Progress was not uncommon. Romanticism was to be regarded an alien mode, as the novelist H. H. Boyesen said, because it subsisted on the social inertia and injustice which America was desined to transcend. To the extent that her authors had accepted realism as their authentically national medium, he concluded, her literature had become "virile, independent, and significant."

Most of the growing body of realists after the Civil War, however, were slow to follow Leland in correlating their literary procedures with the positivistic temper and utilitarian emphases which the Northern victory and the industrial growth of the nation had encouraged. Even when they turned to the city to depict postwar industrialists and politicians, as in Howells' *Silas Lapham* or Twain and Warner's *Gilded Age,* the urban foreground was set against a background of lingering agrarian manners and values. For a time, paradoxically, they recognized the emergent urban-industrial national culture by applying their realistic pens to rural areas; they accepted the new era by devotedly recapturing the old before it passed away. But local color implied both an urban audience and an urban point of view; it was, in essence, for all its meticulous detail and its pretensions to realism, the urban dweller's new romance. Its vogue was grounded in the need of a pragmatic society for the picturesque, and this need could be satisfied, American readers had discovered, not only by Europe (as in Henry James's "Four Meetings") but also by the varied and remote regionalism of a vast new continent. Cable's Creoles, Craddock's Tennessee mountaineers, Eggleston's circuit riders, and Mary E. Wilkins' reticent New Englanders were all the obverse side of Leland's new Utilitaria.

The local colorists, nevertheless, could claim to be an authentic part of the realistic movement by their primary allegiance to observable fact—by professing themselves content, as did Bayard Taylor in writing *Hannah Thurston* (1863), merely to transcribe what seemed to them the neglected peculiarities in the life about them, and to have their transcriptions judged by the principle of fidelity to the American scene. Their aim seems to have been, as Mrs. Stowe phrased it, to make the "mind as still and passive as a looking-glass, or a mountain lake, and then give . . . merely the images reflected there." In accordance with this creed which pushed American writing toward validatable experience, Mark Twain admonished himself to avoid wholly imaginary incidents and "found on a *fact*" in his "personal experience" if he wished to have the created work "seem reality." In this empirical atmosphere even Andrew Carnegie learned to take issue with the classicism of Sir Edwin Arnold on the semantic ground that things and realities and not words and phrases were becoming the stimulus and the referents for the imagination.

Under such principles of realism fiction inclined to become, as Henry James called it, a "history"; and accordingly the national literature consciously moved away from its ante-bellum glorification of American history or principles or aspirations, as Taylor observed, toward an objective recording of the "lesser vibrations" of normal experience. *The Hoosier Schoolmaster* displaced *The Deerslayer* and *Moby Dick* as a model of tone, method, and theme. Eggleston, indeed, insisted that "no man is worthy to be called a novelist who does not endeavor with his whole soul to produce the higher form of history, by writing truly of men as they are, and dispassionately of those forms of life that come within his scope." This creed of local realism, moreover, demanded not merely an eye sharpened for unique pictures but also an ear sensitive to all the nuances of provincial speech. If localism offered the means whereby American writers were to free themselves "from habitual imitation of that which is foreign," as Eggleston maintained, then the use of dialect, as the quintessence of localism, seemed the *sine qua non* of an American literature. Accordingly, in innumerable prefaces, from that of *Huckleberry Finn* down to those of ephemeral regional narratives, post-bellum authors professed their concern for dialectal authenticity. Eggleston's deliberate and successful experiment with "rude characters and a strange dialect perversion" in *The Hoosier Schoolmaster* (1871) signalized the rise of what Hamlin Garland called the "cult of the vernacular," with Gilder as "its high priest." So influential did this "cult" become in the 1870's and 1880's that even the romantically inclined Thomas Nelson Page felt obliged to espouse colloquial realism, and the sentimental Riley became fastidiously contemptuous of the "little minnow poets" who, inept at dialect, were still bound to a traditional poetic diction. Indeed, Henry James was creature enough of his period to suppose that Hawthorne might have been a greater artist had he recorded more faithfully the speech and manners of his region, and that one of Constance Fenimore Woolson's high achievements was the philological exactness with which she recorded Negro speech.

The vogue of local color with its devotion to dialect was a far cry, of course, from the "steam-engine whirling realism" which Leland had besought as the literary correlative of an increasingly urban-industrial culture. To be sure, Rebecca Harding Davis had begun to delve into "vulgar American life" by her sketches of life in the iron mills in the *Atlantic* in 1861. Later Rose Terry Cooke and Sarah Orne Jewett ventured into the life of New England mill workers for their themes, and John Hay involved labor unions and organizers in *The Bread-Winners* (1884). Nevertheless, until the end of the century the human components of America's industrial growth were generally sketched from afar and limited to such respectable "captains" as Howells' Silas Lapham and James's Christopher Newman. With substantial validity Lafcadio Hearn could maintain in the early 1880's that the realists had failed to give distinctive and comprehensive portrayals of life "in the workshops and factories, among toilers on river and rail, . . . in mining districts, . . . in the suburbs of the vast industrial centers, . . . among men who, without culture, have made themselves representatives of an enormous financial force." Even the rich social phenomena of immigration and slum life in New York City remained in this decade virtually untouched, as H. C. Bunner observed; no "deodorized American Zola" had as yet ventured "into the Ninth Ward."

That this "low-life territory" had been neglected by American writers seemed to James L. Ford, Bunner's associate on *Puck,* traceable to the dynasty of genteel taste established by Holland and Gilder. Yet for this hesitancy to approach "the Ninth Ward" probably Howells was also in a measure responsible; for the brand of realism which he proclaimed in the 1870's and 1880's as well as his own earlier fiction scarcely pointed to the "Ninth Ward." Despite the generous encouragement he accorded Crane's and Garland's grim stories of the dispossessed, his greater admiration was for the "divine" Jane Austen and for a realism that exemplified "prudence, obedience, reason." Striving for a generation as editor, novelist, and critic to expel what he regarded as an irresponsible romanticism from American writing, Howells became equally concerned that a new transatlantic morbidity under the guise of realism should not become the vogue. The principle of realism which he at length outlined and defended in *Criticism and Fiction* (1891) was less strenuous and less doctrinaire than the "steam-engine whirling realism" for which young Leland had spoken in *Sunshine in Thought* three decades earlier. Whereas Leland's prospectus for a national literature had many affinities in temper and theme with Whitman's Prefaces, Howells considered himself a disciple of the Emerson who had urged American "scholars" to emancipate themselves from alien models by embracing the low and common aspects of the native scene. *Criticism and Fiction,* relatively innocent of the thoroughgoing positivism on which Leland had based the realistic temper, served rather as an apology for the less pretentious fidelity to some typical segment of national behavior, and this fidelity in the aggregate seemed to Howells the most valid conception of the Great American Novel.

Despite their differences, however, the two authors were clearly in common revolt against the morbid and decadent and sentimental states of mind in which they supposed romanticism to have its diseased roots. Both espoused a realism which was indigenous in the sense that in method and temper it seemed best adapted to express a progressive republicanism and the high average of happiness of their countrymen. Hence Leland's reiterated principle that the new realism must bespeak geniality and common sense, was echoed in Howells' more famous dictum: "Our novelists, therefore, concern themselves with the more smiling aspects of life, which are the more American, and seek the universal in the individual rather than the social interests." As Leland rejected the element of sorrow in Christianity as an outmoded response to human suffering, so Howells contended that fiction revolving about sin, suffering, and shame could not be regarded as representative national literature, since such themes were inconsistent with the "large cheerful average of health and success and happy life" peculiar to America.

Although Howells at times regarded any attempt of "our novelists to try to write Americanly . . . [to] be a dismal error," and although he advised them to be only as American as they "unconsciously" could, his *Criticism and Fiction* in effect proposed a national literary norm of wholesomeness, confidence, and fidelity to American experience. Literature would fulfill its obligations to democracy, he felt in his earlier years, not so much by expounding a political point of view as by devoting itself to an everyday "sense and truth." Furthermore, realism seemed to him the most democratic of the literary modes because its claims to "sense and truth" could not be tested so readily by learned critics as by the mass of readers who had the basis of judgment in the observable world about them. It was in fine consistency with this literary creed that Howells judged Twain to be the "Lincoln of our literature." More than the works of any other author, he felt, Twain's books at once embodied the "vast kindliness and good-will" as well as the "shrewdness" of the American character. The fact that the "ordinary minds" had embraced Twain sustained Howells' democratic faith that the American people would appreciate any literature which comes close to life.

From the literary postulates of Howells and his fellow realists, American writers worked with increasing confidence and success in the post-bellum decades. By the 1890's they had fitted in the details of varied phases of the national life in every region from Maine to California and from Michigan to Louisiana. To be sure, their prescriptions had not entirely been fulfilled. The geniality that Leland and Howells had hoped for was missing in Garland's somber pictures of toil and poverty on the middle border, as well as in Howe's *Story of a Country Town,* Kirkland's *Zury,* and Twain's *Pudd'nhead Wilson.* Moreover, city and industrial life were still to be adequately treated in a later generation which could accept Dreiser and Farrell. Their most crucial deficiency in the eyes of contemporary critics, however, lay in their very method—a method which by its dispassionate localism precluded their works from expressing that "genius" of America whose titanic utterance Emerson had so memorably invoked. Contemporary realism mirrored life in its lesser manifestations, ignoring "old tyrannies and . . . new hypocrisies," said Julian Hawthorne, and it conveyed little of "the characteristic mission of America to mankind." This "shallow Americanism" the Hoosier novelist Maurice Thompson indicted more specifically: what impression would a foreigner receive from the accumulation of realistic dialect stories and personal sketches, he asked, other than that America was a land of insignificant, vulgar people; from the sum of this trivial and enervating realism what awareness could come of the heroic purpose of the most robust people on earth? Moreover, under the impact of this realism American poetry as well as fiction, Stedman feared, was losing some of its "feeling" and "vision." The radical quality of any national literature is not determined by objects and scenes, however meticulously copied, he reminded the realists; for the spirit and not the letter giveth life, and literary fruit is to be judged not by its color and form but by its flavor.

Despite the strictures of the romanticists at the end of the century, however, the realists clearly, within their own postulates, had both broadened and refined the literary expression of the national mind.

Both Howells and Twain worked consciously within its assumptions to create a substantial canon of distinctively American works—distinctive enough, indeed, for Hemingway to call *Huckleberry Finn* the first *American* novel; and Henry James not only had praise for the realistic precision of Howells and Woolson but also created many of his characters, like Newman and Ransome, within the spirit and method of the movement. Perhaps an equally notable gain of post-bellum realism for the national literature, however, lay in its nurturing a host of competent though second-level writers whose skilful exploitation of various regions deepened the popular interest in native materials and prepared the public for the richer realism and naturalism of the next generation. Jewett, Garland, Cable, Howe, and many another perceptively and distinctively grounded their writing in the life about them and, for all their varying tones and purposes and stylistic art, set the direction for Crane, Dreiser, Norris, and Cather almost as surely as Twain prepared for Hemingway. Even their exercises in dialect served to show how the range and tones of American speech could enhance the color and enrich the characterization of American fiction. In the scope and variety of realism, as Howells said at the turn of the century, the nation at last had spoken in all its diverse accents.

The Great American Novel

With the emergence of prose fiction as the dominant literary mode of the late nineteenth century, it was inevitable that American aspirations for a great national literature should have adjusted to this development. Whereas the nationalists of the post-Revolutionary generation had fixed their literary ambitions on the Great American Epic and those of the ante-bellum period on the expression of the Great Idea of democracy, the focus of nationalistic reference in the two decades after the Civil War was the Great American Novel. The coining of the phrase probably belongs to the 1860's. In the latter part of the decade the novelist De Forest used it in referring to a friend's ambition to produce a work of fiction of which the American people in general could say: "That is my picture." In one of the few thoughtful discussions of the requisites for such a work De Forest evolved a definition which would no doubt have been accepted by most of his literary contemporaries: the Great American Novel will be one so broad that every American can say that it is a likeness of something he knows. The nearest approximation to this specification he found in *Uncle Tom's Cabin,* with its national breadth and natural dialogue. But two subsidiary criteria also emerged from De Forest's analysis: as a realist, whose *Miss Ravenel's Conversion* (1867) is sometimes credited with being America's first realistic novel, he required an American Balzac or Trollope who would "picture the ordinary emotions and manners of American existence"; as a Northern humanitarian and a reader of Taine he required that the progressive American soul be focally implicit behind the tableau of manners. None of the romantic writers— he did not mention Melville—could he consider seriously as the Great American Novelist. And since America was still a "changing infant" whose soul had not fully matured, he placed the writing of the Great American Novel in some indefinite future.

De Forest's skepticism regarding the imminent appearance of the Great American Novel was generally shared by his fellow realists in the postwar generation. One might suppose that these ascendant realists, with their concern for an indigenous fiction, would have seized the phrase for their own use. The contrary, however, was true. Indeed, the dream of the Great American Novel was essentially conceived from a romantic matrix—from the assumption that the national "genius" can invigorate the imagination with a unifying power capable of fusing apparent diversity into a singleness of meaning. Such had been Cooper's doctrine: that the Americanization of fiction is contingent upon application of American principles to plot and character, whatever the milieu. Shaping his materials steadily by principle, the American novelist could move indifferently into past or future or into transatlantic society (as Cooper consciously did in *The Headsman* and *The Heidenmauer*) with a communication of nationality as valid as he who focused on current behavior in his native land. Something of this view was echoed by Thomas Sergeant Perry in the early 1870's when he asserted that whether the Great American Novel were laid on the prairies or on Fifth Avenue, it must transcend geographical boundaries. The most cogent and spirited apologist for the Cooper thesis, however, was Julian Hawthorne. When the Great American Novel arrives, he predicted, it will rest not on the episodic and fluid externals of the national life but on the moral and intellectual eman-cipation which defines the American mind. It might appropriately be set abroad, he added, provided it treated its persons and places and ideas "from an American point of view." It might, in other words, be *The Marble Faun* or *The Wings of the Dove.*

The realists, on the other hand, committed as they were to the plane of manners within the writer's own observation, were increasingly em-barrassed by the obligation, which the Great American Novel imposed, to find a representative nationality in any given segment of American society. Romantic writers like Cooper and Paulding and Kennedy whose characters were founded on an idea or a myth of America seemed to De Forest to have created mere "ghosts"; to found on fact, as the realists professed to do, was to discover no clear outline of an American soul amid the conflicting provinces which composed the Union. It is not surprising, therefore, that most of the slurs on the aspiration for such a masterwork came from the realists. Nevertheless, they asserted their claims. "In every town there is material for the great American novel so long expected, but no one appears to write it," declared Edgar Howe, whose *Story of a Country Town* was ac-claimed at times as having met the test for the honor. But what Howe implied by his statement was merely that a great novel could be writ-ten in America. For him the affective and cultural focus was not to be national but universal; the American locale would be of interest not as a distinctive provincial community but as a microcosm of human motives and behavior.

Among the major spokesmen for realism, Howells and Eggleston and Garland, the nationalistic note was more emphatic, though they agreed with De Forest that the appearance of the Great American Novel was contingent on the development of a more homogeneous society. Moreover, they suspected that any single novelist would find it almost impossible to comprehend the vast American scene, however homogeneous it might be. Such a national novel could achieve its proper encyclopaedic form, Howells sardonically wrote, only by con-gressional appointment of novelists under one editorial director! Con-temporary American writers could best contribute toward the Great American Novel, the realists believed, by a conscientious depiction of the localities and regions which they knew. This conviction Eggleston summarily stated in his 1892 Preface to *The Hoosier Schoolmaster* when he said that regionalism "has made our literature really national by the only process possible," and that the "'great American novel,' for which prophetic critics yearned so fondly twenty years ago, is appearing in sections."

To examine the comments on the Great American Novel in the post-bellum decades is to conclude that the term was more nearly a shibboleth than a critical concept. It nurtured few new insights into the nature or sound development of American literature. In general it merely provided a focus for realists and romancers to reiterate the case for their discrete methods of establishing an American literature. Indeed, when any writer or critic discussed it, he merely applied to fiction whatever definition of nationality he had previously evolved, fixing the quintessence of the Great American Novel in idea or style, in method or theme, according to his predilection. Yet however thin the critical atmosphere that surrounded it, the call for the Great American Novel had surely not been reduced by 1880 to the contemptible level of "comic Prophecy" to which the novelist-playwright Edgar Fawcett assigned it. Although the extravagant hopes of the 1870's for a national masterwork have even yet not been realized, the writing of the Great American Novel has continued to be the vague and consuming dream—usually as ill defined as the term itself—of thousands of young authors. How persistently it has continued to arouse the imagination of amateur writers has recently been attested by Clyde Brion Davis's fictional treatment of a journalist's literary aspiration in *The Great American Novel* (1938). Even though by the 1880's the more seasoned writers like Howells were satisfied that a national literature was being steadily achieved, the more earnest nationalists still fondly yearn (to use Eggleston's phrasing) for the definitive *magnum opus* of American fiction.

The End of the Novitiate

The year 1892, the *Dial* predicted on the following New Year's Day, will in the future be known as the *Annus Terribilis* of the nineteenth century. This dark prophecy was prompted by the editor's sense of the loss which American letters had sustained during the previous year through the deaths of Whittier, Whitman, Parsons, and Curtis. Had the year 1891 also been included, with the names of Lowell and Melville added to the necrology, he would have had additional reason to observe that the first great age of American writing had come signally to a close, and that to its achievements the future of American letters would in no small measure be indebted. Just before his death in 1892 Curtis could report that the "hearts of men who were young then [in 1837] still vibrate[d]" to Emerson's declaration of literary independence in "The American Scholar"; but a year later there were few living authors except Higginson and Holmes who could testify that they had been directly influenced by the famous address more than a half century earlier.

During the years between "The American Scholar" and the *Annus Terribilis,* however, much of what Emerson had envisioned as a national literature had been achieved—indeed, a great deal more than the critics of 1892 in their confident assessments perceived. They inclined to find the American strain chiefly in such elements as the homely detail and humanitarian spirit of Whittier, in the affirmative moralism and cisatlantic narratives of Longfellow, in the self-reliant ethic of Emerson or of Cooper's heroes or Lowell's Biglow. They also reckoned the aggregate of local color a considerable advance in portraying the diversity of American character. A few found the New World voice in the radical democracy expressed in Thoreau's sinewy style or in Whitman's varied idiom. But Emerson's call for the treatment of the familiar and low had been answered by Twain with an art that the critics of 1892 had not adequately measured; and Emerson's tribute to American household verse had been vindicated by Emily Dickinson with an art of which the critics of the time were unaware. Nor did they perceive that the tonic raciness of native humor, which Emerson had suggested to be a proper substratum for the national utterance, had been transmuted into a sharp indigenous perspective in *Moby Dick* and *Huckleberry Finn.* And though they might find "art" in Hawthorne and James, they generally suspected (as did Alcott and De Forest of Hawthorne) that their antihumanitarian outlook placed them apart from the central expression of the national mind. Yet for all these omissions—or so the mid-twentieth century would view them —the national literary atmosphere of 1892 held an assurance in sharp contrast to the doubts of 1842 when even Bryant felt obliged to say that American letters had fallen on their darkest days. The next two literary generations, to be sure, still felt the need to alter the direction or to enrich the substance of nationality. Moreover, in the early years of the twentieth century some American writers were to complain for a time, as did Van Wyck Brooks, that they lacked a "usable past"; and in those same years students of literature in American universities could scarcely find curricular provision for instructing them in the subtler ramifications of their native literary tradition.

Yet despite such lingering skepticism, the American public and the major American writers had for their part concluded by the beginning of the 1890's that a reputable and distinctive American literature had been established. That such was the consensus is attested by several volumes devoted to the issue in the early 1890's. The strides of indigenous realism were traced in Howells' *Criticism and Fiction* (1891); the "independent and organic development" of the whole national literature beyond the "pallid reflection of literary fashions" of Europe was outlined in Greenough White's *A Sketch of the Philosophy of American Literature* (1891); Brander Matthews' *Americanisms and Briticisms* (1892) signified the growth of an academic acceptance of American modes and idiom as a distinctive utterance which could not be measured or comprehended solely by transatlantic standards; and T. W. Higginson's *The New World and the New Book* (1891) affirmed in Emersonian tones that American writing was no longer "merely an outlying portion of the literature of Europe." No doubt the recently published eleven volumes of Stedman and Hutchinson's *A Library of American Literature* (1888–90), unsound though some of its interpretations of a "true home school of authorship" may have been, provided the occasion for many of the confident reappraisals of the national literary achievement; and the magnitude of the work compared with that of the Duyckincks' *Cyclopaedia* a generation earlier afforded a reassuring index to the steady expansion of independent literary activity in the American scene.

To this confidence there was other abundant testimony, despite the apprehensions of native authors in the decade after the Civil War. No longer could the literary mind of the New World be claimed as a literary outpost in the empire of some foreign author or school, as in the eighteenth century it had been claimed for Pope; nor did any transatlantic Kames or Blair hold dogmatic sway over American style. American writers, to be sure, still looked with appropriate veneration to the literary experience of Europe; but they initially took a native stance and they learned from Chaucer as well as Dickens and Tennyson, and from Tolstoi and Zola as well as from the English masters. Even the English critics themselves, in such journals as the London *Saturday Review* and the *North British Review,* proclaimed after the Civil War that America had at last come of literary age and was properly reflecting the humanitarianism and experimentalism and irreverence that seemed to them to mark the popular American mind. In fact, under the influence of Taine, critics both at home and abroad inclined to turn a more generous eye toward American writing, for under Tainean principles they could assess it in the context of epoch, race, and milieu rather than by a priori literary standards.

If the post-bellum aspiration for a national literature was less clamorous and extravagant than it had been in the ante-bellum years, it gradually emerged on the other hand, more stable and mature. Most writers and critics had come to feel, with Horace Scudder, that the stridency and "posture" of earlier literary nationalism were outmoded and that a sufficient nationality would reside in "a plain expression of positive organic life." Confidently accepting this organic view of Americanism in literature the major magazines in the post-bellum years tended to concur in *Putnam's* announced policy of encouraging a "broad, generous nationality": *Harper's* refused to put its faith in any single formula or set of themes as the "egg" from which a purely American literature would ineluctably be born; the *Nation,* under E. L. Godkin's discriminating editorship, repudiated the Know Nothing school of American poetry, which relied for nationality on stock symbols like the bald eagle and the buffalo; *Scribner's* avowed its lack of interest in the "geyser school" of native writing; and *Puck* jestingly lamented the fact that Joaquin Miller "the Boundless" and the Sweet Singer of Michigan (Julia A. Moore) had betrayed those who yearned for a completely original American literature.

In accepting the matrix of American life as the ultimate determinant of the national texture and flavor of the country's literature, post-bellum authors were also disposed to accept the fact that the American mind and utterance were organically fixed in and conditioned by the cultural past, especially that of England. Such conspicuous proponents of an indigenous literary emphasis as Whitman and Howells, as has been noted, conceded this debt and this bond. Howells' conception of American literature as a "condition" of English literature Lowell in his later years elaborated and modified in figures implying the same organic development of Americanism in literature as that to which his younger contemporaries generally subscribed. In his youth, Lowell said, American writers were bringing earth from the mother country to pot their imported literary plants, but near the end of the century they could "feel solid and familiar earth" under their feet. And again he proudly remarked the achievement of intellectual independence of the Old World through literary works which were no longer parasitic plants but "new growths from seeds the mother tree has dropped." But if American writing were thus a "part of English literature," Lowell concluded, yet it was so "with a difference," and this difference lay in the increasing infusion of a "new Spirit" and in a growing self-trust. A few years earlier Emerson had employed the same phrase ("new spirit") to applaud the distinctively cisatlantic element in Ellery Channing's long colloquial poem *The Wanderer* (1871)—a poem which expressed the hope that the America of the post-bellum era would sing its own gods and not the vain myths of classic times.

The "difference" which Lowell and his New England contemporaries saw steadily distinguishing American literature from that of Europe involved mainly an ethical tone and spirit. Across the continent, however, an autochthonous "difference" was developing with a more earthy turn of mind that both required and nurtured its own fresh idiom. With the mid-century national expansion, both geographical and industrial, not only new words and phrases but also a whole new linguistic texture and temper emerged across the land. That this patois was amenable to the literary imagination Mark Twain amply demonstrated in the 1870's and 1880's. The Transcendentalists had approvingly observed a generation earlier, of course, that the novel activities and procedures of American politics, commerce, and religion were nurturing a living and vibrant language which would afford the imagination richer aliment than the worn and pretentious diction of academies and pulpits; and to this view Lowell had later lent emphasis in the Second Series of *The Biglow Papers* (1867) by reminding native writers that there was "death in the dictionary." This hopeful literary omen which Lowell found in the color and flexibility of popular speech was soon thereafter given academic sanction by the philologist Maximilian Schele De Vere's *Americanisms; the English of the New World* (1872). Not content with a mere scholarly compilation of American additions to the mother tongue, Schele De Vere affirmed the indigenous divergences and mutations to be a boon to the imaginative writer. Especially in the songs and tales of the Negroes and Westerners he found an "intensified, impulsive language" which contained, as he said in quoting Lowell, "poetry in the egg." In view of such increasing academic sanction, it is not surprising that by the 1890's Howells felt the status of native idiom sufficiently well established to urge that "our novelists, . . . being born Americans, . . . use 'Americanisms' whenever these serve their turn."

Accentuation of the "difference" which Lowell found between American and English literature was also beginning to be felt in the post-bellum period from an influence of which he scarcely took account: the mid-century tide of immigration from the Continent. Previous literary analysts of American nationality as diverse as Crèvecoeur and Longfellow had counted this fusion of racial strains an asset, supposing that thereby a distinctive universality would accrue to American literature. No doubt owing to Taine's emphasis on race as one of the three determinants of the character of a nation's literature, this factor received increasing attention in the closing decades of the century. Though no major author or school had yet appeared to justify their fears, Anglophile critics like Richard Grant White and Thomas Bailey Aldrich darkly prophesied that the pure English heritage then dominant in American writing would be polluted by the taste and idiom of immigrant masses. But those American critics who were concerned for the vigor and independence rather than a traditional purity in the national literature welcomed what Stedman called a continual supply of raw ingredients. So long as these diverse races were not assimilated, Charles Dudley Warner reminded his contemporaries, they could provide those substantial contrasts in manners and character for which American novelists had perennially longed. But the greater benefit would be conferred, so the prophecies generally went, through the addition of fiber and sinew to an American imagination which otherwise, through a kind of colonial inbreeding, would become merely "thinned-out English." Had the authors of these prophecies lived well into the next century, they would no doubt have pointed to such writers as Dreiser, Sandburg, and Mencken as validating their sanguine view of the immigrant as not merely picturesque material for Anglicized pens but rather an imaginative force of tonic breadth and, at times, wholesome vulgarity.

The "difference" in English and American writing which Lowell noted was of course to be sharpened and deepened by still other factors after the turn of the century, especially by America's new dominance as a world power. But by 1892 few critics either at home or abroad were disposed to argue that under any reasonable tests a national literature did not exist. Through the art of the native realists, as Twain observed in the 1880's, "a procession of originals" had marched out of the ark of American literature; and through an indigenous conversion of the romantic mode Cooper, Melville, Hawthorne, and Whitman had in their several ways expressed that complex of freedom and moral order and manifest destiny that had lain at the center of the American mind since colonial days. Moreover, the American writer's emancipation from the stultifying deference to British criticism, according to Holmes's testimony in *Over the Teacups* (1891), had become "pretty well established." That the years at the turn of the century would be a relaxed period wherein the national literary forces would be redeployed—a *fin de siècle* "interregnum"— Stedman among others perceived. Nevertheless, he voiced the critical consensus of his major contemporaries when he asserted in the 1880's that in literature America had clearly "come of age" and that "our novitiate has ended."

Coincident with this national literary maturity came an additional stimulus toward further independence in the passage in 1891 of the first International Copyright Law. Since the early years of the Republic nearly every American writer of prominence had followed Tom Paine and Noah Webster in arguing that so long as an author's work (American or British) could be pirated by foreign publishers, a national literature could scarcely be sustained. Whereas in the ante-bellum decades the gifted native writers had often been impoverished through hopeless competition with cheap reprints of English works, in the latter half of the century popular authors like Mrs. Stowe were in turn robbed of veritable fortunes by unscrupulous publishers abroad. Passed as the result of a resurgent campaign in the 1880's led by the publisher Henry Holt and by Gilder, Eggleston, Stedman, and a host of other authors, the Copyright Law of 1891 appreciably reduced the hazards of a literary career in America. That the Law directly enhanced the indigenous flavor of American writing, however, is open to question. For though by 1892, as Brander Matthews then reported, the majority of works coming from American presses were by native authors, and though some native works were issued in the hundreds of thousands, these best-sellers of the Marion Crawford era often romantically eschewed the American scene and temper. At any rate, at the beginning of the last decade of the century so rapidly was the volume of American works increasing that H. C. Bunner remarked his inability to revert to the mood of the late 1870's when, as editor of *Puck*, he had published solemn articles on "Who Will Write the American Novel?" and "Will There Ever Be an American Drama?"

Amid the richer accretion of American writing in the mid-twentieth century, it may be even more difficult to sense the relevance of such questions as Bunner recorded. Yet the very fact that nearly all native authors of stature during the first century of the Republic felt obliged to answer them may suggest their necessary function as a critical exercise prerequisite to the free play of the literary imagination in America. Certainly in an era in which nationalism was a focus of values, the writers of a self-conscious young republic eager to surpass the civilization of the Old World could scarcely be indifferent to the interdependence of their art and their society. In essence the long campaign for an American literature was an attempt to define the place of the writer in a particular culture which for the first time conjoined a massive New World prospect and a massive Old World heritage. To suppose that without Emerson's "The American Scholar" and Whitman's Prefaces American writing would have as readily achieved its cumulative "independence and vigour"—to quote the title-page of the one-hundred-page supplement of the London *Times* devoted to American literature in 1954—is to deny the directive role of socioliterary criticism and to put the imagination wholly at the disposition of silent cultural forces. The radical independence of the work of Hemingway and Faulkner and Cummings is perhaps ultimately rooted in the subsoil of thousands of forgotten essays and addresses on the character of a national literature. It may well be that only a century's zealous analysis of the cultural climate and responsibilities of an expansive New World republic could provide the American imagination with the reassurance and direction required for the "natural" literature that Lowell bespoke. In literature as in politics the achievement of independence is not unrelated to declarations of independence.

Bibliography

I. Primary Sources

ADAMS, BROOKS. *International Review,* IX (1880).

ADAMS, JOHN. *Works,* ed. C. F. Adams. 10 vols. Boston, 1850–56.

ADAMS, JOHN QUINCY. *Lectures on Rhetoric and Oratory.* 2 vols. Cambridge, 1810.

———. *Memoirs,* ed. C. F. Adams. 12 vols. Philadelphia, 1876.

———. *Writings,* ed. W. C. Ford. 7 vols. New York, 1913.

ALCOTT, A. B. *Journals,* ed. Odell Shepard. Boston, 1938.

———. *Orphic Sayings.* . . . Mt. Vernon, N. Y., 1939.

———. *Ralph Waldo Emerson.* . . . Boston, 1888.

———. *Table-Talk.* Boston, 1877.

ALLEN, PAUL. *Original Poems.* Salem, 1801.

ALSOP, RICHARD. *The Charms of Fancy* . . . , ed. T. Dwight. New York, 1856.

American Apollo, I (1792).

American Magazine and Historical Chronicle, II (1745).

American Museum, II (1787); V (1789); XI (1792); XII (1792).

American Review, I (1811); IV (1812).

AMES, FISHER. *Works.* 2 vols. Boston, 1854.

AMES, J. W. *Overland,* XI (1873).

AMES, NATHANIEL. *The Essays, Humor, and Poems of Nathaniel Ames, Father and Son,* ed. Samuel Briggs. Cleveland, 1891.

Analectic Magazine, II (1813).

APPLETON, NATHANIEL. "A Sermon . . . October 9, 1760." Boston, 1760.

ARNOLD, MRS. W. J., ed. *The Poets and Poetry of Minnesota.* Chicago, 1864.

ATWATER, CALEB. *Writings.* Columbus, 1833.

AUDUBON, J. J. *Audubon and his Journals,* ed. Maria R. Audubon. 2 vols. New York, 1897.

AUSTIN, WILLIAM. *Literary Papers.* Boston, 1890.

BACON, LEONARD. *Biblical Repository,* 2nd ser. III (1840).

BACON, LEONARD. "Oration. . . ." Hanover, 1845.

BACON, W. T. *Poems.* Cambridge, 1848.

BAGBY, GEORGE W. *Selections from the Miscellaneous Writings.* . . . 2 vols. Richmond, 1885.

BALDWIN, J. G. *The Flush Times of Alabama and Mississippi.* New York, 1853.

BANCROFT, GEORGE. *American Quarterly Review,* II (1827).

———. *Life and Letters,* ed. M. A. DeWolfe Howe. 2 vols. New York, 1908.

———. *North American,* XIX (1824); XXIV (1827).

BANCROFT, H. H. *Essays and Miscellany.* San Francisco, 1890.

———. *Literary Industries.* San Francisco, 1891.

BARKER, JAMES NELSON. *The Indian Princess.* Philadelphia, 1808.

———. *Polyanthus,* II (1813).

———. *Tears and Smiles.* Philadelphia, 1808.

BARLOW, JOEL. *Advice to the Privileged Orders.* . . . London, 1793.

———. *The Columbiad.* Paris, 1813.

———. "Oration" on July 4, 1787. *American Museum,* II (1787).

———. "A Poem, Spoken at . . . Yale College . . . September 12, 1781." Hartford, 1781.

———. "The Prospect of Peace. . . ." New Haven, 1788.

———. *The Vision of Columbus.* . . . Hartford, 1787.

BARTLETT, ROBERT. *Monthly Magazine,* III (1840).

BARTLETT, W. C. *A Breeze from the Woods.* [Oakland] 1880.

BEECHER, H. W. *Norwood.* . . . New York, 1868.

BELKNAP, JEREMY. *History of New-Hampshire.* 3 vols. Boston, 1792.

BENÉT, STEPHEN VINCENT. *John Brown's Body.* New York, 1928.

BENJAMIN, PARK. *Southern Literary Messenger,* V (1839).

BERESFORD, RICHARD. *A Plea for Literature.* Charleston, 1793.

BERKELEY, GEORGE. *Works,* ed. A. C. Fraser. 4 vols. Oxford, 1901.

BEVERLY, ROBERT. *The History and Present State of Virginia.* London, 1705.

Biblical Repository, XXIV (1852).

BIDWELL, BARNABAS. *The Mercenary Match.* New-Haven [1785].

BIERCE, AMBROSE. *Selections from "Prattle,"* ed. C. D. Hall. Book Club of California, 1936.

BINCKLEY, J. M. *Lakeside Monthly,* IX (1873).

BIRD, R. M. Cf. "Celebration of the Forty-seventh Anniversary of the First Settlement of Ohio." Cincinnati, 1835.

———. *Nick of the Woods,* ed. C. B. Williams. New York, 1939.

BLAIR, HUGH. *Lectures on Rhetoric and Belles Lettres.* Philadelphia, 1854.

BLEECKER, ANN ELIZA. *Posthumous Works,* ed. Margaretta V. Faugères. New York, 1793.

BOKER, G. H. *Königsmark.* . . . Philadelphia, 1869.

——. *Our Heroic Themes.* Boston, 1865.

——. *Poems of the War.* Boston, 1864.

——. *Sonnets,* ed. S. Bradley. Philadelphia, 1929.

Boston Magazine, I (1783–84).

BOYESEN, H. H. *Independent,* XLIV (1892).

——. *Literary and Social Silhouettes.* New York, 1894.

——. *North American,* CXLVIII (1889).

BRACKENRIDGE, H. H. *Gazette Publications.* Carlisle, Pa., 1806.

——. *United States Magazine,* I (1779).

BRAINARD, J. G. C. *Literary Remains,* ed. J. G. Whittier. Hartford, 1832.

BREVOORT, HENRY. *Letters . . . to Washington Irving,* ed. G. S. Hellman. 2 vols. New York, 1916.

BRISTED, CHARLES A. *Pieces of a Broken-Down Critic.* 4 vols. Baden-Baden, 1858–59.

BRISTED, JOHN. "An Oration on the Utility of Literary Establishments." New York, 1814.

——. *The Resources of the United States.* . . . New York, 1818.

BROOKS, C. T. *Christian Examiner,* XXXVIII (1845).

[BROOKS, J. G.] *Knickerbocker,* V (1835).

BROOKS, VAN WYCK. *Scenes and Portraits.* New York, 1954.

Brother Jonathan, I (1842); II (1842); VI (1843).

[BROWN, C. B.] *American Register,* I (1806–07).

——. *American Review and Literary Journal,* I (1801).

BROWN, C. B. *Clara Howard.* Boston, 1827.

——. *Edgar Huntly,* ed. D. L. Clark. New York, 1928.

——. *The Rhapsodist and Other Uncollected Writings,* ed. H. R. Warfel. New York, 1943.

——. *Weekly Magazine,* I (1798).

BROWN, SOLYMAN. "An Essay on American Poetry. . . ." New Haven, 1818.

BROWN, WILLIAM H. *Ira and Isabella.* Boston, 1807.

——. *The Power of Sympathy.* 2 vols. Boston, 1894.

BROWNSON, ORESTES. *Boston Quarterly Review,* I (1838); II (1839); III (1840).

——. *Brownson's Review,* I (1844); III (1846); IV (1847).

——. *Literary, Scientific, and Political Views,* ed. H. F. Brownson. New York, 1893.

BRYAN, DANIEL. *The Appeal for Suffering Genius.* . . . Washington, 1826.

BRYAN, DANIEL. *The Mountain Muse.* Harrisonburg [Va.], 1813.

BRYANT, W. C. "An Address . . . in behalf of the American Copyright Club," New York, 1843.

———. *Life and Works,* ed. Parke Godwin. 6 vols. New York, 1883–84.

———. *Poems,* ed. W. Irving. London, 1832.

BUCKINGHAM, J. T. *Specimens of Newspaper Literature.* 2 vols. Boston, 1850.

BUCKMINSTER, JOSEPH S. *Monthly Anthology,* VII (1809).

BULFINCH, S. G. *Southern Literary Journal,* I (1835).

BULKLEY, JOHN. Preface to Roger Wolcott, *Poetical Meditations. . . .* New London, 1725.

BUNNER, H. C. *Century,* XXVI (1883).

———. *Life and Letters,* ed. G. Jensen. Durham, 1939.

BURROUGHS, JOHN. *Birds and Poets.* New York, 1877.

———. *Christian Union,* XL (1892).

———. *Life and Letters,* ed. C. Barrus. 2 vols. Boston and New York, 1925.

———. *Notes on Walt Whitman as Poet and Person.* New York, 1867.

BUSHNELL, HORACE. "Oration." Cambridge, 1848.

BYLES, MATHER. *Poems on Several Occasions,* ed. C. L. Carlson. New York, 1940.

[BYLES, MATHER?] Introductory Essay, *American Magazine and Historical Chronicle,* II (1745).

CALIFORNIAN, I (1880).

CAMERON, K. W., ed. *Emerson the Essayist.* 2 vols. Raleigh, 1945.

CARNEGIE, ANDREW. *Cf.* Moncure Conway, *Autobiography.* 2 vols. Boston, 1904.

CHANNING, E T. *Lectures Read to the Seniors in Harvard College.* Boston, 1856.

———. "On Models in Literature." *North American,* III (1816).

CHANNING, WALTER. *North American,* I (1815).

CHANNING, W. E. "On National Literature." *Old South Leaflets.* Vol. VI. Boston, 1903.

———. *Works.* Boston, 1886.

CHANNING, W. ELLERY. *Poems of Sixty-five Years.* Philadelphia, 1902.

———. *Thoreau: the Poet-Naturalist. . . .* Boston, 1873.

———. *The Wanderer. . . .* Boston, 1871.

———. *The Woodman, and Other Poems.* Boston, 1849.

CHILD, LYDIA MARIA. *Letters,* ed. J. G. Whittier. Boston, 1883.

CHIVERS, T. H. *Eonchs of Ruby. . . .* New York, 1851.

———. *Nacoochee.* New York, 1837.

CHOATE, RUFUS. *Addresses and Orations.* Boston, 1883.

CHURCH REVIEW, III (1850).

CLARKE, J. F. *Autobiography, Diary,*

and Correspondence, ed. E. E. Hale. Boston, 1891.

——. "The Pilgrim Fathers." Boston, 1843.

——. "Poem. . . ." Boston, 1846.

——. *Western Messenger,* V (1838).

CLEMENS, S. L. *Letters,* ed. A. B. Paine. 2 vols. New York, 1917.

——. *Notebook,* ed. A. B. Paine. New York, 1935.

——. *Cf.* Advertisement, E. W. Howe, *The Story of a Country Town.* New York, 1917.

CLIFFTON, WILLIAM. *Poems Chiefly Occasional.* New York, 1800.

——. "A Poetical Epistle. . . ." *Cf.* William Gifford, *The Baviad and Maeviad.* Philadelphia, 1799.

CLINTON, DEWITT. "An Introductory Discourse. . . ." New York, 1815.

COAN, T. M. *Appleton's Journal,* II (1869).

COBB, J. B. *The Creole.* . . . Philadelphia, 1850.

——. *Leisure Labors.* . . . New York, 1858.

——. *Mississippi Scenes.* Philadelphia, 1851.

COCKE, A. W. *Southern Magazine,* VIII (1871).

COGGESHALL, W. T. "The Protective Policy in Literature. . . ." Columbus, 1859.

COLE, THOMAS. "Essay on American Scenery." *American Monthly Magazine,* N.S. I (1836).

COLMAN, BENJAMIN. "The Government & Improvement of Mirth. . . ." Boston, 1707.

——. *Cf.* Samuel Penhallow, "The History of the Wars of New-England. . . ." Boston, 1726.

Columbian Magazine, I (1786).

CONDIT, J. B. "Address. . . ." Portland, 1841.

CONWAY, MONCURE. *Autobiography.* 2 vols. Boston, 1904.

COOKE, EBENEZER. *The Maryland Muse,* ed. L. C. Wroth. *Proceedings of the American Antiquarian Society,* N.S. XLIV (1934).

C[OOKE], E[BENEZER]. *Sotweed Redivivus.* . . . *Cf. Maryland Historical Society, Fund Publication,* No. 36. Baltimore, 1900.

COOKE, J. E. *Bonnybel Vane.* New York, 1883.

——. *The Virginia Comedians.* 2 vols. New York, 1855.

COOKE, P. P. *Cf.* R. Griswold, *Passages from the Correspondence of . . . Griswold.* Cambridge, 1898.

COOPER, J. F. *The American Democrat.* Cooperstown, 1838.

——. *Brother Jonathan,* I (1842).

——. *Correspondence,* ed. J. F. Cooper. 2 vols. New Haven, 1922.

——. *Gleanings in Europe,* ed. R. E. Spiller. 2 vols. New York, 1928–30.

——. *A Letter to His Countrymen.* New York, 1834.

——. *Notions of the Americans.* 2 vols. New York, 1850.

COOPER, J. F. *Works.* Household Ed. 32 vols. New York, 1876–84.

COTTON, JOHN. *Singing of Psalms.* . . . London, 1647.

COUES, ELLIOTT, ed. *History of the Expedition under the Command of Lewis and Clark.* 4 vols. New York, 1893.

COX, WILLIAM. *Crayon Sketches.* 2 vols. New York, 1833.

CRANCH, C. P. *Ariel and Caliban.* . . . Boston, 1887.

———. *Life and Letters,* ed. Leonora C. Scott. Boston, 1917.

———. *Western Messenger,* IV (1837).

CRÈVECOEUR, HECTOR ST. JOHN DE. *Letters from an American Farmer.* Everyman's Ed. London, 1913.

CROZIER, R. H. *The Confederate Spy.* Louisville, 1884.

Current Literature, VIII (1891).

CURTIS, G. W. *Early Letters . . . to John S. Dwight,* ed. G. W. Cooke. New York, 1898.

———. *From the Easy Chair.* New York, 1892.

———. *Prue and I.* New York, 189–.

CUSHING, CALEB. "An Oration before the Literary Societies of Amherst College." Boston, 1836.

———. "Reply to the Letter of J. Fenimore Cooper." Boston, 1834.

DABNEY, RICHARD. *Poems, Original and Translated.* Philadelphia, 1815.

Daily National Intelligencer, XLI (1853).

DAKE, O. C. *Midland Poems.* Lincoln, Neb., 1873.

DANA, CHARLES. Cf. *Whittier Correspondence from the Oak Knoll Collections . . .* , ed. J. Albree. Salem, 1911.

DANA, R. H. *North American,* V (1817).

DAVENPORT, JOHN. "A Discourse about Civil Government. . . ." Cambridge, 1663.

DAVIDSON, LUCRETIA. *Poetical Remains.* Philadelphia, 1847.

DAVIES, SAMUEL. *Sermons on Important Subjects.* 3 vols. New York, 1841.

DAVIS, JOHN. *Travels of Four Years and a Half in the United States,* ed. A. J. Morrison. New York, 1909.

DAWES, RUFUS. *Geraldine.* . . . New York, 1839.

De Bow's Review, XVI (1854); XXII (1857); XXIV (1858).

DE FOREST, J. W. "The Great American Novel." *Nation,* VI (1868).

DE KAY, CHARLES. *Hesperus, and Other Poems.* New York, 1880.

Democratic Review, I (1837); XI (1842); XX (1847); XXIV (1849).

[DENNIE, JOSEPH.] *Farmer's Weekly Museum* (1799).

DENNIE, JOSEPH. *The Lay Preacher,* ed. Milton Ellis. New York, 1943.

———. *Letters . . .* , ed. L. G. Pedder. Orono, Maine, 1936.

———. *Port Folio,* I (1801); II (1802); III (1803).

DEXTER, FRANKLIN. *North American,* XXVI (1828).

Dial, VII (1887); IX (1889); XIV (1893).

DRAKE, BENJAMIN. "An Address . . . September 27, 1831." Cincinnati, 1831.

DRAKE, DANIEL. "Discourse on . . . the West." Cincinnati, 1834.

――――. "Remarks on . . . Literary and Social Concert. . . ." Louisville, 1833.

DRAYTON, MICHAEL. *Poetical Works* . . . , ed. Robert Anderson. Edinburgh, 1793.

DUCHÉ, JACOB. *Caspipina's Letters.* 2 vols. Dublin, 1792.

[DUGANNE, A. J. H.] *Parnassus in Pillory.* New York, 1851.

DUNLAP, WILLIAM. *André.* New York, 1798.

――――. *Diary,* ed. D. Barck. 3 vols. New York, 1930.

――――. *The Father.* . . . New York, 1789.

――――. *A History of the American Theatre.* New York, 1832.

――――. *The Life of Charles Brockden Brown.* 2 vols. Philadelphia, 1815.

DU PONCEAU, PETER S. "A Discourse on the Necessity and the Means of Making our National Literature Independent of That of Great Britain." Philadelphia, 1834.

DUYCKINCK, E. A. *American Whig Review,* I (1845); IV (1846).

DUYCKINCK, E. A. AND G. L. *Cyclopaedia of American Literature.* 2 vols. Philadelphia, 1877.

DWIGHT, JOHN SULLIVAN. *Christian Examiner,* XV (1842).

DWIGHT, THEODORE, JR. *Things as They Are: or Notes of a Traveler.* New York, 1834.

DWIGHT, TIMOTHY. *The Conquest of Canaan.* . . . Hartford, 1785.

――――. "The Critics. A Fable." *Cf.* V. L. Parrington, ed., *The Connecticut Wits.* New York, 1926.

――――. "Epistle to Colonel Humphreys." *Cf.* E. Smith, ed., *American Poems.* Litchfield, 1793.

――――. *Greenfield Hill.* . . . New York, 1794.

――――. *Travels; in New-England and New-York.* 4 vols. New-Haven, 1821–22.

――――. "Valedictory Address." *American Magazine,* I (1787).

Eclectic Review, N.S. VI (1867).

EGGLESTON, EDWARD. *The Circuit Rider.* New York, 1902.

――――. *The Hoosier Schoolmaster.* New York, 1892.

――――. *The Mystery of Metropolisville.* New York, 1873.

EGGLESTON, G. C. *The First of the Hoosiers.* Philadelphia, 1903.

――――. *Recollections of a Varied Life.* New York, 1910.

ELLIOT, JAMES. *Poetical and Miscellaneous Works.* Greenfield, 1798.

[ELLIOT, JAMES.] "The Rural Wanderer." *Port Folio,* I (1801).

EMERSON, R. W. *Complete Works.* Riverside Ed. 12 vols. Boston, 1888.

——. *The Correspondence of Thomas Carlyle and . . . Emerson . . .*, ed. C. E. Norton, 2 vols. Boston, 1897.

——. *Democratic Review,* IX (1841).

——. *Dial,* I (1840–41); III (1842–43); IV (1843–44).

——. *Journals,* ed. E. W. Emerson and W. E. Forbes. 10 vols. Boston, 1909–14.

——. *Letters,* ed. R. W. Rusk. 6 vols. New York, 1939.

——. *Uncollected Lectures,* ed. C. Ghodes. New York, 1932.

Essays from the Critic. Boston, 1882.

EVANS, NATHANIEL. *Poems on Several Occasions.* Philadelphia, 1772.

EVERETT, ALEXANDER. "An Address to the Phi Beta Kappa Society of Bowdoin College." Boston, 1834.

——. *North American,* XXXIII (1831).

EVERETT, EDWARD. *American Poets.* Cambridge, 1812.

——. *North American,* XIII (1821).

——. *Orations and Speeches on Various Occasions.* Boston, 1836.

EWING, THOMAS. "An Address . . . before the Union Literary Society. . . ." Cincinnati, 1833.

FAUGÈRES, MARGARETTA, ed. *The Posthumous Works of Ann Eliza Bleecker.* New York, 1793.

FAWCETT, EDGAR. *Californian,* I (1880).

FAY, T. S. *Dreams and Reveries of a Quiet Man.* 2 vols. New York, 1832.

——. *Norman Leslie.* 2 vols. New York, 1835.

"Female Writers of the South, The." *The Land We Love,* II (1867).

FESSENDEN, T. G. *Pills, Poetical, Political, and Philosophical.* Philadelphia, 1809.

FIELD, EUGENE. *Culture's Garland.* Boston, 1887.

FIELDS, ANNIE. *Authors and Friends.* Boston, 1893.

FISHER, WALT. *Overland,* XV (1875).

FISKE, JOHN. *The Unseen World.* Boston and New York, 1900.

FLAGG, EDMUND. *The Far West.* 2 vols. New York, 1838.

FLINT, TIMOTHY. *Athenaeum* (1835).

——. *Francis Berrian. . . .* Philadelphia, 1834.

——. *George Mason. . . .* Boston, 1829.

——. *The History and Geography of the Mississippi Valley.* 2 vols. Cincinnati, 1832.

——. *Knickerbocker,* II (1833).

——. *The Life and Adventures of Arthur Clenning.* Philadelphia, 1828.

——. *Recollections of the Last Ten Years.* Boston, 1826.

——. *Western Monthly,* I (1827); II (1828).

FORD, J. L. *The Literary Shop.* New York, 1899.

FORREST, EDWIN. "Oration." New York, 1838.

FOSS, S. W. *Cf.* H. Traubel, *With Walt*

Whitman. . . . 3 vols. Boston and New York, 1906–14.

Four Dissertations on the Reciprocal Advantages of a Perpetual Union between Great-Britain and her American Colonies. Philadelphia, 1766.

FRANKLIN, BENJAMIN. *Writings,* ed. A. H. Smyth. 10 vols. New York, 1905–07.

FRENEAU, PHILIP. *The Last Poems,* ed. Lewis Leary. New Brunswick, 1945.

———. *Miscellaneous Works.* Philadelphia, 1788.

———. *Poems,* ed. F. L. Pattee. 3 vols. Princeton, 1902–07.

———. *Time-Piece,* II (1797).

———. *Unpublished Freneauana,* ed. C. F. Heartman. New York, 1918.

"Friend, The." *American Museum,* V (1789).

[FRY, J. R.?] *Western Monthly Magazine,* V (1836).

FULLER, MARGARET. *Dial,* III (1842–43).

———. *Life Without and Life Within.* . . . ed. A. B. Fuller. Boston, 1859.

———. *Memoirs,* ed. R. W. Emerson, *et al.* 2 vols. Boston, 1874.

———. *Papers on Literature and Art.* 2 parts. New York and London, 1846.

———. *Woman in the Nineteenth Century.* . . . ed. A. B. Fuller. New York, 1869.

———. *Writings,* ed. Mason Wade. New York, 1941.

GALLAGHER, W. D. *Erato, Number III.* Cincinnati, 1837.

———. *Hesperian,* I (1838).

GARDINER, W. H. *North American,* XV (1822).

GARLAND, HAMLIN. *Literary News,* IX (1888).

———. *Roadside Meetings.* New York, 1930.

———. *A Son of the Middle Border.* New York, 1928.

GARNETT, J. M. ("Oliver Oldschool"). *Southern Literary Messenger,* III (1837).

GAYARRÉ, CHARLES. *Louisiana; Its Colonial History and Romance.* New York, 1851.

GEORGE, LUCAS. *Cf.* John Davis, *Travels of Four Years and a Half in the United States,* ed. A. J. Morrison. New York, 1909.

GILDER, R. W. *Letters,* ed. Rosamund Gilder. Boston, 1916.

GILMAN, SAMUEL. *Contributions to Literature,* Boston, 1856.

GODFREY, THOMAS. *Juvenile Poems.* . . . Philadelphia, 1765.

GODKIN, E. L. *Life and Letters* . . . , ed. Rollo Ogden. 2 vols. New York, 1907.

———. *Reflections and Comments.* . . . New York, 1895.

GODWIN, PARKE. *Out of the Past.* New York, 1870.

Golden Era, III (1855).

GOODRICH, SAMUEL. *Recollections of a Lifetime.* 2 vols. New York, 1856.

GOOKIN, DANIEL. *Historical Collections of the Indians.* . . . Boston, 1792.

GRADY, HENRY W. *Cf.* J. C. Harris, ed. *Life of Henry W. Grady.* New York, 1870.

Graham's Magazine, XXII (1843).

GRAY, J. C. *North American,* XIII (1821).

GREELEY, HORACE. *Recollections of a Busy Life.* New York, 1869.

GREGORY, E. S. *Southern Magazine,* IX (1871).

GRIDLEY, JEREMIAH. *The Weekly Rehearsal* (1731). *Cf.* J. T. Buckingham, *Specimens of Newspaper Literature.* Boston, 1850.

GRIMKÉ, T. S. "Oration on . . . Grecian and American Eloquence." Cincinnati, 1834.

———. "Oration on the Advantages . . . of the Bible. . . ." New Haven, 1830.

GRISWOLD, RUFUS W. "The Cyclopaedia of American Literature. . . . A Review." New York, 1856.

———. *The Female Poets of America.* Philadelphia, 1849.

———. *Passages from the Correspondence . . . of Rufus W. Griswold,* ed. W. M. Griswold. Cambridge, 1898.

———. *The Poets and Poetry of America.* Philadelphia, 1855.

———. *The Prose Writers of America.* Philadelphia, 1847.

HALE, SARAH J. *Selections from the Writings of Mrs. Sarah Hale.* Philadelphia, 1833.

HALL, H. G., ed. *Benjamin Tompson, 1642–1714.* Boston and New York, 1924.

HALL, JAMES. "An Address . . . before the Erodelphian Society of Miami University." Cincinnati, 1833.

———. *Legends of the West.* New York, 1853.

———. *Letters from the West.* . . . London, 1828.

[HALL, JAMES?] *Western Monthly Magazine,* I (1833); II (1834); III (1835); V (1836).

HALL, JAMES. *The Western Souvenir.* Cincinnati, 1829.

HALIBURTON, T. C. ("Sam Slick"). *Literary World,* XI (1853).

HALLECK, FITZ-GREENE. *Life and Letters,* ed. J. G. Wilson. New York, 1869.

———. *Poetical Writings* . . . , ed. J. G. Wilson. New York, 1873.

Harper's Magazine, XXXVII (1868); L (1875).

HARRIS, JOEL C. *Joel Chandler Harris: Editor and Essayist* . . . , ed. Julia C. Harris. Chapel Hill, 1931.

———. *Life and Letters* . . . , ed. Julia C. Harris. Boston and New York, 1918.

———, ed. *Life of Henry W. Grady.* New York, 1890.

HARTE, BRET. *Cf. American Literature,* XIX (1948).

———. *Cornhill,* N.S. VII (1899).

HARTE, BRET. *The Heathen Chinee* . . . , ed. Ina Coolbrith. San Francisco, 1934.

——. *Lectures,* ed. C. M. Kozlay. Brooklyn, 1909.

——. *The Luck of Roaring Camp.* . . . Boston, 1871.

——. *Overland Monthly,* I (1868); II (1869).

——. *Poetical Works.* Boston, 1882.

HAWTHORNE, JULIAN. *North American,* CXXXIX (1884).

——. *Princeton Review,* N.S. XIII (1884).

HAWTHORNE, NATHANIEL. *The American Notebooks,* ed. Randall Stewart. New Haven, 1932.

——. *Complete Works.* Riverside Ed. 12 vols. Boston, 1888.

——. *Doctor Grimshawe's Secret.* . . . Boston, 1883.

——. *The English Notebooks,* ed. Randall Stewart. New York, 1941.

——. *Letters to . . . Ticknor.* . . . 2 vols. Newark, 1910.

——. *Salem Advertiser* (1846). *Cf. American Literature,* V (1934).

HAY, JOHN. *Addresses.* New York, 1906.

——. *Cf.* G. C. Eggleston, *Recollections of a Varied Life.* New York, 1910.

HAYNE, P. H. *A Collection of Hayne Letters,* ed. D. M. McKeithan. Austin, Texas, 1944.

——. *Russell's Magazine,* II (1857); III (1858).

——. *Southern Magazine,* XIV (1874).

HAZARD, EBENEZER. *Cf.* "Belknap Papers," *Collections of the Mass. Historical Society,* 5th series. Boston, 1877.

HEADLEY, J. T. *Miscellanies.* New York, 1850.

HEARN, LAFCADIO. *Editorials,* ed. C. W. Hutson. Boston, 1926.

——. *Letters from the Raven . . . ,* ed. M. Bronner. New York, 1907.

——. *Writings.* 16 vols. Boston, 1922.

H[EATH, J. E.]. *Southern Literary Messenger,* I (1834); II (1836).

HEDGE, F. H. *"Conservatism and Reform."* Boston, 1843.

——. *Dial,* I (1840–41).

HELPER, H. R. *The Impending Crisis.* . . . New York, 1857.

HEMINGWAY, ERNEST. *Green Hills of Africa.* New York, 1935.

Hesperian, I (1838).

HIGGINSON, FRANCIS. *New-Englands Plantation.* . . . London, 1630.

HIGGINSON, JOHN AND THOMAS THACHER. *Cf.* Nathaniel Morton, *New-England's Memorial.* . . . Boston, 1772.

HIGGINSON, T. W. *Atlantic Monthly,* XIX (1867); XX (1867); XXV (1870).

——. *Christian Union,* XLIII (1891).

——. *Nation,* LIV (1892).

——. *The New World and the New Book.* Boston, 1892.

HILLARD, G. S. *North American,* XXXII (1831).

HILLHOUSE, JAMES. *Dramas, Discourses, and Other Pieces.* 2 vols. Boston, 1839.

Historical Magazine, IV (1860).

HITCHCOCK, ENOS. *Memoirs of the Bloomsgrove Family.* 2 vols. Boston, 1790.

HOFFMAN, CHARLES FENNO. *Greyslaer.* . . . New York, 1849.

HOFFMAN, DAVID. *Viator.* . . . Baltimore, 1841.

HOLLAND, J. G. *The Bay-Path.* New York, 1864.

——. *Every-Day Topics, Second Series.* New York, 1882.

——. *Plain Talks on Familiar Subjects.* New York, 1866.

HOLMES, O. W. Cf. *Correspondence of John Lothrop Motley,* ed. G. W. Curtis. 3 vols. New York and London, 1900.

——. *Ralph Waldo Emerson.* Boston, 1885.

——. *Writings.* Riverside Ed. 14 vols. Boston, 1891.

HOLT, HENRY. *New Englander,* LXVIII (1888).

HOME, HENRY (LORD KAMES). *Elements of Criticism,* ed. A. Mills. New York, 1871.

HONEYWOOD, ST. JOHN. *Poems, with Some Pieces of Prose.* New York, 1801.

HOOKER, THOMAS. *A Survey of the Summe of Church-Discipline.* London, 1648.

HOPKINSON, FRANCIS. *Miscellaneous Essays.* . . . 3 vols. Philadelphia, 1792.

HOPKINSON, JOSEPH. Cf. *Duyckincks' Cyclopaedia.* . . . 2 vols. Philadelphia, 1877.

HOVEY, RICHARD. "On the Threshold." *Independent,* XLIV (1892).

HOWE, E. W. *Plain People.* New York, 1929.

HOWELLS, W. D. *Atlantic Monthly,* XXIII (1869).

——. *Criticism and Fiction.* New York, 1891.

——. *Current Literature,* VIII (1891).

——. *Harper's,* LXXXIII (1891); LXXXVI (1892-93).

——. *Life in Letters . . . ,* ed. Mildred Howells. 2 vols. New York, 1928.

——. *Literary Friends and Acquaintance.* New York, 1900.

——. *Literature and Life.* New York, 1902.

——. *My Mark Twain.* . . . New York, 1910.

HUBBARD, WILLIAM. *A Narrative of the Troubles with the Indians.* . . . Boston, 1677.

HUMPHREYS, DAVID. "The Glory of America." Philadelphia, 1783.

——. *Miscellaneous Works.* New York, 1804.

HUTTON, JOSEPH. *The Orphan of Prague.* New York, 1810.

Illinois Monthly Magazine, I (1831); II (1831).

INGERSOLL, CHARLES J. *A Discourse Concerning the Influence of America on the Mind.* . . . Philadelphia, 1823.

———. *Inchiquin, the Jesuit's Letters.* . . . New York, 1810.

———. *Cf.* W. R. Alger, *Life of Edwin Forrest.* 2 vols. Philadelphia, 1877.

INGRAHAM, J. H. *Southern Literary Messenger,* IV (1838).

———. *Southern Magazine,* XVII (1875).

IRVING, WASHINGTON. "The Catskill Mountains." *Literary World,* IX (1851).

———. *Cf.* "Celebration of the Forty-seventh Anniversary of the First Settlement of Ohio." Cincinnati, 1835.

———. *Letters* . . . *to Henry Brevoort,* ed. G. S. Hellman. 2 vols. New York, 1915.

———, ed. *The Poetical Works of Thomas Campbell.* Baltimore, 1810.

———. *Cf.* C. O. Parsons, "Washington Irving Writes from Granada." *American Literature,* VI (1935).

———. *Works.* Hudson Ed. 27 vols. New York, 1902.

JACKSON, DANIEL ("I. Mitchell"). *The Asylum.* . . . Poughkeepsie, 1811.

JACKSON, HELEN H. *Cf.* Moncure Conway, *Autobiography.* 2 vols. Boston, 1904.

JAMES, ALICE. *Alice James, Her Brothers—Her Journal,* ed. Anna R. Burr. New York, 1934.

JAMES, HENRY, SR. "The Social Significance of Our Institutions." Boston, 1861.

JAMES, HENRY, JR. *The American Scene.* London, 1907.

———. *The Art of the Novel* . . . , ed. R. P. Blackmur. New York, 1934.

———. *Harper's Weekly,* XXX (1886).

———. *Hawthorne.* New York, 1879.

———. *Letters,* ed. P. Lubbock. 2 vols. New York, 1920.

———. *Notebooks,* ed. F. O. Matthiessen and K. B. Murdock, 1947.

———. *Notes of a Son and Brother.* New York, 1914.

———. *Novels and Tales.* 26 vols. New York, 1907–17.

———. *Partial Portraits.* London, 1888.

———. *William Wetmore Story and His Friends.* . . . 2 vols. Boston, 1903.

JEFFERSON, THOMAS. *Writings.* Library Ed. 20 vols. Washington, 1903–04.

JEWETT, I. A. "Themes for Western Fiction." *Western Monthly Magazine,* I (1833).

JEWETT, SARAH O. *Letters,* ed. Annie Fields. Boston, 1911.

JOHNSON, R. U. *Remembered Yesterdays.* Boston, 1923.

JONES, J. B. "Thoughts on the Literary Prospects of America." Baltimore, 1839.

JONES, W. A. *Characters and Criticisms.* 2 vols. New York, 1857.

——. "Nationality in Literature." *Democratic Review,* XX (1847).

JUDD, SYLVESTER. *Margaret.* . . . Boston, 1845.

KEESE, JOHN. *The Poets of America.* New York, 1840–42.

KENNEDY, JOHN P. *At Home and Abroad.* . . . New York, 1872.

——. *Memoirs of the Life of William Wirt.* . . . 2 vols. Philadelphia, 1856.

——. *Swallow Barn.* . . . New York, 1851.

KENNEDY, W. S. *Californian,* III (1881).

KETTELL, SAMUEL, ed. *Specimens of American Poetry.* . . . 3 vols. Boston, 1829.

KIRKLAND, CAROLINE. *Forest Life.* . . . 2 vols. New York, 1842.

——. *A New Home—Who'll Follow?* . . . New York, 1839.

——. *Cf.* Preface to Mary Eastman, *Dahcotah.* New York, 1849.

K[IRKLAND], J[OSEPH]. *Dial,* XIII (1892).

[KNAPP, FRANCIS?] *"Gloria Britannorum.* . . ." Boston, 1723.

——. "A New England Pond." *Cf.* Duyckincks' *Cyclopaedia.* . . . 2 vols. Philadelphia, 1877.

KNAPP, JOHN. *North American,* VIII (1818–19).

KNAPP, SAMUEL. *Knickerbocker,* V (1835).

——. *Letters of Shahcoolen.* . . . Boston, 1802.

Knickerbocker, I (1833); II (1833); V (1835).

LADD, JOSEPH B. *American Museum,* II (1787).

LANIER, SIDNEY. *Atlantic Monthly,* LXXXIV (1899).

——. *Southern Magazine,* VIII (1871).

——. *Works.* Centennial Ed., ed. C. R. Anderson. 10 vols. Baltimore, 1945.

LARCOM, LUCY. *Life, Letters, and Diary,* ed. D. D. Addison. Boston, 1894.

LAZARUS, EMMA. *Letters to Emma Lazarus,* ed. R. L. Rusk. New York, 1939.

LEGARÉ, HUGH S. *Southern Literary Gazette,* I (1829).

——. *Writings.* . . . 2 vols. Charleston, 1846.

LEGGETT, WILLIAM. *A Collection of the Political Writings of William Leggett* . . . , ed. T. Sedgwick, Jr. 2 vols. New York, 1840.

LELAND, C. G. *Memoirs.* New York, 1893.

——. *Sunshine in Thought.* New York, 1862.

LEWIS, RICHARD. "Muscipula. . . ." Annapolis, 1728. *Cf. Maryland Historical Society, Fund Publication,* No. 36. Baltimore, 1900.

"Life and Death of Old Father Janus . . . , The." Boston, 1726.

LINN, JOHN BLAIR. *Literary Magazine and . . . Register,* IV (1805).

[LINN, JOHN BLAIR.] *Miscellaneous Works . . . by a Young Gentleman of New-York.* New York, 1795.

LINN, JOHN BLAIR. *The Powers of Genius.* . . . Philadelphia, 1802.

LIPPARD, GEORGE. *Cf.* E. P. Oberholtzer, *The Literary History of Philadelphia.* Philadelphia, 1906.

Literary Magazine and American Register, II (1804).

Literary World, I (1847); VIII (1851).

LODGE, H. C. *Studies in History.* Boston, 1884.

LONGFELLOW, H. W. *Complete Writings.* Craigie Ed. 11 vols. Boston, 1904.

————. "Defense of Poetry." *Cf. Essays from the North American Review,* ed. A. T. Rice. New York, 1879.

————. *Graham's Magazine,* XX (1842).

LONGFELLOW, SAMUEL. *Life of Henry W. Longfellow.* 2 vols. Boston, 1886.

LONGSTREET, A. B. *Georgia Scenes.* . . . New York, 1852.

LOW, SAMUEL. *Poems.* 2 vols. New York, 1800.

[LOWELL, J. R.] *Atlantic Monthly,* III (1859).

LOWELL, J. R. *Cf.* Elizabeth R. Pennell, *Charles Godfrey Leland.* . . . 2 vols. Boston and New York, 1906.

————. *Democracy and Other Addresses.* Boston, 1887.

————. *Graham's Magazine,* XXVII (1845).

————. *Letters,* ed. C. E. Norton. 2 vols. New York, 1894.

————. "Lowell's Letters to Poe." *Scribner's,* XVI (1894).

————. *New Letters,* ed. M. A. DeWolfe Howe. New York, 1932.

————. *North American,* LXIV (1847); LXIX (1849).

————. *Pioneer,* I (1843).

————. *Works.* Standard Ed. 13 vols. Boston, n.d.

McCOY, JOSEPH. *The Frontier Maid.* . . . Wilkesbarre, 1819.

M'KINNON, JOHN D. *Descriptive Poems.* New York, 1802.

MADISON, JAMES. *Letters and Other Writings.* 4 vols. Philadelphia, 1865.

Magnolia, III (1841).

MANN, HORACE. *Life and Works.* 5 vols. Boston, 1891.

————. *Cf.* C. A. Bristed, *Pieces of a Broken-Down Critic.* 4 vols. Baden-Baden, 1858–59.

MARKOE, PETER. *The Storm.* Philadelphia, 1788.

MARSH, GEORGE P. *Cf.* Duyckincks' *Cyclopaedia.* . . . 2 vols. Philadelphia, 1877.

————. *Life and Letters,* ed. Caroline

Marsh. 2 vols. New York, 1888.
MASON, JOHN. *A Brief History of the Pequot War*. . . . Boston, 1736.
Massachusetts Magazine, I (1789); III (1791).
MASTERS, E. L. *Across Spoon River*. . . . New York, 1936.
MATHER, COTTON. Dedicatory Epistle to *Memorable Providences* (1689). *Cf.* G. L. Burr, ed. *Narratives of the Witchcraft Cases 1648–1706*. New York, 1914.
————. *Diary*. 2 vols. *Collections of the Mass. Historical Society*, 7th ser., Vols. VII, VIII. Boston, 1911–12.
————. *Magnalia Christi Americana*. 2 vols. Hartford, 1853, 1855.
————. *Manuductio ad Ministerium*. . . . Boston, 1726.
————. "A Poem Dedicated To the Memory of . . . Mr. Urian Oakes." Club of Odd Volumes, *Early American Poetry*, Vol. III. Boston, 1896.
MATHEWS, CORNELIUS. *Graham's Magazine*, XXII (1843).
————. *Cf.* W. R. Alger, *Life of Edwin Forrest*. . . . 2 vols. Philadelphia, 1877.
————. *Magnolia*, N.S. II (1843).
————. *Various Writings*. New York, 1843.
MATTHEWS, BRANDER. *Cosmopolitan*, XIII (1892).
MEAD, CHARLES. *American Minstrel*. . . . Philadelphia, 1828.
————. *Mississippian Scenery*. . . . Philadelphia, 1819.

MEEK, A. B. "Americanism in Literature." Charleston, 1844.
————. *Romantic Passages in Southwestern History*. . . . New York, 1857.
MELLEN, GRENVILLE. *North American*, XXXVII (1833).
MELVILLE, HERMAN. *The Apple-Tree Table*. . . . Princeton, 1922.
————. *John Marr and Other Poems*, ed. H. Chapin. Princeton, 1922.
————. *Pierre*. . . . New York, 1949.
MILLER, JOAQUIN. *Joaquin, et al.* Portland, 1869.
————. *Poetical Works*, ed. S. P. Sherman. New York, 1923.
MILLER, SAMUEL. *A Brief Retrospect of the Eighteenth Century*. . . . 2 vols. New York, 1803.
MITCHELL, DONALD G. *The Lorgnette*. 2 vols. New York, 1851.
————. *Works*. Edgewood Ed. 15 vols. New York, 1907.
MONROE, HARRIET. *Lippincott's*, XXXIX (1887).
Monthly Anthology, V (1808); VII (1809); VIII (1810); IX (1810).
Monthly Magazine and American Review, I (1799); III (1800).
Monthly Register and Review, I (1806).
MORRELL, WILLIAM. *New-England; or a Briefe ENARRATION*. . . . Club of Odd Volumes, *Early American Poetry*, Vol. II. Boston, 1895.
MORRIS, GOUVERNEUR. "An Inaugural Discourse. . . ." New York, 1816.

MORTON, SARAH. *Beacon Hill.* . . . Boston, 1797.

——. ("Philenia"). *Ouâbi: or the Virtues of Nature. An Indian Tale.* Boston, 1790.

——. *The Virtues of Society. A Tale, Founded on Fact.* Boston, 1799.

MOTLEY, J. L. *Correspondence,* ed. G. W. Curtis. 3 vols. New York and London, 1900.

——. *Merry-Mount.* . . . Boston, 1849.

——. *Morton's Hope.* . . . 2 vols. New York, 1839.

——. *North American,* LXIX (1849).

MURDOCK, KENNETH, ed. *Handkerchiefs from Paul.* . . . Cambridge, 1927.

MURRAY, JUDITH SARGENT. *The Gleaner.* . . . 3 vols. Boston, 1798.

——. *Cf.* Sarah Wood, *Dorval.* . . . Portsmouth, N. H., 1801.

Nation, IV (1867); VI (1868); XI (1870).

NEAL, JOHN. *American Writers* . . . , ed. F. L. Pattee. Durham, 1937.

——. *Brother Jonathan.* . . . 3 vols. Edinburgh and London, 1825.

[NEAL JOHN?] *Brother Jonathan,* I (1842); VI (1843).

NEAL, JOHN. *Errata.* . . . 2 vols. New York, 1823.

——. *Rachel Dyer.* Portland, 1828.

——. *Randolph.* . . . N.p., 1823.

——. *Wandering Recollections of a Somewhat Busy Life.* Boston, 1869.

[NEAL, JOHN?] *Yankee and Boston Literary Gazette,* N.S. II (1829).

NEWCOMB, C. K. *Journals,* ed. Judith Johnson. Providence, 1946.

New Eclectic Magazine, V (1869); VI (1870).

New England Magazine, V (1833); VI (1834).

New-Haven Gazette, and the Connecticut Magazine, I (1786); II (1787).

New Mirror, III (1844).

New York Mirror and Ladies' Literary Gazette, I (1823).

NOAH, M. M. MS letter in Schoolcraft Papers, Vol. XX. Library of Congress.

North American, III (1816); XXVIII (1829).

NORTON, C. E. *Letters,* ed. Sara Norton and M. A. DeWolfe Howe. 2 vols. Boston, 1913.

NOYES, NICHOLAS. *New-Englands Duty and Interest.* . . . Boston, 1698.

——. "A Prefatory Poem." Cotton Mather, *Magnalia.* . . . Hartford, 1855.

OAKES, URIAN. "An Elegie upon . . . Mr. Thomas Shepard. . . ." Club of Odd Volumes, *Early American Poetry,* Vol. IV. Boston, 1896.

ODIORNE, THOMAS. *The Progress of Refinement.* . . . Boston, 1792.

"On Novelty in Literature." *Literary Magazine and American Register,* V (1806).

Overland Monthly, VIII (1872); IX (1872); 2nd ser. XIX (1892).

PAGE, THOMAS N. Lippincott's, XLVIII (1891).

PAINE, ROBERT TREAT. Works, ed. Charles Prentiss. Boston, 1812.

PAINE, THOMAS. Life and Works. Patriots' Ed. 10 vols. New Rochelle, 1925.

PALFREY, J. G. North American, XLV (1837).

Palladium. Cf. Port Folio, I (1801).

PARKE, JOHN. The Lyric Works of Horace. . . . Philadelphia, 1786.

PARKER, THEODORE. Works. Centenary Ed. 15 vols. Boston, 1907.

PARKMAN, FRANCIS. Cf. A. T. Rice, ed. Essays from the North American Review. New York, 1879.

PARSONS, T. W. Poems. Boston, 1893.

PARTON, JAMES. Atlantic Monthly, XXII (1867).

PAULDING, JAMES K. AND W. I., eds. American Comedies. Philadelphia, 1847.

PAULDING, JAMES K. "Americanisms." Analectic, III (1814).

———. American Quarterly Review, I (1827).

———. The Backwoodsman. . . . Philadelphia, 1818.

———. Cf. "Celebration of the Forty-seventh Anniversary of the First Settlement of Ohio." Cincinnati, 1835.

———. A Christmas Gift from Fairyland. New York, 1838.

———. Koningsmarke. 2 vols. New York, 1823.

———. The Lay of the Scottish Fiddle. . . . New York, 1813.

———. Letters from the South. . . . 2 vols. New York, 1817.

———. The Puritan and His Daughter. 2 vols. New York, 1849.

———. Salmagundi: Second Series. 3 vols. New York and Philadelphia, 1819–20.

———. Southern Literary Messenger, I (1834).

———. Tales of the Good Woman. 2 vols. New York, 1836.

———. The United States and England. . . . New York and Philadelphia, 1815.

PAULDING, W. I. The Literary Life of James K. Paulding. New York, 1867.

———. "Madmen All. . . ." American Comedies. Philadelphia, 1847.

PEIRCE, THOMAS. The Muse of Hesperia. Cincinnati, 1823.

PENDLETON, P. C. Magnolia, III (1841).

PENNELL, ELIZABETH. Charles Godfrey Leland. 2 vols. Boston and New York, 1906.

PERCIVAL, J. G. Clio, Number II. New Haven, 1822.

———. "Poem." Boston, 1826.

———. Poetical Works. 2 vols. Boston, 1859.

[PERKINS, J. H.] New York Magazine, V (1839).

PERRY, T. S. *North American,* CXV (1872).

——. *Selections from the Letters of . . . Perry,* ed. E. A. Robinson. New York, 1929.

[PHILLIPS, WILLARD.] *North American,* VI (1818).

PHILOMATHES. *Some Thoughts on Education.* . . . New York, 1752.

PICKERING, JOHN. *A Vocabulary . . . Peculiar to the United States.* . . . Boston, 1816.

Pietas et Gratulatio Collegii Cantabrigiensis. . . . Boston, 1761.

PIKE, ALBERT. "An Address. . . ." Little Rock, 1852.

Pioneer, III (1855).

POE, EDGAR ALLAN. *Complete Works,* ed. J. A. Harrison. 17 vols. New York, 1902.

——. *Letters,* ed. J. W. Ostrom. 2 vols. Cambridge, 1948.

——. "The Poe-Chivers Papers." *Century,* LXV (1903).

——. *Southern Literary Messenger,* II (1836).

——. *Works,* ed. R. Griswold, *et al.* 10 vols. New York, n.d.

Poet Lore, II (1890).

POLLOCK, EDWARD. *Pioneer,* II (1854).

Polyanthus, I (1812–13).

POPE, JOHN. *A Tour through the Southern and Western Territories.* . . . New York, 1888.

PORTER, NOAH. *Biblical Repository,* 3rd ser. III (1847).

Port Folio, II (1802); V (1805).

Port Folio, N.S. I (1809); VII (1812).

Port Folio, 2nd N.S. IV (1817); VII (1819).

PRENTISS, CHARLES. *Child of Pallas.* Baltimore, 1800.

——, ed. *Works . . . of the Late Robert Treat Paine, Jun. Esq.* Boston, 1812.

PRESCOTT, W. H. *Biographical and Critical Miscellanies.* New York, 1845.

——. "The Life of Charles Brockden Brown." *American Biography,* ed. Jared Sparks. Vol. VII. New York, 1902.

——. *North American,* XXI (1825); XXIX (1829); XXXIII (1831); XXXV (1832).

PRESTON, MARGARET JUNKIN. *Life and Letters,* ed. Elizabeth P. Allen. Boston and New York, 1903.

"Proposals for a Poem." *Boston Magazine,* I (1784).

Puck, II (1878).

PUTNAM, G. H. *Memories of a Publisher.* . . . New York, 1915.

Putnam's Monthly, N.S. I (1868); V (1870).

RAMSEY, DAVID. "Oration on the Advantages of American Independence." *United States Magazine,* I (1779).

READ, T. B. *The New Pastoral.* Philadelphia, 1855.

——. *Poetical Works.* Philadelphia, 1894.

REED, SAMPSON. *Cf.* K. W. Cameron,

ed. *Emerson the Essayist.* 2 vols. Raleigh, 1945.

RICE, A. T., ed. *Essays from the North American Review.* New York, 1879.

[RICHARDS, W. C.] *Orion,* I (1842).

RICKETSON, DANIEL. *Autobiographic and Miscellaneous,* ed. Anna and Walton Ricketson. New Bedford, 1910.

———. *The Autumn-Sheaf.* New Bedford, 1869.

RILEY, J. W. *Letters,* ed. W. L. Phelps. Indianapolis, 1930.

———. *Pipes o' Pan at Zekesbury.* Indianapolis, 1891.

RIPLEY, GEORGE. *Dial,* I (1840–41).

ROANE, A. *De Bow's Review,* XXIV (1858).

ROBIN, ABBÉ C. C. *New Travels through North-America.* . . . Philadelphia, 1783.

ROSE, AQUILA. *Poems on Several Occasions.* Philadelphia, 1740.

ROWSON, SUSANNA. *Charlotte and Lucy Temple.* Philadelphia, 1864.

———. *Charlotte's Daughter.* Boston, 1828.

———. *Miscellaneous Poems.* Boston, 1804.

———. *Slaves in Algiers.* . . . Philadelphia, 1794.

Royal American Magazine, I (1774).

[RUSH, BENJAMIN.] *American Museum,* IV (1788); V (1789).

RUSH, BENJAMIN. *Essays, Literary, Moral, and Philosophical.* Philadelphia, 1806.

Russell's Magazine, I (1857); II (1857); V (1859).

SANBORN, F. B. AND W. T. HARRIS. *A. Bronson Alcott.* . . . 2 vols. Boston, 1893.

SANBORN, F. B. *The Life of Henry David Thoreau.* Boston and New York, 1917.

SANDS, ROBERT C. *Writings.* 2 vols. New York, 1834.

SANDYS, GEORGE. *Ovid's Metamorphosis Englished.* . . . Oxford, 1632.

SCHELE DE VERE, M. *Americanisms.* . . . New York, 1872.

SCHOOLCRAFT, HENRY ROWE. MS letters of May 26, July 3, and November 17, 1845 in Schoolcraft Papers, Vols. XXI, XXII. Library of Congress.

———. *Personal Memoirs.* . . . Philadelphia, 1851.

———. *The Rise of the West.* . . . New York, 1841.

S[COTT], W. C. *Southern Literary Messenger,* XI (1845).

SCOTTOW, JOSHUA. "A Narrative of the Planting of the Massachusetts Colony. . . ." *Collections of the Mass. Historical Society.* 4th ser., Vol. IV. Boston, 1858.

Scribner's Monthly, X (1875); XVIII (1879).

SCUDDER, H. E. *Atlantic Monthly,* LVII (1886).

———. *James Russell Lowell.* . . . 2 vols. Boston, 1901.

SCUDDER, H. E. *Men and Letters.* . . . Boston, 1887.

———. *Noah Webster.* Boston, 1883.

SEDGWICK, CATHARINE. *Clarence.* . . . New York and Boston, 1854.

———. *Letters from Abroad to Kindred at Home.* 2 vols. New York, 1841.

———. *Life and Letters,* ed. Mary E. Dewey. New York, 1871.

———. "Lucretia Maria Davidson." *Cf. American Biography,* ed. Jared Sparks. Vol. VII. New York, 1902.

———. *A New England Tale.* . . . New York, 1852.

———. *Redwood.* . . . New York, 1824.

———. *Tales and Sketches.* Philadelphia, 1835.

SELLMAN, H. S. *Cf.* James Woodmansee, *Wrinkles from the Brow of Experience.* Cincinnati, 1860.

SEWALL, SAMUEL. *Phaenomena Quaedam Apocalyptica.* . . . Boston, 1697.

———. *Proposals Touching the Accomplishment of Prophecies.* . . . Boston, 1713.

SEWARD, W. H. *Works.* 5 vols. New York, 1853–84.

SHEPPARD, N. *Western Magazine,* I (1869).

[SHINN, MILICENT.] *Overland Monthly.* 2nd ser. II (1883).

SIGOURNEY, LYDIA. *Letters of Life.* New York, 1866.

SILL, E. R. *Californian,* I (1880).

SILSBEE, E. A. *The Life and Services to*

Literature of Jones Very. Salem, 1881.

SIMMONS, J. W. "American Literature." *Southern Literary Journal,* III (1836).

———. *The Maniac's Confession.* . . . Philadelphia, 1821.

———. *Southern Literary Gazette,* I (1829).

SIMMS, W. G. *Castle Dismal.* . . . New York, 1844.

———. *The Damsel of Darien.* 2 vols. Philadelphia, 1839.

———. *Guy Rivers.* . . . 2 vols. New York, 1834.

———. *Katharine Walton.* . . . New York, 1884.

———. *Magnolia,* III (1841); IV (1842); N.S. II (1843).

———. *Mellichampe.* . . . 2 vols. New York, 1836.

———. *The Partisan.* . . . 2 vols. New York, 1835.

[———.] *Southern and Western Monthly Magazine* . . . , I (1845); II (1845).

SIMMS, W. G. *Southern Literary Messenger,* X (1844).

[———.] *Southern Quarterly Review,* XVII (1850); XVIII (1850).

SIMMS, W. G. *Southward Ho.* . . . New York, 1854.

———. *Views and Reviews.* . . . 2 vols. New York, 1845.

———. *The Wigwam and the Cabin.* . . . 2 vols. New York, 1845.

———. *The Yemassee.* 2 vols. New York, 1835.

SIMPSON, STEPHEN. *The Author's Jewel.* Philadelphia, 1823.

——. *Portico,* II (1816).

——. *The Working Man's Manual.* Philadelphia, 1831.

SMITH, EAGLESFIELD. *William and Ellen.* . . . New York, 1811.

SMITH, ELIHU, ed. *American Poems.* . . . Litchfield, 1793.

——. "Epistle." *Cf.* Erasmus Darwin, *The Botanic Garden.* New York, 1798.

——. "Occasional Address." *Monthly Magazine and American Review,* I (1799).

SMITH, ELIZABETH OAKES, ed. *The Mayflower.* Boston, 1847.

SMITH, ELIZABETH OAKES. *The Newsboy.* New York, 1854.

——. *Selections from the Autobiography of Elizabeth Oakes Smith,* ed. Mary A. Wyman. Lewiston, 1924.

——. *Shadow Land; or, the Seer.* New York, 1852.

SMITH, SEBA. *The Life and Writings of Major Jack Downing.* . . . Boston, 1833.

——. *Powhatan.* . . . New York, 1841.

SMITH, WILLIAM (1727-1803). *American Magazine.* . . . I (October, 1757).

——, et al. *Four Dissertations.* . . . Philadelphia, 1766.

[——.] *Indian Songs of Peace.* . . . New York, 1752.

SMITH, WILLIAM. *Works,* 2 vols. Philadelphia, 1803.

SMITH, WILLIAM (1728-1793). *The History of the Province of New-York.* London, 1757.

SNELLING, W. J. *Tales of the Northwest.* . . . Boston, 1830.

SNOWDEN, RICHARD. *The Columbiad.* . . . Philadelphia, 1795.

Southern Ladies' Book, I (1840).

Southern Literary Gazette, I (1828-29).

Southern Literary Messenger, XXIII (1856).

Southern Magazine, IX (1871); XI (1872).

Southern Presbyterian Review. Cf. New Eclectic, V (1869).

Southern Review, N.S. VII (1870).

[SPARHAWK, E. V.] *Southern Literary Messenger,* I (1835).

SPARKS, JARED. *North American,* XX (1825).

Spirit of the Times. Cf. Literary World, I (1847).

SPOONER, W. J. "An Address. . . ." Boston, 1822.

SPRAGUE, CHARLES. *Poetical and Prose Writings.* Boston, 1876.

SPRAGUE, W. B. "An Oration. . . ." Albany, 1851.

STEDMAN, E. C. *Life and Letters,* ed. L. Stedman and G. M. Gould. 2 vols. New York, 1910.

——. *Poets of America.* Boston and New York, 1885.

——. *Scribner's,* XXII (1881).

STEERE, RICHARD. "A Monumental Memorial of Marine Mercy. . . ." Boston, 1684.

STERLING, JAMES. "A Pastoral." *American Magazine,* I (1758).

[STICKNEY, JOHN.] *Monthly Anthology,* IX (1810).

STILES, EZRA. "The United States Elevated to Glory and Honour." Worcester, 1785.

STODDARD, R. H. *Poems.* New York, 1880.

———. *Recollections.* . . . New York, 1903.

STORY, JOSEPH. *Miscellaneous Writings.* Boston, 1852.

———. "The Power of Solitude." Salem, 1804.

STORY, W. W. *He and She.* . . . Boston, 1884.

———. *Nature and Art.* . . . Boston, 1844.

———. *Poems.* 2 vols. Boston, 1856.

STOUGHTON, WILLIAM. "New-Englands True Interest; Not to Lie. . . ." Cambridge, 1670.

STOWE, C. E. *Harriet Beecher Stowe.* . . . Boston, 1891.

STOWE, HARRIET BEECHER. *Cf.* Annie Fields, *Authors and Friends.* Boston, 1893.

———. *Dred.* . . . 2 vols. Boston, 1856.

———. *The Mayflower, and Miscellaneous Writings.* Boston, 1883.

———. *The Minister's Wooing.* Boston and New York, 1902.

———. *Oldtown Folks.* Boston, 1869.

STREET, A. B. "Our State." New York, 1849.

SUMNER, CHARLES. "The Scholar, the Jurist, the Artist, the Philanthropist." Boston, 1846.

SWINTON, WILLIAM. *Cf.* H. Traubel, *With Walt Whitman.* . . . 3 vols. Boston and New York, 1906–14.

TARDY, MARY F., ed. *The Living Female Writers of the South.* Philadelphia, 1872.

TAYLOR, BAYARD. "The American Legend." Cambridge, 1850.

———. *A Book of Romances, Lyrics, and Songs.* Boston, 1852.

———. *The Correspondence of . . . Taylor and . . . Hayne,* ed. C. Duffy. Baton Rouge, 1945.

———. *Critical Essays, and Literary Notes.* New York, 1880.

———. *The Echo Club.* . . . New York, 1895.

———. *Hannah Thurston.* . . . New York, 1903.

———. *Home Pastorals.* . . . Boston, 1875.

———. *John Godfrey's Fortunes.* . . . New York, 1864.

———. *Life and Letters,* ed. Marie Hansen-Taylor and H. Scudder. 2 vols. Boston, 1895.

———. "The National Ode. . . ." N.p., 1876.

———. *Poetical Works.* Boston, 1892.

TAYLOR, BAYARD. *The Poet's Journal.* Boston, 1863.

——. *The Story of Kennett.* New York, 1894.

——. *The Unpublished Letters . . . ,* ed. J. R. Schultz. San Marino, 1937.

TAYLOR, EDWARD. *Poetical Works,* ed. T. M. Johnson. New York, 1939.

TERHUNE, MARY VIRGINIA. *Marion Harland's Autobiography. . . .* New York, 1910.

THACHER, S. C. *Monthly Anthology,* II (1805).

THOMAS, F. W. *East and West.* Philadelphia, 1836.

——. *John Randolph, of Roanoke.* . . . Philadelphia, 1853.

THOMPSON, J. R. "Education and Literature in Virginia." Richmond, 1850.

——. *Poems,* ed. J. S. Patton. New York, 1920.

——. *Southern Literary Messenger,* XVI (1850).

THOMPSON, MAURICE. *Current Literature,* II (1889); III (1889).

——. *North American,* CXLIX (1889).

——. *Public Opinion,* V (1888).

THOREAU, H. D. *Collected Poems,* ed. Carl Bode. Chicago, 1943.

——. *Dial,* IV (1843–44).

——. *Writings,* Manuscript Ed. 20 vols. Boston, 1906.

TICKNOR, GEORGE. *Life, Letters, and Journals,* ed. Anna Ticknor and G. S. Hillard. 2 vols. Boston, 1877.

Time-Piece, II (1797).

TIMROD, HENRY. *Essays,* ed. E. W. Parks. Athens, Ga., 1942.

——. *The Last Years of Henry Timrod . . . ,* ed. J. B. Hubbell. Durham, 1941.

TODD, C. B., ed. *Life and Letters of Joel Barlow. . . .* New York, 1886.

TRAUBEL, HORACE. *With Walt Whitman in Camden.* 3 vols. Boston and New York, 1906–14.

TROWBRIDGE, J. T. *My Own Story. . . .* New York and Boston, 1903.

TRUMBULL, JOHN. "An Essay on the Use and Advantages of the Fine Arts. . . ." New-Haven, 1770.

TUCKER, GEORGE. "Discourse on American Literature." *Southern Literary Messenger,* IV (1838).

[TUCKER, GEORGE.] *Essays on Various Subjects of Taste, Morals, and National Policy.* Georgetown, 1822.

TUCKERMAN, HENRY, ed. *The Boston Book.* Boston, 1836.

TUCKERMAN, HENRY. *Leaves from the Diary of a Dreamer.* London, 1853.

——. *The Life of John Pendleton Kennedy.* New York, 1871.

——, ed. *A Memorial of Horatio Greenough. . . .* New York, 1853.

——. *North American,* LXXXII (1856).

——. *The Optimist.* New York, 1850.

——. *Rambles and Reveries.* New York, 1841.

——. *Selections from the Writings*

of Henry Theodore Tuckerman. For Private Circulation. N.p., 187–.

TUDOR, WILLIAM. *Letters on the Eastern States.* New York, 1820.

——. *Monthly Anthology,* IX (1810).

——. *North American,* II (1815).

TURELL, EBENEZER. *Memoirs of the Life and Death of . . . Mrs. Jane Turell.* . . . London, 1741.

TYLER, ROYALL. *The Algerine Captive.* . . . London, 1802.

——. *The Yankey in London.* . . . New York, 1809.

UMPHRAVILLE, ANGUS. *The Siege of Baltimore.* Baltimore, 1817.

UPHAM, T. C. *American Sketches.* New York, 1819.

WALKER, AMASSA. *New England Magazine,* V (1833).

WALSH, ROBERT. *Brother Jonathan,* II (1842).

——. *Didactics.* 2 vols. Philadelphia, 1836.

WALTER, THOMAS. "The Sweet Psalmist of Israel." Boston, 1722.

WARD, J. H. *Life and Letters of James Gates Percival.* Boston, 1866.

WARNER, C. D. *A Little Journey in the World.* New York, 1889.

WARREN, MERCY. *Poems, Dramatic and Miscellaneous.* Boston, 1790.

WASHINGTON, GEORGE. *Writings.* . . . Bicentennial Ed. 39 vols. Washington, 1931–44.

W[ATERHOUSE, BENJAMIN]. *Monthly Anthology,* II (1805).

WATTERSTON, GEORGE. *The Child of Feeling.* George Town, 1809.

WEBSTER, DANIEL. "The State of our Literature." *Writings and Speeches.* . . . National Ed. 18 vols. Boston, 1903.

WEBSTER, NOAH. *American Museum,* XII (1792).

——. *A Collection of Essays and Fugitiv [sic] Writings.* Boston, 1790.

——. *A Collection of Papers on Political, Literary, and Moral Subjects.* New York, 1843.

——. *A Compendious Dictionary of the English Language.* New-Haven, 1806.

——. *Dissertations on the English Language.* Boston, 1789.

——. *A Grammatical Institute . . . Part I.* Hartford, 1783.

——. *Letters to a Young Gentleman.* . . . New-Haven, 1823.

Weekly Magazine, III (1798).

WEISS, JOHN. *Atlantic Monthly,* IX (1862).

Western Magazine, I (1869); II (1869).

Western Monthly Magazine, I (1833); II (1834); V (1836).

Western Monthly Review, II (1828).

Western Souvenir, The. Cincinnati, 1829.

WHARTON, CHARLES. *A Poetical Epistle to . . . George Washington.* . . . London, 1781.

WHARTON, G. M. *North American,* LII (1841).

WHIPPLE, E. P. *Essays and Reviews.* 2 vols. Boston, 1856.

———. *Harper's,* LII (1876).

WHITAKER, ALEXANDER. *Good Newes from Virginia.* London, 1613.

WHITAKER, DANIEL. "The Necessity of a Southern Literature." *The Charleston Book.* Charleston, 1845.

———. *Southern Literary Journal,* I (1835).

———. *Southern Rose,* VII (1839).

WHITE, R. G. *The Fate of Mansfield Humphreys.* . . . New York, 1884.

———. *Galaxy,* XXIV (1877).

———. *National Hymns.* New York, 1861.

———, ed. *Poetry . . . of the Civil War.* New York, 1866.

[WHITE, T. W.] *Southern Literary Messenger,* IV (1838).

WHITING, HENRY. *Cf.* H. R. Schoolcraft, *Personal Memoirs.* . . . Philadelphia, 1851.

WHITMAN, WALT. *An American Primer,* ed. H. Traubel. Boston, 1904.

W[HITMAN], W. *Brother Jonathan,* I (1842).

WHITMAN, WALT. *Complete Prose Works.* Boston, 1907.

———. *Complete Writings,* ed. R. M. Bucke, T. B. Harned, and H. L. Traubel. 10 vols. New York, 1902.

———. *Criticism.* . . . Newark, 1913.

———. *The Gathering of the Forces* . . . , ed. C. Rodgers and J. Black. 2 vols. New York, 1920.

———. *I Sit and Look Out* . . . , ed. E. Holloway and V. Schwarz. New York, 1932.

———. *Leaves of Grass.* Brooklyn, 1856.

———. *New York Dissected* . . . , ed. E. Holloway and R. Adimari. New York, 1936.

———. *Notes and Fragments* . . . , ed. R. M. Bucke. London, Ont., 1899.

———. *Poetry and Prose.* Inner Sanctum Ed. New York, 1950.

———. *Rivulets of Prose* . . . , ed. C. Wells and A. Goldsmith. New York, 1928.

———. "Three Uncollected St. Louis Interviews. . . ." *Cf.* R. R. Hubach, *American Literature,* XIV (1942).

WHITTIER, J. G. *Correspondence from the Oak Knoll Collections, 1830–1892,* ed. John Albree. Salem, 1911.

———. *Legends of New-England.* Hartford and Boston, 1831.

———. *Literary Recreations.* . . . Boston, 1854.

———. *Writings,* ed. H. Scudder. 7 vols. Boston, 1888–89.

WIGGLESWORTH, MICHAEL. *The Day of Doom* . . . , ed. Kenneth Murdock. New York, 1929.

WILDE, R. H. *Hesperia.* . . . Boston, 1867.

WILLIAMS, ROGER. *A Key into the Lan-*

guage of America . . . , ed. H. M. Chapin. Providence, 1936.

WILLIS, N. P. *American Scenery.* . . . 2 vols. London, 1840.

———. *Athenaeum* (1835).

———. *Hurry-Graphs.* . . . Auburn and Rochester, 1856.

———, ed. *The Legendary.* . . . 2 vols. Boston, 1828.

WILLIS, N. P. *Letters from Under a Bridge.* . . . London, 1840.

———. *Paul Fane.* . . . New York, 1857.

WILMER, L. A. *The Quacks of Helicon.* . . . Philadelphia, 1841.

WILSON, ALEXANDER. *Memoir and Remains* . . . , ed. A. B. Grosart. 2 vols. Paisley, 1876.

WINTHROP, F. W. "Beauty." *North American,* VII (1818).

WINTHROP, THEODORE. *Cecil Dreeme.* Boston, 1862.

WIRT, WILLIAM. *The Letters of the British Spy.* Baltimore, 1817.

———, ed. *The Rainbow; First Series.* Richmond, 1804.

WITHERSPOON, JOHN. *Works.* 4 vols. Philadelphia, 1802.

[WITHINGTON, LEONARD.] *The Puritan.* . . . Boston, 1836.

WOLCOTT, ROGER. *Poetical Meditations.* . . . New-London, 1725.

WOOD, SARAH. *Dorval.* . . . Portsmouth, N. H., 1801.

WOODWORTH, SAMUEL. *The Champions of Freedom.* . . . 2 vols. New York, 1816.

Worcester Magazine, II (1786–87).

II. Secondary Sources

ADKINS, N. F. *Fitz-Greene Halleck.* New Haven, 1930.

ALGER, W. R. *Life of Edwin Forrest.* 2 vols. Philadelphia, 1877.

ANDERSON, C. R. "Gayarré and Hayne: The Last Literary Cavaliers." *American Studies in Honor of William Kenneth Boyd.* Durham, 1940.

BARNES, H. F. *Charles Fenno Hoffman.* New York, 1930.

BARRUS, CLARA. *Whitman and Burroughs, Comrades.* Boston and New York, 1931.

BAYLESS, JOY. *Rufus Wilmot Griswold.* . . . Nashville, 1943.

BEATTY, R. C. "Lowell's Commonplace Books." *New England Quarterly,* XVIII (1945).

BENEDICT, CLARE, ed. *Constance Fenimore Woolson.* London, 1932.

BOLWELL, ROBERT. "Concerning the Study of Nationalism in American Literature." *American Literature,* X (1939).

BOYS, RICHARD C. "The Beginnings of the American Poetical Miscellany, 1714–1800." *American Literature,* XVII (1945).

BRADLEY, SCULLEY. *George Henry Boker.* . . . Philadelphia, 1927.

BRAWLEY, B. G. *Paul Laurence Dunbar.* . . . Chapel Hill, 1936.

BROWN, H. R. "The Great American Novel." *American Literature,* VII (1935).

BROWNSON, H. F. *Orestes A. Brownson's Early Life.* . . . 2 vols. Detroit, 1898–90.

BRYCE, JAMES. *The American Commonwealth.* 2 vols. New York, 1888.

CAIRNS, W. B. "On the Development of American Literature from 1815 to 1833." *Bulletin of the University of Wisconsin.* Vol. I. Madison, 1901.

CARDWELL, GUY. *Charleston Periodicals, 1795–1868.* . . . Unpublished University of North Carolina dissertation, 1936.

CHARVAT, WILLIAM. *The Origins of American Critical Thought, 1810–1835.* Philadelphia, 1936.

CLARK, H. H. "The Influence of Science on American Literary Criticism, 1860–1910, Including the Vogue of Taine." *Wisconsin Academy of Sciences, Arts, and Letters,* LIV (1955).

———. "Literary Criticism in the *North American Review,* 1815–1835." *Wisconsin Academy of Sciences, Arts, and Letters,* XXXII (1940).

———. "Nationalism in American Literature." *University of Toronto Quarterly,* II (1933).

COBERLY, J. H. *The Growth of Nationalism in American Literature, 1800–1815.* Unpublished George Washington University dissertation, 1949.

COLE, CHARLES W. *The Beginnings of Literary Nationalism in America, 1775–1800.* Unpublished George Washington dissertation, 1939.

COOK, E. C. *Literary Influences in Colonial Newspapers, 1704–50.* New York, 1912.

COOKE, G. W. *An Historical and Biographical Introduction to . . . the Dial.* . . . 2 vols. Cleveland, 1902.

COTTMAN, G. S. "The Western Association of Writers." *Indiana Magazine of History,* XXIX (1933).

COWIE, ALEXANDER. "John Trumbull as a Critic of Poetry." *New England Quarterly,* XI (1938).

———. *John Trumbull: Connecticut Wit.* Chapel Hill, 1936.

CURRENT-GARCIA, E. " 'Mr. Spirit' and *The Big Bear of Arkansas.* . . ." *American Literature,* XXVII (1955).

CURTI, MERLE. *The Growth of American Thought.* New York, 1943.

———. "Young America." *American Historical Review,* XXXII (1926).

DALLMAN, W. P. *The Spirit of America . . . in the Works of Charles Sealsfield.* St. Louis, 1935.

DUNN, W. H. *The Life of Donald G. Mitchell: Ik Marvel.* New York, 1922.

ELLIS, MILTON. *Joseph Dennie and his Circle.* . . . Austin, 1915.

ENTRIKIN, ISABELLE. *Sarah Josepha Hale and Godey's Lady's Book.* . . . Philadelphia, 1946.

FLEWELLING, H. L. *Literary Criticism in American Periodicals, 1783–1820.* Unpublished University of Michigan dissertation, 1931.

FORD, E. E. F. *Notes on the Life of Noah Webster,* ed. E. E. Ford Skeel. 2 vols. New York, 1912.

GEORGE, J. MISHELL. *James Kirke Paulding: A Literary Nationalist.* Unpublished Master's thesis, George Washington University, 1941.

GORMAN, H. S. *A Victorian American, Henry Wadsworth Longfellow.* New York, 1926.

GREENSLET, FERRIS. *The Life of Thomas Bailey Aldrich.* Boston and New York, 1908.

——. *Under the Bridge.* . . . Boston, 1943.

GRIFFIN, CONSTANCE. *Henry Blake Fuller.* . . . Philadelphia, 1939.

HALL, L. S. *Hawthorne: Critic of Society.* New Haven, 1944.

HART, J. D. *The Popular Book.* New York, 1950.

HASSOLD, E. C. *American Literary History before the Civil War.* Unpublished University of Chicago dissertation, 1935.

HASTINGS, L. "Emerson in Cincinnati." *New England Quarterly,* XI (1938).

HAYES, CARLTON J. H. *Essays on Nationalism.* New York, 1926.

HEROLD, A. L. *James Kirke Paulding, Versatile American.* New York, 1926.

HOUTCHENS, L. "Charles Dickens and International Copyright." *American Literature,* XIII (1941).

HOWARD, LEON. *The Connecticut Wits.* Chicago, 1943.

HUBBELL, JAY B. "Literary Nationalism in the Old South." *American Studies in Honor of William Kenneth Boyd.* Durham, 1940.

——. *The South in American Literature.* . . . Durham, 1954.

HUMPHREYS, F. L. *The Life and Times of David Humphreys.* 2 vols. New York, 1917.

INGRAM, J. H. *Edgar Allan Poe.* . . . 2 vols. London, 1880.

JACKSON, D. K. "Philip Pendleton Cooke." *American Studies in Honor of William Kenneth Boyd.* Durham, 1940.

JANTZ, HAROLD S. *The First Century of New England Verse.* Worcester, 1944.

JOHNSON, M. O. *Walt Whitman as a Critic of Literature.* Lincoln, Neb., 1938.

JONES, HOWARD M. *The Theory of*

American Literature. Ithaca, 1948.

————. *Ideas in America.* Cambridge, 1944.

KEISER, ALBERT. *The Indian in American Literature.* New York, 1933.

KENNEDY, W. S. *The Fight of a Book for the World.* West Yarmouth, Mass., 1926.

KING, J. L. *Dr. George William Bagby.* . . . New York, 1927.

KNIGHT, G. C. *James Lane Allen and the Genteel Tradition.* Chapel Hill, 1935.

KOHN, HANS. *The Idea of Nationalism.* New York, 1944.

LEARY, LEWIS. *That Rascal Freneau.* . . . New Brunswick, 1941.

LELAND, L. P. *Theories of Fiction in America, 1789–1870.* Unpublished Ohio State University dissertation, 1940.

LONG, O. W. *Frederick Henry Hedge.* . . . Portland, Me., 1940.

————. *Literary Pioneers.* . . . Cambridge, 1935.

McCLOSKEY, J. C. "The Campaign of Periodicals after the War of 1812 for a National American Literature." *PMLA,* L (1935).

————. "A Note on the *Portico.*" *American Literature,* VIII (1936).

McMASTER, HELEN. "Margaret Fuller as a Literary Critic." *University of*

Buffalo Studies. Vol. VII (1928).

McWILLIAMS, CAREY. *Ambrose Bierce.* . . . New York, 1929.

MADDOX, N. S. "Literary Nationalism in *Putnam's Magazine,* 1853–57." *American Literature,* XIV (1942).

————. *Phases of Literary Nationalism in American Magazines, 1855–1890.* Unpublished Ohio State University dissertation, 1940.

MATTHIESSEN, F. O. *American Renaissance.* . . . New York, 1941.

MENCKEN, H. L. *The American Language.* . . . New York, 1936.

MILLER, PERRY. *The New England Mind: the Seventeenth Century.* New York, 1939.

MILLER, PERRY AND T. M. JOHNSON. *The Puritans.* New York, 1938.

MORSE, W. I. *Bliss Carman.* . . . Windham, Conn., 1941.

MOTT, F. L. *A History of American Magazines.* 3 vols. Cambridge, 1938.

MURDOCK, KENNETH B., ed. *A Leaf of Grass from Shady Hill.* Cambridge, 1928.

MUSSER, P. H. *James Nelson Barker.* . . . Philadelphia, 1929.

NEWLIN, C. M. *The Life and Writings of Hugh Henry Brackenridge.* Princeton, 1932.

OBERHOLTZER, E. P. *The Literary History of Philadelphia.* Philadelphia, 1906.

Open Court, X (1896).

PARKS, E. W. *Charles Egbert Craddock.* Chapel Hill, 1941.

PATTEE, F. L. *The Feminine Fifties.* New York, 1940.

PEARCE, ROY HARVEY. "The Eighteenth-Century Scottish Primitivists: Some Reconsiderations." *ELH*, XII (1945).

——. *The Savages of America.* Baltimore, 1953.

PERRY, BLISS. "Emerson's Most Famous Speech." *The Praise of Folly.* . . . Boston, 1923.

PERRY, R. B. *The Thought and Character of William James.* . . . 2 vols. Boston, 1935.

PLEADWELL, F. L. *The Life and Works of Joseph Rodman Drake.* Boston, 1935.

RHEA, LINDA. *Hugh Swinton Legaré.* . . . Chapel Hill, 1934.

ROTHERT, O. A. *The Story of a Poet: Madison Cawein.* . . . Louisville, 1921.

ROURKE, CONSTANCE. *American Humor.* . . . New York, 1931.

——. *The Roots of American Culture.* . . . New York, 1942.

RUSK, R. L. *The Life of . . . Emerson.* New York, 1949.

——. *The Literature of the Middle Western Frontier.* 2 vols. New York, 1925.

SEDGWICK, W. E. "The Materials for an American Literature." *Harvard Studies and Notes in Philology and Literature*, XVII (1935).

SHAFER, BOYD C. *Nationalism: Myth and Reality.* New York, 1955.

SHEPHARD, ESTHER. *Walt Whitman's Pose.* New York, 1938.

SILVER, R. G. "Walt Whitman Interviews Himself." *American Literature*, X (1938).

SIMPSON, L. P. "A Literary Adventure . . . The Anthology Society and the *Monthly Anthology*." *New England Quarterly*, XXVII (1954).

SIXBEY, G. L. "Chanting the Square Deific. . . ." *American Literature*, IX (1937).

STAFFORD, JOHN. *The Literary Criticism of "Young America."* Berkeley and Los Angeles, 1952.

STARKE, A. H. *Sidney Lanier.* . . . Chapel Hill, 1933.

STREETER, R. E. "Association Psychology and Literary Nationalism in the *North American Review*, 1815–25." *American Literature*, XVII (1945).

TAGGARD, GENEVIEVE. *The Life and Mind of Emily Dickinson.* New York, 1930.

THOMPSON, LAWRANCE. *Young Longfellow.* . . . New York, 1938.

THOMPSON, RALPH. *American Literary Annuals & Gift Books: 1825–1865.* New York, 1936.

TICKNOR, CAROLINE. *Hawthorne and His Publisher.* Boston, 1913.

TRACY, T. J. *The American Attitude toward American Literature . . . 1800–1812.* Unpublished St. John's University dissertation, 1941.

TRENT, W. P. *William Gilmore Simms.* Boston, 1892.

WADE, J. D. *Augustus Baldwin Longstreet.* New York, 1924.

WALKER, FRANKLIN. *San Francisco's Literary Frontier.* New York, 1939.

WARFEL, HARRY. *Noah Webster, Schoolmaster to America.* New York, 1936.

WARREN, AUSTIN. "Mr. Pope: Letters from America." *PMLA,* XLVIII (1933).

WHITE, G. L., JR. "H. H. Boyesen: A Note on Immigration." *American Literature,* XIII (1941).

WILLARD, C. B. *Whitman's American Fame. . . .* Providence, 1950.

WILSON, J. G. *Bryant, and His Friends. . . .* New York, 1886.

WOODBERRY, G. E. *The Life of Edgar Allan Poe. . . .* 2 vols. Boston, 1909.

WRIGHT, LOUIS B. "The Classical Tradition in Colonial Virginia." *Papers of the Bibliographical Society of America,* XXIII (1939).

WRIGHT, T. G. *Literary Culture in Early New England. . . .* New Haven, 1920.

WROTH, LAWRENCE C. *An American Bookshelf, 1755.* Philadelphia, 1934.

ZUNDER, T. A. *The Early Days of Joel Barlow. . . .* New Haven, 1934.

Index

Inasmuch as the sixty-odd divisions in the Contents indicate the major topics treated in the volume, the Index is in the main confined to names of persons, magazines, and significant places. Topics listed in the Contents have generally not been repeated in the Index, but other recurrent themes and allusions have been included to provide additional analytic approaches to the development of nationality.

235, 239–240, 245, 248, 249–250, 270,
271, 280, 283, 285, 287, 288, 295,
309, 316, 317–318, 319, 321, 322
Neal, John, 76, 77, 92, 94, 102, 103,
105, 125, 129, 131–132, 133, 134,
143–144, 145, 146, 196, 197, 211, 292
Negro and Negroes, 37, 97, 167, 228,
229, 271, 281, 324, 336
Neo-classicism, 7, 8, 13, 20, 22, 33, 34,
35, 36, 38, 41, 47, 48, 53, 55, 60, 61,
82, 83, 86–87, 91, 109, 120, 122, 131,
132, 135, 150, 151, 164, 190, 199, 201,
205, 206, 212, 270, 278, 319
New Eclectic, 275, 276
New England Courant, 18
New England Weekly Journal, 18
New Hampshire, 48–49, 165
New Mirror, 85
New York (State), 21, 38, 67, 99, 154,
207, 280
*New York Mirror and Ladies' Literary
Gazette,* 76
Newcomb, Charles K., 189
Newton, Isaac, 23, 169, 208
Niagara, 13, 48, 49, 97, 102, 108, 111,
164
Niles' Weekly Register, 75
Nineteenth Century, 275
Noah, M. M., 148
Norris, Frank, 288, 328
North American Review, 63, 74, 76,
83, 86, 140, 147, 197
North British Review, 334
Norton, Charles E., 242, 248, 290, 291,
298, 309, 317
Novel, 40, 41, 54, 109, 116, 133, 134–

139, 146, 200–201, 203, 205, 259–260,
263, 274, 293, 309, 310–311, 316, 324,
325, 328–331, 336, 338
Noyes, Nicholas, 14

Oakes, Urian, 6
Odiorne, Thomas, 35, 69
Ohio, 133, 138, 254, 256, 281, 282, 287,
288
Ohio River and Valley, 23, 50, 69, 79,
99, 141, 161, 178, 279, 281, 286, 288,
318
"Old Father Janus," 18
Oration and Oratory, 54, 57, 58–59, 75,
131, 133, 134
Oregon, 167, 177
Originality, 26, 28, 29, 31, 34–35, 39,
196–197, 269
Orion, 269
Ossian, 104, 105, 108, 190, 191
Overland Monthly, 244, 284, 288, 314

Page, Thomas N., 261, 324
Paine, Robert T., 38
Paine, Thomas, 12, 67, 143, 337
Palfrey, J. G., 87, 122
Palladium, 57
Park, William, 143
Parke, John, 35, 38, 52
Parker, Theodore, 87, 113, 118–119,
122, 125, 127, 153–154, 156, 157, 169,
173, 174, 175, 189, 193–194, 292
Parkman, Francis, 112
Parsons, T. W., 209, 265, 304, 332
Pastoral, 50, 85, 108, 169, 223, 260, 268,
279, 317